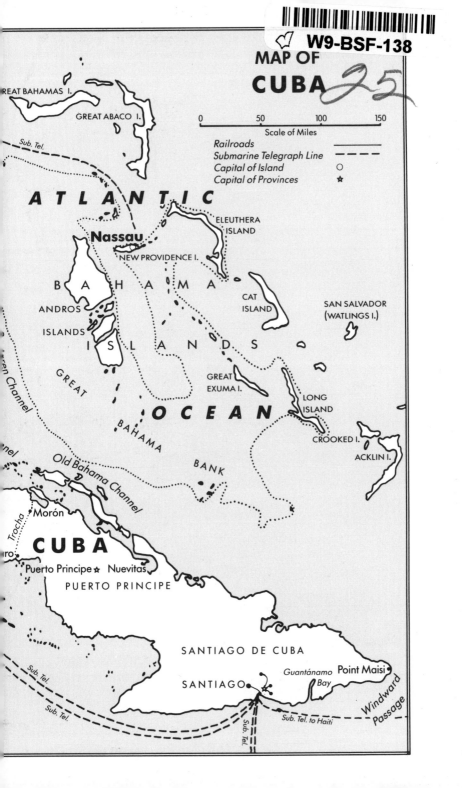

MAP OF
CUBA

GREAT BAHAMAS I.

GREAT ABACO I.

Sub. Tel.

| 0 | 50 | 100 | 150 |

Scale of Miles

Railroads
Submarine Telegraph Line
Capital of Island   ○
Capital of Provinces   ☆

A T L A N T I C

Nassau

ELEUTHERA
ISLAND

NEW PROVIDENCE I.

B A H A M A

ANDROS

CAT
ISLAND

SAN SALVADOR
(WATLINGS I.)

ISLANDS

I S L A N D S

GREAT

GREAT
EXUMA I.

O C E A N

LONG
ISLAND

BAHAMA

CROOKED I.

BANK

ACKLIN I.

Old Bahama Channel

Trocha   Morón

ro

CUBA

Puerto Principe ☆ Nuevitas

PUERTO PRINCIPE

SANTIAGO DE CUBA

Guantánamo   Point Maisi
Bay

SANTIAGO ●

Sub. Tel.

Sub. Tel.

Sub. Tel. to Haiti

Windward
Passage

Sub. Tel.

A
SHIP
TO
REMEMBER

A
SHIP
TO
REMEMBER

The *Maine* and the Spanish-American War

MICHAEL BLOW

WILLIAM MORROW AND COMPANY, INC.
New York

ISBN 0-688-09714-6

Printed in the United States of America

BOOK DESIGN BY BERNARD SCHLEIFER

ENDPAPER MAPS BY ARLENE GOLDBERG SCHLEIFER

In remembrance of my grandfather,
George Preston Blow, and his
shipmates on the *Maine*.

PREFACE

WHEN WE WERE GROWING UP in Virginia, time was defined by the order of bells. At noon, my brothers and I ran for the house as the clapper of a great brass bell outside the front door pealed a ten-minute tocsin for lunch. Inside, ship's clocks ticked away and struck the vespers of the evening, five bells for supper, eight for bedtime. On special occasions, a little brass bell on the dining room table signaled the kitchen for help. It had a flat, round handle with the inscription: *The brass in this bell was recovered from the wreck of the MAINE.*

Apparently, a long time ago, a ship had sunk; there was some mysterious family connection. As a child, this intelligence seemed trivial compared to the recent news from Pearl Harbor. Later I was told that the *Maine* was an American battleship that blew up just before the Spanish-American War in Cuba. According to a brother wed to melodrama, my grandfather was on board; indeed, he died in the explosion.

That was interesting. Later still, I became intrigued by the mystery of the *Maine* and the meaning of the war it triggered.

Ambassador John Hay, in his debonair way, called it a "splendid little war," and in many ways it was. It lasted less than four months; battle deaths numbered 379, not many more than died in the explosion on the *Maine*. It tore the shroud of isolation that had fogged the nation's world view almost since its inception, brought the United States increased respect in the international community, and immeasurably widened the frontiers of the country at a time when the once-wild West was tamed. It freed Cuba from almost four centuries of offensive Spanish dominion.

But it also brought responsibilities and perils we have yet to wholly grasp, and an "insurrection" in the Philippines as dreadful as that in Vietnam. The Philippine war was won, but at enormous cost, and it left the United States with a vulnerable outpost in the Pacific seven thousand miles from the coast of California and two thousand miles from Japan. It is a forgotten war now but was not in 1907 when Theodore Roosevelt, who bushwhacks through the pages of this book, observed: "The Philippine Islands form our heel of Achilles. They are all that makes the present situation with Japan dangerous."

This book begins, in Madrid, Washington, D.C., and Havana, on February 15, 1898, the day the *Maine* died. Her short and tragic life—she was in commission for only two and a half years, but was raised from the waters of Havana Harbor and properly buried in 1912—frames an era of American conflict and expansion in the Caribbean and the Far East. The mystery of the *Maine* endures, though readers may draw valid conclusions from the evidence presented here. She should be remembered for what she was, a fine ship with a brave crew, but more than that as a symbol of all the wars we have forgotten, and all the mysteries left unsolved.

Remember the *Maine*. Let her bells of warning sound once more.

M.B.

ACKNOWLEDGMENTS

SPECIAL THANKS ARE DUE the dedicated and skilled staff members of the following institutions, all of which made contributions in words or pictures to this book.

The New York Public Library
The Library of Congress
The National Archives
The Naval Historical Center
The Naval Historical Foundation
The Greenwich [Connecticut] Library
The New-York Historical Society
The Sterling Memorial Library, Yale University
The Library of the Yale Club of New York
The New York Society Library
The Nimitz Library, United States Naval Academy

My thanks, also, to the many people who contributed family papers and valuable insights to this story, especially

John Winthrop Aldrich, Martha C. Brown, William Astor Chanler, Jr., Dorothy S. Rudkin, and Roy C. Smith III. I am grateful to Richard Preston Blow for his editorial suggestions, to George Blow for research assistance on family papers, and to Frank Cheney Platt whose unflagging encouragement and perceptive comment sustained this project from the start. Finally, a deep bow to my wife, Diane. Without her empathic and logistical support this book could never have been finished.

CONTENTS

A
SHIP
TO
REMEMBER

I

THE
LAST
SUPPER

THE MORNING OF Tuesday, February 15, 1898, dawned clear and cold in Madrid, but the brisk morning weather did little to lift the spirits of the Spanish minister of marine, Segismundo Bermejo y Merelo. The former admiral found the intricacies of his bureaucratic life increasingly vexing, his days arduous. Even on a Sunday, he noted, "which the Lord has set aside as a sacred day of rest," he was apt to begin work at eight o'clock in the morning; often he did not leave his office until nine at night.

On this morning, as Bermejo sat down at his ornate desk, there was, as always, a stack of ciphered telegrams, confidential letters, and office memoranda to cope with. The file that particularly concerned him, however, contained the anxious—and often anguished—communications from Rear Admiral Pascual Cervera y Topete, commander of the Spanish squadron at Cartagena, its Mediterranean base.

Cervera was an old and dear friend. The distinguished

fifty-nine-year-old nobleman had joined the navy in 1851 at
the age of twelve. For forty-seven years, from the coast of Morocco to the shores of the Philippines, he had fought valiantly
to preserve Spain's shrinking colonial empire. He was much
decorated and greatly respected, an able leader, a steady
hand at the wheel. Even so, Cervera had not been able to
steer his way through the riptides of Madrid politics. Appointed minister of marine when Prime Minister Práxedes
Mateo Sagasta took power in October of 1897, he had soon
resigned, saying that his colleagues in government placed political expediency above national interests. Reluctantly, Bermejo had taken his place. Now he had to cope with the
bureaucracy, army and church meddling, the whims of the
Queen Regent, and a critical press.

Reviewing the secret Cervera file, it seemed to Bermejo
that the crisis in Cuba and the growing threat of war with the
United States had unnerved his fleet commander. The admiral's reports over the past several months pointed only to
problems. There were severe shortages of all kinds of naval
stores from coal for the ship's boilers to sea biscuits, navigational charts, and playing cards for the crew. The cruiser
Cristóbal Colón was without her main battery; the 9.8-inch
guns provided by the Italian firm of Ansaldo had been tested
and found unsatisfactory. The engines of Cervera's flagship,
the Infanta María Teresa, gulped coal at an "unreasonable"
rate. The Vizcaya had not been dry-docked for a year, and the
long filaments of weed that clung to her barnacle-encrusted
bottom slowed her speed by four knots. It had not been possible to scrape and paint her underbody before sending her off
on January 29 for a courtesy call to New York to return the
"friendly" visit of the American battleship Maine to Havana
Harbor on January 25.

Then there was the matter of money. Cervera wrote that
he lacked funds to pay his crews. The men "trust their admiral will look after them," he wrote. "I beg and implore that
you will be kind enough to remedy this evil." There was little Bermejo could do about that. Spain was virtually bank-
rupt; the Ministry of Marine had no funds. Every month
sixteen million pesos had to be sent to Cuba where two hundred thousand Spanish soldiers—or what was left of them
after malaria, yellow fever, and Cuban bullets had taken their

toll—fought the rebellion that had flared up in 1895. Even so, most of the soldiers had not been paid for months. In his new post Bermejo fretted constantly about the "excitable" press. Cervera argued that the "bad" Italian guns should be accepted—accept "hard bread rather than none." Bermejo felt he could not. If the press found out the navy had paid for faulty guns, then so would the Cortes—the Spanish parliament—and that would bring it down on his head. To make matters worse, Segismundo Moret y Prendergast, the minister of colonies, was talking indiscreetly to journalists. Brimming with false optimism, he disparaged the American navy and exalted the defective Spanish fleet.

Bermejo wondered whether Premier Sagasta had been right in recalling General Valeriano Weyler from Cuba. El Coyote waged war without giving quarter, but then so did the Cubans. Given a little more time, Weyler's *reconcentrado* plan—herding the Cuban peasants into fortified camps to keep them from supporting the insurgents—might have worked. And if Weyler had quelled the rebellion, Sagasta's offer of limited autonomy for the Cubans might have been accepted. Instead, it was rejected out of hand. "*¡La Victoria o el sepulcro!*"—"Victory or the tomb!"—the Cuban revolutionary José Martí had cried.

The Americans were growing increasingly emotional over Spanish "atrocities," as the New York press had it. Recently, the bulk of their Atlantic fleet had been concentrated at Key West, only ninety miles from Havana, for "naval exercises." And three weeks ago the battleship *Maine* had defiantly entered Havana Harbor. The *Alfonso XII* was moored only two hundred yards from the *Maine*, but the aging cruiser was a virtual derelict. Her boilers had been out of operation for over a year. Havana was at the mercy of the American warship.

Cervera's recent dispatches had been entirely negative. He spoke of "critical periods which seem to be the beginning of the end." He anticipated a maritime disaster should the fleet come to grips with the American squadron in U.S. waters. In Madrid, one of his captains complained, talk of "a second Trafalgar" was commonplace. If Cuba were to be lost, a sacrifice to national honor was required. The fleet would provide a suitable offering. Admiral Méndez Núñez had set the stage for all this during the bombardment of Callao, Peru, in 1866.

"Better honor without ships," he had said, "than ships without honor." With his personal honor at stake, Cervera rejected this path. In his view, the fleet must be preserved. On February 12 he advised Bermejo that the American squadron "is three or four times as strong as ours." Therefore, "the best thing would be to avoid war at any price." Four-inch rope, he noted, was not to be found at Cartagena.

Bermejo read Cervera's latest communication and pushed it aside. The admiral's timidity irritated him. If peace with honor could be achieved, fine, but the prospects were not bright. If it came to war, Cuba would have to be defended vigorously. The French journalist Charles Benoist had perceived the problem: "Cuba—it is the flesh of the flesh of Spain; it is part of the history, the glory and the grandeur of Spain." On February 15, Bermejo began a reply to the admiral.

First the details. The Italian navy, through the Ansaldo Company, might propose alternate guns for the Colón to replace those found not acceptable. An emissary had been dispatched to England to hasten the delivery of cartridge cases. Some Bustamente torpedos would be sent. "The decks of cards asked for are on the way." Then he came to what was foremost on his mind. "As to the war with the United States, I will tell you my ideas about it." A division of several large ships and destroyers would stay in Spain in the vicinity of Cádiz on the Atlantic coast. The six most effective vessels, together with destroyers, torpedo boats, and "the eight larger vessels of the Havana Navy Yard, would take up a position to cover the channels between the Gulf of Mexico and the Atlantic and try to destroy Key West, where the United States Squadron has established its principal base of provisions, ammunition, and coal."

It was a bold plan, one designed to bring out the aggressor instinct in his reticent admiral. Yet the venture Bermejo outlined seemed to tire the minister of marine, and he ended on a dispirited note. "My life is getting to be a burden," he wrote, "for to all that is already weighing upon me under the circumstances are now added the elections and candidates for representatives."

Bermejo was a student of naval history. Perhaps, for a moment, a vision of Philip II came before him. In 1588, when his advisers told him how easy it would be for the Armada to conquer England, the king of the greatest empire the world had ever seen replied, "¡Disparo!" (Nonsense!).

As the sun rose over Washington, D.C., that Tuesday, the comfortable house on N Street opposite the British embassy came to life as the assistant secretary of the navy cheerfully prepared for his day and swiftly dispatched hard-boiled eggs, rolls, and coffee. Theodore Roosevelt had his mind on a number of important navy matters, but he could hardly wait to write his fellow Porcellian Club member Benjamin Harrison Diblee about taking "Brother-honorary Homans for a slashing walk across country last Sunday, which gave him cramps in his legs afterwards." Almost exultantly, Roosevelt had told Homans that he would never become a sybarite while he was around.

As a child, Roosevelt had been frail and asthmatic, but that was over now. His small, rimless spectacles gave him a nearsighted look—out west, they had called him "Four-eyes"—but he could play ninety games of tennis in a day, exhausting several opponents in the process, and he astonished sedate Washingtonians with his spirited "scrambles" through Rock Creek Park. He felt—and even looked, with his stocky frame and large white teeth—like a bull moose, and the broad Washington political and intellectual arena was hardly spacious enough for his varied interests and activities.

Roosevelt had graduated magna cum laude from Harvard in 1880. A year later he was elected a New York State assemblyman. He was a prolific and skilled wordsmith, and began his career as a writer in 1882 with a highly regarded study, The Naval War of 1812. Devastated by the death of his first wife, Alice Hathaway Lee, in 1884, he spent several years ranching in the Dakota Territory, six more as civil service commissioner in Washington. By 1895 he had all but finished four volumes of his epic history, The Winning of the West. That effort was followed by a two-year tour as New York City Police Commissioner.

In 1897, frustrated by Tammany Hall politics, aware that he was "playing against stacked cards," Roosevelt had nibbled cautiously at the suggestion of his good friend and political mentor, Henry Cabot Lodge, Republican senator from Massachusetts, that he become secretary of the navy in the new McKinley administration. Lodge couldn't quite swing the appointment. Prudent by nature, McKinley was wary of the impulsive police commissioner, who had called Grover Cleveland's refusal to annex Hawaii "a colossal crime." But with the aid of Senator Redfield Proctor of Vermont, Lodge did secure the assistant secretaryship, and Roosevelt eagerly accepted the post. "Cabot Lodge plus Proctor & a few others got me in," he wrote a friend. The *Washington Post* commented: "He is a fighter, a man of indomitable pluck and energy, a potent and forceful factor...."

In April of 1897, Roosevelt was summoned to Washington by McKinley's new secretary of the navy, John Davis Long. Long did so with some reluctance—Roosevelt was a self-professed jingo with strong views on Cuban independence and an almost casual attitude toward war with Spain—he did not think it would "cause much strain on the country." Even so, Long wrote in his diary, Roosevelt was the "Best man for the job."

In Washington, where he put up at the Lodges while the N Street house was readied for his family, Roosevelt took to his duties like a duck to water. He immersed himself in problems of armament, steel procurement, and turret design. He studied the location of coal bunkers and magazines on ships, and the advisability of putting them next to each other—spontaneous combustion of coal was a persistent problem. He questioned traditional naval views on the importance of sails, and even involved himself in such minutiae as the amount of "gold lace" officers should wear on their sleeves.

The assistant secretary soon enlisted his old western colleague Frederic Remington to the navy's cause. The distinguished artist had devoted himself to portraying, in bronze and oil, the drama of the frontier. Roosevelt allowed him his love for the vitality of the horse and rider, but added, "I can't help looking on you as an ally from henceforth on [sic] in trying to make the American people see the beauty and the majesty of our ships...." Remington responded favorably, and Roosevelt lured him down to a naval exercise at Hampton Roads, Virginia. The artist "was very nearly blown up," Roosevelt wrote his friend Rudyard Kipling, "through incautiously getting too near the blast line of one of the 13-inch guns when it was fired. . . ."

Above all, the assistant secretary pursued his dream of building up the navy. The Congress "should at once give us six new battleships," he told Secretary Long. "A great navy does not make for war, but for peace. It is the cheapest kind of insurance." He warned that Japan threatened to surpass the United States, and that Germany, hungry for colonies, would have to be faced down. Long responded in a placid, noncommittal way. He had little interest in adding ships to the fleet; he considered Roosevelt impulsive. From time to time, the secretary felt it necessary to gently lecture Roosevelt on the virtue of prudence.

Long had graduated from Harvard in 1857, practiced law in Boston, served as governor of Massachusetts for four years, and spent six years in the Congress. He was an able public servant and Roosevelt developed a genuine fondness for him—"Long is just a dear," he wrote Lodge. But Long was not, in Roosevelt's mind, a "doer." At a critical time when Roosevelt believed decisive action was required, Long procrastinated. Roosevelt chafed at the bit, confiding to a friend, "I wish to heaven we were more jingo about Cuba and Hawaii!"

In the matter of jingoism Roosevelt and the distinguished president of Harvard, Charles William Eliot, disagreed. Eliot thought Lodge and Roosevelt "degenerated sons of Harvard." And philosopher William James, who had taught Roosevelt comparative anatomy at Harvard, later considered his former student to be "still mentally in the *Sturm und Drang* period of early adolescence . . . . [he] gushes over war as the ideal condition of human society. . . ." Roosevelt fired back: "Eliot is a flabby timid type of character which eats away the great fighting features of our race."

There was opposition to expansion in the Congress as well. The razor-tongued speaker of the house, Thomas Brackett Reed of Maine, called Cabot Lodge "thin soil highly cultivated," and he would say to Roosevelt, who had few doubts about what was right and what wrong: "Theodore, if there is one thing for which I admire you, it is your original discovery of the ten commandments." But the tide of Manifest Destiny was cresting in the Congress, along with a growing sympathy for the afflicted Cuban people, and Reed's hortatory pleas for caution were increasingly ignored. For Roosevelt, John Long—not the so-called anti-imperialists—was the proximate roadblock to naval expansion, and in the summer of 1897 the secretary all but took himself out of the debate on naval policy.

The fifty-nine-year-old Long had recently suffered a nervous breakdown. Like his opposite number in Madrid, Minister of Marine Segismundo Bermejo, he was weary, and he longed to vacation at his family farm—"Hotel Long"—in Buckfield, Maine. After suffering through the heat of a Washington July, he left the sweltering city for an extended rest at the farm, where life was calm and people in town hailed him on the street with a friendly, "Well, Johnnie, how be ye?"

Unlike Roosevelt, Long had made it a point not to trouble himself with detail. He felt the range of naval knowledge "so enormous I could make little progress, and that at great expense of health and time, in mastering it." He would leave such matters to the bureau chiefs and other officers: "What is the need of my making a dropsical tub of any lobe of my brain, when I have at hand a man possessed with more knowledge than I could acquire?"

In the wake of his swift departure Long left a vacuum that Roosevelt, with his fierce interest in every aspect of naval affairs, cheerfully filled. At first, rejecting the temptation to assume authority that was not his, the assistant secretary was circumspect. He wrote detailed letters to Long explaining problems and asking for decisions. But his dutiful reports seemed to exhaust Long, and on August 9, Roosevelt promised not to bother him save on matters of first importance. "You must be tired," he wrote Long, "and you ought to have an entire rest."

By now Roosevelt was well on his way to becoming the "hot-weather secretary." As the dog days of August dragged by, he began to indulge Long. "Now stay there," he advised, "just exactly as long as you want to." The president was away, Congress was not in session, "and there is nothing of any importance on hand." It was a refreshingly cool summer, he informed several friends, but wrote Long that September was "not a pleasant month in Washington." When September arrived, he observed that it brought "the hottest weather we have had," and added, "I don't want you to shorten your holiday by a day."

Toward the end of September, Roosevelt dropped a note to Lodge: "Long . . . has wanted me to act entirely independently while he was away." In fact, from time to time, the secretary had tried to rein in his deputy, but it was like trying to anchor a battleship with a lunch hook. Roosevelt had momentum: "I am having immense fun running the Navy."

One of his projects was to educate the president on naval affairs. The Navy Department building was only minutes from the Executive Mansion, and when McKinley invited him around, Roosevelt would pelt across the street and over the White House lawns to take a carriage ride or to dine with the president. On these occasions he briefed his commander in chief on the navy's state of readiness and told him explicitly what should be done with the fleet in the event of war with Spain. To further lobby the president on the vital importance of building up the navy, Roosevelt prepared an article for the Naval Institute *Proceedings* and sent a copy to McKinley. Its message was clear: Great presidents had expanded the navy; failed presidents had not.

By September 21, Roosevelt felt that he had achieved a good deal in Long's absence, and he sent off a cheerful letter to his friend John Hay, ambassador to Great Britain: "My chief has been taking a holiday for two months . . . I have really greatly enjoyed it for I have been able to do two or three things in the Department which I have long really wished to do."

One of those things concerned the appointment of a naval officer to head up the Asiatic Squadron. The assistant secretary favored fifty-nine-year-old George Dewey, who had served under Farragut in the Civil War. Roosevelt was persuaded that Dewey had taken resolute action in 1891 "at a time when there was a threat of trouble with Chile." He thought Dewey immune to cautious, "red tape minds."

Another candidate was being considered by the Senate. Roosevelt sent Commodore Dewey around to see Senator Redfield Proctor of Vermont, the expansionist who had backed his own appointment. Proctor, favorably impressed, spoke to McKinley. When Secretary Long finally returned from Maine on September 28, he found on his desk the president's recommendation that Dewey be given the Asiatic command. Unaware of the competition for the post, Long promptly acted on McKinley's request. Roosevelt was delighted.

On Long's return, Roosevelt immediately pushed him on the question of battleships. At first, Long demurred, but in November he did ask the Congress for one battleship. Surprisingly, Roosevelt took an optimistic view of this hesitant concession. One ship was not enough; clearly, however, Long's request extended the naval building program that had begun in 1883. Keeping that "principle" in force was of critical importance.

Shortly before Christmas that year Roosevelt received a letter from Lieutenant Commander Richard Wainwright, executive officer of the *Maine*, which had arrived off Key West on December 15. Roosevelt knew and admired the forty-nine-year-old Wainwright. Before joining the *Maine* he had served as chief intelligence officer in Washington and had helped to forge an operations plan to be put into effect in the event of war with Spain. He wrote back: "As you are unwise enough to want a picture of mine, I send it," and added, "I wish there was a chance that the *Maine* was going to be used against some foreign power. . . ." Roosevelt had Germany in mind. The kaiser was acting a bit paranoid. He seemed to think that "foreigners" begrudged Germany her rightful place in the sun, and recently he had swaggered several warships around the Caribbean and the Pacific. But Roosevelt was not particular—"I'd take even Spain if nothing better offered."

Almost at the same time Roosevelt received a communication from Captain Charles Dwight Sigsbee, the commanding officer of the *Maine*. Knowing of Roosevelt's interest in the configuration of modern warships, Sigsbee addressed the assistant secretary on the matter of whether they should carry sails. One of the first designs for the *Maine* called for a full suit on three masts, but as launched, she had two masts and no canvas to hoist. Sigsbee was convinced sails were an anachronism.

Roosevelt responded enthusiastically: "We must face the

fact that sails have gone just as three centuries ago oars went. Your letter is most admirable."

Setting that matter to rest, Roosevelt turned to more important issues. He was increasingly frustrated by McKinley's "flabby" approach to Spanish tactics in Cuba. Thousands of Cubans were dying in General Weyler's concentration camps. This was "not 'war' at all," he felt, "but murderous oppression." Cuba should be freed and made independent, peaceably if possible, but "one way or the other."

In the middle of January 1898, Roosevelt sent Long an exhaustive memo on preparedness. He proposed that a flying squadron be assembled. In the event of war, it could be sent to the Canary Islands, pass through the Strait of Gibraltar, and destroy Spanish shipping in Barcelona. Then he wrote to a friend, "Between ourselves, I have been hoping and working ardently to bring about our interference in Cuba. If we could get the seven Spanish ironclads together against our seven seagoing ironclads on this coast we would have a very pretty fight. . . ."

On January 24, McKinley ordered the *Maine* to Havana. There had been riots in the city on January 12, and the president wrote, "In view of the possibility of danger to American life and property, some means of protection should be at hand." Roosevelt entirely approved. Sigsbee and Wainwright were fine officers; and the formidable *Maine* would stabilize the situation. The Spanish press fulminated. On February 6 a Madrid newspaper cartoon depicted a demented Uncle Sam lobbing shells from the *Maine*. But the situation was now calm; there were no further demonstrations. Roosevelt did not think the "flurry" in Havana would trigger war. Still, he worked hard on war preparations "on the mere chance of having to strike."

Of course, he had no way of knowing, on February 15, that Minister of Marine Segismundo Bermejo had outlined to his fleet admiral a plan for the destruction of Key West. On paper at least, Roosevelt's "pretty fight" was taking shape.

In Havana Harbor that morning, Captain Charles Sigsbee's peacekeeping duties were almost over. The *Maine* had been on station for three weeks and was scheduled to show the flag at Mardi Gras celebrations in New Orleans in a few days. So far, all had gone well. Clearly, the Spanish regarded her as a "gunboat calling card," yet they had shown every courtesy. On the surface at least, Havana seemed peaceful.

When Sigsbee had boldly steamed into Havana on the morning of January 25, he had not known what to expect. At Dry Tortugas, where the fleet was on maneuvers the day before, Captain French E. Chadwick of the *New York* had warned, "Look out that those fellows over there don't blow you up"—there were rumors that the bottom of the harbor was covered with mines and torpedos. "Don't worry," Sigsbee replied, "I've taken precautions against that."

A pilot boat conned by Julian García Lopez met the *Maine* at the harbor entrance. Sigsbee asked Lopez for the buoy occupied by the *Alfonso XII*—he judged that berth "would be free from harbor defense mines." That was not possible, Lopez said—the *Alfonso* was incapacitated. Instead, Lopez guided the *Maine* to a little-used mooring east of the Havana Navy Yard. On Sigsbee's chart of Havana Harbor this was buoy number 5. Oddly, the barrel-shaped mooring had been given the number 4. Lopez gave no explanation for the discrepancy.

Considering his situation, Sigsbee realized his ship could be blown up, as he put it, "from outside," and he took extraordinary precautions. The crew was confined to ship, and the standard anchor watch upgraded to a quarter watch— fully one quarter of the crew were available for duty at a moment's notice. Night deck crews manned rapid-fire guns. Watertight doors were kept closed. "Hogging" lines were run under the ship so that collision mats could be lowered at a moment's notice. Enough steam was kept in the after boilers to operate the main 10-inch turrets. Ammunition for the 1- and 6-pounders was stowed on deck. Visitors were kept under close surveillance as they toured the ship.

The novelty of being in Havana wore off quickly for the three hundred and fifty crewmen confined to the poorly ventilated ship. After a few days the officers had been allowed to venture ashore, but Sigsbee feared his thirsty crew (grog had been abolished on U.S. Navy ships in 1862) might precipitate an incident. The ship's officers kept the sailors busy. On the *Maine*'s broad teak decks, under canvas that shaded them from the tropical sun, they performed over and over the "single-stick" exercise, a kind of mock fencing drill with hickory swords. Squads of sharpshooters, kneeling and standing, practiced loading and aiming their navy revolvers. Some of the coal passers brought shovels on deck and had their picture taken cradling the instruments of their trade, banjo style. The contingent of twenty-four marines went over plans to repel boarders.

When Christopher Columbus entered Havana Harbor on October 28, 1492, he wrote ecstatically: "This is the most beautiful land ever beheld. . . . Never could my eyes weary of gazing upon the beautiful verdure." Four centuries later the harbor was not quite the paradise Columbus had viewed. On February 15 the trade wind from the east was dying; it was hot, sultry, and overcast—almost dark. A stench rose from the polluted harbor waters. Despite the heat, Sigsbee's executive officer, Richard Wainwright, roamed the deck keeping a close eye on local shipping and activity at the naval depot—Roosevelt had asked him to gather intelligence on the harbor's defenses.

Like Sigsbee, Wainwright was aware that the sight of the *Maine* was "odious" to the Spaniards. The passengers on a ferryboat that passed close by the *Maine* had jeered at her crew. Wainwright had seen handbills calling on "good" Spaniards to kill the "Yankee Pigs." He was not alarmed by these taunts. They were to be expected, and the *Maine* had clearly defused the explosive situation that existed in January.

Wainwright was, however, concerned about the danger of mines. As a former intelligence officer, he knew the Spaniards used them extensively. At Santiago, on Cuba's southeast coast, there were said to be scores of fixed-bottom mines. Despite the crew's vigilance, it was certainly feasible for the Spaniards to get a small mine under the ship. The possibility of being blown up was constantly discussed in the wardroom.

The *Maine* was moored, at high tide, in about thirty-six feet of water; she drew twenty-two. Hence only about fourteen feet separated the keel of the ship from the harbor bottom. Even "if a mine should cause us to seek the mud with our bottom," Wainwright felt, "there would be left sufficient buoyancy to keep our guns above water. With our turrets and the way to the magazines clear, Havana would still be at our mercy." If the "ultra-Spanish" planned treachery, Wainwright thought it more likely to find expression in a direct attack. Ferryboats and lighters constantly plied the harbor, often passing close to the *Maine*. The executive realized a boatload of determined armed men could board the ship. They would be driven off by the ship's sailors and marines, but there might be serious casualties.

Only the day before, on Monday, a lighter had been observed steaming to a transatlantic steamer nearby. She appeared to have facilities on board for hanging mines and stowing cable, and Wainwright considered her erratic course across the harbor suspicious. The lighter was carefully tracked until she disappeared from view around a point of land near the Havana arsenal.

But Tuesday seemed an exceptionally quiet day to Wainwright. The only incident he found worthy of notice was the entry into harbor of the Ward Line steamer *City of Washington* with Captain Frank Stevens at the helm. She came in swiftly and dropped anchor smartly off the *Maine*'s quarter. It was a pretty bit of seamanship, Wainwright noted, "quite a contrast to the Spanish steamers that entered and left the harbor slowly, and anchored only after much backing and filling." If there were to be war with Spain, he reflected, seamanship would prove invaluable.

Clara Barton spent that day visiting hospitals in and around Havana, doing what she could to help the starving patients, most of them lingering victims of General Weyler's concentration camps. It was a dismal business. Barton had tended the wounded at Bull Run. She had worked in Paris during the Franco-Prussian War when the city's desperate citizens had consumed the animals in the city's zoo and even the rats on the streets. In 1892 she had taken a relief expedition into Turkey when the Armenians were being slaughtered. She had been in Cuba only six days, and her experience was confined to the greater Havana area, but now the massacre in Armenia seemed "merciful in comparison" to what she saw. Starving vagrants filled the streets, begging for food. The only Spanish provisions that seemed in good supply were the black coffins piled up in the streets outside the overcrowded hospitals.

Beyond Havana, she realized, the suffering must be far greater. In fact, only a few days before she arrived in the city, the cruiser *Montgomery* had put in at several Cuban ports. After visiting Santiago on February 8 her skipper, Commander George A. Converse, had dispatched an alarming report on the victims of the *reconcentrado* camps. Fourteen thousand homeless were without food, clothing, or shelter. Most of them were women and children, he noted, "all emaciated, sick and almost beyond relief, unless they could have the benefit of regular treatment in the hospitals." But even the hospitals, Barton saw, were only the penultimate step on the tragic path from starvation to death.

Barton's concern for the plight of the Cubans was of long standing. In 1874, during the Ten Years' War, she wrote to a friend that Spain "has been so tyrannical and so careless of [her colonies'] welfare that she has lost nearly all. And Cuba, you know, has an insurgent army of so-called rebels fighting for their freedom. If she ever gets free, she must come to the United States, as she is too small to stand alone. . . ."

The war came to an end in 1878. The Treaty of Zanjón offered reforms to the Cubans while preserving Spanish sovereignty. But the reforms failed to materialize and insurrection flared up again over the years. In February of 1896, Prime Minister Antonio Cánovas reluctantly sent Valeriano Weyler to Cuba, knowing him to be a soldier in the ruthless tradition of the American Civil War and Indian war general he so admired—William Tecumseh Sherman. And as Weyler's concentration-camp policy took hold, the death toll steadily rose.

Not surprisingly, the American press took aim at Weyler's policy of "extinction," especially in New York, where William Randolph Hearst's *Journal* and Joseph Pulitzer's *World* fought a bitter war of their own—in circulation. When the *Journal* lamented Weyler's "thirst for American gore," his "carnal, animal brain," and his "tortures and infamies and bloody debauchery," the *World* rose to the occasion and spelled out the atrocities. Sylvester Scovel, the paper's star correspondent in Cuba, wrote that "the skulls of all [the Cubans] were split to pieces down to the eyes. Some of these were gouged out . . . the arms and legs of one had been dismembered and laced into a rude attempt at a Cuban five-pointed star. . . . The tongue of one had been cut out and placed on the mangled forehead. . . . The Spanish soldiers habitually cut off the ears of the Cuban dead and retain them as trophies."

Many of the atrocity stories were fanciful. Still, the situation in Cuba was appalling. By the middle of 1897, a Spanish report estimated, at least a third of the rural population—some 400,000 *reconcentrados*—had died. President McKinley tried to get an objective fix on Weyler's handiwork. In May of 1897 he sent attorney William J. Calhoun on a fact-finding tour of Cuba. Calhoun's report was devastating. Cuba, it said, was "wrapped in the stillness of death."

Against this background, Clara Barton took direct action. In July she went to the White House and asked to see the president. A secretary told her that McKinley was tied up in a meeting with Secretary of State John Sherman; perhaps an appointment could be arranged. As Barton prepared to leave, she heard the president's voice saying, "Wait a minute, Miss Barton." Asked in, she found that McKinley and Sherman had been discussing what might be done to alleviate the suffering in Cuba.

Barton was seventy-five, and she wheezed and puffed from bronchitis, but she was still full of fire. "You need no looking after," the president remarked. "You will stand without hitching." It was immediately arranged that the American Red Cross would handle volunteer relief for the Cubans. As Barton noted matter-of-factly, they decided "to form a committee in New York to ask money and material of the people at large to be shipped to Cuba for the relief of the *reconcentrados*."

Six months later she was in Havana. She brought with her J. K. Elwell, who had been a merchant in Santiago and spoke Spanish fluently. They settled into a villa with a view of the harbor. Barton inspected the hospitals, organized food distribution, made arrangements with Cuban bakers to turn flour into bread, and met with Spanish authorities, begging them to allow the *reconcentrados* to plant crops within the fortified camps. The Spanish were unfailingly courteous—and evasive. The Spanish soldiers had their orders; perhaps in time the autonomy policy would work.

On her way into Havana Harbor on February 9, Barton had noted with pride "the shining battleship *Maine.*" Four days later, on Sunday, February 13, she was invited to lunch aboard the warship. Sigsbee's gig picked her up, and she was received with ceremony. The crew, "strong, ruddy and bright," went through a deck drill to entertain her, and at lunch she chatted amiably with the officers about her relief assignment. The Red Cross was at their service, Barton told Lieutenant Commander Wainwright. On a warship, in action or otherwise, someone was bound to be hurt. Touched by her mannerly offer, Wainwright thanked Barton on behalf of the crew.

Consul General Fitzhugh Lee had worked his way through a number of crises since the unnerving riots in Havana on January 12. One of his tensest moments had come when the *Maine* made her sudden appearance in the harbor on the twenty-fifth. To the Spanish hawks, he thought, her arrival was a bit like waving a red flag in front of a bull. But the weeks since had passed peacefully, and on the afternoon of February 15 he was almost complacent about the situation in the city. Recently, he had cabled Washington via the undersea wire to Key West: "The *Maine* has greatly relieved by her presence the Americans here."

At sixty-two, Lee looked the model of a colonial planter in his tropical whites, but favored derby hat and cutaway for ceremonial occasions. A favorite photograph showed him resplendent in the uniform of a major general of Confederate cavalry. The portrait displayed a portly man in an almost belligerent pose; his white hair was parted in the middle, and he stared into the distance with a stern, patrician mien.

Indeed, Lee's Virginia credentials were as imposing as his appearance. He was the grandson of Henry "Light-Horse Harry" Lee of Revolutionary War fame, the nephew of Robert E., and had fought under Wade Hampton and J.E.B. Stuart. After the war he wrote a biography of his uncle and served a term as governor of Virginia. He fancied himself as a historian as well as a soldier, politician, and diplomat, and had begun to chronicle the four-hundred-year period of Cuba's struggle against Spain.

In this effort, he left little doubt about where his sentiments lay. Spain's Siglo de Oro—the golden age of overseas expansion that began with Columbus—had brought about a worldwide empire greater than Rome or England had assembled. But Spain had developed no colonial policy such as England's and had forfeited her rights to absentee ownership. Now, Lee wrote, "we can almost see the spirit of Columbus and hear the clanking of his handcuffs in the forefront of the most dramatic picture in all history. The flag which has floated unchallenged over thousands of square miles for . . . centuries is about to be lowered." And if it was to be lowered, he felt, the United States should be there to pick up the standard.

Lee was, in fact, a known jingoist who supported an expansionist foreign policy. This hardly endeared him to Grover Cleveland, who took a cautious approach to intervention in the Caribbean. But Lee was also an honest administrator and a loyal Democrat who had worked hard to bring the South back into the Union. Cleveland appointed Lee to his post in June of 1896, toward the end of his administration—and almost immediately regretted his decision as the peppery, independent Lee showed his colors. On his arrival in Cuba, Lee began pushing for U.S. intervention—as Cleveland saw it, "rolling intervention like a sweet morsel under his tongue." The new consul general deplored Weyler's "blood-bath"; he did not think the hodgepodge structure of mother-country control would ever work in Cuba; he felt Spain could neither put down the insurrection by force nor find a way out through reform.

When McKinley took office in 1897, he told the Congress that Spain must be given time—at least limited time—to find a Cuban solution. He spoke cautiously of "the horrors and dangers to our own peace." Lee felt this "cowardly, heartless and idiotic." He stepped up his series of doleful reports from Havana. Fifty-two thousand reconcentrados had died in Havana Province—not including the city of Havana. Governor-General Ramón Blanco, who had taken over from Weyler, should be given just thirty days to relieve the suffering. If he could not, the United States must intervene, for the new

Spanish pledge of autonomy would never be put into effect. In this view, at least, he found significant Spanish support. Madrid's minister to Washington, Enrique Dupuy de Lôme, wrote, with some indiscretion, that autonomy existed "for the purpose of printing it in the newspapers."

Cleveland had suspended "courtesy" visits to Cuban ports for fear of offending the Spaniards. Lee argued that they be resumed. American lives and property were at risk. On January 12, 1898, his fears seemed to be realized. Lee wired John Sherman at the State Department: "Mobs, led by Spanish officers, attacked today the offices of the four newspapers here advocating autonomy." Whether anti-American or not, the riot was not reassuring. The crowd threw rocks, broke windows, and shouted out, "*Viva* Weyler! Death to Blanco!"

Now Lee was more than every convinced that the concessions offered by the liberal Sagasta government in Madrid would not be carried out by the conservative Spanish authorities in Havana. Indeed, it seemed that Governor-General Blanco could not even control his own army. Lee thought a warship might be needed. At Key West, Sigsbee wrote to his wife: "In certain events, the *Maine* is to be the chosen of the flock."

But as the excitement in Havana quieted, Lee had second thoughts. The immediate danger seemed to have passed. The *Maine* might only rekindle anti-American sentiment. He cabled Washington on January 24 that a warship would not be required. The message arrived too late. Earlier that day Secretary Long had written in his journal, "Situation normal. We can resume visits."

At eleven o'clock the next morning the *Maine* glided placidly past crowds lining the *malecón* that circled the waterfront. Lee was surprised to see her but called Washington: "Ship arrived at 11 A.M. today. No demonstration so far." Perhaps that was too alarmist. He added, "Peace and quiet reign." As the days went by, Lee grew accustomed to the *Maine's* imposing presence. Now he remembered her entrance into harbor "as a beautiful sight and one long to be remembered."

True, resentment still smoldered behind Havana's calm facade. Lee and Sigsbee, returning from a bullfight, had been especially struck by a large poster that showed the *Maine* being blown up by a mine. That was possible, Sigsbee said. It could be done. But he did not take the poster seriously. Explosives in Havana were forbidden except to the military. No doubt some rum-sotted follower of Weyler's had found the poster a way to express his hostility.

Early on the evening of the fifteenth, George Bronson Rea, a correspondent for the *New York Herald*, left his top-floor room at the Gran Hotel Inglaterra and walked through the Parque Central to a café near the waterfront. When he arrived, the streets were still thronged with Cubans anticipating the Mardi Gras, but as night came on, the city began to quiet. The harbor was especially still. Looking through the café windows, Rea could barely make out any activity on the merchant vessels, but he did notice sentries aboard the *Maine* "mechanically pacing to and fro."

Rea, twenty-nine, was perhaps the most knowledgeable correspondent on Cuba. Before turning to journalism he had worked in the countryside as an engineer for five years. Since 1896 he had covered the war not, as so many of his press colleagues did, from the bar at the Inglaterra, but in the field with General Máximo Gómez and the other guerrilla leaders. He sympathized with the Cubans, deplored their poverty, but was outraged by the "lies" American newspapers printed to boost their circulation.

In 1897, based on his travels with the *insurrectos*, Rea had published a book called '*Facts and Fakes About Cuba*' in which he tried to set the record straight. It was highly critical of his press colleagues who, he suggested, were trying to "embroil the United States in a war with Spain." Too much sentiment, he wrote, has been wasted on the Cuban rebellion. Many of the atrocities attributed to El Carnicero—"Butcher" Weyler—were actually committed by the insurgents. General Gómez's scorched-earth policy was the real cause of the starvation in Cuba. The rebels were bandits and rapists "who burn, plunder and destroy," and "the atrocity rot is but a cock-and-bull story learned by rote from *laborantes*."

Weyler, Rea felt, was a much maligned general. The stories about him feeding prisoners to the sharks were pure invention. His *reconcentrado* decrees were probably legal.

True, he burned down farmers' houses, but these were only shacks. As for Gómez, to whom Rea had taken an instinctive dislike (the general had threatened to have him shot), he was not the "martial-looking old gentleman" he had expected to find, but "a chocolate-colored, withered old man who gave one the idea of a resurrected Egyptian mummy," and "an inflated bundle of vanity." Rea called the revered Cuban leader "the Dictator of the Cuban Republic."

Rea was soon joined at the café by the *World's* Sylvester Scovel. Scovel had spent almost as much time in the field as Rea but had come to different conclusions. On one assignment he had devoted several months to documenting Spanish atrocities, and found the mutilation of dead Cuban bodies "so beastly, so indecent, no Apache could have conceived anything equal to it." He gave the *World* exactly what it wanted—gory, detailed accounts of atrocities—but there is no evidence that they were invented or even embellished. In the end, he concluded, "Extermination of the Cuban people under the cloak of civilized warfare is Spain's settled purpose."

In Rea's view, Scovel had "not fully realized Cuban duplicity." But whatever their differences of interpretation, the two newspapermen—often working together—had risked their lives in the Cuban mountains and jungles, and they were closely bonded by shared experiences. They sat at the café chatting, perhaps drinking a Cuba libre, as they looked out over the harbor. The situation was, they felt, *tranquilo.*

Across the still harbor, aboard the *Maine,* the ship's chaplain finished his office of the day and prepared to retire. It was just nine o'clock, however, and John Chidwick decided to read for a few minutes. He picked up a copy of George Rea's '*Facts and Fakes About Cuba*' and sat down on his bunk.

The Reverend John P. Chidwick had joined the navy in 1895 at the age of thirty-two. Soon afterward, he was assigned as chaplain to the *Maine.* That September he attended her long-awaited commissioning and, new to the service and "wholly ignorant" of his duties, anxiously tried to behave in naval fashion at the impressive ceremony. After that excitement, however, Chidwick began to wonder why he had signed up. The ship's complement was only about 360 men and, aside from morning service and occasional choir practice, there didn't seem much to do. To make matters worse, he was a poor sailor. In any kind of weather, he noted dryly, "I threw my bread upon the passing waters."

But one morning, as the *Maine* calibrated navigational gear in the fog off New York, he thrilled to a sound echoing across the pewter-dark sea. Then the cruiser *New York* loomed out of the billowing mist. Assembled on the main deck, their brasses glistening, the ship's band was playing "The Star-Spangled Banner." That emotional moment was a turning point for the chaplain. From then on he felt part of his ship and part of the navy.

As he settled more comfortably into shipboard routine, Chidwick began to truly enjoy naval life. He had a ready smile and a cheerful mien, and the sailors affectionately called him the Padre, or Sky Pilot. When the *Maine* sailed up to Portland to receive her silver service from the city fathers, he heartily joined the celebration. Maine was a dry state, and instead of the customary punch bowl and goblets, she was presented with a soup tureen. It was filled for the guests, the chaplain observed with thinly concealed delight, with "a peculiar quality of soup with no meat or vegetable components." There were no complaints, he noted.

When the *Maine* entered Havana Harbor on January 25, Chidwick observed anxiously that the crew was at battle stations. He was confident the ship could handle any emergency. Still, he took his own precautions, advising the men to make an act of contrition every night with their prayers; it was important to be spiritually as well as militarily armored. Chidwick didn't pay much attention to the scuttlebutt about Spanish mines, but there were other unsettling rumors. On the evening of February 14 the men were saying that some "great event" was about to happen in Havana. Somehow, they had heard there was to be a Cuban raid.

The Padre had already started George Rea's book, and puzzled over his independent viewpoint. His secular commander in chief had been severely critical of the Spanish policy of extermination. Yet Rea, who had spent two years with Cuban guerrilla forces, took an understanding, even sympathetic, view of Valeriano Weyler's tactics, placing the blame for starvation squarely on the Cubans. Their "barbarous crimes" had brought about the suffering. It may have seemed an extreme view to Chidwick, but the book was fascinating. He found his place and began to read.

It had been an exhausting day for Clara Barton, and in the steamy night air she was bothered by her bronchitis. Late as it was, however, she and Elwell sat at their writing tables doing clerical chores—filling out requisition forms, paying invoices. The villa grew very still as the street noises faded. To Barton's right a large glass door opened onto a veranda facing the harbor. There the "beautiful *Maine*" rode gently at her mooring. Barton's visit to the ship was still vivid and bright in her mind—"those polished tables, the glittering china and cut glass, with the social guests around."

The scene was unforgettable. But in only a few minutes now, that sparkling impression would shatter, and for the rest of her years she would be haunted by a nightmarish vision of the Last Supper.

The tide had almost finished ebbing; a gentle tradewind barely riffled the water. The *Maine* hunkered up to the mooring buoy that had been designated by the harbor master and, for perhaps the first time since her arrival three weeks before, pointed west by north. Now her big 10-inch bow guns aimed directly at the city. Lights began to twinkle on the *City of Washington*, some two hundred yards off the port quarter. The *Alfonso XII* was off the starboard bow, closer in to the docks. One of the *Maine*'s launches hung slackly to her davits on the glassy water.

Captain Sigsbee, smoking a rich Cuban cigar on the poop—Governor-General Blanco had been most generous—noted the new heading of his ship. The *Maine* was now in the most likely spot for a mine, he reflected, and it was obvious that if it came to a fight only a mine could save the Spanish. Lieutenant John J. Blandin, his deck officer, was organizing the quarter watch and the petty officers were making routine eight o'clock reports: storerooms locked; security orders carried out; galley fires out. Following dinner in the messes, most of the officers had retired to their cabins to write letters home.

The evening air was still misty, but as darkness fell, bright tropical constellations began to spangle through the overcast. Sigsbee lingered on the poop, listening idly as an off-duty sailor strummed a mandolin up forward; there was lively music ashore, too, at the waterfront cafés, but this gradually muted. He moved to the rail and darted his cigar over the side, carefully watching its glow extinguish in the dark water. Then he climbed easily down the steel stairs to his quarters on the main deck.

The *Maine* was originally designed as a flagship, and her aft main deck featured identical admiral's and captain's cabins, port and starboard. Sigsbee used the admiral's cabin to write another report to the assistant secretary of the navy. This time the subject was whether to put torpedo tubes on battleships. (The *Maine* carried torpedoes, but their warheads were not armed.) There were two portholes in the cabin, but it was dark enough to warrant the cabin lights. As Sigsbee wrote, his dog Peggy lay quietly at his side in the heavy night air.

Sigsbee paused, called his mess attendant James Pinkney, and asked him to bring his thin "civilian" coat to replace his heavier uniform blouse. Pinkney, a cheerful black man, did so and then retired to his berth in the forward section of the ship. Sigsbee stuck his hand in the pocket of his coat and, to his embarrassment, pulled out a letter his wife had asked him to mail ten months ago. He finished his report to Roosevelt and began a letter of apology.

As a ship's clock chimed two bells for nine o'clock, Marine bugler C. H. Newton began to play Taps, signifying lights out, turn in, and keep quiet. Newton had played it countless times, "fully and correctly," Sigsbee thought, but also with flair and the captain always enjoyed his rich phrasing. On this quiet night, it seemed to him especially beautiful in the oppressive stillness. He put down his pen for a moment and listened. During Newton's dramatic pauses, "echoes floated back to the ship with singular distinctness repeating the strains of the bugle fully and exactly."

Soon afterward Sigsbee noticed the executive officer passing his cabin. Wainwright had heard Lieutenant Blandin mustering the watch and ordering sailors to their gun sta-

tions. Then he went below to write his own "home letter."
Now he was on his way to the captain's office to find muci-
lage for some stamps that refused to stick to the envelope. In
the office he found Naval Cadet Jonas Hannibal Holden, the
captain's aide. Wainwright glued the stamps to his letter and
the two began to chat. Sigsbee could dimly hear them over
the hum of the ship's dynamos. He was congratulating himself, even "feeling a bit merry" over his skillful apology.
Folding the paper with the *Maine*'s red, white, and blue logo
embossed at the top, he began to put it in an envelope.

The ship's clock had chimed three bells for nine-thirty. It
ticked steadily on for ten more minutes but would never
strike again.

II

PEARL
OF THE
ANTILLES

> It is my duty ... to prevent, through the independence of
> Cuba, the U.S.A. from spreading over the West Indies and
> falling with added weight upon other lands of Our
> America. . . . I know the Monster, because I have lived in its
> lair—and my weapon is only the slingshot of David.
>
> —José Martí

> I candidly confess that I have ever looked on Cuba as the
> most interesting addition which could ever be made to our
> system of states.
>
> —Thomas Jefferson

I T WAS HARD, windy, wet going as the little British mail
steamer *Karnak* ploughed down the Bahama Channel
toward Havana through rough winter seas. Many of the passengers were feeling seasick. One of them was the Bostonian
Julia Ward Howe, who later noted in her travel articles for
the *Atlantic Monthly*, "We have jolted for three weary days
over the roughest of ocean highways." She was relieved
when the vivid green waters of the harbor finally hove into
sight. On entering she observed: "Here is the Morro Castle
which guards the entrance to the harbor, here go the signals

... here comes the man with the speaking trumpet [a harbor pilot] who yells out to our captain. . . ."

"Any Americans on board?"

"Yes, thank heaven, plenty."

"How many are Filibusters?"

"All of them."

"*Caramba*," says the Spaniard.

"————," says the Englishman.

Howe had little sympathy for Spanish rule over the island. The officious customs inspectors who came on board reminded her of agents of the Inquisition. She found Havana colorful: street vendors sold peeled oranges, horses bathed in the harbor shallows, and *volantes* dashed by jangling silver-studded harnesses. But there was little else to catch her fancy. The city was as hot as "Dante's inferno" and full of "mosquitoes, howling of dogs and chattering of negroes." Breakfast was an ordeal for her. It consisted of "fish, rice, beefsteak, fried plantains, salt cod with tomatoes, stewed tripe and onion, indifferent claret," all served under the "attendance, or non-attendance, of negro and half-breeded waiters, who mostly speak no English and neither know nor care what you want."

There were other drawbacks. The railroads were expensive, the U.S. consul incompetent, the Jesuit College closed to women, and the island seemed to have run out of tea. There was a scorpion in her hotel room and, in general, conditions were unsanitary. Touring a sugar plantation, Howe observed "a huge pit of fermenting molasses, in which rats and small negroes occasionally commit involuntary suicide." There was a fascination to the making of sugar, however, and she watched avidly as steam-powered rollers crushed the cane and the juice flowed into copper caldrons to be boiled and skimmed by the slaves.

This was 1859, and the abolitionist from New England (three years later, in an early morning trance, she would inspire the armies of the North by turning an old camp song into the "Battle Hymn of the Republic") was appalled by the cruel conditions endured by slaves on the sugar plantations. Suicide seemed the only alternative to despotism. Even so, blacks and whites mingled freely in Cuba and their exchange was by private sale rather than public auction. Howe doubted their lot would be improved by "possible future occupation of the island by Americans."

What bothered her most, however, was the corrupt Spanish bureaucracy. It was all a question of plunder. "Not content with taxes ... the home government looses on the Colony a set of officials who are expected to live by peculation." Angrily, she railed against the Spanish military with their "villainous foreheads." It wouldn't take long, she thought, for "a handful of resolute Yankees to knock them all into ———."

Then, chiding herself, she reflected, "You are not a Filibuster, you know."

But in a very real way she was. In 1890 her popular travel pieces were gathered together and published in book form, and what she had to say about Spanish colonial rule helped to fuel the zeal of filibusters and the Cuban revolutionary movement in the United States.

Smugglers and ships—English, French, Dutch, and American—bearing contraband had been poking into nooks of the long Cuban coastline for hundreds of years. The word "filibuster" (from the Spanish *filibustero*) began to be used around 1850 when a Venezuelan-born soldier of fortune named Narciso López, in alliance with southern politicians favoring the annexation of both Cuba and Mexico, planned an invasion of the island. In New Orleans, López grandly announced that the star of Cuba (he designed the flag adopted by Cuba in 1902) would soon be admitted "with glory into the splendid North American constellation where destiny leads it."

Shortly, he mounted two illegal expeditions against the island. The first failed when Cuban support for his beachhead assault failed to materialize. López executed a deft withdrawal and soon made another try, landing at Bahía Honda. This time he was captured by the Spanish, tried for treason (he had once held the rank of general in the Spanish army), and garroted to death. If his military efforts were a fiasco, he had at least shown that the extensive Cuban coastline was as vulnerable to freebooting in the nineteenth century as it had been in the sixteenth.

Filibustering became commonplace during the Civil War, continued throughout the Ten Years' War, diminished after the Treaty of Zanjón, and picked up again in the 1890's with the renewed Cuban struggle for independence. Of all the filibusters over the years, a man named John (later "Dynamite Johnny") O'Brien was the most daring and the most dedicated, both to his vocation and to Cuba.

O'Brien was born in 1837 of Irish parents in the old Dry Dock section of New York, a stone's throw from the East River. The first thing O'Brien ever really looked at was a tall ship, and then the sea. He liked to say that he had "never known a ship that was a liar or a coward." At the age of thirteen he ran away from home, shipping out as a cook on a fishing sloop. He joined the navy during the Civil War. Afterward, he earned his first nickname, "Daredevil Johnny," piloting ships through the wicked currents of Hell Gate, connecting the East River and Long Island Sound.

In 1885, O'Brien accepted an offer to take a cargo of arms and ammunition to Colombian revolutionaries. From that day, although he occasionally went back to piloting the East River (where he watched the *Maine* being built on the Brooklyn waterfront), he was a confirmed filibuster, making arms deliveries to Honduras, Mexico, Haiti, Panama, and Cuba. The illegal nature of these operations did not faze him. After all, he said, "we were rebels once ourselves."

The Panama venture was perhaps the most dangerous. His ship carried hundreds of inch-thick dynamite sticks packed in sawdust. For an entire day the ship passed through an intense electrical storm, bright lightning crackling through an ozone-green sky. O'Brien realized that if the yards were struck by a bolt of lightning, only small pieces of the vessel and its crew would remain. They were lucky, and after that they called him "Dynamite Johnny." He passed it off lightly. "Being Irish," he said, "I was favorably disposed toward dynamite on general principles."

O'Brien had sympathized with the Cubans during the Ten Years' War, and he knew of a patriot named José Martí who made his headquarters on the Lower Manhattan waterfront and often spoke for the cause at Hispanic meetings in New York. Originally, Martí was a poet; as a teenage boy during the Ten Years' War, he honed his eloquence penning anti-

Spanish essays and published a newspaper, *La Patria Libre.* The Spanish rewarded these literary experiments with a sentence of six years' hard labor in a rock quarry. Martí served it in Cuba and Spain, studied afterward in Madrid, became a journalist in South America, and eventually made his way to New York.

Now Martí's mission was to organize a Cuban junta. He traveled widely, visiting Cuban social clubs in Chicago, Charleston, New Orleans, Tampa, Jacksonville, and Key West, persuading the cigar makers to contribute 10 percent of their wages to the revolutionary war chest. Of all the Cuban revolutionaries he was the most fluent. In New York, in July of 1893, he spoke at a Hispanic dinner honoring the centennial of the birth of Simón Bolívar and offered a toast to those still in bondage. He spoke with passion on the great Latin American liberator, and ended; "Let him who has a country honor it; and let him who has no country conquer it!" The *New York Times* commented in 1895, "The most alarming Cuban revolutions have occurred in New York for many years—in speeches."

Martí did not hesitate to use the United States as a base for fund-raising and gunrunning, but he did not see the American eagle as a solution to his problems. Indeed, he viewed Yankee expansionism as a threat; his fear that the United States intended to annex Cuba permeated the ranks of the top echelon of Cuban exiles.

The second Cuban revolution was planned for February 24, 1895. In January three boats assembled at the deepwater port of Fernandina, Florida. One went to Santo Domingo to pick up the seventy-two-year-old General Máximo Gómez, another veteran of the Ten Years' War, who had always considered the Treaty of Zanjón to be a "shameful" document. A second steamed for Costa Rica to embark General Antonio Maceo—the famed "Titan of Bronze." The third boat, with Martí on board—the poet-patriot insisted on landing with the military leaders—was to set off for Key West to pick up a party of Cuban exiles. The three groups planned landings at different sites in Cuba.

Something went wrong. O'Brien thought there had been a leak; in any event, Martí's vessel was impounded in San Fernandina and two key insurgents were arrested in Havana.

The insurrection began without its leaders, but the first shots—the *grito*, or "shout," of independence—were fired on schedule near a little village in Oriente Province.

On March 31, Antonio Maceo managed to get safely ashore just west of Cape Maisí, Cuba's easternmost point. Ten days later, not far away, a small boat was lowered into turbulent seas from the davits of a German freighter. José Martí wrote in his diary of wind and torrential rain as he and five other men rowed desperately for the rugged southeast shore of Cuba: "Another downpour. Rudder lost . . . We strap on our revolvers. Steer towards clearing. Moon comes up red . . . we land on a rocky beach."

Then the six men in the group, which included General Gómez, strapped on their heavy packs and began to hack their way through the jungle. Martí was "radiant with pride and satisfaction," Gómez remembered, for the civilian party leader was holding his own with the military men. Martí had come because he had "preached the need for dying" for the cause. He felt a responsibility to risk his own life. "For me the hour has come," he wrote.

In Madrid the Conservative minister Antonio Cánovas del Castillo considered his options in Cuba. Cánovas was a political veteran and a passionate advocate of keeping Cuba in the remains of the once great Spanish Empire. He had served as minister, off and on, since the end of the Ten Years' War. At first, his rule had been almost dictatorial. The Cortes tried with some success to modify his powers, but in 1881, when Cánovas again led the country toward absolutism, he was unseated by the Liberal party under Práxedes Mateo Sagasta. From then on, the two parties alternated in power according to staged "elections." This was the *turno pacifico*, the peaceful exchange of ministerial authority between Liberals and Conservatives.

During the Ten Years' War, Cánovas had given token support to autonomy. Now he took a hard line on Cuba, announcing that the nation's blood and pesetas would have to be spilled and spent before Spain would let "anyone snatch from it even one piece of its sacred territory." Cuba was the gift of God to Spain, after all, a divine reward for hurling the Islamic Moors out of Europe.

His first move that March was to appoint a new governor-general for the colony. General Arsenio Martínez Campos had served him well during the Ten Years' War. Afterward, he had soldiered with distinction in the Philippines and Morocco. Now Cánovas once again dispatched Spain's most illustrious soldier to Cuba with a fresh infusion of troops. More than seven thousand soon embarked on the *Reina Mercedes*. They were young, some only fifteen years old, with little or no training, but they sang with the optimism of youth:

> "With the beard of Maceo
> We will make brooms
> To sweep the barracks
> Of the Spanish troops."

Martínez Campos had no need to splash ashore under cover of rain and darkness. The old soldier landed in Havana in April to a hero's acclaim. Salutes were fired, bands played the "March of Cádiz," and huge crowds cheered him and his young recruits along the broad plazas of the city. But Martínez Campos was a realist. The situation in Cuba was worse than he had expected; he had an unsettling feeling that the new insurrection might be "the last that Spain has to endure in America."

At this stage of the uprising, Spanish regulars and Cuban loyalist troops outnumbered the insurgents by more than eight to one. They had little trouble defending the towns and protecting railroad lines and telegraph wires, but in the countryside, in the mountains, plains, and jungles, Martínez Campos found a hostile climate and a higher degree of rebel organization than he had observed in 1876. "The leaders know more and their manner of waging war is different."

Then Martínez Campos got lucky. In Oriente Province the man thought of as the "soul" of the revolution fell dead.

Somehow, ever since he had captured and imprisoned José Martí in 1876, his destiny and that of the Cuban patriot had been connected. Both had served their country with distinction in Cuba; they had returned to the island within a few days of each other. Martí had joined up with the forces of Antonio Maceo near Guantánamo. Martínez Campos had taken to the field near Santiago, just down the coast. And on May 20, Martínez Campos's troops bushwhacked the Bronze Titan's band near the little town of Dos Ríos.

Martí was conspicuous on a big white horse, advancing in front of the troops. There was a sudden burst of firing; Maceo's foot soldiers dived for cover. It was too late for Martí. He had taken a bullet through the heart. Probably, he was dead before he hit the ground. Martí had been right. His hour had come.

The news of Martí's death elated the Spanish as it devastated the morale of the Cuban revolutionaries on the island and in the United States. For a moment the revolution faltered, but Tomás Estrada Palma, with Martí's departure for Cuba the chief U.S. representative of the Cuban Junta, held the movement together as Máximo Gómez rallied his troops. The propaganda machine of the junta, stretching from Havana and Key West up the American coast to Boston, went into high gear. Most readers of the American press believed the accounts they were fed of Cuban battle victories and Spanish casualties. Actually, they were not battles but skirmishes, and the Cuban freedom fighters rarely stayed around long enough to make body counts. But the stories had the desired effect. Cuban forces were actively engaging the enemy and growing in numbers. Martí, more valuable as a martyr than as a soldier, would be avenged by the sword.

During the Ten Year's War, Martínez Campos had shown a delicacy in his approach to guerrilla war that put him at a disadvantage in the Cuban jungles. His mission was to defeat the Cuban rebels, but this desirable end did not, he felt, justify the means employed by his predecessors. One of these was General Blas Villate, count of Valmaseda, whose brutal approach to war in 1869 left little to the imagination: "Not a single Cuban shall remain on this island, because we shoot all those we find in the fields, on their farms and in every hovel. . . . We do not leave a creature alive where we pass, be it man or animal. . . . So everyone receives what he deserves, the men with bullets, the animals with the bayonet. The island will remain a desert."

That was not Martínez Campos's way. He believed that

peace was attainable; the concessions in the Treaty of Zanjón had been enacted partly on his recommendation. But after only two months on the island, he had few illusions that his less than total approach to war had any prospect of succeeding in Cuba. In June he wrote to Premier Cánovas in Madrid: "Even the timid will soon follow the orders of the insurrectionary chiefs . . . I cannot, as a representative of a civilized country, be the first to give an example of . . . intransigence. I must hope that they begin it. We could reconcentrate the families of the countryside in the towns . . . but much force would be needed . . . the misery and hunger would be terrible. . . . Perhaps we will come to this, but only as a last resort and I think I lack the qualities to carry through such a policy."

But Martínez Campos knew—just as Cánovas knew—of a respected general who had no compunctions about this kind of war: General Valeriano Weyler, who had served under Villate. Almost eagerly, Campos thrust Weyler's name forward: "Among our present generals, only Weyler has the necessary capacity for such a policy. . . . Reflect my dear friend, and if . . . you approve the policy I have described, do not delay in recalling me. . . . I retain certain beliefs and . . . they forbid me to carry out summary executions and similar acts."

No such qualms afflicted Máximo Gómez. Soon after Martí's death he made his position clear. Those who were not for him were against him; all laborers who continued to work the plantations that supported the economy of Cuba would be considered traitors and shot; all plantations would be destroyed. Heading relentlessly westward through Oriente and Camagüey, Gómez began to set them afire. "Blessed be the torch," he said. It would render Cuba worthless to Spain.

Cane is easy to burn, an American correspondent in Cuba remarked. "One person can burn cane, and 4000 cannot stop it." A reporter for the New York World, William Shaw Bowen, who had made a determined effort to describe the war realistically from the field, filed a vivid dispatch on Gómez's tactics: "A very reign of terror prevails throughout the rural districts. 'If you work I will have you hanged,' say the rebel commanders to the laborers. 'You may have 500 troops to guard your place,' says Gómez to the planter, 'but I will find a way to destroy it sooner or later.'"

Martínez Campos tried to bring Gómez and Maceo to battle. To find them he had only to follow the oily black clouds that rose over scorched fields of sugar cane. But the guerrillas proved elusive. "They hid in the jungle and attacked from ambush," a Spanish officer wrote, and were supported by sympathetic *laborantes*. If they were not sympathetic, the officer observed, "the machete, the torch and the rope are good arguments."

Martínez Campos was a professional, and his hardy troops could march with the Cubans. In July he nearly trapped Antonio Maceo near Bayamo, but the Bronze Titan slipped through his net. In October, Gómez and Maceo combined their forces and made a bold dash westward through Spanish defenses stretching from Júcaro to Morón. Now some fifteen hundred infantry and cavalry were loose in the rich plains and valleys of Santa Clara Province. An American planter complained: "It has been a perfect roaring hell of fires all the way to the hills of Trinidad and the sea and we could see nothing but smoke and smouldering ruins. . . ."

As the Plant Line steamer *Olivette* quietly entered Havana Harbor on November 20, 1895, the twenty-year-old soldier-newsman on deck felt like Long John Silver gazing on Treasure Island. "Here," he mused, "I might leave my bones." He was astonished by the beauty of the scenery and for a moment wondered why his ancestors had let the "Pearl of the Antilles slip through their fingers one absent-minded morning." (An English expedition had in fact breached Morro Castle and captured Havana in 1762.) He lit a cigar, a habit he had picked up in New York on his way to Havana, and in his mind began his first dispatch from Cuba to the London *Daily Graphic*: "High up on the cliffs, as the ship enters the narrows, one sees the fortress of El Morro commanding the channel to the port. It is now used only as a prison. . . ."

Soon the ship docked and the young man and his brother subaltern, Reginald Barnes, had their kit taken to the Gran Hotel Inglaterra. The Inglaterra was convenient, it had a good restaurant, a lively café, and a lot of English-speaking correspondents stayed there on their way to cover the war in the interior. Some, indeed, seemed to cover the war *from* the bar. It was a good spot to collect war stories, true or fancied.

In this casual way Winston Spencer Churchill thrust himself into the war between Spanish army regulars and Cuban guerrillas that had flared up in the eastern provinces. The adventure—"a kind of World's Fair with shooting," as one observer put it—had begun in England only a few months before. Churchill, a recent graduate of Sandhurst and a subaltern with Her Majesty's Fourth Hussars, had brooded about soldiers and war "from very early youth." Now he was a soldier—but there was no war. "The Empire," he noted sadly, "had enjoyed so long a spell of almost unbroken peace that medals and all they represented in experience and adventure were becoming extremely scarce in the British Army." But at last the peace, "in which mankind had for so many years languished," broke down in Cuba. It was not a real war, but it would do. Churchill's colonel agreed, rating the Cuban fracas "as good or almost as good as a season's serious hunting."

Through family connections in Spain, Churchill wangled permission to accompany Spanish troops under Martínez Campos as an observer. His specific objective was to check out "the effect of the new bullet." By this he meant the smokeless powder shells the Spanish army used in their German rifles—"Dr. Mauser's pills." When it was all arranged, he wrote to his mother, "Now I hope you won't mind my going my dear Mamma." The trip was, he said, safer than "cruising the fences of the Vale of Aykesbury on horseback."

Off he went to New York on the Cunard Royal Mail steamship *Etruria*. The weather was vile; shortly before reaching New York on November 8 the future lord of the admiralty again wrote his mother: "I do not contemplate ever taking a sea voyage for pleasure." New York, however, proved far more stimulating than he had imagined it could be. Churchill and Barnes stayed in the comfortable Fifth Avenue apartment of the remarkable Bourke Cockran, a New York attorney and sometime congressman with British connections. Cockran showed Churchill the town—everything from a tour of the cruiser *New York* to supper at the Waldorf.

But the most rewarding hours of his short stay were those spent in earnest communion with Cockran. He found the Irish attorney to be the most remarkable man he had ever met. "I have never seen his like, or in some respects his equal . . . his conversation, in point, in pith, in rotundity, in antithesis, and in comprehension, exceeded anything I have ever heard." The young subaltern and the forty-one-year-old politician talked on into the night, smoking cigars, sipping Cognac, discussing Tammany Hall, the American press, the Cuban Junta in New York. Churchill was awed by Cockran's intellect and eloquence. The young subaltern with ambitions to someday fill his father's seat in Parliament learned from Cockran "how to hold thousands in thrall. . . ."

As for the Cuban expedition, Churchill spoke of "tomfoolery," but Cockran did not take the situation there lightly. Despite the death of José Martí, the cause of Cuba Libre seemed to be gaining momentum. Cockran did not approve of Gómez's policy of torching the countryside, but he had little sympathy for Spain and a foreign policy that "stooped to exact tribute."

Still, it was not until Churchill reached Santa Clara in central Cuba after a long trip by armored train ("when firing broke out, as was usual, you had only to lie down on the floor of the carriage") that he began to appreciate the seriousness of the situation in Cuba.

Churchill and Barnes reported in to Martínez Campos commanding a Spanish force of almost four thousand infantry and cavalry. Campos turned the two uniformed subalterns over to one of his staff officers, who told them that if they wanted to see fighting they should join a mobile column. Unfortunately, one had just left for Sancti-Spíritus about forty miles away. Churchill suggested that he and Barnes could easily overtake it, but the young lieutenant shook his head and told them they would not get five miles into the jungle.

"Where, then, are the enemy?" Churchill asked.

"They are everywhere and nowhere," the Spaniard replied. Obviously, the tactics of the insurgents were not those taught at Sandhurst.

They finally reached Sancti-Spíritus three days later after a circuitous but safe train and boat detour. General

Suáres Valdéz welcomed them, and they set out early the next morning in pursuit of the legendary Gómez, thought to be encamped near Iguara with a large band of insurgents. Churchill admired the perseverance of the Spanish troops in their dusty white cotton uniforms and Panama hats. "These tough Spanish peasants, sons of the soil, could jog along with heavy loads over mere tracks with an admirable persistence."

At daylight the long Spanish column came to a halt and fires were lit. It was time for breakfast and a siesta. To the British subalterns it seemed more of a picnic. "The General's aide-de-camp produced a long metal bottle in which he made a beverage which he described as 'runcatelle.'" (Years later, Churchill realized this was a rum cocktail.) After eating and drinking, everyone slept for four hours—a practice Churchill, who later adopted a variation of the theme, found admirable. He observed that a long day should be broken into two parts. "The Latins are wiser and closer to Nature in their way than the Anglo-Saxons or Teutons."

It soon became apparent, however, that the search-and-destroy mission assigned Valdéz was no picnic. On November 30, Churchill's twenty-first birthday, near the little village of Arroyo Blanco, as the column moved off into the morning mist, Gómez's troops opened fire. "For the first time," Churchill noted delightedly, "I heard shots fired in anger and heard bullets strike flesh." Fortunately, he observed, the rebels tended to shoot high. The Cubans were masters, however, of hit-and-run, and for the next three days Gómez's troops first bushwhacked the Spaniards, then melted into the jungle.

Near the village of Iguara, Churchill "heard enough bullets whistle and hum past to satisfy me for some time to come." For once the insurgents held their ground and the Spanish infantry could advance according to textbook patterns. General Valdéz and his staff, accompanied by Churchill and Barnes, rode up to within four hundred yards of the Cuban picket line. "During this period," Churchill noted, "the air was full of whizzings, and the palm trees smitten by the bullets yielded resounding smacks and thuds."

The rebels were "not good soldiers," Churchill later

summed up, "but as runners would be hard to beat." Even
so, he was impressed by their mobility. He noted that the
nature of the country was against the Spanish and that the
Cubans were supported by the civilian *laborantes*. The spring
rains, bringing with them the dreaded yellow fever and malaria, would certainly work to the advantage of Gómez and
force the Spanish to grant major concessions. He did not see
how thousands of troops wandering around in the endless,
humid jungle—a world of "impalpable hostility" several
thousand miles from their home base—could win.

Churchill hoped that Spanish concessions would not include independence. "A Cuban government would be worse"
than Spain's—"equally corrupt, more capricious and far less
stable. Under such a government revolutions would be peri-
odic, property insecure, equity unknown." He later wrote to
Bourke Cockran, "If the States care to take Cuba—though this
would be very hard on Spain—it would be the best and most
expedient course for both the island and the world in general. But I hold it a monstrous thing if you are going to
merely procure the establishment of another South American
Republic. . . ."

After filing dispatches to Joseph Pulitzer's *New York
World* and the London *Daily Graphic*, Churchill returned to
England. For his sangfroid under fire at Iguara, General Valdéz diplomatically recommended him for the Spanish Red
Cross, an officer's decoration. After the paper work was completed, it was sent to Churchill by Martínez Campos. British
army regulations forbade his wearing it, but the young subaltern had his medal all the same. And he had found a war
that seemed, in retrospect, quite real.

On December 7, as Churchill began his long voyage back
to England, Tomás Estrada Palma, the chief U.S. representative of the Cuban Junta, sent a long letter to Richard Olney,
secretary of state under Grover Cleveland. He began by saying
that every promise of reform embraced in the 1878 Treaty of
Zanjón had been broken by the Spanish. Suffrage was re-
stricted by exorbitant poll taxes. Cubans had no security of
person or property. Freedom of speech, the press, and religion did not exist.

"The Army of liberation," Estrada Palma claimed, was well organized and well drilled. General Gómez was commander in chief, General Maceo second in command. "The discipline of the Army was strict."

All classes—not just the lower—were involved in the struggle. He warned that the sacrifices of the Cuban people entitled them to fight oppression with any means at hand, including Gómez's torch. The end justified the means. "Puerile scruples and fears" would not be tolerated. But in fact, the burning was "simply a blockade, so to speak, on land. . . ."

Estrada Palma's letter was an attempt to legitimize the Cuban revolution and the scorched-earth tactics employed by its commanders in the field. Later, with American business interests on his mind, Richard Olney found a single word to describe them: "arson."

By early January 1896, Gómez had almost reached Havana and Maceo was somewhere ahead of him. Martínez Campos, still reluctant to follow in the footsteps of Villate, unable to bring the rebels to decisive battle, tendered his resignation to Premier Cánovas in Madrid and confessed to the army that he had not resolutely implemented the government's war policy. He was given a cold reception in Spain. Politically, it was now expedient for Cánovas to take a hard line. The whip must be cracked before the carrot was tendered. The next governor-general of Cuba would be Valeriano Weyler y Nicolau, Marquis of Tenerife, Villate's protégé.

Weyler made no attempt to embroider his image: "Mercy has no place in war," he wrote. "I care not what is said about me. I am not a politician. I am Weyler." There was hard, ruthless work ahead of him if Cuba was to be saved for Spain. "How do they want me to wage war?" he asked. "With bishops' pastorals and presents of sweets and money?" He enjoyed pointing out that he had taken his first lessons in tactics from the great American general William Tecumseh Sherman.

Weyler had served as a military attaché in Washington during the Civil War. He saw Sherman's march through Georgia as the dedicated work of a professional soldier. In Washington he could hardly have been unaware of the army song

"John Brown's Body" and the inspiring new words put to it by Julia Ward Howe after visiting the camps of McClellan's Army of the Potomac: "He hath loosed the fateful lightning of his terrible swift sword . . ." Ward had based her lyrics on the Old Testament text of Isaiah: "I have trodden the wine-press alone; and of the people there was none with me, for I will tread them in mine anger, and trample them in my fury." Ward's God—and Weyler's—was a God of vengeance quite different from the one before whom Martínez Campos genuflected.

Born in Majorca in 1838, Weyler was of German descent, and there was a streak of the Puritan in him. In the field he slept on a thin, hard mattress and ate his soldiers' mess—bread and sardines—with an occasional cup of wine. He did not smoke or drink hard liquor. Ruthless to men, he loved animals and in Spain maintained a horse farm where aging cavalry mounts, destined for the glue factory, could live out their days.

Weyler arrived in Havana on February 10, 1896, to the usual cannonades and moved into the Governor's Palace. His reign of terror began only six days later as he swiftly imposed the first of a series of harsh *bandos*, or decrees. The first, which applied to sections of Oriente and Camagüey provinces, ordered all those not already living in fortified towns to move into them within eight days. Their cattle would be confiscated; they were not allowed to bring food; their houses would be burned. Anyone found outside the towns after an eight-day grace period would be treated as a rebel. Soon afterward, *reconcentrado* decrees were issued covering the other provinces.

In theory, the peasant farmers might survive within the fortified towns and cities. In practice, they starved and succumbed to malaria and yellow fever. Without their animals, forbidden or unable to plant crops in the urban neighborhoods, plagued by the diseases of the rainy season that began in April, they died by the thousands. The tactical benefits to Weyler were clear: The rebels would be deprived of their base of peasant support—guerrilla recruits, food, military intelligence.

The second prong of Weyler's plan was designed to contain the so-called Army of Liberation. The Júcaro-to-Morón *trocha*—literally a ditch—had been slashed through the jungle at the western end of Camagüey Province with slave labor during the Ten Years' War. Weyler set out to restore and expand this fifty-mile-long system of forts, blockhouses, abatis, and barbed wire. A second *trocha* would be built across a narrow neck of Cuba west of Havana between Mariel and Majana to seal off Maceo's insurgents in the westernmost province of Pinar del Río. Both *trochas* would be heavily manned by Spanish regulars. In addition to containment, the *trochas* would give Weyler massive anvils on which his troops, spreading to the east and west from the central provinces, could hammer the guerrilla forces.

For William Randolph Hearst, the thirty-three-year-old owner of the *New York Journal*, Weyler's arrival was heaven-sent. The enterprising newspaper tycoon's career had already had its ups and downs. Hearst had become enthusiastic about journalism while working on the Harvard *Lampoon*. Expelled from Harvard for various pranks (in one, gilded chamber pots were presented to certain of his professors, perhaps to contain their scholarly offerings), he spent a year working on Joseph Pulitzer's *New York World*. Equipped with the *curriculum vitae* of breezy yellow journalism, he took over the *San Francisco Examiner*, a paper his father had bought to promote his political fortunes. The dreary *Examiner* was awash in red ink when Hearst arrived, but he soon had it headed for the black. In September of 1895 he bought the *Journal* and took up editorial arms against his old mentor, Joseph Pulitzer, and the New York *World*.

The "Yellow Kid," as he came to be called—it was the name of a racy comic strip that ran in the *Journal*—soon realized the potential of the Cuban struggle and began to recruit the best available talent for the fray. When Spanish artillery saluted the arrival of Valeriano Weyler in February, the big guns on the *Journal* boomed. "The Butcher," as Weyler was promptly dubbed, was also a "fiendish despot ... pitiless, cold, an exterminator of men ... there is nothing to prevent his carnal, animal brain from ... inventing tortures and infamies of bloody debauchery."

The *Journal* was practicing what Hearst preached. "Newspapers," he said, "form and express public opinion. They suggest and control legislation. They declare wars."

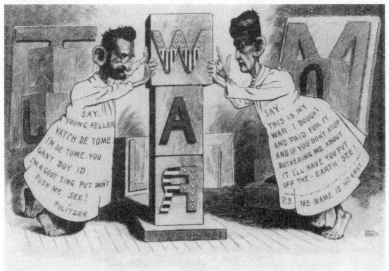

THE BIG TYPE WAR OF THE YELLOW KIDS.

Hearst and Pulitzer battle for circulation.

Throughout 1896 the *Journal* continued to pepper "the most cruel and bloodthirsty general in the world." Late that year Hearst signed on western artist Frederic Remington and the well-known writer Richard Harding Davis to document Weyler's "Reign of Terror."

Remington had been to Havana once before as a tourist ("The shops were full of gentle-minded idiots buying those absurdly-painted bull fight fans") and he looked forward to returning to the city he felt was now becoming the center of the universe. He and Davis, whom the former cowboy, frontier scout, mule rancher, saloon owner, and Yale football player considered something of a dandy, took a train down to Key West and got on board the *Vamoose*, a yacht Hearst had chartered to filibuster the Spanish blockade. "Things so arranged themselves that I was expected to go to Cuba to illuminate the genius of Mr. Richard Harding Davis," Remington observed.

Remington was leery of the sophisticated Davis, famed for his popular stories about an eleemosynary socialite named Cortland Van Bibber—"the dandy, who goes rowing in Central Park with children from the tenement houses . . . never . . . losing the air of wearing an orchid in his buttonhole," as the publisher's blurb had it. Davis also modeled for Charles Dana Gibson's "man," the handsome, craggy-jawed companion to the Gibson girl. He was the Beau Brummel of foreign correspondents. When Davis took his trench coat off, a reporter for the *World* spoofed, he was "attired in a Norfolk jacket with 24 pockets, golf trousers, cavalry boots, hat and gauntlets, a field glass, a note book, a revolver, a cartridge belt, and a practicable flask."

"We tried to run the Spanish blockade with a very narrow-waisted yacht," Remington wrote, "but the sailors did not like their job." The weather was foul, the seas high, and the thirty-five-year-old Remington began to feel that he had not been "caught young enough to develop a love for the sea." He watched a Chinese sailor hammering a raft together from timbers and thought, "If we capsize I'll throttle him and take it from him." The storm grew worse and the "damn tub" turned back and deposited Remington and Davis once again in Key West. Davis wrote to his mother that what he did not know "about the Fine Art of Filibustering now is unnecessary."

Their objective had been to land on the Cuban coast in Santa Clara and somehow join up with Gómez. Having failed to get in through what Remington called "the coal cellar window," "Richard the Lion-Harding," as Davis was often called, decided to try the front door. "Davis has the true newspaper impudence," Remington observed, "so we arranged passage on the regular line steamer *Olivette* for Havana." Their passports were bogus, "made out on some sort of custom-house blanks by a friend in Key West, but plastered with gold seals and draped with ribbons like May Queen's." Somehow they worked.

Hearst's crack team arrived on January 9, 1897, and the doughty Fitzhugh Lee managed to get them an interview with Weyler. Lee escorted the two Hearst correspondents to the Governor's Palace near the waterfront in the walled old city. The grandeur of Weyler's headquarters held little appeal to Remington. "To my simple democratic soul, the marble stairway of the palace which we entered looked like the Gates of Heaven. . . . There were gold-laced officers, black-robed church dignitaries, sentries and couriers coming and going. . . .

"After being introduced," Remington continued, "General Lee sat on a sofa, which he filled with his impassive presence; Weyler teetered in a cane rocking-chair nervously; Davis squinted at the scene for future reference, and I made the only profile of Weyler on this side of the Atlantic on my cuff." The artist in Remington saw Weyler in dark tones: "A little man. A black apparition—black eyes, black hair, black beard—dark, exceedingly dark complexion; a plain black attire, black shoes, black tie, and soiled standing collar and not a relief from the aspect of darkness anywhere on his person."

The painter's impression of Weyler may have been colored by his association with the *Journal*. Still, the *reconcentrado* decrees spoke for themselves. Remington viewed them as nothing less than a means of extermination. In Havana he saw "the *reconcentrados* being hurried in by mounted [Spanish] guerrillas, and the country was a pall of smoke from their burning homes." He saw "scarred Cubans with their arms bound stiffly behind them being marched to the *cabañas*. They were to face the black line in the Laurel Ditch." Remington thought it his obligation as well as his job to document the atrocities. "Davis will tell and I will draw," he wrote a friend, but felt handicapped by the poor print quality of his newspaper: "Can't do much in a Yellow Kid Journal." Still, the sketches printed in the *Journal* were vivid. So were the captions. One read: ". . . the blood curdles in my veins as I think of the atrocity, of the cruelty, practiced on these helpless victims."

In anger and frustration Remington decided to leave Cuba. The story told by a *Journal* reporter has it that he wired Hearst: "Everything is quiet. There is no trouble here. There will be no war. I wish to return." And Hearst cabled the reply: "Please remain. You furnish the pictures and I'll furnish the war."

Remington left anyway. As his ship passed El Morro at the narrow entrance to Havana Harbor, he shook his fist at the receding city and thought, "I won't come again except with United States soldiers."

That was exactly how he would come.

Davis stayed on. He wrote to his mother on January 15, "There is a war here and no mistake." Remington may have thought him dandified, but the trench-coated Gibson boy had a sharp eye for a story and he showed exceptional perseverance. For his part, Davis was happy to see Remington go: "He was a splendid fellow but a perfect kid and had to be humored and petted all the time." He had also, Davis complained, a weakness for cafés and "it always took him 15 minutes before he got his cocktails to suit him."

Davis had abandoned the idea of joining up with Gómez—"it is too dangerous to seek for Gómez"—but he was determined to see what was going on outside Havana. He talked Weyler into letting him survey the country by train—with a police escort—and he made the most of his journey across the eight-hundred-mile-long curve of Cuba. The country was studded, he noted, with little forts, "as is the sole of a brogan with iron nails." And it was clearly divided into two camps, one "within the forts, the other scattered over the fields and mountains outside." The insurgents controlled the outside, but only "as a mad bull may be said to have control over a ten-acre lot when he goes on the rampage."

The forts were built on the outskirts of towns, usually within a hundred yards. Outside this core defense was a circle of smaller forts built on high ground. Davis noted that "you are either inside one circle of forts or passing under guard by rail to another circle . . . or you are with the insurgents." From these fortified areas the Spanish sent out flying columns of regulars and guerrilleros, the irregulars recruited in Cuba, in pursuit of the rebels. Fearing ambush, they usually returned to their fortified camps at night and seldom managed to vigorously assault the enemy. Davis thought the Spanish tactics ineffective. During the Mexican border war, U.S. cavalry had gone into the field for three months at a time.

Davis's train trips through the open areas outside the circles of fortifications proved hazardous and depressing. Both sides were now burning the sugar plantations and smaller farms, the Cubans to make the country economically worthless and to intimidate the *pacíficos*, the Spanish to enforce the *reconcentrado* decrees and to put a stop to the payment of tribute to the insurgents by planters who wanted to save their plantations from Gómez's torch. The land was "blotted with grim and pitiable signs of war. The sugar cane has turned to a dirty brown where the fire has passed through it. . . . Sometimes the train passes for hours through burning districts, and the heat from the fields along the track is so intense that it is impossible to keep the windows up . . . we seemed to be moving through the white steam of a Russian bath."

Weyler's harsh policies seemed, to Davis, to be counterproductive. The savage machete-wielding irregulars killed for sport; the ground Davis walked seemed to reek with blood. The old and the infirm were rounded up and taken to the filthy squalor of the towns. "No one was vaccinated, no one was clean." At Cárdenas, a seaport town, the *reconcentrados* were penned up in warehouses over the water. High tide brought in a green slime of sewage—"deadly stenches and poisonous exhalations. The people are living over a death trap." All this could only generate sympathy for their plight.

At Cienfuegos on the south coast the intrepid Davis managed to ditch the spies and police who had accompanied him. Hopping aboard a Spanish troopship bound for Santiago, on which "roosters and buglers vied with each other," he jumped ship at Júcaro and was taken ashore on a lighter. There he persuaded the Spanish officer in charge that his pass from Weyler to "fortified places" included the Júcaro-to-Morón *trocha*; he was given a ride north toward Morón, some fifty miles distant, on a boxcar.

Davis thought the fortified *trocha* not just a rampart, but an "important piece of engineering." A path up to two hundred yards wide had been cleared through the jungle. The trees that had been felled were piled in two parallel rows on either side "forming a barrier of tree trunks and roots and branches as wide as Broadway and higher than a man's head." There was no way a horse could cross it.

The single-track railroad ran between the trees and a maze

of barbed wire. Alongside, a system of forts, large and small, filled the clearing. Every half-mile there was a major fort, two stories high, built of stone and adobe, with a cellar below and a watchtower above. From the watchtower a sentry could observe three of these forts on either side, and also block-houses placed half the distance between them. Between each fort and each blockhouse there were three smaller fortifications built of mud and planks, surrounded by a ditch. Each held five men, who were within hailing distance of the adjoining fortification. Stout wooden stakes and a cat's cradle of barbed wire filled the intervening spaces.

The extensive defensive line had proved pregnable the previous fall when Gómez and Maceo had both crossed the *trocha,* but it was still unfinished. Soon the Spanish hoped to emplace calcium searchlights and mines with trip wires to deter night infiltration. In a few months, he thought, the *trocha* would be impassable.

Arriving at Ciegó de Avila, an army center, Davis realized he had not had a bath in days. He felt sorry for the Spanish recruits, some of whom had endured these hot, dusty conditions for eighteen months. In April, when the rains came, he thought, Cuba would be "one huge plague spot . . . and the farmer's sons whom Spain has sent over here to be soldiers . . . are going to die by the hundreds."

Eventually, Davis made his way back to Havana and to Florida where, at the end of January, he began to file his stories. In one, called "The Death of Rodriguez," he told how a Cuban patriot was shot by a firing squad: Afterward, "as I . . . looked back [I saw] the blood from his breast sinking into the soil he had tried to free." He painted the plight of the *reconcentrados* in grim terms. "This is not war, it is a state of lawless butchery." Hearst was delighted.

Finally, Davis told a story he had heard on the *Olivette* on his way to Key West. Three young Cuban women, exiles on their way to the United States, were taken to a cabin on a vessel "with an American flag hanging from the stern," where they were "stripped and searched by brutal Spaniards." The story, vividly illustrated by Remington (who had gone "on the water wagon for fair and [was] working like a mad man") was inaccurate and would prove an embarrassment to Remington and Davis, if not to Hearst. Remington claimed he had only illustrated what Davis had written; Davis announced, "I never wrote that she was searched by men. Mr. Frederic Remington, who was not present . . . is responsible for the idea." Outraged, Davis broke with Hearst—"I am quit with him."

When the fabrication was gleefully exposed by Pulitzer's *World*, Hearst's campaign against Spanish turpitude paused momentarily, then picked up steam. First came an incident involving Dr. Ricardo Ruiz, a Cuban with American citizenship papers. Ruiz, who had aided the insurgents, was jailed near Havana and, in February of 1897, found dead in his cell. George Eugene Bryson, one of Hearst's men in Havana, thought the death suspicious and examined the body. On the basis of his report that Ruiz may have been murdered, the *Journal* called for war. "War is a dreadful thing, but there are things more dreadful even than war, and one of them is dishonor. . . ."

McKinley was not ready to go to war over Ruiz's alleged murder, and Hearst shortly came up with a far more dramatic story. Before he was finished with the "Cuban Joan of Arc," as Evangelina Cosio y Cisneros came to be called, he had enlisted in his crusade the president's mother, Clara Barton, Julia Ward Howe, the pope, and even the queen of Spain.

Bryson and George Clark Musgrave, a correspondent for the *London Chronicle*, found the story as they strolled the "lower quarters" of Havana one hot June morning. Musgrave wrote, "We visited the Real Casa de Recojidas, a prison for abandoned women of the lowest class. . . . Penned within was the most frightful horde of women I have ever seen. Repulsive black viragos raved, swore and scolded . . . they resembled beasts rather than human beings."

All except one: "There suddenly appeared in their midst a white face, young and pure and beautiful. . . ." With her "masses of dark hair" and glowing complexion, the languorous Cisneros reminded Musgrave of "the Madonna of an old master, inspired with life but plunged into Hades." Bryson and Musgrave instantly saw the possibilities in the Cuban beauty's plight. Obviously, she was of high station, perhaps of royal birth, since she came from Puerto Principe (Camagüey) Province, "where the old Castilian grandees settled." Now she had been cast among "the vilest class of abandoned women of Havana" because she steadfastly resisted the bestial advances of Spanish officers.

The story reached Hearst in August. According to one of his editors, he slapped his knee, laughed, and exulted, "We've got Spain now!"

In fact, the eighteen-year-old Cisneros was the daughter of an underground Cuban revolutionist from Camagüey who had been captured and sentenced to life imprisonment at the Ceuta prison colony in Morocco by General Weyler. Somehow, Evangelina Cisneros had persuaded Weyler to reduce the sentence, and to send her father to a lower-security facility on the Isle of Pines. Cisneros was allowed to join her father there, and one evening she used her undeniable charms to lure the Spanish commandant to her quarters. Colonel José Berriz was promptly set upon by Cubans, bound, gagged, and beaten before guards rescued him and foiled the escape attempt. The quality of Weyler's mercy had been strained. Cisneros was dispatched to Recojidas to await trial.

Hearst (whom some thought truly moved by Evangelina's plight as well as by her news value) determined to free her. He wired Bryson: "Rescue Evangelina Cisneros from the Recojidas, no matter what it costs." But Bryson was unable to carry out his mission. Weyler, incensed by his inflammatory stories in the *Journal*, expelled him from Cuba. Hearst gave the assignment to another enterprising reporter, Karl Decker, and sent him to Cuba to effect the jailbreak. "At this juncture," wrote Musgrave, now also reporting for the *Journal*, "Mr. Karl Decker arrived in Havana. He is a Viking by nature and appearance."

Meanwhile, Hearst ordered his reporters and stringers across the country to rally American women to the Cisneros cause: "Get up a petition to the Queen Regent of Spain for this girl's pardon," he told editor Sam Chamberlain. "Enlist the women of America. Have them sign the petition. . . . Have distinguished women sign first. . . ."

The newsmen fell to with enthusiasm and produced an astonishing flood of influential names for Hearst's "Roll of Honor." John Sherman's wife signed up, and McKinley's mother, and the widows of Jefferson Davis and Ulysses S. Grant. Clara Barton and Julia Ward Howe enrolled. The aging Howe, swayed by the *Journal's* vivid portrait of the pitiful

Cisneros, no fonder of the Spanish than she had been on her visit to Cuba in 1859, wrote: "How can we think of this pure flower of maidenhood condemned to live with felons and outcasts, without succor, without protection, to labor under a torrid sky suffering privation, indignity and torment worse than death?" On August 26, the *Journal* announced that fifteen thousand American women of distinction had signed petitions for Cisneros's release.

Hearst had staked out a claim on Cisneros. The *World*, scooped again, fought back, asking Consul Fitzhugh Lee to make an impartial investigation of the case. Lee discovered that Cisneros had been well treated, had two rooms at the Recojidas and was allowed considerable freedom of movement. She admitted complicity in the insurrection on the Isle of Pines. On vacation in New York to see his son at West Point, Lee tried to correct "a false and stupid impression which has been created by some newspapers." He called the whole affair "tommyrot."

A few paid attention; most bought the *Journal*, consumed its breathless prose, and waited anxiously as the tens of thousands of petitions and signatures Hearst's newsmen had gathered were sent to Pope Leo XIII. The buck did not stop at the Vatican. Leo forwarded his letters on to Queen María Cristina, who was intimidated by their sheer numbers. She suggested to Weyler by cable that Cisneros be placed in a convent. Weyler ignored her plea.

Decker, meanwhile, planned a rescue effort that seemed to have been lifted from the pages of a dime novel. After putting up at the Inglaterra, he rented a house adjacent to the Recojidas prison and stocked it with a ladder, a hacksaw, sleeping potions (to knock out Evangelina's roommates), and a briefcase full of money to bribe prison guards. On the evening of October 6 he somehow pulled it off. After bribing the guards the ladder was placed from the roof of the house over the street to Recojidas. Decker himself scrambled across and sawed the bars to Evangelina's cell; the correspondent and the maiden then made a shaky retreat back across the ladder.

Decker took Cisneros to a safe house, hid her for two days, cloaked her in the uniform of a sailor from a Ward Line steamer about to sail for New York, and followed her down the waterfront to the ship's gangplank. Seaman Cisneros stepped smartly aboard and Decker repaired to the nearest bar. Shortly, the steamer sailed out of Havana Harbor into international waters. Cisneros was free.

When the bewildered eighteen-year-old arrived in New York, she was given a hero's welcome. Hearst laid on a suite at the Waldorf, dinner at Delmonico's (a crowd of 120,000 packed the streets around the restaurant), and an extravaganza in nearby Madison Square featuring military bands, fireworks, searchlights, and speeches. Later, Cisneros was taken to a reception in Washington where President McKinley, possibly at his mother's behest, shook her hand.

Altogether, as the *Journal* modestly pointed out, it was "the greatest journalistic coup of this age." The paper had succeeded where diplomacy had failed and put to rout "monster" Weyler and his toadies: BAFFLED WEYLER RAGES AT THE JOURNAL, the headlines crowed. Meanwhile, "d'Artagnan Decker," as the paper now called him, arrived back in the United States (using forged credentials aboard a Spanish ship) and proudly passed out "Weylers"—Cuban cigars banded with the general's name.

Gradually, the *Journal* let the story slip off the front page. The Cuban Joan of Arc had used up her news value, and Hearst had even bigger fish to fry.

"Dynamite Johnny" O'Brien had observed Valeriano Weyler's *reconcentrado* decrees with a critical eye. "The Butcher's" unflinching application to total war had been known to him since the end of the Ten Years' War. His own illegal activities seemed to him more than ever justified. Throughout 1897 he continued to filibuster. To him this was simply the moral act "of surreptitiously conveying munitions of war to a people . . . who are in rebellion against a government . . . inefficient, corrupt, or both."

The filibustering business was becoming more hazardous. To enforce the law, the United States had assigned the navy, the Revenue Cutter Service, customs officers, and treasury and Secret Service agents. O'Brien and his colleagues in freebooting also faced the challenge of Spanish warships, hired Pinkerton detectives, and an army of Spanish spies, all determined to put a stop to the filibusters. None of this daunted O'Brien.

In March of 1897, O'Brien made a large delivery of guns, ammunition, and explosives at Banes Bay, a hundred miles west of Point Maisí. There was a narrow three-mile-long entrance into the bay, and Dynamite Johnny had to thread the narrow passage at night. Fearing that a Spanish gunboat might block the channel, he mined its entrance with two five-gallon demijohns of nitroglycerin connected to wires running to the shore where a Cuban stood watch. No Spanish ships showed up, but it was a good demonstration of Dynamite Johnny's versatility with explosives.

Valeriano Weyler was not amused when he heard of the Banes Bay expedition. He announced that he was going to capture O'Brien and "have him hanged from the flagpole at Cabañas in full view of the city." O'Brien, who had a spy in the Spanish legation in Washington, soon heard of the boast. He knew the reputation of Cabañas, the old fortress on the east bank of Havana Harbor where Cubans were lined up against a wall and shot, the "granite blocks spattered with blood and nicked by tens of thousands of Mauser bullets." O'Brien picked up the gauntlet and threw it back at Weyler: "To show my contempt for you . . . I will make a landing within plain sight of Havana on my next trip to Cuba."

"It was a duty to me to keep my promises," O'Brien said, On the night of May 24, he conned the blacked-out *Dauntless* past a gaggle of steamships off the Morro at Havana. There were no warships among them, and after waiting for the moon to go down, O'Brien steamed for a landing site one and one half miles east of Morro Castle. Every time the powerful Morro light came around, the *Dauntless* was outlined by the flash; as it continued turning, he could see Spanish sentries pacing the wall of the Cabañas fortress. Shortly, the tug hove to offshore and the dynamite, packed in fifty-pound water-tight boxes, was rowed ashore. Some of it went overboard in the surf and was thrown up onto the rocky beach. None of it exploded. The insurgents soon used some of it to blow up a railroad car Weyler was thought to be on. Fortunately for the governor-general, he was on the following train.

As Weyler hauled his naval chiefs and the commanders at El Morro and Cabañas over the coals, Ambassador Dupuy de Lôme in Washington observed that O'Brien had made a mockery of Spanish coastal defenses. Perhaps Weyler should be replaced. As it turned out, only two months later, a more compelling reason for the governor-general's recall presented itself.

In the summer Prime Minister Antonio Cánovas moved the government to the pleasant resort town of San Sebastián on the Bay of Biscay. On Sunday August 8, after attending mass, he was sitting at a hotel café when a young man approached his table. Cánovas looked up and saw the man pull a pistol from his pocket. The gun fired three times. Cánovas, mortally wounded, lived less than an hour.

The assassin was an Italian anarchist named Miguel Angiolillo. Apprehended, he claimed the shooting was an act of vengeance for the execution of five anarchists in Spanish prisons. As it turned out, there was more to the plot than that. Traveling from Italy to Spain, Angiolillo had detoured to Paris where he met with a Cuban agent named Ramón Emeterio Betances. They discussed the killing of Queen Regent María Cristina and the heir to the throne, eleven-year-old Alfonso XIII. But their power was limited; if the regime was to be overthrown, the obvious target was Premier Cánovas. Without Cánovas, Weyler would have no solid power base in Madrid; without Weyler, the hard-pressed Cuban cause might gain a respite. Betances gave Angiolillo five hundred francs and sent him to Spain.

In New York the president of the Cuban Junta disclaimed responsibility but shed no tears. Indeed, Estrada Palma, in an interview with the *World*, expressed a certain satisfaction: "While I have no sympathy for the assassin, I cannot help but feel the act was one of retribution. He [Cánovas] was the cause of the cruelties of the Spanish troops in Cuba. I cannot help but feel I am benefitted by it."

Once again, Práxedes Sagasta came to power, and there were liberal appointments to the ministerial ranks. Segismundo Moret, who favored dominion status for Cuba, took over the colonies; Pascual Cervera the navy; Pio Gullón foreign affairs. Weyler, whom Sagasta disliked, resigned on October 31. He was replaced by General Ramón Blanco y Erenas, whom

Weyler considered indecisive and an appeaser. Arriving in Havana, Blanco announced that he had come to offer self-government. Militarily, he assumed a defensive posture.

Sagasta, viewing Spain's situation on his resumption of power, may have felt the need for compromise. The Spanish treasury was empty. Revolution had flared up in the Philippines. In Cuba there had been some military success (Maceo had been killed late in 1896), but Weyler's harsh tactics had pushed many influential Americans into the camp of Cuba Libre. Tentatively, stalling for time, the premier extended an olive branch. Noting that Cánovas's projected reforms embraced the principle of autonomy, he announced, "Let us go on, then, to autonomy."

In Washington the assistant secretary of the navy saw practical as well as humane reasons for getting into a scrap with Spain. Writing to Lieutenant Commander William Wirt Kimball on November 19, Roosevelt observed, "with a frankness which our timid friends would call brutal," that he would "regard a war with Spain from two standpoints: first, the advisability on the grounds both of humanity and self-interest of interfering on behalf of the Cubans, and of taking one more step toward the complete freeing of America from European dominion; second . . . the benefit done our military forces by trying both the Navy and Army in actual practice."

There was no question in his mind as to how that action should be carried out. That fall the heavily favored Harvard football team unaccountably lost to Yale. Roosevelt, who had exulted to John Davis Long, "By George, Harvard ought to beat Yale football this year!" was crestfallen. He wrote to the newly elected Crimson captain, Norman Winslow Cabot, that the team must pay "more attention to aggressiveness in attack. . . . Fight with 'devil,' as they say in the boxing ring."

The ships that Roosevelt contemplated sending out to the field against Spain's well-regarded fleet had, for the most part, been in commission only a few years. Their development and construction were due, in no small measure, to the influence of a naval scholar and theorist named Alfred

Thayer Mahan, who had recently received—to Roosevelt's huge satisfaction—a degree from Harvard University.

It was later said that while Mahan taught Roosevelt, the whole nation went to school under Roosevelt. Still, it was Mahan who wrote the text. The son of a West Point professor, Mahan had entered the Naval Academy at the age of sixteen and been given a year's advanced standing—a unique concession. He graduated from Annapolis in 1859 and served in the Civil War. In 1886 his intellectual vigor and instinctive grasp of geopolitics earned him the presidency of the Naval War College in Newport, Rhode Island, only recently founded as a navy think tank. There he lectured that "the sea is a great highway over which one may pass in all directions"—assuming one controls it. Maritime strength is needed to protect this highway and determine the outcome of great events—indeed, the survival of nations. The struggle between Carthage and Rome might have turned out differently had Hannibal been able to invade Italy by sea. He could not. Rome's control of the Mediterranean "forced Hannibal on a long, perilous march through Gaul." Elephants could be useful; ships were essential.

The lesson seemed an obvious one, but no one had ever quite spelled it out. At a time when the "earth hungry" European powers and Japan were prowling the world's major oceans in search of fruitful possessions, Mahan's imperative, though couched in rather ponderous prose, became required reading for naval expansionists. One of Mahan's corollaries made particular sense to the imperialist nations. Ships making long passages across the broad ocean highways needed to be resupplied; hence the value of colonies, attached like England's to the mother country, which provide "the surest means of supporting abroad the sea power of a country." Without overseas coaling stations, he stressed, United States ships in wartime "will be like land birds, unable to fly far from their own shores."

In the United States, conventional wisdom had it that they did not have to. The world view of the founding fathers was limited; British naval supremacy during the War of 1812, and Horatio Nelson's victory over a combined French-Spanish fleet at Trafalgar in 1805, which shattered Napoleon's dream of total European conquest, made little impression on the conservative military strategists of the day.

During the Civil War the importance of controlling the coastline and cutting off the South's access to war matériel and food supplies from Cuba and England became self-evident. Lincoln realized the importance of "Uncle Sam's web feet." Once the South had been sealed off by a wall of sea power stretching from the Rio Grande, around Florida, and up to Chesapeake Bay, the Confederates could eat cotton. Naval construction was given important support. Thus, when the surrender was signed at Appomatox in 1865, the newly reunified states possessed a fleet of several hundred ships, many ironclad monitors of advanced design, comprising perhaps the most powerful navy in the world.

Afterward, however, it seemed a time for pulling in horns. Most of the ships were mothballed. Those left in commission, and the few ships built during this period of the "doldrums," were assigned to coastal defense. The enemy—should there be one—would come to American waters where the slow and unseaworthy monitors could, with the support of shore batteries, protect seaports. For two decades most of the enormous energy and invention of the nation was devoted to railroads and the thrust into the western territories. Without congressional support, the navy rusted at its moorings, falling behind England, Germany, France, Russia, and Japan—even Chile, Mahan judged—not just in numbers of ships, but in marine engineering, architecture, metallurgy, and explosives technology.

At the time, England was building the world's largest and most effective fleet to protect her colonies and the ocean highways that led to them. British observers considered the United States Navy a laughingstock. A leading journal commented, "The scream of the American Eagle [is] no more alarming than that of a parrot." Another remarked, "There never was such a hapless, broken-down, tattered, forlorn apology for a Navy as that possessed by the United States."

Admiral David Dixon Porter, operating chief of the navy, admitted the ridicule was merited. The fleet was "nearly worthless for war purposes." If the remaining ironclads went to sea, he observed, it would have to be at the end of a towline. Should they presume to engage a modern warship, their smooth-bore, muzzle-loading cannon would be at the mercy of European breech-loading rifles.

Slowly, the tide had turned. In 1883, on the recommendation of a Naval Advisory Board appointed by President Chester Alan Arthur, Congress abandoned the patch-up policy that had prevailed for eighteen years and authorized the construction of four steel ships: the cruisers *Atlanta*, *Boston*, and *Chicago*, and the gunboat *Dolphin* (hence, the ABCD fleet). They carried two or three masts and a full set of square sails that gave them a speed under canvas of less than four knots in a strong wind. Even under power, they were disappointingly slow. It was also clear that even the largest vessel of the ABCD fleet, the 4,500-ton *Chicago*, would be blown out of the water by a single broadside from the *Inflexible*, one of Britain's forty-one battleships. Still, in many respects they were an enormous improvement over the lumbering monitors of the post–Civil War era. Commissioned between 1885 and 1889, they became the building blocks of what was called "the new navy."

By this time Mahan was preaching the gospel of expansion at the Naval War College. He began his lecture series *The Influence of Sea Power Upon History* in 1887. Published in 1890, they became a cornerstone for the expansionist visions of a number of prominent Americans, including Henry Cabot Lodge and Roosevelt. Mahan's conclusions filled in key blanks on Lodge's blueprint for national prosperity: a strong fleet built around capital ships; strategically located territories such as Hawaii; and an Isthmian canal to link the East and West coasts. Once the canal was built, "the island of Cuba will become a necessity."

Roosevelt, then still a civil service commissioner, picked up an early copy of Mahan's book and immediately wrote to him. "During the last two days I have spent half my time, busy as I am, reading your book. . . . I can say with perfect sincerity that I think it . . . a *very* good book—admirable; and I am greatly in error if it does not become a naval classic."

Three years later, on the theory that old sea dogs must occasionally wet their feet, the navy gave Captain Mahan command of the *Chicago* and sent him off to Europe on a flag-waving tour. He went reluctantly, preferring the challenge of the classroom to the demands of a steel ship. Arriving in England, however, the tall, spare intellectual found that his strong convictions on the importance of sea power had been fervently embraced by the British. Under the force of his argument (which provided them with an objective base for colonial policies) Parliament had voted a huge new appropriation to expand the already formidable Royal Navy. Mahan dined with Queen Victoria and the prince of Wales. Within a single week Oxford and Cambridge presented him with degrees.

The Influence of Sea Power Upon History had made an even greater impact upon Kaiser Wilhelm II, emperor of Germany, and a convert "navalism." He was so taken by its message that he made a serious attempt to memorize the 540-page study. "It is on board all my ships and constantly quoted by my Captains and Officers," The Kaiser wrote. He invited Mahan aboard his yacht the *Hohenzollern*, anchored at Cowes, on the Isle of Wight.

In August of 1886, the year Lodge was elected to the House of Representatives, Congress had authorized the construction of two larger warships. The plans for the battleship *Texas* were obtained in Europe; the old masters had still to be imitated before an original concept could be developed. The armored cruiser *Maine* embodied European concepts, but was designed by the navy's Bureau of Construction and Repair. She would be built at the New York Navy Yard in Brooklyn after the launching ways had been lengthened to accommodate the 324-foot ship, and sheathed in American armor and steel. Final plans were approved in November 1887.

To envision the construction of a steel battleship, an engineer wrote, "place the skeleton of a herring upon its back. The backbone will represent the keel and each pair of ribs a 'frame.' Connect the ribs with four horizontal wires and we have deck beams. Connect the ribs and also these wires by other wires parallel to the backbone and [you have] longitudinals and stringers."

As simple as that sounded, the *Maine* was on the cusp of American technology, and the navy was awash in red tape and bureaucratic inertia. Months passed and, as Navy Secretary William C. Whitney observed angrily in Washington, the keel had not even been laid. Finally, he dispatched Commander Robley D. Evans to Brooklyn to "get things moving."

Evans had superb credentials for the assignment. Although a Virginian, he had stuck by "the old flag" in the Civil War. In the furious assault on Fort Fisher off Cape Fear, North Carolina, Evans took three bullets in his legs. One passed through his right knee, gave him a gimp for life, and temporarily put him on the retired list.

As a boy in western Virginia, he had loved to hunt, and after the war, as navy ships made social visits to foreign ports, Evans was able to take advantage of the local sport: shorebirds in Japan, red-legged partridge in Morocco, wild boar in Tangier. He served on the Lighthouse Board and as an inspector of matériel. In Pittsburgh, Evans suggested to Andrew Carnegie that he build a plant to make first-class steel plate for ships. Carnegie had been selling the navy cheaper pot metal, but he respected Evans and began to meet the higher specifications the navy officer insisted on.

When Whitney gave him the *Maine* assignment, Evans commuted to New York from his post in Washington on the Lighthouse Board. He took a train to New York on Monday, spent two days working on the armored-cruiser project, and returned to Washington Wednesday evening. It was a grueling schedule. "I had always held," Evans said, "that it is better for an officer to wear out rather than rust out."

The *Maine*'s massive double keel was finally laid on October 11, 1888, almost a year after her plans were given final approval. From that moment work went more swiftly. The *Maine* was ready for launching in two years. Even then, she was without her superstructure. Still, she looked imposing with her ram bow thrusting far out of the huge shed.

On November 18, 1890, twenty thousand people turned up at the Navy Yard to attend the launching ceremonies. The new secretary of the navy, Benjamin F. Tracy, stood on a platform draped with red, white, and blue bunting with his granddaughter Alice Tracy Wilmerding, who nervously eyed a bottle of champagne. Even the grapes for the wine had been made in America, in San Bernardino, California.

At eleven o'clock two gangs of workmen began to drive ten-foot oak "ram" wedges between the ship and her keel-blocks. The blocks were knocked out and the still-to-be-named ship rested in her cradle on greased ways. At this stage only friction kept her from gathering momentum and sliding into the East River. The rams were removed, and the gangs used block-and-tackle gear to get the ship underway. Alice Wilmerding quickly raised the bottle of champagne and crashed it against the bow: "I name thee *Maine*." And the *Maine*, glistening in a new coat of red paint, the largest ship ever built at a U.S. Navy yard, slid majestically down the ways into the water as a navy band played and the crowd cheered. The American flag placed on her bow carried forty-five stars.

It seemed to go unnoticed, but Wilmerding had crashed the champagne bottle hard into the number "13" painted on the vessel's Plimsoll line.

From launching to commissioning took almost five years as Naval Constructor William L. Mintoyne of Construction and Repair, together with the Bureaus of Ordnance, Steam Engineering, and Equipment, worked out the problems of new systems and materials the ship would incorporate: nickel steel for her waterline armor belt; turret motors; electrical lightning (Thomas Edison had not made a practical lamp at his Menlo Park laboratory until 1879, but the *Maine* would have some four hundred fixtures); inverted, triple-expansion engines; and critical safety devices such as the heat sensors and "annunciators" that relayed dangerous bunker and magazine temperatures to the ship's control center.

By September 17, 1895, when the *Maine* was at last ready for commissioning, she had been redesignated a "Second-Class Battle Ship." The awesome forms of bigger and more powerful battleships of the *Indiana* class were on the ways, but the *Maine*'s four 10-inch breech-loading rifles were bigger than any armament carried by a cruiser. On that September day, she was the virtual peer of any U.S. fighting ship afloat.

In addition to the 10-inch rifles, the *Maine* armament included half a dozen 6-inch guns at bow, stern, and amidships on the battery deck, seven rapid-firing 6-pounders, four deck torpedo tubes, and a miscellany of 1-pounders and Gatling guns. The inventory of small arms listed "150 swords."

Normally loaded, her displacement was 6,682 tons. Eight boilers gave her two engines over 9,000 horsepower. These drove twin three-bladed screws, each 15 feet in diameter. She could load over 800 tons of coal in her bunkers, enough, at cruising speed, for 7,000 miles of steaming. As originally designed, she carried sails for auxiliary propulsion to extend her cruising range. These were abandoned in the final configuration. The *Maine* would depend on coaling stations rather than wind. The navy listed her design speed at 17 knots, though Frederick Jane, the English publisher whose first U.S. edition of *Jane's Fighting Ships* came out in 1898, rated her at 15 knots. Still, for an "armored cruiser," as Jane still classified her, that was impressive.

Compared to the ships under construction, the *Maine* had an unusual appearance. Instead of poking out of ports along the side, or being placed in a centerline configuration, the 10-inch gun turrets were placed *en echelon* on rounded sponsons extending over the side of the ship's main deck, to port and starboard. The starboard turret was about 100 feet aft of the bow; the port gun platform about 120 feet from the stern. Had the ship's superstructure been continuous, the guns could have fired through an angle of only 180 degrees. To make them more versatile, the superstructure was constructed in three separate sections; thus the big 10-inch guns could rotate and fire across the deck through an angle of 64 degrees as well as point fore and aft and sweep the sea on the side of the ship on which they were placed.

The Spanish-Cuban war had begun to make headlines, and almost certainly the *Maine* would be assigned filibustering duty if it dragged on, but this was still peacetime. The rust-preventive red paint that covered the *Maine* at her launching had been overlaid with a combination of more subtle hues. Hull and boats were white, the superstructure—including the tall twin stacks and the masts with their fighting tops—a dark straw, the guns a businesslike black. Varnished brightwork gleamed around the bridge.

September 17 was a Tuesday, a working day, but a huge crowd gathered for the commissioning ceremonies, many crossing the East River from Manhattan on John Roebling's twelve-year-old Brooklyn Bridge, another marvel of the age. Chaplain John Chidwick, brand new to the navy (he had enlisted earlier in the year after serving at Saint Stephen's Church in New York), found the nautical celebration inspiring. The entire ship's company of 355 officers and men was assembled on the quarterdeck, and after speeches were delivered, Captain A. S. Crowninshield read the *Maine's* orders, then looked out over the neat ranks of sailors and said: "I will expect every man to do his duty." The bugler sounded colors and the American flag was raised smartly to the top of the mainmast. A navy band broke into the national anthem and the entire crew, at ramrod attention, saluted what Chidwick called "our glorious ensign."

After the bugler sounded retreat, the ceremonies were over and the job of getting the ship ready for sea duty began again. Chidwick purchased a small organ and rehearsed the choir in a room near the dynamos, and the ship took on supplies and checked her navigational gear. On November 5 the *Maine* was off for Newport to be inspected by Captain George Dewey.

No one, least of all Chaplain Chidwick, knew that her life at sea would be pitifully short. It had taken nine years to design and build in *Maine*. She would be in commission for less than twenty-nine months.

III

"A BURST OF THUNDER"

In my opinion, the arrival of the *Maine* has caused the United States Government to dominate the situation. It has reduced to absurdity the warnings and threats published from Spanish sources previous to the arrival of the vessel.

—CAPTAIN CHARLES D. SIGSBEE to
Secretary of the Navy John D. Long

You might as well send a lighted candle on a visit to an open cask of gunpowder.

—MRS. RICHARD WAINWRIGHT

E N ROUTE TO THE presidency, William McKinley had run on a plank of peace and prosperity. Shortly before his inauguration he told Grover Cleveland at the White House that he would be happy if he left the office knowing "that I have done what lay in my power to avert this terrible calamity." By that he meant intervention in Cuba and war with Spain. Neither prospect could serve the interests of the nation. McKinley had, in any case, a visceral abhorrence of killing. He had served in the Civil War, fought on the bloody fields of Antietam where over twenty thousand fell, seen "the bodies piled up." Devoutly religious, he hoped there would be no more slaughter in God's name or any other. He wanted to bind up wounds, not open them.

The morning of his inauguration on March 4, 1897, was clear and breezy. McKinley wore a frock coat and a new pair of shoes made by a cobbler in Canton who had drummed the Twenty-third Ohio Volunteers into the carnage at Gettysburg. The new president took his oath of office before "the Lord Most High." In his address McKinley made no mention of Cuba, though he alluded to the difficult situation in the nation's backyard. "We have cherished," he said, "the policy of non-interference with the affairs of foreign governments. . . . We want no wars of conquest . . . we must avoid the temptation of territorial aggression . . . peace is preferable to war in almost every contingency."

William Randolph Hearst, who had a picture of Napoleon hanging in his office, thought the president's address "vague and sapless."

Nine months later, on December 6, 1897, in his first annual message to the Congress, McKinley was—as Hearst and Roosevelt hoped he would be—a shade more truculent. He applied the word "extermination" to the appalling death rate in the Spanish concentration camps, then noted that Sagasta had recalled "brutal" Weyler and "modified the horrible order of reconcentration." Rejecting intervention, recognition of the insurgents, or forcible annexation—this would be "criminal aggression"—he urged that Spain be given time to carry out her reforms, adding that peace and order must soon be restored. If not, the United States might face an obligation "to ourselves, to civilization, and humanity to intervene with force. . . ."

But that was an option, as the president made clear, of last resort. There was another—outright purchase—and McKinley gave it serious consideration. It was not, after all, a radical idea. Five of his predecessors in the White House had made documented offers, and virtually every American president since Washington had hoped to acquire Cuba in one way or another. Nothing came of their initiatives but the idea would not die, perhaps because it offered a simple solution to a long-standing problem. McKinley added his name to the long list of suitors. Predictably, the Spanish balked. Sagasta may have been tempted, but for him there was no easy way out. Any Spanish administration that accepted an offer for the Pearl of the Antilles would be signing its own death warrant—and that of the monarchy as well. Cuba was sacred territory. "Spain is not a nation of merchants capable of selling its honor," he replied.

Enrique Dupuy de Lôme, the sad-eyed Spanish minister to the United States, viewed McKinley's negotiations with the poise of a veteran poker player. The cards he held were not high; he kept them close to the vest. But he sensed that if he played them deliberately and stretched the game out, the Spanish military advantage in Cuba could turn the tables for Spain. Then he would have a strong hand to play in working out a compromise.

Dupuy de Lôme was an experienced negotiator, shrewd, skilled in the subterfuge of diplomacy, but also arrogant, haughty, and on occasion blunt. A conservative, he had survived the cabinet changes made by the new Sagasta government, but he had no sympathy for Moret's policy of conciliation. Though few knew it, he despised McKinley. Around the middle of December, some ten days after the president gave his annual message, Dupuy de Lôme made this plain in a letter to a close friend. This breach of ministerial discretion was to cost him—and Spain—dearly, turn doves into hawks, and present William Randolph Hearst with another windfall.

The five-page handwritten letter was penned in Washington and addressed to José Canalejas, the influential editor of the Madrid *El Heraldo*, who was then in New York negotiating unofficially with the Cuban Junta. Canalejas had not answered the letter when he left New York for Havana. Unwisely, he took it with him. Unwisely again, he hired a temporary secretary in Havana, Gustavo Escoto, who may have been an agent of the junta. Escoto came across Dupuy de Lôme's indiscretion, took a steamer for New York and delivered it to Tomás Estrada Palma. Palma passed it along to Hearst and the State Department.

Dupuy de Lôme's bitter remarks about McKinley's character were triggered by the president's annual message. He wrote: "Besides the natural and inevitable coarseness [grosería] with which he repeats all that the press and public opinion in Spain have said of Weyler, it shows once more that McKinley is weak and catering to the rabble [*débil y populachero*] and, in addition, a hack politician [*politicrasto*] who desires to leave a door open to himself and to stand well with the jingoes of his party."

Canalejas must have known that the letter had disappeared, along with Escoto, and perhaps informed Dupuy de Lôme. Faced by the possibility of being unmasked and embarrassed by the Cubans, the minister carried on. Handling the public relations turmoil that followed the riots in Havana on January 12 proved particularly trying, but the crisis eased when it became apparent, even to Consul General Lee, that they were not anti-American in nature. Lee wired Navy Secretary Long that warships were no longer necessary, though the *Maine*, on standby at Key West since the middle of December, should be available for emergencies.

On January 20, Dupuy de Lôme called at the State Department and made clear his government's position on the matter of a U.S. warship visiting Cuba. It would be regarded as an unfriendly act. Autonomy was working and peace could be achieved by May 1. There was no need to upset the delicate balance of power that existed in Havana. Doing so might bring about a break in relations between Spain and the United States.

De Lôme had played a high card, but the Assistant Secretary of State, Judge William R. Day, filling in for the ailing Secretary John Sherman (the *New York Times* had characterized Sherman as palsied, doddering, and imbecile) turned up an ace: Governor-General Blanco seemed unable to control his own army. How could Spain object if the United States sent a warship to protect its citizens and property?

Four days later, at 10 A.M. on the morning of Monday, January 24, Dupuy de Lôme was summoned to the State Department by Day, who told him that the president had decided to resume the practice (abandoned by Grover Cleveland) of sending American ships on friendly visits to Cuban ports. It would be curious, Day now said, if visits did not take place, since Spain and the United States were at peace. Señor Dupuy could only concede the point.

When Dupuy de Lôme had left, Day went to the White

House and met with the president and Long. No records of the meeting were kept, but soon afterward Day cabled Lee in Havana that the *Maine* would arrive "in a day or two," and that afternoon he so informed a puzzled Dupuy de Lôme. It was arranged that a Spanish ship, probably the *Vizcaya*, would make a reciprocal visit to New York.

Lee received Day's late-morning cable and immediately responded: "Advise visit be postponed six or seven days to give last excitement more time to disappear." But he did not receive that day a second cable from Washington advising that "*Maine* has been ordered. Will probably arrive at Havana some time tomorrow, Tuesday." Later he was understandably perplexed by the haste with which the *Maine* was dispatched.

In his journal that night Long, perhaps sensing that history might require an explanation, made it all seem casual and offhand:

> I have favored for some time suggesting to the Spanish Minister here that his government recognize the wisdom of our sending a ship in a friendly way to Havana ... to resume the usual practice ... to exchange courtesies ... and thus to emphasize the change and the improved condition of things which have resulted from the new Spanish policy. Today, the Spanish Minister assented to this view. . . . Judge Day and I called upon the President and we arranged that the *Maine* should be ordered at once to Havana, notice having been given by the Spanish Minister to his people, and by our Department to our Consul.
>
> It is a purely friendly matter. There is, of course, the danger that the arrival of the ship may precipitate some crisis or riot; but there is far less danger of this than if the ship went in any other way. I hope, with all my heart, that everything will turn out all right.

Chaplain John Chidwick enjoyed watching the *Maine*'s baseball team play its matches with the nines from other ships. The team was especially strong on the mound. "Our pitcher was a colored man named Lambert," Chidwick reported, "a master of speed, curves and control." William

Lambert was a fireman from Hampton, Virginia, and on the afternoon of January 12, at Key West, as rioting erupted in Havana, he was practicing his usual deception when a gun on the *Maine* sounded recall; he and his teammates trotted off the field and returned to the ship.

The gun boomed because Charles Sigsbee had received a message from Lee—"Two dollars"—that the two had worked out and tested over the telegraph wire connecting Havana and Key West. When received, Sigsbee would ready his ship for a dash to Havana as soon as the second part of the signal—"Vessels might be employed elsewhere"—arrived. If it did not, the sortie would be canceled.

On that afternoon the follow-up message was not received. The *Maine* stayed quietly at anchor. Sigsbee and several of his officers relaxed and went to a dance ashore. The days of waiting passed slowly. Swatting an insect in the wardroom one evening, Cadet Wat T. Cluverius thought that the ship must be on station to pursue mosquitoes as well as filibusters.

On Sunday January 23, some of the big new ships arrived at Key West: the *New York*, the *Indiana*, the *Iowa*, the *Massachusetts*, and the *Texas*. All the battleships except the *Oregon*, on the West Coast, were now gathered under Admiral Montgomery Sicard's command. It was the largest fleet assembled since the Civil War, and the reef-fringed, outside anchorage was crowded by the new arrivals. The next day they sailed for the Dry Tortugas, some sixty miles to the west.

The Tortugas had been acquired from Spain in 1819 along with Florida and the keys. A huge fort named after Thomas Jefferson had been built on Garden Key—a "Gibraltar" guarding the entrance to the Gulf of Mexico—and served an important role during the Civil War. Afterward, the Tortugas were all but abandoned until they became winter "drill ground" for the North Atlantic Squadron.

Around 6 P.M. on the twenty-fourth the squadron anchored ten miles southeast of the entrance to Tortugas Roads. Sicard ordered his ships to bank fires. The tense situation in Havana seemed to have quieted; Sigsbee now anticipated only routine maneuvers in the Gulf of Mexico until February when the *Maine* was to proceed to New Orleans for Mardi Gras festivities.

That starry night, at about nine o'clock, the watch on the *Maine* sighted the red and green running lights of a ship approaching from the east at speed. She proved to be the torpedo boat *Dupont*, which steamed directly to the *New York*. Shortly, the flagship signaled Sigsbee to come aboard. On a hunch, Sigsbee ordered steam up before taking his gig over to the *New York*. Sicard showed him a message from Long: "Order the *Maine* to proceed to Havana, Cuba, and make friendly call—Pay his respects to authorities there—Particular attention must be paid to usual interchange of civility. . . ."

Returning to the *Maine*, Sigsbee climbed to the bridge and ordered Wainwright to take her out. The anchor was hauled up around eleven and the ship cruised slowly south toward Cuba. Sigsbee didn't want to arrive furtively at dawn, rather "when the town was alive and on its feet."

The morning of January 25 dawned "clear and pleasant," Cadet Cluverius observed, "and on the starboard bow stretched the deep blue line of the Cuban Coast." As they steamed for Havana, the officers debated whether the *Maine* would be greeted by normal peacetime protocol—or by broadsides from the guns of La Punta and El Morro. Anticipating a worst-case scenario, the ship was discreetly put in fighting trim: main and secondary batteries supplied with ammunition; rifles brought topside from the armory; rifle belts filled with cartridges; and a landing party organized in case American citizens had to be evacuated. As the heights of El Morro loomed off the bows, the ship went to general quarters. These precautions alarmed Chaplain Chidwick, but he felt better for having provided his flock with spiritual armor.

Around 10 A.M. there was only a little breeze as the ship approached the narrow channel that led to the inner harbor. On the starboard hand, Cluverius noted, the La Punta battery appeared to be composed of antique artillery. To port, however, El Morro, built on jagged rock, looked as imposing as it had seemed to French and English raiders over the centuries. Philip II had ordered the great fortress built in 1589, a year after the Armada was shattered. As the *Maine* glided by, Cluverius looked up to the heights and saw the yellow and red colors of Spain floating over the battlements.

Past Morro Castle, along the high cliffs lining the eastern shore, Cluverius saw the white-stone fortifications known as El Cabaña where, he had heard, captured filibusters were incarcerated. Just below the fort, he wrote, "on the hillside, was the Laurel Grove where doomed insurgents were shot; and farther down, on the water's edge, was the town of Casa Blanca."

To starboard of the *Maine* the situation was less threatening. Here was the old walled city with its colorful hotels, parks, office buildings, and the Governor's Palace where General Ramón Blanco administered the affairs of the colony. A seawall built of stone blocks bordered the waterfront; beyond it a handsome avenue ran parallel to the water's edge. On this broad street crowds had begun to gather.

Sigsbee was relieved to see the pilot boat approaching. It seemed to him "evidence of good will." Pilot Lopez told him the *Maine* had not been expected, but would be safe in Havana—"a cultured town." Lopez conned the *Maine* her last mile to the buoy the Spanish numbered 4. Sailors on the forecastle shackled a chain to a ring on the buoy. The *Maine* swung peacefully to her mooring, about four hundred yards off the Machina wharf, with its tall, tripod-shaped, lifting shears. The ship's guns fired off ritual salutes to the flag of Spain and to the ensign of Admiral Vincente Manterola flying from the *Alfonso XII.*

A few minutes before the guns of the *Maine* boomed out, correspondent John R. Caldwell of the *New York Herald* left his room on the top floor of the Hotel Inglaterra, walked down the hall, and knocked at the rooms of Consul General Fitzhugh Lee. Lee opened the door—he took Spanish hours seriously and was just putting the finishing touches to his business suit—and asked Caldwell in. The reporter told him he had important news: the *Maine* would be arriving at Havana that morning.

Lee told Caldwell that was nonsense. Nevertheless, Caldwell insisted, she was coming and he told Lee why. Caldwell had needed cartridges for a revolver the New York office had provided him. Since he could not obtain them in Havana—the sale of arms in the city was strictly prohibited by the Spanish—he had coyly wired the *Herald*: "Camera received but no plates; please rush by next steamer." In New York the message had been misinterpreted and literally decoded as "U.S. Consulate under attack." Apparently, the news had been sent to Washington and taken seriously by officials there. Caldwell had just received a wire stating, "Send report Cuban cane crop. Want for main section." That meant, he told Lee, that the *Maine* was on her way.

Lee again scoffed. As he pondered whether to tell Caldwell about his cable to Long advising a week's delay, thuds of gunfire echoed across the harbor and the two men walked over to a window. "There," Caldwell reported, over the rooftops, "we saw the *Maine* entering the harbor, with bulbs of smoke drifting from her saluting battery."

Quickly, Lee excused himself. He would be leaving shortly for the consulate. No doubt Captain Sigsbee would be paying a call.

Cadet Cluverius was watching a throng of Cuban taxi boats and listening to the "jabbering" of the crowd along the shore when Sigsbee ordered him to go to the consulate and see Lee. He took a boat and was put ashore at the Machina dock. Outside the naval station's gate, surrounded by a group of urchins and idlers, he flagged a cabriolet and directed it to Casa Nueva, the modern office building which housed both the U.S. and British consulates. "The general received me," Cluverius reported, "and seemed surprised at our early arrival. I could see that he did not expect a ship—at least not then."

Lee asked if there had been any disturbance as the *Maine* entered harbor. None, the midshipman replied. Again, Lee looked surprised. Cluverius made an appointment for Sigsbee's call and went back to his ship. When he had left, Lee sent his wire to the Navy Department. The *Maine* had arrived at 11 A.M. So far, so good.

That Tuesday, Sigsbee called on Lee and also, in full dress with cocked hat and epaulets, on Admiral Manterola. He was testing the waters. There were no demonstrations, but once a "stolid and sullen" crowd closed around him, and he noted that Spanish soldiers saluted him apathetically—or not at all. On Thursday, however, acting Governor-General Parrado (Blanco was in the field) received him "with great courtesy." Afterward, Parrado and his staff were given a tour of the *Maine*. Cluverius was struck by the "gaudy array" of the Spanish officers. "Not one single uniform matched another. Some wore red coats, light blue trousers with green stripes; some blue coats, red trousers with black stripes; others wore green coats, red trousers with blue stripes—for all the world like the 'soldiers-so-brave' in the comic opera of the period."

Parrado and his technicolored aides, carefully supervised, were shown the *Maine* from top to bottom. The acting governor-general showed his appreciation by sending a case of his best sherry for the officer's messes.

After that, Cluverius observed, there was a constant flow of Cuban visitors to the ship from noon until dusk—pretty girls, scolding duennas, crying children—all awed by the size of the *Maine* and the power of her armament. (At the Machina, there was considerably less enthusiasm. Cluverius overheard a sailor say that if you were to put the *Maine* on the quarter deck of the *Carlos V*, you wouldn't be able to find her.) Topside, it was sometimes difficult to keep track of the throng of visitors. Below decks, however, security was tight. No one toured unaccompanied and the master-at-arms maintained a constant patrol during visiting hours.

A few Spanish soldiers came on board and the young cadet noted that these "mere boys" didn't seem to know the difference between a turret and a capstan. But the Habaneros made no distinction between amateur and professional soldiers. When the young recruits were loaded aboard transports, "the city went wild, rockets fired, flags flying." Ferry boats circled the steamers for hours "with brass bands hammering out 'Cádiz' over and over, and passengers yelling themselves hoarse with cries of '¡Viva Cuba Española!'"

Cluverius, who had learned something about the guerrilla war at Annapolis, felt sorry for this "miserable lot of recruits [who] were landed from a transport one day, sent to the front the next, marching back and forth, through swamps and morasses, living in filth, one meal a day out of a common trough, fallen upon suddenly by insurgent bands, finally brought back, burning with fever, to hospitals, which the majority of them never left again." He had to admire their loyalty and

fortitude, especially as he compared it with the more indo-
lent life of the Spanish naval officers in Havana. They did
not make their quarters aboard Admiral Manterola's flagship
and did not drill or hold target practice. Their ships seemed
to deteriorate from lack of maintenance.

After several days, as the situation remained tranquil, the
officers of the *Maine* began venturing ashore. Though dressed
in civilian clothes, they were easily identified and coolly received. Even the Cuban businessmen kept their distance,
Cluverius observed, since to be seen with us "meant to be
marked as an insurgent sympathizer." The Americans in
town welcomed the officers warmly but warned them to be
careful—the Spaniards were "treacherous."

At the hotels Spanish and French officers (the latter off
the *Dubordieu*) were given preference. The Spanish gave
a reception and ball for the French to which the officers off
the *Maine* were not invited. General Blanco returned
from the field and Sigsbee paid him a courtesy call. It was
not returned. Often, in frustration, the American officers
would rent bicycles and pedal to Vedado to watch baseball
games.

Sigsbee and several other officers did attend the bull-
fights. Mazzantini, one of the great Spanish matadors, was in
town giving a series of corridas at the Plaza de Toros, across
the harbor in Regla. Sigsbee had been warned that the bullfight crowds were excitable, but he still wanted to test "the
true feeling of the people of Havana toward *Maine*." As he,
Lee, and four officers made their way to the ferry-boat landing that Sunday, someone in the crowd pressed a circular
into Sigsbee's hand:

SPANIARDS!

LONG LIVE SPAIN WITH HONOR

What are you doing that you allow yourselves to
be insulted in this way? Do you not see what they
have done to us in withdrawing our brave and beloved Weyler, who at this very time would have fin-

ished with this unworthy, rebellious rabble who are trampling on our flag and on our honor?

The flyer scornfully derided "low-bred autonomists," then got to the heart of the matter:

> And, finally, these Yankee pigs who meddle in our affairs, humiliating us to the last degree, and, for a still greater taunt, order to us a man-of-war of their rotten squadron... Spaniards! The moment of action has arrived. Do not go to sleep! Let us teach these vile traitors that we have not yet lost our pride.... Death to the Americans!... Long live Spain! Long live Weyler!

Lee translated the circular and, in his jocular way, dismissed it. He often received such threatening broadsides. They boarded the ferry for Regla and, at the Plaza de Toros, watched Mazzantini deftly dispatch the small but shifty Cuban bulls. After the fifth was killed—with one still to meet its fate—Lee suggested that they leave to avoid the crowds that would flock to the ferry landing when the fights were over. He was concerned about the tense atmosphere of the corrida. The Habaneros were unpredictable. General Parrado was in a box nearby, and there were guards all around, but Lee felt they should avoid "embarrassing" the general by "mixing with the people." Sigsbee agreed. He got up and the naval party made a discreet exit.

At the end of the first week of February, the old rumor that the *Maine* would be ordered to New Orleans for Mardi Gras resurfaced. The *Dubordieu* had already departed for the festivities and the crew of the American warship, confined to their hot metal quarters for two weeks, looked forward to joining her. But no orders came through. Instead, another rumor swept the berth deck: the *Maine* would have to leave in twenty-four hours or there would be trouble. Nothing came of this, either, though signs of hostility persisted.

On Wednesday, February 9, Dupuy de Lôme's long struggle with William Randolph Hearst and the *New York Journal* came to an abrupt end. The Canalejas letter had found its way to Hearst's doorstep and, as was usual, he had the last word: THE WORST INSULT TO THE UNITED STATES IN ITS HISTORY bannered the *Journal* across the front page. Below that it declared angrily, SEND DE LÔME HOME AT ONCE IN DISGRACE. There was a trace of hypocrisy to that. Dupuy de Lôme had only said in private what Hearst splashed across his front pages. That hardly mattered to the publisher. The Harvard dropout had another impressive scoop and the *Journal* was fast approaching the million-copy mark in circulation.

Palma had thoughtfully also provided the State Department with a facsimile copy of the letter. Doubting its authenticity, Judge Day took it to the Spanish legation and asked Dupuy de Lôme if it was genuine. The ambassador said it was. He seemed to have anticipated Day's arrival and informed the acting secretary that he had already cabled his resignation to Madrid; he intended to return to Spain immediately. That was none too soon for Hearst; the *Journal* intoned:

Dupuy de Lôme, Dupuy de Lôme, what's this I hear of you?
Have you been throwing mud again, is what they're saying
true? . . .
Just pack your few possessions and take a boat for home.
I would not like my boot to use but—oh—get out De Lôme!

There was no need for the boot. Dupuy de Lôme, his bags packed with dress uniforms, gold braid, and the decorations of a Spanish diplomat, was on his way even as Hearst called for prompt intervention in Cuba: "The flag of Cuba Libre ought to float over Morro Castle within a week." If it was any consolation to the ambassador, Friday's *Journal* announced, in bigger and blacker type than that proclaiming his departure, SPAIN MAKES WAR ON THE JOURNAL BY SEIZING THE YACHT BUCCANEER.

Hearst was furious. The 138-foot steel ship, born the *Vamoose* and only recently given a more aggressive name, was a gift from his beloved mother Phoebe who had been flecked by spray aboard the wasp-waisted *Aquila*. The yacht had been enlisted for press duties more than a year earlier and was said to be carrying a special correspondent to Cuba to report on the "famine and suffering" in the concentration camps. The Spanish assumed it was Karl Decker of Cisneros fame, the *Journal* reported, and seized the ship "right under the guns of the *Maine*." Though Sigsbee didn't know it, his ship had precipitated what Hearst called "the Spanish-*Journal* War."

In Key West later that week, correspondent Walter Scott Meriwether of the *New York Herald*, covering the winter maneuvers of the fleet, received a telegram from his publisher, James Gordon Bennett. He was ordered to Havana to replace John Caldwell. Meriwether had just arrived in Key West and he got his gear together and jumped aboard the *Olivette* for the overnight run to Havana. On arrival, he got a room on the third floor of the Inglaterra and went down the hall to greet his colleague.

He found Caldwell incensed at being recalled; the *Herald* was not unsympathetic to Spain. All the same, Caldwell had turned in some blistering copy on Weyler before "the Butcher" was replaced by Blanco at the end of October, and now he thought the Spanish had maneuvered his reassignment. Calming down, he made a "snifter" for Meriwether and they toasted the *Maine*, swinging peacefully at her harbor mooring.

They were soon joined by Freeman Halstead, a Canadian reporter on the *Herald* team, and by Felipe Ruiz, a Mexican reporter and interpreter. The four journalists repaired to the restaurant of the Inglaterra for the late breakfast favored by the Habaneros. They were talking shop when Halstead noticed that Sylvester Scovel and George Bronson Rea were sitting at a nearby table. Halstead pulled out a blank cable form stamped with the censor's mark of approval—a document he had surreptitiously pocketed when the censor was not looking—and mentioned that Scovel had one, too.

After a leisurely breakfast the correspondents wandered over to the Governor's Palace to see Secretary-General Congosto, the bearded Castilian who was in charge of press relations for the Spanish. Meriwether, who had spent ten years in the navy before taking up journalism, excused himself and walked down Obispo Street to the boat landing so that he could visit the *Maine* and see old shipmates.

Later on in the day, back at the Inglaterra, Meriwether ran into an old friend having a drink at the bar with a Spanish officer. Conversation turned to the relative merits of the American and Spanish navies and the officer admitted Cervera's fleet was numerically inferior to Sicard's. However, he said, the Spanish crews were superior in discipline and accuracy of gunfire. Also, American crews were composed of immigrants—"foreigners"—and they would desert in the event of war. Then Spanish ships would lay waste to the American coastline.

Meriwether took that with a grain of salt. It was true that the crew of the *Maine* was multinational—Oriental, Nordic, Teuton, Irish, and Slavic as well as Anglo-Saxon, but some 80 percent were U.S.-born. They would stick if it came to a showdown.

It was February 15, the city was in a festive mood, and Meriwether took a stroll down the Prado, "lovely with greenery and palms, and in the shimmering bay the *Maine* rode to her buoy." The streets, as Julia Ward Howe had observed years before, were splashed with pre-Lenten colors: There were ladies who "abused the privilege of powder and white themselves with *cascarilla* to a degree that is positively ghastly. . . . Parties of maskers . . . went about screaming at the public with high, shrill voices. . . ." There were men in women's clothes, white people disguised as blacks, blacks powdered in white, and aristocrats in full dress swathed in flowers and jewels. Some of the celebrants shook gourds full of *ghirra* seed: "Chick-a-chick, chick-a-chick!"

As he sauntered down Havana's "Broadway," Meriwether's eye was suddenly caught by a crude drawing on the wall of a side street. It showed a strutting, pompous Uncle Sam, eyes averted, while a figure representing Spain slipped a banana peel under his upraised foot.

Meriwether's only duty that evening, if all was peaceful, was to send the file word *tranquillo* over the cable to Key West. Even this had to go through the censor, and at about eight-thirty he and Ruiz took a horse cab to the palace and filed the one-word message just before the office closed for the night. Afterward, they went to a café frequented by "our gang." Meriwether looked forward to comparing notes with Scovel, Rea, and others in the large Havana press corps.

The long tropic day was suddenly over. (As Howe had recorded, "there is no twilight in these parts, and the curtain of the dark falls upon the scene as suddenly as the screen of the theater upon the denouement of the tragedy.") The trade wind, unstable in the winter months, had died to a whisper; what breeze remained came from the north, and the battleship *Maine* slowly drifted to a northwest heading. There was little tide in the harbor—only a three-foot rise and fall at the new moon—and without that force, Cadet Cluverius had observed, the ship rode virtually head to wind.

Chaplain Chidwick had also noted the new direction before going below to read his breviary. "For the first time our ship swung bow on toward the city." On the bridge, the heading was duly entered in the ship's log.

After fifer Newton had piped down the *Maine* and sent the sailors not on watch to their hammocks, the city hushed, too. Clara Barton noticed the stillness as she worked at her records. And then suddenly her writing table shivered and there was "a burst of thunder" followed by the sound of breaking glass. The big door to the veranda overlooking the bay smashed open. Horrified, she looked up and sensed everything in the room moving. Then she looked through the door, across the harbor, and saw "the air was filled with a blaze of light, and this in turn filled with black specks like huge specters flying in all directions. Then it faded away, the bells rang, the whistles blew...."

Walter Meriwether of the *Herald* was just entering the café, looking around for friends, when there was a tremendous explosion. Instinctively, he covered his head as glass and plaster sprayed the room; a split second later the lights went out. Stunned, Meriwether thought a group of Cuban insurgents must have infiltrated the city and blown up the Governor's Palace; a previous attempt had succeeded only in destroying a downstairs bathroom. He pushed gingerly through the darkness, made his way to the Inglaterra, and walked up to his top-floor room. Inexplicably, perhaps because he looked toward the Palace instead of over the bay, he saw nothing unusual.

Meriwether rushed downstairs and reached the street just as a squadron of Spanish cavalry galloped by, bugles blaring. Then he met up with an English friend. It was the *Maine*, the man told him; the *Maine* was gone. Meriwether, his eyes now accustomed to the darkness, ran off toward the waterfront.

Frederick Teasdale was the captain of the British bark *Deva*, berthed at a wharf in Regla about a half-mile south of the *Maine*. He felt the blast before he heard it; the *Deva* staggered and Teasdale thought his ship had been rammed by a steamer. Then—the shock had been so great—he put his hand to his head thinking he might have been shot. He threw open the shattered door of his cabin and rushed on deck as a tremendous explosion hurled debris and gray smoke high over the harbor. Teasdale noticed something—fireworks?—popping and sparkling through the dense smoke.

Aboard the *City of Washington*, moored aft of the *Maine*, Sigmund Rothschild and Louis Wertheimer had unknowingly given themselves ringside seats to disaster. The two American tobacco dealers had gone on deck shortly after 9:30 P.M. and arranged deck chairs so as to have a view of the harbor. Rothschild joked that they were well protected with the guns of the *Maine* commanding the city. The words were barely out of his mouth when Rothschild heard a sound like "a shot." He looked up and to his astonishment saw the bow of the *Maine* rise up out of the water. Then, in the center of the ship, came "a terrible mass of fire and explosion, and everything went over our heads, a black mass. . . . It was all black. Then we heard the noise of falling material on the place where we had been, right near the smoking room. . . ."

Captain Frank Stevens of the *City of Washington* heard a muffled blast—it sounded as if it came from underwater—then a second explosion. Seeing what had happened, he ordered the ship's boats launched. Two of them had been holed by flying debris and had to be winched back into their davits.

*   *   *

Aboard the *Maine*, Cadet Cluverius had taken the deck watch from 4 to 8 P.M., After the eight o'clock reports were made, he went down to his quarters, stripped down to his underclothes, and began to write letters. The *Olivette* was to enter harbor in the morning and he wanted to mail them before the *Maine* left Havana.

As he wrote, the events of the quiet day played back in his mind: the Spanish coasting steamers taking on troops; the wind shift northward and the ship's new heading; the mustering of the watch; sailors dancing in the starboard gangway to accordion music; fifer Newton playing Taps and the boatswain's mates piping the men to quarters. His pen was moving evenly across the paper when a report cracked the stillness—"the firing of a gun it seemed." The ship's lights winked out, and then there was "an indescribable roar, a terrific crash, intense darkness . . ."

Cluverius, propelled to his feet, found his way to the passageway outside his quarters and ran into a classmate from Annapolis, Cadet Amon Bronson, Jr.

"Come on," Bronson said, "we'll make it."

Cluverius felt a draft of air from up forward—apparently the deck was open to the sea in that direction—and the two cadets splashed their way through ankle-deep water toward the junior officers' hatch. It was impossible to see what had happened, but they found it blocked by wreckage. "One exit closed," Cluverius thought. The cadets struggled aft to the engine-room hatch; a torrent of water poured down from the deck above. Second exit closed.

Finally, Cluverius and Bronson found the mangled ladder to the wardroom hatch and climbed topside, then up the after superstructure to the safety of the poop deck. Beneath them, down below, "the poor wretches, pinned down and drowning, mangled and torn, screamed in agony."

After relieving Lieutenant George P. Blow at 8 P.M., John Blandin had organized the new watch. At about 9:30 Blandin walked down the port quarter deck to a position near the aft 10-inch turret. He sat down and looked out toward the city;

the ship's bow was pointing almost directly toward Havana, he noted. The sky threatened rain, and in the humid air the lights of Havana appeared to wink at him. He wondered whether Washington was cutting new orders for the *Maine;* it seemed time to move on.

Lieutenant John Hood came up beside him and jokingly asked if he was asleep.

"No," Blandin replied, "I'm on watch."

It happened only a few seconds later—two sullen, roaring explosions. "It seemed to me that the sound came from port side forward. Then came a perfect rain of missiles of all descriptions, from huge pieces of cement to blocks of wood, steel railings, and fragments of gratings. . . ." Blandin was knocked down by a piece of debris. Dazed, he struggled to his feet as Hood dashed by, saying that he was going to the poop to help launch boats. Blandin staggered after him. The deck was awash, and he had to slosh through knee-deep water and debris. Climbing to the poop deck aft, he found Captain Sigsbee already there, "as cool as if at a ball."

But Sigsbee had been stunned and uncertain as he put the letter to his wife in an envelope and a "bursting, rending, crashing sound or roar of immense volume" shattered the stillness of the night. The *Maine* trembled, tipped by the head and lurched to port; the lights blinked out and smoke filled his cabin. "For a moment the instinct of self-preservation took charge of me," Sigsbee reported. He felt his way out of the admiral's cabin and started up the suddenly canted floor toward the starboard cabin, planning to leave the ship through one of its square portholes. He pulled himself together and took the usual passageway leading to the main deck.

On his way down the passageway he ran violently into Private William Anthony, his marine orderly. Anthony may have saluted—it was hard to tell in the darkness—and told Sigsbee the ship was sinking. Sigsbee followed Anthony outside and was momentarily blinded by the light of an explosion. He blinked his eyes; now he could see by the light of a fire that had broken out amidships. He prepared to assert command. To signal central authority Sigsbee needed a bugler to sound the "silence call"; Newton was not to be found. He shouted an order—sentries should prepare to repel boarders. Then he realized there were no marines on deck to take the duty.

Not that there was much left to defend. By the light of the fires forward he could see that the *Maine*'s stacks had been knocked flat, port and starboard, and the bow was a mass of twisted wreckage. Several officers seemed to have gathered on the poop deck, and he splashed through the water to the ladder. As he climbed, he heard a hubbub on shore. It seemed to him there were cheers and "shouts of exultation." He found the executive officer, Lieutenant Commander Wainwright, on the poop and began to exercise the chain of command. There were "white forms" in the water and he ordered boats lowered.

At 9:40 P.M., Wainwright was still chatting with Cadet Jonas Holden in the captain's office when he felt the vessel stagger under his feet and his senses were stupefied by "a single long crash." Then he heard the sound of metallic impacts on deck and assumed that the *Maine* had been blown up by a mine—and that the *Alfonso XII* was firing on the sinking ship. The cabin door had been smashed shut by the shock wave, but he managed to get it open. With Holden he dashed from the office, planning to get a battery ready to return the *Alfonso*'s fire. When he reached the deck, he heard shrieks and groans from wounded and dying men up forward. The *Maine* was down by the head, and without power he realized it would be impossible to bring guns to bear on the enemy ship. He took the starboard ladder up to the after superstructure.

Sigsbee ordered Wainwright to assemble a damage-control team from the few survivors and flood the ship's magazines. Naval Cadet David F. Boyd and John Hood volunteered, and the three went forward to see what could be done. Because of the fire amidships they could only go as far as the aft end of the central superstructure. Pungent smoke enveloped them. Wainwright thought it smelled like burning cellulose—the ship's waist had been girded with the material as a self-sealant against shell holes. Choked by the acrid fumes, Wainwright was about to repeat the order to open the flood cocks when he looked down the wardroom hatch; even in the smoky darkness he could see a surge of water rushing aft. The ship was sinking rapidly by the head; the harbor waters would soon flood the magazines. There was nothing they could do about the fire. The three officers went back to the poop where Sigsbee was calling out orders to man the boats.

As Chaplain John Chidwick lay in his bunk reading *Facts and Fakes About Cuba,* a loud report boomed through the ship and she lurched suddenly to port. Chidwick thought the Spanish must have fired on the *Maine.* Leaving his room, he made out, by the light of explosions, the figures of officers climbing up to the deck. He followed them. "I was among the last to reach the ladder," he reported, but "as I ascended I heard someone back of me saying, 'For God's sake, hurry up!'"

Chidwick found the deck clear, but the forward part of the ship was burning fiercely. "From the waters and the ship came the heart rending cries of our men: 'Help me! Save me!'" It was well that he had urged them to make an act of contrition every night, asking pardon of God. Now, as he climbed up to the poop, he made the sign of the cross and desperately called out to them over the din to say the name of Jesus; again and again, he gave them absolution from their sins.

Up on the superstructure he found the captain shouting orders at the top of his lungs. Ammunition was still cooking off forward, and the ship was pierced by an angry, high-pitched whistling noise as air burst out of watertight compartments. His altar boy, Frederick Holzer, came up to him, crying over the din, "Look at me, father, I'm all burned." Rescue boats had appeared out of the darkness, and Chidwick told Holzer to get into one of them.

Several ship's officers (only a few crew had mustered on the poop) worked frantically to get boats into the water to help with the rescue work. Only two or three of the fifteen carried seemed to be usable. Apprentice First-Class Ambrose Ham helped to lower the captain's gig and jumped in as it eased toward the water. Lieutenant Blow was manning the forward fall. In the darkness, without his spectacles, Blow assumed the blocks had jammed after the gig went down a few feet. He shouted down to Ham, "Why won't the boat go down?"

"It's afloat, sir!" Ham replied.

Blow ordered Cluverius to take charge of the gig and save what life he could, then helped to lower the ship's barge on the port side. He jumped aboard and found Chidwick, Lieutenant Carl Jungen, and several other officers and crewmen manning oars. They began rowing around the *Maine* looking for survivors. As they passed down the side of the stricken ship toward the inferno forward, they saw a man struggling in the water. Jungen steered the boat through flotsam that reminded him of Mississippi River driftwood, and they pulled him into the boat. By the glare of the fire it seemed to Chidwick that the water was flowing clear through the ship near the central superstructure.

They returned, slowly searching, to their starting point. By now the poop deck on which the captain and a few others stood was only about a foot above the water.

Chidwick's anguished prayers of absolution were heard on shore where Sylvester Scovel and George Bronson Rea stood on the customhouse docks. The two reporters had been relaxing at a café—perhaps the same one Meriwether was entering—when the roar burst over Havana. They rushed outside. In the darkness—all the city's lights seemed to be out—they saw a glare over the harbor punctuated by flashing colored explosions. Flagging a *volante*, they dashed to the waterfront and talked their way through the police cordon, saying they were officers from the *Maine*. Rushing through the baggage-inspection room and out onto the dock, they found the police chief of Havana, Colonel José Paglieri, climbing into a boat. Paglieri said they could join him, and the two reporters jumped aboard. As they approached the *Maine*, exploding ammunition shrieked through the air overhead. Paglieri's terrified oarsmen stopped rowing and begged to turn back. The Spanish colonel hit one of them with his cane; Rea flogged the other with the end of a rope—"they concluded to proceed."

Nearing the holocaust, Rea noted that "the bow had disappeared; the foremast and smokestacks had fallen; and . . .

the mass of wreckage amidships was on fire." Scovel saw "the red glare of flames glancing upon the black water. At first it appeared as if her bow was totally demolished. Then the mass of beams and braces was seen that was blown forward by the awful rending." They pushed on toward the burning ship and began to pick up bodies from the water. Boats from the *Alfonso XII* and the *City of Washington* were all round them.

Aboard the *Maine*, water was lapping at the edge of the canted poop deck. Sigsbee and a few officers and men clustered under the platform holding the big aft searchlight. A sailor appeared with Peggy, the captain's dog; somehow she had found her way out of the wreckage. But there was no sign of the ship's mascot, a cat named Tom.

A light rain began to fall; perhaps, Sigsbee thought, the explosion itself had caused the precipitation. Private Anthony had called out for the gig and Lieutenant Jungen was backing it in at the aft end of the poop. But Sigsbee was reluctant to leave his command. Then Wainwright whispered to him that the 10-inch ammunition, originally stored ninety feet from the bow, might have been thrown back upon the burning central superstructure. "Captain, we had better leave her," he said quietly.

Sigsbee reflected a moment, then turned to the group around him: "Get into the boats, gentlemen." He added that it would be appropriate for him to go last. As the others boarded the gig and the dog was carefully handed over, he climbed up the after rigging a few feet and looked sadly around; he could see no bodies in the water. Then he got down and stepped over the poop railing into his gig.

At 10:15 P.M. the boat pulled quickly away; then the oars were momentarily shipped. John Blandin heard one of his fellow officers call out across the water: "If there is anyone living on board, for God's sake say so!"

Blandin always wanted to—but never could—blot out the reply. "The only answer was an echo from the distant shore which repeated, '*For God's sake . . .*'"

*　　*　　*

Aboard the *City of Washington*, Wainwright supervised a muster. Lieutenant George Holman took a boat over to the *Alfonso XII* and made a count there; others went to the city's hospitals. Four officers who had been ashore at the time of the explosion reported in. When a master list of the missing was compiled, Wainwright was appalled. Only eighty-five survivors had been found. That meant 265 men were dead or missing. He thought it "a wholesale murder of sleeping men!"

The dining saloon of the Ward Line steamer had been turned into a makeshift hospital. Officers, stewards, passengers—anyone who knew anything about nursing—were attending to the wounded, who lay on mattresses on the floor. The ship was crowded with officials—representatives of Governer-General Ramón Blanco, U.S. consular officials. As always, reporters had appeared, including Scovel and Rea, whose boat had followed Sigsbee's gig to the *City of Washington*.

Seaman Ham observed that the captain was "cool but changed. He looked ten years older." When Colonel Paglieri offered his condolences, Sigsbee replied carefully, "I cannot state more than that we are blown up until I closely investigate."

After inspecting the wounded sailors and finding them well cared for, he went out on deck. For a few minutes he watched ammunition explode fitfully over the small section of his ship that remained above water. Then, at Frank Stevens's invitation, he retired to the captain's cabin and, occasionally striking out words or lines, penciled a message to John D. Long on a piece of ship's stationery:

> Secnav—Washington, D.C. *Maine* blown up in Havana harbor at nine forty tonight and destroyed. Many wounded and doubtless more killed or drowned. Wounded and others on board Spanish man of war and Ward Line steamer. Send Light House Tenders from Key West for crew and the few pieces of equipment above water. No one has clothing other

than that upon him. Public opinion should be suspended until further report. All officers believed to be saved. Jenkins and Merritt not yet accounted for.

Sigsbee signed his name. He was informed that a delegation of Spanish army and naval officers had arrived and wished to express condolence. He saw them, returned to Stevens's cabin, crossed out his name, and added: "Many Spanish officers including representatives of General Blanco now with me to express sympathy." He called in Secretary-General Congosto and showed it to him. "Very kind," Congosto murmured. He told Sigsbee the cable office had been opened. Sigsbee gave the message to Rea shortly before 11 P.M. and asked the correspondent to send it for him. Rea put it in his pocket and departed by boat for the dock area.

After Rea had left, Chaplain Chidwick came up and asked permission to go ashore. Chidwick did not voice his fears. He thought there might be a war on and that he would be taken prisoner, but he wanted desperately to minister to the wounded, many of whom might be dying, in the hospitals of Havana. Sigsbee told him to go.

Shortly before 2 A.M., Sigsbee retired, hoping sleep would clear his head for the difficult day ahead. As he lay in a stranger's bunk, he heard rapid-fire ammunition exploding; the stench of the harbor water came over him, and the terrible smell of blood. He listened to the groans of the wounded sailors just outside his stateroom. Eventually, he caught snatches of sleep.

"Mr. Elwell," Clara Barton reported, "was early among the wreckage and returned to give me the news. She is destroyed." Many of the wounded had been taken to the San Ambrosio and Alfonso Trece hospitals. Barton recalled her remark to Commander Wainwright that on a naval vessel someone was bound to be hurt, in action or otherwise. Gathering a few supplies, she rushed out of the house and proceeded to the San Ambrosio Hospital.

There she found perhaps forty of the wounded. They were "bruised, cut, burned; they had been crushed by timbers, cut by iron, scorched by fire, and blown sometimes high in the air, sometimes driven down through the red hot furnace room and out into the water, senseless, to be picked up by some boat and gotten ashore. Their wounds were all over them—heads and faces terribly cut, internal wounds, arms, legs, feet and hands burned to the live flesh."

Then she made an observation that would prove useful to a court of naval inquiry: "The hair and beards [were] singed, showing that the burns were from fire and not steam; besides, further evidence shows that the burns were where the parts were uncovered. If burned by steam, the clothing would have held the steam and burned all the deeper." The men she talked to were certain the explosion could not have been internal; even if it was, she thought, the boilers could not have blown up.

As she passed down the lines of wounded men, she took their names. Most recognized her. One, peering out from the bandages over his face, "looked earnestly at me and asked: 'Isn't this Miss Barton? . . . I knew you were here and thought you would come to us. I am so thankful for us all.'"

It was too much for Barton. Turning her head, she "passed the pencil to another hand and stepped aside."

Walter Scott Meriwether also made the rounds of the hospitals. After confirming that the *Maine* had been sunk, he had dashed to the cable office at the Governor's Palace. It was open, and Congosto had two censors on duty, but nothing was going over the line to Key West. Meriwether left his bulletin with one of the operators and, with his interpreter Felipe Ruiz, went to one of the hospitals. There were guards at the entrance. "Officer from the *Maine*," Ruiz announced in Spanish. Meriwether was immediately allowed in.

The *Herald* correspondent began his rounds of the hospitals at 1:30 A.M. All night long he watched the wounded being carried into the wards on stretchers. He took some of them by the hand and, "with the best voice I could command," tried to cheer them up. "In adjoining cots were a sailor with his face half blown away and another with both legs so badly fractured that he must lose them.

"At the end of the ward was a lusty marine crying, 'For God's sake, let me die!'

"With all possible tenderness and care the Spanish doctors were dressing the face of a fireman. 'There is something in my eyes,' he said. 'Wait and let me open them.' Both eyes were gone."

Meanwhile, at the cable office, Congosto allowed only Captain Sigsbee's dispatch to go over the wire, though Sylvester Scovel, using his stolen cable blank, managed to get a bulletin through and about a hundred words of an Associated Press story slipped past the censor. Unknown to Congosto, however, a Cuban agent working for U.S. naval intelligence had wired Key West shortly after ten o'clock that the *Maine* had been sunk. The message was delivered to Lieutenant Albert Gleaves, commanding the torpedo boat *Cushing*. Gleaves was skeptical; Key West was awash in rumor. Yet the agent was said to be reliable.

Gleaves took the message to Lieutenant Commander William S. Cowles, commanding the *Fern*. With the fleet at sea Cowles was the senior officer afloat at Key West. More than that, as everyone knew, he was married to Theodore Roosevelt's sister Anna. Cowles was inclined to take the message seriously. He and Gleaves went over to the telegraph office where a night operator, Tom Warren, was on duty. They waited for more than an hour, drinking coffee and chewing the breeze, while the telegraph remained silent. Then, just as they were about to discount the rumor and leave, the instrument began tentatively to click.

The message came through unciphered, in the clear. It was from Sigsbee to Long: "*Maine* blown up in Havana harbor at nine forty tonight and destroyed. . . ."

When they had all read it, Warren sat down at the telegraph and began to transmit the news to Washington.

It arrived at the Navy Department slightly before one on Wednesday morning, February 16. The duty officer immediately called for a courier and sent the message to Secretary Long, who was putting up at the Portland Hotel.

It was a cold, blustery night, but the social season in Washington was in full swing. Helen Long, the secretary's daughter, had been to a ball and at 1:30 A.M. had just returned to her father's rooms when the courier appeared at the door. She woke up her father and gave him the dispatch. Long found it "almost impossible to believe." He quickly penciled a note to Captain Francis W. Dickins, acting chief of the Bureau of Navigation, asking him to report immediately to the Portland; he attached Sigsbee's wire, stuck the papers in an envelope, and gave it to the courier. Dickins had been sleeping at his office during the weeks of the emergency; he received it in about twenty minutes.

Dickins hurried through the deserted Washington streets thinking that war was now inevitable. It was nearly 3 A.M. when he reached Long's quarters. After a short discussion, they decided to inform the president at once. Again, Dickins took to the windy streets. By the time he reached the White House, a hint of dawn bleached the horizon. The night watchman let him in and he was ushered upstairs to a large room that adjoined the commander in chief's bedroom. Shortly, McKinley appeared in his dressing gown. Dickins apologized for the early hour and gave him Sigsbee's wire.

The president read it several times. "The *Maine* blown up!" he murmured. "The *Maine* blown up!" Then, grimly, he handed the cable back and told Dickins to let him know of any further developments. It may have seemed to him that the bodies were piling up again.

IV

THE YELLOW KID AND THE CHINA-SHOP BULL

A great nation must have a great navy; and this means that it must accept without undue hysterical excitement the fact that accidents will from time to time befall the ships of its navy. If because of these accidents it stops work, whether on dry docks, battleships or torpedo boats, it will prove that it is not a great nation and that it is not entitled to rank as such in the world.

—THEODORE ROOSEVELT to John Davis Long
February 18, 1898

Our great battleships are experiments which have never yet been tried and, in the friction of a fight, have almost as much to fear from ... some explosion of their own tremendous ammunition as from the foe.

—JOHN DAVIS LONG
February 24, 1898

ABOARD THE *City of Washington*, Charles Sigsbee rose and took reports from his officers on the condition of the wounded in the lounge and the number of survivors mustered. Over 250 men were still missing; only 18 of the 85 rescued seamen were uninjured. As light streaked the sky outside the liner's portholes, he went on deck to take stock of the damage to his ship.

The stench from the water hit him again, but by dawn's first light there was not much to be seen. There were still fires amidships throwing off a pungence of wood, cellulose, and cordite, and a pall of black smoke shrouded the harbor. As visibility improved, Sigsbee could see that even the poop was now awash—either the tide had risen or the ship had sunk into the bottom ooze. A few jagged pieces of metal nicked the surface where the bow of the *Maine* had pointed at Havana. A small detail bothered him. Even the mooring buoy had disappeared. The *Maine* would never need one again, but it was surprising that it had vanished.

The central superstructure looked totally unfamiliar; then Sigsbee realized that part of the forward deck and superstructure, including the bridge and pilothouse, had been blown upward and back over the afterpart. What he now saw, starkly outlined by the slanting rays of the rising sun, was the ceiling of the berth deck. Only the night before, the crewmen had slung their hammocks from that surface. "On the white paint of the ceiling was the impression of two human bodies—mere dust." There were still white objects in the water. They appeared to be parts of bodies.

Shortly afterward, Sigsbee saw Wainwright and Hood take the gig and attempt to make a closer inspection of the *Maine*. A Spanish boat off the *Alfonso XII*, manned by armed sailors, warned them off, but later that morning Wainwright was able to close on the wreckage. He saw immediately what Sigsbee had observed. The forward deck had been violently peeled back as though it were the top of a sardine tin; the conning tower pointed downward; the port 6-inch gun of the central superstructure was perched almost on top of the starboard 6-incher—"the force of the explosion was in a direction from port forward to starboard aft."

The tide was lower now, and Wainwright boarded the *Maine*. Standing on a section of the after decking, he could see "nothing that I could recognize as any part of the ship forward of the crane on the port side of the main deck"— except what appeared to be a piece of bottom plating. But he had the impression that the body of the ship had somehow been bent, with the apex to starboard, "as a stick would show a break if held fast at both ends and pushed from left to right until broken."

Wainwright noted that the aft mast with its armored top was still standing, though slightly askew. Above the crosstree a swab, apparently blown upward from the deck, hung limply from a signal-yard line.

Wainwright returned to the *City of Washington* and reported to Sigsbee. The captain appeared tired but calm, perhaps willing on himself part of the service creed: "An officer in emergency should pour ice water over his personal feelings." They worked out plans to move Sigsbee's headquarters from the Ward Line steamer to the Hotel Inglaterra, meet with Lee, visit the hospitals, send the able-bodied crewmen back to Key West. The dead would have to be buried; Chidwick could make the arrangements with the bishop of Havana.

Sigsbee decided to keep only a skeleton staff in Havana—Wainwright, Holden, Cluverius, Private Anthony, Surgeon Lucien G. Heneberger, and a few others. The Spanish had been sympathetic, but it seemed wise to get most of the men out of Cuba.

In his cable to the Navy Department, Sigsbee had advised that opinion on the cause of the accident be suspended, but after observing the wreckage of the *Maine* the conviction that a mine had caused the disaster took hold of him. He knew that a court of inquiry would investigate. If the explosion had taken place on the *Maine*, if it was internal, the responsibility was his. But if it originated outside the ship, his slate would be cleared.

That morning the punctual *Olivette* steamed into the harbor to deliver passengers and pick up mail. It was instantly obvious there could be none from the *Maine*—and yet there was one piece of mail. Captain Frederick Teasdale of the English bark *Deva*, docked at Regla, later recalled that a storm of paper and small fragments had fallen on his ship after the explosion. One of these was a charred envelope addressed to a Mr. "Silley" or "Seller." If it had been penned by apothecary Walter Sellers, it was his last home letter. Sellers was dead.

The last survivor of the *Maine's* complement was also

found that morning among the wreckage. It was the ship's mascot, the cat named Tom.

William McKinley was late for breakfast that Wednesday morning. He had a houseguest, Myron T. Herrick, a Cleveland banker active in Republican politics. Herrick joshed the president about his tardiness, but fell silent when McKinley told him what had happened to the *Maine*. It was clearly not a morning for levity.

All over Washington the mood was grim. Flags were half-masted, business and social functions canceled, as newsboys hawked the morning papers. Somehow the story had percolated up from Key West over the telegraph wires. Navy Secretary John Long had been harassed until 5 A.M. by telephone calls from reporters trying to confirm the story. Finally, he dressed, went to his office at the Navy Department, and confirmed that Captain Dickins had dispatched relief vessels, including Commander Cowles's *Fern*, to Havana. Then he called the White House and arranged to lunch with the president.

That evening the dog-tired secretary wrote in his journal. "This has been a busy day, a day of gloom and sadness." The entire Spanish delegation to Washington had called to express their regrets. As they did, they must have passed the finely crafted model of the *Maine* outside his office. Workmen took off its glass case, removed the little silk American flag from the peak of the foremast and placed it at half-mast on the backstay.

After lunch with the president and his family, Long observed that opinion on the cause of the explosion was sharply divided on traditional lines. Conservatives thought it an accident; jingoes were sure that it was by design. "My own judgment is . . . that it was the result of an accident, such as every ship of war, with the tremendously high and powerful explosives which we now have on board, is liable to encounter." The naval board of inquiry he had ordered Admiral Sicard to appoint would have to determine the cause and fix the blame.

McKinley was also cautious, not about to be rushed to decision. "My duty is plain," he confided to Senator Charles

W. Fairbanks of Indiana. "We must learn the truth and endeavor, if possible, to fix the responsibility. The country can afford to withhold its judgment and not strike an avenging blow until the truth is known."

The assistant secretary of the navy took a slightly different tack. He felt his first duty was to brief Long on preparedness. "It may be impossible," he wrote, "to ever settle definitely whether or not the *Maine* was destroyed through some treachery on the part of the Spaniards," and he did not presume to anticipate the administration's reaction to the crisis, or to formulate foreign policy. But since the navy would play a critical role in any conflict with Spain, "it seems to me, sir, that it would be well to take all possible precautions."

"For a year and a half now," he warned, "we have been explaining to Spain that we might and very probably would, in certain contingencies interfere in Cuba." She had used that lead time to ready her fleet. With the sinking of the *Maine*, Spain now held the advantage—at least insofar as ships on the Atlantic were concerned. It would be false economy not to press Congress for "an ample Navy."

Sending that down the hall to Long, he dashed off a less circumspect note—"from one Porc man to another"—to his Harvard friend Benjamin Diblee: "Being a Jingo . . . I would give anything if President McKinley would order the fleet to Havana tomorrow. This Cuban business ought to stop. The *Maine* was sunk by an act of dirty treachery on the part of the Spaniards I believe; though we shall never find out definitely, and officially it will go down as an accident."

With his brother-in-law William Cowles on his way to Havana aboard the *Fern*, Roosevelt knew he would have a direct pipeline to Havana, and as news filtered in from Cuba, he became less certain that Spain had blown up the *Maine*.

In New York, however, William Randolph Hearst rushed to judgment. In less than forty-eight hours he knew with certainty what had happened, how, why, and even who had committed the crime.

Hearst first heard about the catastrophe late on Tuesday evening. He had left his office early, probably to go to the theater, and called the *Journal* afterward. The night editor reportedly told him that the *Maine* had blown up and the story was being front-paged along with "other big news."

"There is not any other big news." Hearst announced. "Please spread the story all over the page. This means war."

On Wednesday morning the *Journal's* headline—CRUISER MAINE BLOWN UP IN HAVANA HARBOR—was, if inaccurate (the *Maine* was a second-class battleship) at least factual. The *World* took the news a step further. Sylvester Scovel's brief account of the sinking suggested foul play: "There is some doubt as to whether the explosion took place ON the *Maine*." After that, the *Journal* was never again indecisive.

The evening edition of the *Journal* announced that the Cabinet was meeting to cope with the crisis, and that there was a GROWING BELIEF IN SPANISH TREACHERY. On Thursday, February 17, the Spanish plot was unmasked in an early-edition headline: DESTRUCTION OF THE WARSHIP MAINE WAS THE WORK OF AN ENEMY. Beneath the banner head was a sketch of the *Maine* anchored over a harbor mine. The Spanish had arranged this, and the explosion was initiated through a wire leading from the mine to a shore installation. A later edition put a catchy label on the device; it was AN ENEMY'S SECRET INFERNAL MACHINE.

That evening all doubts regarding the perpetrators of the crime had vanished: WAR! SURE! MAINE DESTROYED BY SPANISH; THIS PROVED ABSOLUTELY BY DISCOVERY OF THE TORPEDO HOLE. The story written by George Bryson reported that all Havana knew what had happened; divers working around the ship had found plates bent inward. This was "undoubted proof of Spanish treachery." Oddly, since Spanish agents were deemed responsible, Hearst offered a fifty-thousand-dollar reward "for the Detection of the *Maine* Outrage."

Captain Sigsbee, the *Journal* said, was practically certain that his ship had been blown up by a mine or torpedo. In this assertion, the *Journal* was somehow right. On February 17, Sigsbee cabled Secretary Long: "Probably the *Maine* destroyed by mine, perhaps by accident. I surmise that her berth was planted previous to her arrival, perhaps long ago." In his mind a device very similar to that pictured by the *Journal* had begun to take shape.

In Cartagena on February 16, Admiral Pascual Cervera wrote yet another lugubrious advisory to Minister of Marine

Bermejo: "To the grave Dupuy de Lôme affair is added the news of the explosion of the *Maine*, which has just been reported to me, and I am constantly thinking of the *Vizcaya*." The Spanish cruiser had sailed a week before and was due in New York that day. As Cervera saw it, he had sent one of his best ships, carrying 150,000 pesetas in gold for troop payments, coal, and other supplies "into the mouth of the wolf." "God grant that no attempt is made against her."

"The explosion of the *Maine*," Cervera wrote the next day "seems to have occurred under circumstances which leave no doubts of its being due to the vessel herself." Since no real investigation of the wreckage had taken place, his conclusion seemed premature. In Havana, Governor-General Blanco and Admiral Manterola had only begun to organize a Spanish naval board of inquiry. Blanco's instructions from the minister of colonies, Segismundo Moret, were unambiguous: "Gather every fact you can to prove the *Maine* catastrophe cannot be attributed to us."

Neither Cervera nor Moret had suspended judgment, but at least their remarks were confidential. In Madrid, however, General Valeriano Weyler bluntly announced that the explosion was due "to the indolence of the vessel's crew." Weyler failed to declare, however, that on January 8 he had written to a friend in Havana strongly suggesting that he had authorized the mining of the harbor before leaving Cuba for Spain. Fitzhugh Lee would testify before the Senate Foreign Relations Committee that Weyler subsequently sent a cable to his correspondent asking him to destroy the incriminating letter.

On the sixteenth Lee cabled the State Department his hope that the American people would "repress excitement," but he was already developing his own theory. The Civil War veteran cobbled up a simple but effective device. A few evil persons, amateurs really, had secretly crammed a buoyant container, perhaps a hogshead or an old wine barrel, with a few hundred pounds of guncotton and placed it where the *Maine* would drift against it. Sigsbee's explanation, as it evolved, was remarkably similar. He thought that a dozen terrorists could have jury-rigged the mine, put it aboard a lighter, and towed it, barely awash, to a position near the *Maine*. His executive, Richard Wainwright, had observed a suspicious vessel passing by the day before the explosion.

Rumors, perhaps spread by the Cuban Junta, seemed to reinforce the mine theory. According to one, a Spanish diplomat in Key West admitted there had been mines underneath the *Maine*—"enough to blow her to hell."

In the U.S. Navy, if not the Spanish, opinion was sharply divided on the cause of the explosion. According to a survey by the *Washington Evening Star*, a majority of naval officers interviewed thought it accidental. They suspected heat generated by internal combustion in a coal bunker adjacent to one of the magazines had cooked off ammunition. Many others, however, espoused the mine theory; a few thought a bomb might have been smuggled aboard.

Most line officers who had friends aboard the *Maine* held the Spanish responsible. Robley ("Fighting Bob") Evans, one of Roosevelt's favorite captains, heard about the explosion in New Orleans. He had a "decided" opinion on the matter. War should be declared on Spain. Diplomatically, Evans kept his judgment to himself, but his gut instinct was to strike hard and fast. He considered Admiral Sicard, who was subject to malarial attacks, too old, sick, and enfeebled to take action. He should have steamed "into Havana the morning after the disaster with his whole fleet and said to General Blanco that he had come to find out why these American officers and men, the guests of Spain, had been foully murdered." Later, in Washington, he candidly told Secretary Long how he would have handled the situation.

"In that event," Long replied sharply, "you would have been promptly recalled and reprimanded."

"Undoubtedly," Evans fired back, "but the people would probably have hailed me as the next president."

In Havana, by the afternoon of the sixteenth, some semblance of order had been restored. The Spanish had been helpful and sympathetic. Flags flew at half-mast from the Governor's Palace and all the ships in the harbor. Blanco—in tears, some said—finally paid a call on Sigsbee at the Inglaterra.

The *Olivette* arrived on schedule and provided logistical support until the *Mangrove*, a lighthouse tender, came in. At 1 P.M., the Plant Line steamer left Havana carrying *Maine* officers and able-bodied crew. Lieutenant George Blow, dressed in a shirt, an old pair of trousers, and a pair of slippers he had been given on the *City of Washington*, was exhausted, but the horrors of the explosion, running through his mind, banished sleep. He wrote to his wife Adele of his miraculous escape. He did not know if the *Maine* had been "torpedoed by the Spanish, blown up by a mine, or whether the Cubans did it to bring on a war—or whether it was one of those spontaneous explosions." But when they reached Key West, he expected "to find that at last the jingoes have had their way and that war is declared. We must do our best!"

Sigsbee put Wainwright in charge of the hulk of the *Maine*. His first assignment was to claim jurisdiction over the wreck; the Spanish were not at first cooperative. Chaplain Chidwick had more success with his negotiations with the bishop of Havana for funeral plots—embalming facilities in the city were almost nonexistent. "We cannot thank too much the Bishop of Havana," Chidwick wrote, "who placed his cemetery at our disposal." This was Colón Cemetery, on the outskirts of the city. There was only one hitch. The bishop insisted that the service be Catholic. Sigsbee indignantly protested the bishop's edict. Each creed, he pressed, needed its own forms. But the bishop would not "concede the point."

By the morning of the seventeenth, only nineteen bodies had been recovered. They were placed in simple wooden coffins and taken to the Havana Municipal Palace to lie in state, flanked by tall torchères and floral wreaths from the Ward Line and other organizations. The most extravagant arrangement announced, on its broad silk ribbon: NEW YORK JOURNAL. Later the coffins were taken outside and placed before the Governor's Palace. Hearses arrived, and at 3 P.M. the funeral cortège moved off through Havana as thousands of Cubans and Spaniards watched from city streets and balconies. On the left were the hearses, some crested with gold-leafed angels, drawn by black horses; on the right were carriages carrying dignitaries, drawn by white horses. Sigsbee took an Episcopal prayer book from his pocket and began reading the Protestant service.

"It was a beautiful spectacle," Cadet Cluverius remembered. "First the marines, then the seamen battalion from the

Alfonso. Behind them came military, naval and civil authorities; then the long line of richly-draped hearses [and] the officers of the *Maine* in carriages. . . . A sorrowful band we were, following our dead shipmates to their graves in foreign soil."

Clara Barton's heart faltered at the sight of the hearses carrying "bodies of martyred heroes," and the sound of muffled drums and tolling bells pierced her with sadness. Her thoughts turned to "homes wailing in bitter grief for these, so lone, so lost"; the sailors had only

> Nodding plumes over their bier to wave,
> And God's own hand in that lonely land
> To lay them in their grave.

At graveside, Father Chidwick solemnly read the Catholic service. Lee stood nearby in derby and morning suit with Sigsbee, Barton, and the others. Governor-General Blanco led the Spanish delegation. After the coffins were lowered into the ground, a volley rang out.

And then it was over, but not for long. Soon after the funeral Sigsbee learned that forty more bodies—most unrecognizable—had been recovered from Havana Harbor. They, too, were buried at Colón. Sigsbee wired the Navy Department: "Friends of dead should realize that we are in tropics."

A cross was later placed over the graves in the Colón Cemetery. It said simply, VICTIMS OF THE MAINE and represented all those who had perished, the known dead, and those still missing: Gustav Anderson, seaman, Uddevala, Sweden; Anthony Conroy, coal passer, Galway, Ireland; Charles Hassel, gunner's mate, Saba, West Indies; Otogira Oshida, steerage cook, Yokohama, Japan; George Mobles, coxswain, Cephalonia, Greece; C. H. Newton, fifer, Washington, D.C.; James Pinkney, mess attendant, Norfolk, Virginia; Michael Salmin, ordinary seaman, Russia; and all the rest.

On the day before the funeral Secretary Long had ordered Admiral Montgomery Sicard, commanding the North Atlantic squadron, to appoint a court of inquiry to investigate the disaster. Under naval regulations such fact-finding bodies were established when blame could not immediately be fixed and criminal acts were suspected. They were composed of four officers, one of whom would serve as judge advocate.

The ailing Sicard, whose future in the navy was even then being determined by a board of medical survey, promptly submitted to Washington the names of four officers from his flagship, the New York. Not one was senior in rank to Sigsbee. Washington rejected two of the appointees and Sicard proposed alternates. As finally comprised, the court included Captain William T. Sampson as president, Captain French Ensor Chadwick and Lieutenant Commander William P. Potter as members, and Lieutenant Commander Adolph Marix as judge advocate.

Sampson, commander of the battleship Iowa, was himself ill (though neither he nor the navy knew how seriously). He was senior to Sigsbee on the navy list and had served as chief of the Bureau of Ordnance and head of the torpedo station at Newport. Chadwick captained the New York and had directed the Office of Naval Intelligence and the Bureau of Equipment. His special areas of expertise included coal and electricity. Potter also had technical experience and was considered an outstanding officer. Marix had been executive officer of the Maine until November 1897, and was thoroughly familiar with her design and organization.

On the evening of February 20 the members of the court and Chief Yeoman Frederick J. Buenzle, who had been appointed stenographer, boarded the Mangrove in Key West and sailed for Havana. They arrived at sunrise the next morning; almost immediately, the court of inquiry went into session. Its four members sat in straight-backed chairs at a round table in the light tender's comfortable, mahogany-paneled saloon.

Yeoman Buenzle, who had known about a dozen men on the Maine, was able to visit the wreck just before the court convened. He ran into Chaplain Chidwick who was still trying to identify bodies. At low tide, Buenzle noted, a hatch opening was flush with the harbor surface. Pieces of wood blocked access to the hatch, but through the "imprisoning barrier" he could see "a tangled mass of bodies . . . a huddle of arms and legs swaying with the motion of the tide. Through a hole that had been blown in the deck extended the frail arm of a boy, tattooed with an armor-pierced heart above a girl's name, 'Beatrice.'"

Buenzle, an expert in shorthand, began to record the proceedings at 10 A.M.

The first witness was Charles Sigsbee. The captain of the *Maine* declined the offer of counsel but asked that he might be allowed to join the proceedings "at such times . . . as he might desire." The court had no objection.

After the formalities were observed, Sigsbee told the court that he had taken command of the *Maine* on April 10, 1897, and brought her into Havana Harbor about 9:30 A.M. on January 24, 1898. He had the date wrong and the time was later than he stated, but the court took no notice, perhaps recognizing that Sigsbee's real trial had begun six days earlier when disaster struck his once proud command.

They had been difficult, emotionally disturbing days. In addition to hospital visits, graves' registration, the funeral, and a blizzard of Washington paperwork, Sigsbee had legal questions to cope with. On Friday the eighteenth, still dressed in civilian clothes, he had tried to approach the *Maine* on one of the *Fern's* gigs. A Spanish patrol boat intercepted him and turned him back. Everything was "*mañana*" as Cadet Cluverius pointed out, and it took Sigsbee a full day to obtain official permission to board his ship.

The question of jurisdiction over the *Maine* and the waters around it plagued Blanco and Manterola as much as it did Lee and Sigsbee. The ship—what was left of it—was American, the harbor Spanish. The Spanish argued that a joint investigation could best determine the cause of the accident. Lee forwarded the Spanish proposal to Washington. At the Navy Department, Roosevelt opposed the request. In a strong memo to Long on Saturday the nineteenth, Roosevelt argued convincingly against "any examination in conjunction with the Spaniards as to the *Maine's* disaster. I myself doubt whether it will be possible to tell definitely how the disaster occurred by an investigation; still it may be possible, and it may be that we could do it as well in conjunction with the Spaniards as alone. But I am sure we never could convince the people-at-large of this fact."

Long and the president agreed, and the State Department wired Lee that the navy's investigation would continue independently. In the meantime, however, the coastal survey vessel *Bache* arrived from Key West carrying navy divers, who set to work on the wreck. The Spanish, who had now established their own inquiry, insisted that their divers accompany them. Sigsbee gave the Spanish plans of the *Maine* and extended other assistance, but refused them permission to dive on the wreck—"a part of the territory of her own country." The Spanish conceded the point but then told Sigsbee that U.S. divers were not to investigate the harbor bottom, which was Spanish. "There it stood," Cadet Cluverius noted. Even the depth of the waters around the *Maine*, which proved to range from 29.5 to 37.5 feet, had at first to be taken from the wreckage itself.

The arrangement did not please Captain Don Pedro del Peral y Caballero, who had been placed in charge of the independent Spanish investigation. If the corpse of the *Maine* was out of bounds for his divers, how could he conduct a responsible postmortem? But in spite of—or perhaps because of—the restriction, Peral was ready with a preliminary report by Sunday. It concluded that the explosion that had blown up the *Maine* was internal. The finding was based on the observations of three officers who rowed around the hulk of the *Maine* in a small boat.

Two days earlier, Captain Antonio Eulate, commanding the magnificent black-hulled *Vizcaya*, approached New York in a heavy fog. On a previous visit to the city, Eulate had received a royal welcome. He did not expect that on this hastily arranged "courtesy call"; relations between Spain and the United States were hardly cordial. But he had no way of anticipating the ugly reception his ship would receive, for he had left Cartagena before the *Maine* exploded and, without wireless, had no way of knowing the news from Havana.

Eulate's weedy-bottomed cruiser had made a slow, coal-saving passage and was further delayed by foul weather off Bermuda. When she finally appeared off Point Pleasant, New Jersey, February 18, a pilot came aboard and took her through the dense fog as far as Sandy Hook, where she anchored to await improved visibility. There Eulate heard about the *Maine*. Stunned, he ordered his colors to half-mast. The members of the ship's band and the Galician bagpipers who had prepared to serenade visitors, put away their instruments.

Two days later, with the weather still windy and foggy, the *Vizcaya* moved as far as the naval anchorage at Tompkinsville, Staten Island—but not to Lower Manhattan as originally planned. Public animosity toward the visit, fanned by the yellow press, made tight security precautions necessary. Even as the *Vizcaya* approached the New Jersey coast, the *World* had warned its readers: "While lying off the Battery, her shells will explode on the Harlem River and in the suburbs of Brooklyn."

The *Journal*, whose headquarters in the Tribune Building on Park Row were well within range of the cruiser's 11-inch guns, fired off incessant editorial volleys at the *Vizcaya*: WAR—SPANISH WARSHIP APPROACHING, it headlined, and after the cruiser arrived, BIG GUNS TRAINED IN NEW YORK HARBOR FORTS ON VIZCAYA. Shortly, Hearst proudly announced "that on account of its too decided Americanism and its work for the patriots of Cuba this newspaper and its reporters have been forbidden entrance on board the Spanish warship. . . . The *Journal* is flattered by these delicate attentions from Spain. . . ." Hearst also offered his readers an entertaining card game in which the battleship *Texas* took on the *Vizcaya*. The object of the game was, of course, to sink the Spanish ship.

A more tangible threat to the cruiser's safety lay docked nearby at the navy yard in Brooklyn. Inventor John Holland's submarine torpedo boat was undergoing sea trials. His latest model appeared to meet or surpass rigid performance requirements imposed by the navy that had plagued him since he built his first submarine in 1881. ("What will the Navy require next," Holland once asked, "that my boat should climb a tree?") Rear Admiral Francis Bunce, commandant of the yard, was told to keep a close watch over Holland's weapon. The submarine's sea trials were canceled until further notice. Police Department launches and navy tugs carrying marines formed a protective cordon around the unpopular Spanish vessel.

The situation alarmed Cervera. If the *Vizcaya* met the same fate as the *Maine*, the odds against his fleet would increase. Eulate was ordered to "judiciously shorten his stay" in New York and "use every manner of precautions, especially in coaling." The captain of the *Vizcaya* did take on coal, but only enough for a safe passage to Havana, and it was closely inspected for explosives. On February 24 he made an earlier-than-planned departure for Cuba.

When William McKinley appointed his Cabinet, critics observed that he seemed to have founded a home for illiterate old men. Only two had a college education; all but two were now over sixty, and the garrulous and doddering John Sherman at State was seventy-five. Even John Long, fifty-nine and Harvard-educated, considered the Cabinet to have four "cripples"—himself included. Though Long considered his assistant secretary aggressive and on occasion impulsive, he still thought Roosevelt competent and responsible. After the afternoon of February 25, however, he had second thoughts.

Long took most of that Friday off. He had suffered from insomnia since the dispiriting news of the *Maine*'s sinking shattered his sleep ten days earlier, and was also afflicted by mysterious aches and pains in his legs and stomach. Therapy in a "mechanical massage" machine operated by a Washington osteopath had proved soothing, and Long went off for a treatment, leaving Roosevelt in charge for the rest of the day. "Whenever I was left as Acting Secretary," Roosevelt later noted, "I did everything in my power to put us in readiness." Now he seized his best opportunity since Long had taken his extended vacation the previous summer.

Roosevelt had himself been under severe pressure for several months. In November, Quentin, his sixth child and fourth son, had been born. Roosevelt, who dashed off on his bicycle to fetch the doctor and the nurse, proudly entered him at Groton less than two hours after he appeared. Edith seemed to recover well, then came down with a fever and neuralgic pains. One of the children also fell ill. "Ted has dreadful headaches each day," Roosevelt wrote to his sister Anna, called Bamie. And "I am not at all easy about Edith."

Doctors were unable to diagnose the illnesses. Roosevelt's torment was so deep that it masked his concern over the *Maine* disaster. He had lost his mother and his first wife

Alice on the same day in 1884; afterward he had scratched a black cross over his diary page for February 14 and written: "The light has gone out of my life." He had turned it back on, but now he again faced the dark prospect of twin deaths in the family.

Gradually, Ted improved; Edith did not. On February 25, she was so feverish and weak Roosevelt decided to have her examined by the famous Canadian physician Sir William Osler, then at Johns Hopkins. In anguish, he went to the office and began his most active day in the navy.

After Long went off to have his legs palpated, Roosevelt began cabling orders to squadron commanders, bureau chiefs, shipyard commandants, and coal-purchasing agents. He moved guns from Washington to New York, authorized the purchase of coal, told captains to have their ships ready to sail immediately, and designated strategic rendezvous for various squadron elements in the event of war.

Roosevelt had long deplored the fragmentation of the navy. For many years, like New York policemen on solitary beats, ships had been sent off "ship by ship, at all kinds of points and in all kinds of ports with the idea of protecting everything everywhere." Along with Mahan he believed in concentration. Roosevelt was concerned about the Asiatic Squadron and, aided by Captain Arent Schuyler Crown-inshield, chief of the Bureau of Navigation and the former commander of the *Maine*, he began framing a cable to Commodore George Dewey in Hong Kong.

Dewey had taken command of the scattered squadron in January, in Nagasaki, Japan, then moved the ships there (his flagship, the *Olympia*, the old ABCD cruiser *Boston*, and the gunboat *Petrel*) to Hong Kong so as have them closer to the Philippines. Roosevelt had great confidence in the doughty commodore. "I knew that in the event of war Dewey could be slipped like a wolf-hound from a leash." (Roosevelt had brought two wolfhounds back from a ranching excursion in North Dakota and admired the swiftness and determination of the breed.) "I was sure that if he were given half a chance he would strike instantly and with telling effect." But three ships did not amount to half a chance.

Roosevelt decided to improve the odds. Sitting at his heavy mahogany desk, carved with replicas of Civil War monitors, he and Crowninshield began to draft an order which, Roosevelt felt, would be "of much importance to subsequent operations."

At that moment Henry Cabot Lodge stopped by. It may have been coincidence, though the two had discussed strategy that morning. At any rate, the senator from Massachusetts read and approved of the contents of the cable. Shortly it went out over the telegraph wire:

> Dewey, Hong Kong: Order the squadron except *Monocacy* [an obsolete paddle-wheeler] to Hong Kong. Keep full of coal. In the event of declaration of war Spain, your duty will be to see that the Spanish squadron does not leave the Asiatic coast and then offensive operations in Philippine Islands. Keep *Olympia* until further orders.
>
> Roosevelt

Two cruisers and a gunboat were ordered to join Dewey at Hong Kong, 620 miles from Manila. The Asiatic Squadron was soon poised to strike.

Before going home, Roosevelt stopped off at Long's hotel and reported, apparently in vague terms, on the events of the day. Long thought it a commendable demonstration of loyalty. He slept peacefully that night, and in the morning felt well enough to go to the office.

When he saw copies of the cables Roosevelt had issued in his afternoon absence, Long was angered, stunned, and embarrassed. The assistant secretary had assumed extraordinary powers. Long confided to his journal: "Roosevelt, in his precipitate way, has come very near causing more of an explosion than happened to the *Maine*. His wife is very ill and his little boy is just recovering from a long and dangerous illness; so his natural nervousness is so accentuated that I really think he is hardly fit to be entrusted with the responsibility of the Department at this critical time . . . the very devil seemed to possess him yesterday afternoon."

Long considered at length the orders Roosevelt had issued. They were, he realized, the logical extension of strategic planning formulated at the Navy Department. In the end, he let them stand. But Roosevelt, "like a bull in a china shop," had gone too far; something had to be done. Long gave the assistant secretary a slap on the wrist: "Do not take any such step affecting the policy of the Administration without consulting the President or me. I am not away from town, and my intention was to have you look after the routine of the office while I got a quiet day off."

Later that weekend Long went to the White House and spent some time talking and "grumbling psalm tunes" with the president. The effect may have been calming, but in addition to Roosevelt's volcanic outbursts, Long was increasingly concerned about the "earthquaky" situation in Cuba. As reports from Lee, Cowles, and others in Havana filtered up from Key West, he began to doubt that the *Maine* explosion had been internal: "It might have been an accident or might have been by design." Curiously, the thinking of his volatile aide seemed headed in the opposite direction. It was "inadvisable," Roosevelt wrote his chief of ordnance Charles O'Neil, "for any person connected with the Navy Department to express his opinion publicly in the matter" while the court of inquiry was in session. Lieutenant Philip Rounseville Alger, a professor of mathematics at the Naval Academy, had done so, and Roosevelt felt he had taken "the Spanish side." Most naval experts agreed that "whether probable or not, it certainly is *possible* that the ship was blown up by a mine which might, or might not, have been towed under her."

But it also seemed to him possible that the catastrophe was accidental. Spontaneous combustion was a known threat to the navy's new ships. Only three months earlier, Roosevelt had recommended to Long that a study be made of the causes of the phenomenon in coal bunkers. Now he wrote his sister Bamie: "No one can tell as yet what the cause of the disaster was. Even if it were due to Spanish treachery it might be impossible ever to find it out."

It annoyed Roosevelt that William Randolph Hearst, not content with putting words in Sigsbee's mouth, had casually enlisted the assistant secretary to the ranks of those who blamed Spain for the *Maine* sinking. Queried by Judge Day at the State Department about a newspaper story, Roosevelt responded: "The alleged interview to which you refer is, I presume, the one in the New York *Journal* . . . [it] was an absolute fake." Roosevelt went on to say that he "had not seen or spoken to any *Journal* reporter, and had not expressed . . . any public opinion as to the cause of the accident; and I may add that I had not expressed such private opinion, for the excellent reason that I had not formed any."

This was not entirely true—at least immediately following the *Maine* explosion—but Roosevelt had no intention of letting Hearst tell the country what he thought. On many issues the two agreed, but the *Journal's* flagrant irresponsibility—and what he considered its antinavy bias—had gotten under his collar. Twice in September he had warned Lieutenant Commander Kimball, who was organizing the navy's first torpedo-boat flotilla, not to allow *World* or *Journal*—but especially *Journal*—reporters aboard the ships. Their instructions were to seek the sensational and try "to discredit the navy by fake stories."

Hearst let Roosevelt go for a few weeks (in March he would brazenly attribute to the assistant secretary remarks commending the honesty and patriotism of the *Journal*) and put his mind to other projects. One of his illustrators, Charles Johnson Post, designed a *Maine* medal, though no one quite knew why it was to be struck. Reporters began interviewing the mothers of the *Maine's* dead; many, according to the *Journal*, cried out for revenge. The newspaper began a subscription drive for a *Maine* memorial on Columbus Circle. Hearst seeded the pot with a one-thousand-dollar contribution, then asked Grover Cleveland for a donation. The ex-president's reaction was to the point: "I decline to allow my sorrow for those who died on the *Maine* to be perverted to an advertising scheme for the New York *Journal*."

There were scattered voices of reason. The Associated Press, alluding to the hysterics of the *World* and the *Journal*, issued a blanket denial of the Yellow Press's speculations: "The cruiser *New York* has not been ordered to Havana, Consul General Lee has not been assassinated . . . the situation is decidedly quiet." But it was Edwin Lawrence Godkin, editor of the *Nation* and the *New York Evening Post*, who most firmly assailed Pulitzer and Hearst: "Nothing so disgraceful as the behavior of these two newspapers . . . has ever been known in the history of journalism." He accused them of "gross misrepresentation of facts, deliberate invention of tales calculated to excite the public, and wanton recklessness in the construction of headlines . . ." Their proprietors were base, corrupt, and satanic.

Godkin was a feisty, bearded, Anglo-Irish muckraker who edited the *Evening Post* for "sober-minded people." If these were accurately represented by circulation figures, there were only twenty-five thousand in the city, but they were opinion makers. When a newspaperman deprecated the *Post*'s small circulation, a fellow journalist rebuked him: "You idiot, don't you know there isn't a decent editor in the United States who doesn't want to find out what it has to say . . . before getting himself on record in cold type."

Many considered the *Nation* the best journal in the country; others deplored its antiexpansionist views. Roosevelt thought Godkin an unpatriotic and dishonest editor afflicted, as he once wrote Henry Cabot Lodge, by "a species of moral myopia, complicated with intellectual strabismus." He complained to Alfred Thayer Mahan, "What fearful mental degeneracy results from reading . . . the *Nation* as a steady thing." But he would certainly have agreed with Godkin when the irrepressible Celt flayed Hearst for luring influential members of the Congress into the *Journal*'s camp.

What the Yellow Kid had done at the end of February was to corral five senators and congressmen and send them off to Cuba on the *Anita*, at 170 feet his largest press boat. The titular leader of the "Journal Commissioners" was Senator John M. Thurston of Nebraska, chairman of the 1896 Republican National Convention and the man who had seconded McKinley's nomination. Thurston took his ailing wife along on the junket, which was entirely at Hearst's expense. Perhaps he thought the sea air would improve her health.

The *Journal* printed regular reports on the progress of the "Congressional Cuban Commission." Its members, lauded for their courage—they "faced death to get at the truth in Cuba"—wrote their own accounts of suffering in the concentration camps, and so did Mrs. Thurston. The *Anita* reached Havana on March 11, and shortly afterward she penned an emotional appeal, in the fashion of Julia Ward Howe, to the *Journal*'s readers: "Oh! Mothers of the Northland, who tenderly clasp your little ones to your loving hearts! Think of the black despair that filled each Cuban mother's heart as she felt her life-blood ebb away, and knew that she had left her little ones to perish. . . ."

Three days later, at Matanzas, Mrs. Thurston died of a heart attack occasioned, the *Journal* announced, by the horrors she had seen in the Cuban camps. The commissioners calmly returned to Washington, spoke to their fellow legislators of what they had seen, and continued writing signed stories for the *Journal*. Perhaps that was what most incensed Edwin Godkin.

When Hearst "offers a yacht voyage," he wrote in the *Evening Post*, "with free wine, rum and cigars, and a good bed, under the guise of philanthropy, or gets up a committee for Holy purposes, and promises to puff it, it can get almost anyone it pleases to go on the yacht voyage and serve on the committee. . . . Every one who knows anything about 'yellow journals' knows that everything they do and say is intended to promote sales. . . . No one—absolutely no one—supposes a yellow journal cares five cents about the Cubans, the *Maine* victims, or any one else."

In Havana, meanwhile, divers kept arriving. Seamen off the *Iowa* and the *New York* (trained at Newport, Rhode Island, they normally performed ships' maintenance duties) were followed by commercial divers on the salvage vessels *Right Arm*, *J. J. Merritt*, and *F. R. Sharp* and underwater teams dispatched by three New York newspapers. Spanish divers also circled the *Maine*, probing the skirts of the wreckage. At times, three or four groups of divers explored the murky waters at the same time.

Both the *World* and the *Journal* had tried to send down divers on the morning of February 19. They had Sigsbee's permission but were denied access by the Spanish. The *Journal* took umbrage: "Vultures now hover over the wreck of the *Maine*, picking to pieces the portions of the bodies of American sailors which rise to the surface. Spain, by refusing to permit [our] divers to search the wreck and rescue the bodies, occupies the position of protecting these foul birds."

Once the question of jurisdiction was settled, navy divers were lowered into the polluted water shrouding the *Maine's* secrets. It was exhausting, dangerous work. Near the bottom it was so dark they could not see the numbers of the two-foot rulers they took along for measurements. The dim red glare from the electric hand lamps they carried kept winking out; at times the divers were guided solely by touch.

The slimy bottom mud was several feet thick in places, and divers sank up to their knees in the ooze. Jagged pieces of metal in the wreckage posed a threat to lifelines and air hoses. Wainwright was in charge of salvage operations. At one point, he reported, diver Andrew Olsen had his lifeline caught above him and his air hose below; only cool thinking saved him. When the divers emerged from the filthy water, they were disinfected—along with anything they had brought with them. Most clothing retrieved was burned, some went to the poor of Havana.

Nearby, on the *Mangrove*, Sigsbee continued his testimony, hoping to show that the explosion was not due to accident or carelessness. Sabotage seemed a remote possibility, but he had considered it. Access to the powder magazines and shell rooms could only have been gained with his keys. These were tagged by metal plates in the shape of Maltese crosses and kept in canvas bags that hung from a bulkhead at the foot of his bunk. On the morning of February 15, as was usual, the keys had been called for at quarters. Afterward, Sigsbee was certain they had been returned to his cabin.

A diver carefully scanned plans showing the passageway to the cabin, then was lowered with infinite care into the wreckage. Slowly, carefully shepherding his air hose, he groped down the passageway through the opaque, debris-filled water and entered the captain's quarters on the starboard side. By the flickering light of his lamp he made a painstaking search. Finding important papers—cipher codes and signal books—he took them topside. They were burned.

But he had not found the keys; they were not where they were always kept.

They sent a diver down again. This time he moved more surely. He found a hook on the bulkhead; the key bags were not attached. Then he realized that the bunk mattress was floating on the cabin ceiling. Cautiously, he moved one hand over the mattress top; the keys were there. He took them to the surface.

"I have had divers down in the cabin," Sigsbee told the court, "and have recovered by that means the cipher code and magazine keys."

On the evening of March 1, the Vizcaya made a dramatic entrance into Havana Harbor after a five-day passage from New York. Her massive ebony hull, the elaborate scrollwork on her stern capped by the golden eagle of Spain, impressed the Habaneros. When Cadet Cluverius arrived at the waterfront, he saw a flotsam of small craft flying streamers and flags. As the Spanish cruiser steamed slowly in, bands played, salutes were fired, fireworks exploded, and thousands along the shore cheered an emotional welcome to Eulate and his crew.

On March 5, the Vizcaya was joined by the Almirante Oquendo, which Admiral Cervera had sent to the city from Cartegena. Minister of Marine Bermejo had written on February 23 that his general plan was "to establish two centers of resistance, one in Cuba, the other in the peninsula; and by the end of April our position will probably have [improved]. We shall have to be very careful, and if possible avoid until then any conflict with the United States."

Little more than two weeks earlier, the 10-inch guns of the Maine had commanded Havana. Now only the tangled wreckage of the stern—the black searchlight and the tilted straw-colored mast—broke the surface of the water. Those aboard the Mangrove and the Fern, the diving teams in barges around the wreckage, and the Americans in the city viewed the formidable Spanish cruisers with apprehension.

But Cervera could see only the dark side. His fleet was not ship-shape, and the absence of two of his best vessels severely impaired his ability to defend the Canaries and the coast of Spain. In the event of war, Spain's outlook was bleak. "It is one thing to meet with energy and manliness whatever may befall us and another thing to indulge in illusions." He felt uneasy about making himself "an accomplice in adventures which will surely cause the total ruin of Spain. And for what purpose? To defend an island which was ours, but . . . is now no more than a romantic ideal." The American fleet was superior in numbers, tonnage, and firepower; he did not think the situation would improve by April; he favored a defensive posture around the peninsula.

Replying, Bermejo said he found Cervera's remarks "painful." The admiral had misunderstood the situation regarding "the island of Cuba. Our flag is still flying there, and the Government, to meet the sentiments of the people, even at the cost of many sacrifices, desires that this Spanish colony should not be separated from our territory. . . ." Havana, with its fortifications and dock facilities, could become a major naval base for Spain, the other Cuban ports closed with mines.

The disparity in strength between the two fleets was exaggerated by Cervera. The powerful *Oregon* was in the Pacific, guarding San Francisco and San Diego. Moreover, "In your estimate you do not count for anything the effect of homogeneous troops, well-trained and disciplined, as against the United States crews of mercenaries, and you might find historical facts, evoking sad memories for us, to confirm what I say."

In his reply to Bermejo on March 7, Cervera put the matter bluntly: War was coming. Spain could expect only defeat, "which may be glorious, but all the same defeat." Again, he recited a doleful litany of the inadequacies of the fleet. "Our want of means is such that some days ago three men went overboard while manning the rail for saluting, through the breaking of an old ridge rope. A new line had been asked for 50 days ago. . . ." As for the American mercenaries, he did recall a sad historical fact: "I may say that the crews that defeated our predecessors at Trafalgar had been recruited in the same way."

News of the deliberations of the naval court filtered into the newspapers. The *Journal* took extraordinary liberties with the little hard information it had received. On March 11 it printed a bald-faced lie: "The court of inquiry finds that Spanish government officials blew up the *Maine*. . . . There will be a war with Spain as certain as the sun shines unless Spain abases herself in the dust. . . ."

Illustrator Charles Post, who had designed Hearst's *Maine* medal, thought the *Journal* had an incendiary effect on public opinion. "This reporting was fragrant with circulation re-sults"—the paper had sold over a million copies the day *Vizcaya* arrived in New York—while we common folk began to boil and seethe with ardor to kill a Spaniard." Indeed, Spanish statesmen had been burned in effigy in several states; so had McKinley, for allowing the *Maine* to be de-stroyed.

An Episcopalian minister in Washington lamented the "wild clamor for blood, blood, blood." So did Secretary Long, who had received several crude notes from angry citi-zens. One read, "If we wer [sic] in Spaines place and they in ours they would wipe us of the map as regards the Maine it was a planed plot and De Lome is at the bottom of it . . . wake up the president people in general will not stand it much Longer." Another lashed out at the "demagoges" who had "caused the Glorious Maine to be blown up . . . Why on earth don't you resign you *old fosil?*"

Still, it was hard to tell whether the yellow press was making public opinion—or simply reflecting it. Godkin could call Hearst "the blackguard boy," but there was something else in the wind that had to do with a new American mood, a caldron of agitated feelings and instincts that suddenly came to a boil: patriotism; the urge to expand beyond conti-nental borders; impatience with Old World imperialism; sympathy for the underdog; humanitarian fervor; a need to flex the growing national muscle. The *Washington Post* took note: "A new consciousness seems to have come upon us—the consciousness of strength—and with it a new appe-tite. . . . The taste of empire is in the mouth of the people even as the taste of blood in the jungle."

McKinley was aware of the national mood—and the polit-ical risks of fighting the tide. Still, he struggled to keep the ship of state out of needless conflict, and he took comfort from what Long and other advisers told him: even if the court decided the *Maine* had been destroyed by a mine, the Span-ish could not be criminally implicated. He was still "bent on peace," as Roosevelt saw it.

The assistant secretary had downgraded the president's backbone; it now had the firmness not of an eclair, but of a jellyfish. The *Maine* itself was not the only, perhaps not even the central concern, but only a part "of the whole Cuban business." Whatever the result of the naval inquiry, Roosevelt felt the genocide in Cuba "intolerable to the conscience of mankind." Decisive military action, not diplomatic waffling, was the surest and swiftest way to end it. Yet he appreciated McKinley's difficult position and realized it would be hard to press on with peaceful means if the court of inquiry, as Washington now suspected, found the explosion had been deliberate. He wrote his brother-in-law Douglas Robinson (he was married to Roosevelt's sister Corinne) on March 6: "In a week or so I believe we shall get [the court's] report; if it says the explosion was due to outside work, it will be very hard to hold the country...."

That Sunday, William Osler, the Johns Hopkins specialist, operated on his wife. He found, Roosevelt wrote Bamie, "a large abscess, in the psoas muscle, reaching down to the pelvis. Everything went well; but of course it was a severe operation.... She behaved heroically; quiet, and even laughing, while I held her hand until the ghastly preparations had been made."

That evening President McKinley also demonstrated a good measure of intestinal fortitude. He called Joseph ("Uncle Joe") Cannon, his personal and political friend and the chairman of the House Appropriations Committee, to the White House. When the two were secluded in the library, McKinley began to pace the floor with quick, nervous strides. Then he abruptly told Cannon, "I must have money to get ready for war." He did not wish to torpedo the diplomatic initiatives then underway in Madrid, but the country was unprepared and must be strengthened. Spain was not the only threat.

Cannon agreed to introduce a bill if the president would prepare it. He watched, astonished, as McKinley "walked over to the table and wrote on a telegraph blank a single sentence: 'For national defense, fifty million dollars.' It wasn't a bill nor a message nor an estimate, but it was the President's memorandum as to what he wanted done, and I put the slip of paper in my pocket."

The next day Cannon introduced what became known as the "Fifty Million Bill." On Tuesday the House voted, 311 to 0, to appropriate the funds; on Wednesday the Senate passed the bill 76 to 0. There was not a single dissenting vote in the entire Congress. Cannon observed that "more unanimity, more harmony and more real enthusiasm" had been shown than he had ever seen.

In Madrid, Ambassador Stewart L. Woodford cabled that the appropriation "has not excited the Spaniards—it has stunned them." Queen María Cristina was prepared to negotiate the sale of Cuba to the United States.

The president, who had resurrected purchase as perhaps the last and best alternative to war, was pleased by the impact of the huge national defense appropriation on his diplomatic initiatives. Hearst was pleased for a different reason. The *Journal* headlined: FOR WAR! $50,000,000!

V

COURT
OF
INQUIRY

An officer whose life is spent in the naval service is keenly alive in all matters affecting his official record.

—CAPTAIN CHARLES D. SIGSBEE

From his testimony emerges the portrait of an individual who was unfamiliar with his ship. He might have been a good seaman and a brave man, but perhaps also the victim of the new technology which was transforming the Navy.

—ADMIRAL HYMAN G. RICKOVER

As CHARLES SIGSBEE began to testify before the court of inquiry on the Monday morning of February 21, he was aware that he and his ship were, "in a measure, under fire by the court." The fifty-three-year-old captain's record was exemplary in most respects, but not without blemish. An 1863 graduate of the Naval Academy, he had fought in Civil War engagements at Mobile Bay and Fort Fisher. During the long peace that followed, as the navy deteriorated, he had shown a special talent for oceanography and hydrography. Working with the world-renowned marine biologist Alexander Agassiz in the Gulf of Mexico, he had discovered the

Sigsbee Deep and invented several devices for measuring and recording deep-sea data.

His observations on this important research were published in 1880 in his highly regarded *Deep-Sea Sounding and Dredging.* One of his inventions was exhibited in Machinery Hall at the Columbian Exposition in Chicago in 1893. A distinguished Spanish naval officer named Víctor Concas, an awards' judge at the exposition, wanted to present Sigsbee with a medal for his ingenious device, but by the rules in effect the medal was given instead to the United States. Still, his work had been acknowledged, and in the quiet postwar period when promotions were slow to come, he rose steadily through the ranks to captain. His commission was signed on April 10, 1897, when he took over the *Maine.*

There were, however, two questionable reports in his fitness file. The first, in 1886, when he commanded the *Kearsarge,* found the ship shabby and admonished Sigsbee for failing to enforce regulations on ordnance and the drilling of his marine detachment. There were extenuating circumstances, however. The Civil War vessel was old and, when inspected, had just come through a storm.

A more serious incident occurred shortly after Sigsbee took command, when he attempted to con the *Maine* through New York's treacherous East River without a pilot. After successfully navigating through Hell Gate and passing the New York Navy Yard, he tried to pass to starboard of a tug towing the steamer *Colorado.* An errant excursion steamer packed with tourists barged into the *Maine's* path. To avoid hitting her, Sigsbee tried to veer back to port, then backed full speed on both engines. He managed to miss the excursion boat but, in the strong tide, could not help ramming into a barge and a railroad pier along the shoreline. As her collision signal sounded and watertight doors were closed, the *Maine* backed away. Damage to her bows proved to be superficial.

The inquiry that followed exonerated Sigsbee. Indeed, he was awarded a letter of commendation for prompt, lifesaving action. But some officers thought Sigsbee had failed to take proper precautions in guiding his ship through crowded, tide-ripped waters.

The *Maine* had also suffered indignities, earning a reputation in the fleet as something of a Jonah ship. She had caught fire while under construction, run aground in 1896, and lost three sailors in a gale off Cape Hatteras in 1897. Then came the collision with the pier in New York's East River. And now she lay destroyed on the bottom of Havana Harbor.

As he observed the wreckage of his command through the *Mangrove's* stateroom window, Sigsbee must have thought it ironic that he had presented a copy of *Deep-Sea Sounding and Dredging* to General Parrado shortly after the *Maine* took her mooring. And Concas, he knew, was captain of Cervera's flagship, the *Infanta María Teresa* in Cartagena. Because of what had happened in Havana, the two might meet again. That would depend, of course, on whether the members of the court decided the explosion had been internal—his responsibility—or external—Spain's.

Judge Advocate Adolph Marix—Sigsbee's former executive officer—cleared the court and read its letters of precept and authority. He swore in the president of the court, Captain Sampson, and then Captain Chadwick and Lieutenant Commander Potter. After Sigsbee gave his name and command, Marix began to establish the groundwork for the court's investigation.

> MARIX: Upon your arrival, did you take a pilot?
> SIGSBEE: I did; I took an official pilot sent off by the captain of the port of Havana.

Marix asked if the pilot had berthed the *Maine*. Sigsbee replied that he did and added: "The berth is in the man-of-war anchorage off the *Machina*, or the Shears . . . my recollection is the pilot said that it was buoy number 4. Our bearings, taken soon after mooring, did not place it exactly according to the charted position of buoy number 4, but no note was taken of this because it was assumed the . . . buoys might have been changed somewhat in the examinations of the moorings."

Marix asked, "Do you know if you were placed in the usual berth for men-of-war?"

Apparently not, Sigsbee replied. After the explosion Captain Stevens of the *City of Washington* informed him "that he had never known in all his experience, which covers visits to Havana for five or six years, a man-of-war to be anchored at that buoy, and that he had rarely known merchant vessels to be anchored there, and that it was the least-used buoy in the harbor."

In his first hour of testimony, Sigsbee expressed himself with caution and uncertainty. "I can not now recollect" how often the ship's ashes were dumped in the harbor. "I can not personally recollect" a certain coal bunker under the forward turret. It was his "recollection" that turpentine and other inflammables were stored forward inside the superstructure, and that the magazine and shell-room keys had been "called for that morning at quarters in the usual way. I can not recollect any other call for the keys on that day."

MARIX: Were the keys properly returned after quarters?

SIGSBEE: Yes, so far as I can recollect . . .

And, as he testified, the keys for all the magazines and shell rooms, both those in daily use and the spare keys, had been found by the divers reconnoitering the *Maine* earlier that morning.

Sigsbee offered a general impression on the location of the blast. "The center of the explosion appears to have been beneath and a little forward of the conning tower, and on the port side . . . in the region [of] the six-inch reserve magazine . . ."

On many crucial points, however, Sigsbee's recall of events was exact. The *Alfonso XII* was moored 250 yards to the north and west of the *Maine*. His ship had taken on 150 tons of coal from a government pile at Key West within a week of entering Havana. The coal was carefully inspected before it was brought on board. There was no flaring of the lights before the explosion, rather "a total and sudden eclipse." Two boilers in the after fireroom were in use at the time of the disaster. Marines checked the ship's posts twice each night. Packages brought on board were inspected for explosives. The *Maine's* heading on the night of the fifteenth was approximately northwest, somewhat to the right of the Shears, near Admiral Manterola's quarters.

Marix asked where he had been at the time of the

explosion. Sigsbee relived the events, telling how he had immediately known that the *Maine* had blown up. He had left the admiral's cabin, run into Private Anthony, and made his way to the poop. He recalled little details—the poop awning was baggy and covered with debris, there were no marines to post as sentries, there were "white, floating bodies" in the water.

Marix asked him what he had heard when the *Maine* blew up. Sigsbee said he had the impression of one "overwhelming explosion."

MARIX: Was there any smokeless powder [on board]?
SIGSBEE: There was no great gun smokeless powder ammunition, [just] ordinary brown powder.

Sigsbee testified that in his opinion the temperatures in the magazines never approached the danger point, even in the stifling heat of Havana. The highest temperature he could remember was 112 degrees, and that was in the aft magazines, which were generally hottest. Brown prismatic powder was considered obsolete by many navy experts, certainly when compared to the increased power of the new smokeless explosives—the "fancy powder," as Sigsbee called it—which had nitrocellular components. But brown powder was stable and could be heated to almost 600 degrees with impunity.

In Havana on February 15 the safety margin in the powder magazines was apparently close to 500 degrees.

It was almost 1 P.M. Before the court adjourned for the day, Sigsbee was asked a final question: Were the coal bunkers near the forward magazines full? The engineer could best answer that, Sigsbee said, but added that "all the bunkers were ventilated through air tubes, examined weekly by the chief engineer . . . and were connected electrically to the annunciator near my cabin door."

Adolph Marix questioned his former commander for three grueling hours. While Sigsbee's testimony was unclear in some respects, the parameters of the mysterious explosion were established. There was a long way to go, however. The court would be in session for a month, taking testimony on twenty-three of those days from officers, crewmen, and expert witnesses. Marix strolled on deck with the other members of the court to get some fresh air, and they had their picture taken. The judge advocate wore a white jacket to distinguish him from the other members of the court, who wore blue jackets and white caps. They did not smile; the business was too serious. They had only begun, but already the country clamored for their report.

On Tuesday morning Marix first questioned Lieutenant George F. W. Holman, navigator and ordnance officer, who had served on the *Maine* since September 17, 1895—the day of her commissioning. Holman stressed the extraordinary precautions taken on the ship when the magazines were opened. Lights were put out, cigarettes extinguished. There was no public-address system on board, but word was hailed all over the ship. The galley was sealed off. The inspecting crew put on antistatic slippers—an innovation pioneered by Sigsbee.

Holman testified that the temperatures of the magazines and the shell rooms were taken daily, after quarters, and that the highest temperatures—110 degrees—had been recorded in the aft 10-inch magazine. The thermometers were actually located inside the magazines. The chief gunner's mate opened a small plate, reached in, took the thermometer out and recorded the temperature. The bulkheads of these rooms were steel. The powder was stored in tanks set in chocks; the shells were stowed in racks, rather like wine bottles. Electric lamps in the rooms were sealed off by a double plating of glass, so there could be no grounding effect. There were no steam pipes nearby.

It was all according to standard procedures.

At the time of the explosion, Holman said, he had been in the messroom with Lieutenants Carl Jungen and Friend W. Jenkins and Chief Engineer Charles Howell. There was "a low grumbling explosion which shook the ship violently, followed by a heavy booming explosion." It was "like a submarine explosion such as I have heard only on a larger scale." The lights blinked out. "I called to the rest, 'we have been torpedoed. Get up on deck.'" In the darkness they moved to an aft stairway. Jenkins never made it up; his body had yet to be found.

Holman had had experience with underwater explosives at the torpedo school in Newport. Marix asked him if he had any thoughts on what had caused the explosion.

"My impression," Holman volunteered, "is that a very heavy mine went off under the *Maine's* bottom."

The word "mine" had been used for the first time. Marix picked him up on it, asking if there might be another explanation. Yes, Holman admitted, the explosion of a "down low magazine" might sound like a mine.

On Tuesday afternoon, Lieutenant Commander Richard Wainwright was sworn in. Wainwright told the judge advocate what Marix already knew—that he had relieved him as executive officer of the *Maine* at Norfolk, Virginia, on December 7, 1897. He described the scene in the captain's office with Cadet Jonas Holden at the time of the explosion, saying that he only remembered "one very heavy shock," then a list to port. Divers had been exploring the wreck, he reported, and they had brought to the surface a copper powder tank from the 10-inch magazine. It was ruptured by pressure but otherwise intact. That magazine apparently had not exploded.

Cadet Holden remembered the scene differently. He recalled two explosions, the second "of far greater force, and a terrible shaking."

On Wednesday, Chief Engineer Charles P. Howell testified. Curiously, a new stenographer listed him as "a witness for the prosecution" rather than "a witness before the court," as was usual.

Howell explained the location of the ship's forward coal bunkers, magazines, and shell rooms. Bunker A-16, which held a full complement of coal taken on in Newport News several months before, was outboard of the 6-inch reserve magazine on the port side, A-14-M. It could only be accessed by passing through bunkers B-4 and B-6. But these had been empty for some time before the explosion and had recently been scraped down and painted by crewmen. They would certainly have felt or sensed any heat buildup in A-16. Moreover, wing passages passed between the hull and the bunker's outboard walls. Howell himself had often put his hands on the steel walls of A-16 and there had never been any signs of undue heat in that bunker—or any other—during his two-year service on the *Maine*.

The bunker was three decks deep, extending down to the ship's double bottom. If there had been a fire at the base of A-16, Howell said, where magazine A-14-M abutted, heat would have diffused upward to a point where it could be felt through escape hatches on the bunker walls.

The chief engineer vividly described the explosion itself. The ship experienced "convulsions." Then there was the sound of metal tearing and "a tremendous crash." The deck "waved" and the *Maine* listed about five degrees to port.

Marine Private William Anthony confirmed the ominous shaking that had racked the ship. Anthony had been on orderly duty on the main deck aft. He remembered making his report to Sigsbee that the magazines "were in proper condition." At nine-forty there was a trembling and bucking of the decks followed by "a prolonged roar." Then he saw "an immense sheet of flame" forward of the superstructure, more to port than amidships, but no column of water. As he ran off to find Sigsbee, the *Maine* dipped to port and forward: "It apparently broke in the middle . . . and surged forward, and then canted over to port."

When Anthony concluded his testimony, Sigsbee shared with the court his experience with bunker A-16. He noted that it was exposed on three sides at the forward end of the port wing passage, and on the fourth side by the B bunkers where the men had been painting. Their hands had rested on the bunker wall; they had felt no heat. Moreover, he had gone through the passageways a day or two before the explosion and observed that one of the dogs on the bunker's manhole escape cover was not firmly wedged in place. "I put my hand on the dog and there was no appearance of undue heat." Satisfied, he ordered the cover secured.

As the court continued taking testimony, Gunner's Mate Charles Morgan of the *New York*, diving over the *Maine*, made what appeared to be a significant discovery. Exploring

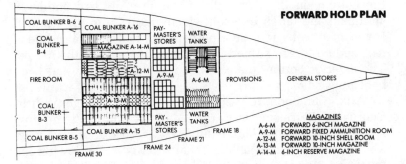

FORWARD HOLD PLAN

COAL BUNKER B-6

COAL BUNKER A-16

PAY-MASTER'S STORES

WATER TANKS

COAL BUNKER B-4

MAGAZINE A-14-M

FIRE ROOM

A-12-M

A-9-M

A-6-M

PROVISIONS

GENERAL STORES

A-13-M

COAL BUNKER B-3

COAL BUNKER B-5

COAL BUNKER A-15

PAY-MASTER'S STORES

WATER TANKS

FRAME 18

FRAME 21

FRAME 24

FRAME 30

MAGAZINES

A-6-M   FORWARD 6-INCH MAGAZINE
A-9-M   FORWARD FIXED AMMUNITION ROOM
A-12-M   FORWARD 10-INCH SHELL ROOM
A-13-M   FORWARD 10-INCH MAGAZINE
A-14-M   6-INCH RESERVE MAGAZINE

Forward hold plan of the *Maine* shows the location of the suspect coal bunker A-16, port side, and the adjacent six-inch reserve magazine A-14-M.

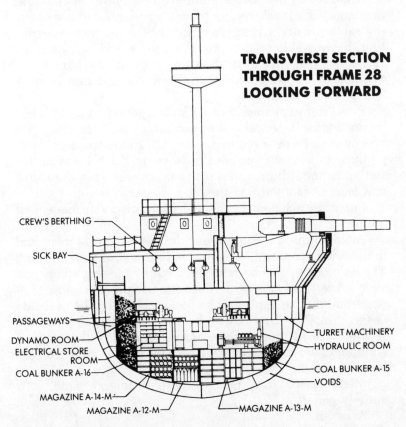

TRANSVERSE SECTION THROUGH FRAME 28 LOOKING FORWARD

CREW'S BERTHING

SICK BAY

PASSAGEWAYS

DYNAMO ROOM
ELECTRICAL STORE ROOM

COAL BUNKER A-16

MAGAZINE A-14-M

MAGAZINE A-12-M

MAGAZINE A-13-M

TURRET MACHINERY

HYDRAULIC ROOM

COAL BUNKER A-15

VOIDS

Cutaway view of the *Maine*, looking toward the bow. Passageways are to port of coal bunker A-16.

the bottom on the port side of the ship, he had suddenly stumbled and fallen into soft, slushy mud up to his armpits. He seemed to be in a hole perhaps six feet deep and fifteen feet wide. Morgan shined his light on the side of the *Maine*. The exterior bottom plates looked as though they had been bent upward.

After the noon recess on February 23, Ensign Wilfrid Van Nest Powelson told the court of Morgan's finding. Powelson was not a *Maine* survivor, or an expert sent from Key West, but a line officer aboard the *Fern*. Following his four-year stint at Annapolis, where he was first in his class, Powelson planned a career as a naval constructor and took a six-month course in the architecture of ships at Glasgow, Scotland. This background proved invaluable to the ongoing salvage work. Given blueprints of the *Maine's* construction, he was able to interpret the diver's findings. Even so, as he testified, his intimate knowledge of the *Maine* surprised and impressed the court. Marix asked him how he had gained his insight.

Powelson explained that he had expected to be attached to the *Maine* when she was commissioned. He was on a nearby vessel and "used to go over to the ship frequently and go through her, with an idea of learning. Then I was on the staff of Admiral Bunce, and made an inspection of the *Maine* and learned more at that time."

Purely by accident the court had found a valuable expert witness.

After telling the court about the depression Morgan had found, Powelson said he gave this information "no weight." The hole might have been scooped out by the ship's bow ram as it twisted and crashed to the bottom. Still, it was his "impression" that an explosion had taken place on the port side of the ship. Powelson related how he had dragged a twenty-seven-foot lead line over the *Maine* forward of the inverted conning tower and found that "as you go in across the ship there is nothing."

Marix asked, "You think the ship on the port side . . . is entirely gone?"

"Yes, sir."

"Entirely blown out?"

"Yes, sir."

Marix seemed impatient to flesh out Powelson's impression that an explosion had taken place well to port of the *Maine*'s midship line. That could not be so difficult to establish. He pointed out the window: "You see, the divers are even now down . . ."

Powelson would not be rushed. Yes, he replied, "they see things there but they do not know exactly what they are . . ."

The twenty-five-year-old ensign was excused to work on his renderings of the ship's exploded sections.

On Friday, February 25, the day Roosevelt put the navy on a war footing, Powelson's impressions were reinforced by divers' testimony. Gunner's Mate Thomas Smith of the *Iowa*, who had spent almost eight hours in the water, said that he could find no trace of the forward part of the 6-inch reserve magazine—it seemed to him to have "completely blown away" to starboard. There was a hole through the ship but the 10-inch magazine, starboard side, had not exploded; intact powder tanks and shells had been lifted to the surface.

Gunner's Mate Carl Rundquist off the *New York* said he had gone down aft and followed the bottom plates of the *Maine* toward the bow. Crawling through the bottom sediment thirty feet down, he could hardly see anything, but could identify the bottom plating from its green antifouling paint. He came to a hole in the ship's side. Shining his lantern, peering intently, touching with his hands, he found that the ragged edges of the plates had been bent inward.

Marix cautioned the diver: "You must be very careful when you say that the edge of it was turned inboard."

Rundquist stood his ground: "My opinion is, I believe she was blown up from the outside and in, because there was no explosion from the inside could make a hole like that. . . ."

Rundquist's eyewitness testimony confirmed Powelson's impression that a hole had been punched in the *Maine*'s bottom from the outside.

*   *   *

Powelson was due to return with sketches he had made after discussions with the divers, but first the court took the testimony of a mystery witness. There had been a number of rumors about Spanish plots; one, referred to the court by Fitzhugh Lee, seemed worth investigating.

The name and address of the man who had agreed to testify were "suppressed by agreement with the witness that his identity should not be revealed." Probably, he was Cuban; at any event he spoke Spanish and Henry Drain of the American consulate interpreted for him.

Marix began the questioning: "I have heard that on Tuesday morning [February 15] you overheard a certain conversation in a ferryboat which referred to the possible sinking of the *Maine*. Will you please state to the court all you can in regard to that matter."

The witness responded that at about seven-thirty that morning he was crossing from Havana to Regla, seated in the bow of the ferry, when he overheard a conversation between three Spanish officers and a stout, moustached civilian in a derby hat. One of the army officers said that in the Circulo Militario, the military club on the Prado, he had heard that the sinking of the *Maine* was "nearly arranged." Her presence was "a shame to Spain." She would "simply explode." There was no danger to Havana because the vessel would open up and she would immediately sink.

One of the others said, "I will take plenty of beer on that occasion!"

Another officer spoke. "Then if you blow her up, there would be another one come."

"No," the first officer said, "they would take care not to send another."

Marix questioned the witness closely. The man said he was positive about the conversation. One of the officers had two stripes and a belt, which meant he was a general staff officer. The civilian wore a large diamond ring. He did not know who he was but could find out.

The witness was excused. His story was pure hearsay, but the court had put evidence on the record of a possible Spanish plot.

*   *   *

Later that day Ensign Powelson returned to the *Man-grove*. This time he went beyond surmise. Illustrating his testimony with blueprints and sketches based on divers' findings, he reported that some sixty feet aft of the bow, the double-plated keel of the battleship had jackknifed up almost to the surface of the water in the form of an inverted V. "I have also succeeded in identifying a part of the bottom plating which is now about four feet above water." The court was clearly riveted by this testimony, but Powelson's sketches were incomplete and he was excused to finish the renderings.

On Saturday the twenty-sixth, Powelson again took the stand. Diver Andrew Olsen, who had been exploring the inverted V configuration of the *Maine's* keel and bottom plating, was asked to stand by and confirm that the ensign's testimony accurately reflected what he had seen.

Marix asked Powelson what he now made of the findings. Powelson replied that he thought an explosion had occurred "somewhere about frame 18, center of impact." (The frames, or ribs, of the *Maine* were numbered from bow to stern; number 18 would be about sixty feet from the bow.) The center of impact, Powelson continued, "was under the ship, a little on the port side."

"How far from the keel?" Marix asked.

About "15 feet in a horizontal line," Powelson replied.

Marix questioned why there was such immense damage next to the 6-inch reserve magazine that stretched aft from frame 24.

"My idea" Powelson said, "is that after the ship was raised up at frame 18, the magazines, one or all of them, after that were exploded." The mine did not have to be very close to the plates lifted up, he added. "It seemed to me that the mine was somewhat removed, and the pressures came through the water . . . a cushioned sort of pressure."

Sampson intervened. Perhaps there were two mines, he suggested, one driving the keel up into its inverted V configuration, the other exploding plates inward.

Since its inception, the court had seriously considered the

possibility that the *Maine* had been devastated by a mine. There was every reason to do so. The Spanish were thought to have sent a supply of the weapons to Cuba. Santiago was known to be mined; certainly Havana would be. Holman had first used the word "mine," and Gunner's Mate Rundquist had indicated the explosion must have been external. Circumspectly, the court had discouraged speculation. Now, as Powelson elaborated on the divers' findings, the court's suspicions came to a boil.

That Saturday, as Powelson testified, *Scientific American* tutored its readers on the effects of mine explosions and spontaneous combustion. "We are of the opinion that if a torpedo or mine exploded immediately in the vicinity of the magazines, the shock would be quite sufficient to detonate the explosives within the magazines...." There were bunkers adjacent to magazines, and there had been spontaneous combustion in coal on other ships. In these cases, however, the steel plates of the bunkers had become red hot. "If such a fire occurred in the adjoining bunkers, it is inconceivable that it should not have been discovered when the nightly inspection ... was made."

There were various types of mines, the weekly subsequently explained. The observation mine was detonated when seen to be in the vicinity of an enemy vessel; the automatic mine self-fired when struck. In the electrical contact mine, a cable led from an igniting charge to an observation station on shore.

Some mines were cylindrical, with rounded ends, some conical. Some—known as ground mines—were laid on the bed of a harbor; buoyant mines floated on the water or were anchored so as to be suspended beneath the surface. Either kind, the magazine reported, could have sunk the *Maine*.

On February 28 the *New York Herald* reported what correspondents in Havana already knew: "Never in the history of similar proceedings have such precautions been taken to guard the facts from public scrutiny. Never have officers of either arm of the service remained more consistently reticent under the orders of their chief." That was largely true, yet the shroud of security that covered the deliberations aboard the *Mangrove* had torn in at least two places. One rent may have resulted from the close working relationship that had developed between Charles Sigsbee and Fitzhugh Lee. Both were certain a mine had blown up the *Maine*. Their conviction somehow seeped through to Long and others in Washington. Since Sigsbee was attending most of the sessions of the court of inquiry, his opinion carried special weight.

The second leak seemed to spread slowly from sailors in Havana to correspondents and then on to New York.

Walter Scott Meriwether's naval service was still paying dividends. Gunner's Mate Charles Morgan was an old friend and shipmate. At the Inglaterra one evening he told Meriwether that a piece of the *Maine*'s keel had exploded upward to "within 18 inches of the surface." Sooner or later, Meriwether felt, that finding meant war. He had a scoop, but knew the story would not hold long. Other correspondents would soon piece the story together from waterfront scuttlebutt or their own sources. Sylvester Scovel of the *World* was always nosing around the wreck of the *Maine*, and he had friends in the navy.

The *Herald*'s dispatch boat would not depart for Key West until the following morning; that might be too late. Meriwether decided to try to get the news past the Spanish censors. All the correspondents had become adept at subterfuge, and he cleverly camouflaged the news in a coded cable: "An important story will be filed from dispatch boat in Key West tomorrow. Please note that main story is mine."

Meriwether took the message to the cable office at the palace and gave it to one of Congosto's censors, who eyed it suspiciously and asked why it was so vital that the story be attributed to Meriwether. The *Herald* reporter replied that he badly needed the credit.

"You can tell that to your marines," the censor said.

Meriwether sent the news out by boat the next day, but Scovel, as he had feared, uncovered the story, and his elliptical cable, written in the form of a banal space filler, slipped by the censor. Scovel wrote of the gentle trade winds in Havana and weather so tranquil there were "buzzards roosting on the keel of the *Maine*."

In the *World's* New York office, an editor failed to read between the lines of Scovel's eye-closing copy. The dispatch was spiked.

Spanish censorship was growing increasingly heavy-handed and Scovel could only watch in dismay as words were chopped out of his copy. There was, for example, the Red Cross story. On February 26 a congressional delegation arrived in Havana aboard the *Olivette*, this one spearheaded by Senator Redfield Proctor, the Vermont legislator who had been so instrumental in securing Dewey's command of the Asiatic Squadron. Proctor conferred with Sigsbee, dined with Lee at his table at the Inglaterra, and added Clara Barton to his delegation before heading off to Artemisa for a look at Spanish concentration camps.

Scovel did a story on Barton's efforts to relieve the famine and sickness in Cuba. It was 233 words long when he gave it to the censor. When he got it back, there were 105 words.

Still, the important news trickled out of Havana. Anybody who read the newspapers and believed them knew by the end of February that a mine had sunk the *Maine*. At that time the *Mangrove* left Havana for Key West to take testimony from the *Maine* survivors who had been sent back to Florida.

Theodore Roosevelt thought it would be difficult—if not impossible—for the court to reach a clear-cut verdict. But even if the court's findings were inconclusive, Roosevelt felt, war was likely and he had no intention of sitting it out in an office. For eleven months he had struggled to ready the navy for war; for three years he had thought about—even made plans for—his own role in the conflict.

Little more than a month after the *grito* of independence sounded in Cuba in February 1895, Roosevelt had written to Governor Levi Parsons Morton of New York: "In the very improbable event of a war with Spain I am going to beg you with all my power to . . . get me a position in New York's quota of the force sent out. Remember, I make application now. I was three years captain in the 8th Regiment N.Y. State militia, and I must have a commission in the force that goes to Cuba!"

On September 14, 1897, Roosevelt went for a carriage ride with the president and told him that if war should come, the navy needed warning so that "the Department would be in the best possible shape that our means permit" when war began. The president, who had no intention of going to war, was amused when Roosevelt added, "I myself would go to the war." McKinley asked what his wife would think of that. Roosevelt replied that she would regret it—and so would the president—"but that this was one case where I would consult neither." McKinley laughed and jollied Roosevelt, saying he would do what he could. As the carriage returned to the White House, the talk turned to torpedo boats.

The thought of missing out on a scrap pressed on Roosevelt. The next day he wrote to Colonel Francis Vinton Greene, a commander in the New York National Guard: "There is always a possibility, however remote, that we will have war with Spain . . . I suppose you would be going, would you not? . . . What I should like to do if it were possible would be to go . . . with you as Colonel, and with me as Lieutenant Colonel. . . . Would this suit you should the need arise?"

In December he wrote to General C. Whitney Tillinghast, adjutant general of the National Guard, saying that in the event of "trouble" he wanted to go with the New York contingent. On January 13, following the riots in Havana, Roosevelt again queried Tillinghast, volunteering his services. That same day he wrote to Greene reporting that "trouble with Spain" seemed possible and asking if he could go with him as a major.

After the *Maine* disaster, the urge to enlist consumed Roosevelt. On February 25 he warned Tillinghast that conditions were "threatening" and begged him to "remember that in some shape I want to go." Tillinghast told him that the role of the National Guard in any conflict with Spain had not been determined, so Roosevelt touched yet another base. In March he wrote to Greene again and also to his close friend William Astor Chanler, asking if he planned to raise a regiment. "I shall chafe my heart out if I am kept here instead of being at the front ... I have a man here, Leonard Wood, who is also very anxious to go. He is an Army surgeon, but he wants to go in the fighting line. He is a tremendous athlete."

Roosevelt was high on Wood, who served in Washington as an attending surgeon to McKinley. Wood had graduated from Harvard two years after Roosevelt, then joined the army and won a Medal of Honor fighting against Geronimo in the Indian Wars. Roosevelt, once sickly and anemic, prided himself on his vigorous cross-country treks, but he was no match for Wood. The assistant secretary wrote Bellamy Storer, who had helped to persuade McKinley to appoint him to the Navy Department, that his new "playmate ... fairly walked me down in the course of a scramble home ... down the other side of the Potomac over the cliffs." That was really no disgrace since, Roosevelt said, Wood was one of just three men in the army "who could march as well as the Apaches, week in and week out, over the deserts."

Often on a Sunday, Roosevelt and Wood took their children for a spirited hike through Rock Creek Park. On one occasion Roosevelt was showing his children and a number of their friends and relatives how to cross a deep pool by climbing over a fallen tree. Somehow he fell in. One of Wood's children dashed back to the surgeon's side crying out, "Oh, Father, the father of all the children has fallen in the water."

Chanler, the great-great-grandson of John Jacob Astor, was also a man with the sort of credentials Roosevelt approved. Orphaned at an early age (along with nine brothers and sisters), he developed a fierce independence. After schooling in England, he attended Phillips Exeter Academy—for three weeks—then left to hunt and wrestle alligators in the Florida Everglades. In the fall of 1886 he matriculated at Harvard, joined the Porcellian Club (his older brother Winthrop and Roosevelt had been fellow Porcs), and considered playing polo. But he was an indifferent student and when he turned twenty-one, at the end of his sophomore year, abandoned Harvard and his academic career.

Chanler was handsome, bold, energetic, self-assured—and wealthy. After traveling through Europe, he went big-game hunting in Africa. Back in New York "the mighty Nimrod," as Winthrop called him, set off with his brother on another hunting jaunt to Colorado. Out West Chanler consorted with Butch Cassidy and other bank robbers, and struck up a friendship with John G. Follansbee, who managed the Hearst ranches. Jack Follansbee had roomed with Hearst at Harvard and the two were close.

After Colorado, Chanler did some steeplechasing in England, then set out to explore the "terra incognita" of British East Africa. The elephant-hunting trip had been "fun." The expedition, a serious scientific investigation into the geology and geography of a remote, forsaken area of East Africa, was not. Chanler barely made it back. He and his party were attacked by natives and rhinos and suffered from dysentery, fever, and starvation. Still, the twenty-month expedition mapped six hundred miles of unknown territory and put Chanler Falls on the map of Africa.

Chanler sympathized with the Cuban insurgents, and in 1896 he got to know Horatio Rubens, the lawyer who later maneuvered Dupuy de Lôme's exit from Washington by delivering a copy of the ambassador's indiscreet remarks on McKinley's ineptitude to Hearst. It may have been Rubens, or Estrada Palma, heading up the Cuban Junta, who put him in touch with "Dynamite Johnny" O'Brien. Early in 1897, Chanler helped O'Brien organize one of the filibuster expeditions of the *Bermuda*, shipping out on the thousand-ton steamer as "Mr. White." Dodging Spanish gunboats and American antifilibuster patrols, the *Bermuda* successfully landed her cargo of guns, machetes, and dynamite in Cuba.

Chanler admitted to being young and reckless, but was deeply concerned by the suffering in Cuba. "I sympathize with the Cubans in their gallant efforts in behalf of liberty and . . . being an American, feel it necessary to do what I can to separate entirely this continent from Europe." Rubens gave him letters of introduction to Máximo Gómez and other Cuban generals ("He has contributed much but would even give his life for the cause . . .") and Chanler again set off for Cuba. He failed to link up with Gómez in the cause of Cuba Libre, but did reach Havana. On his return to New York, he took a sabbatical from the Cuban wars, dabbling in Tammany politics. That fall he was elected to the New York State legislature.

Late in December he received a "Private and Confidential" letter from Roosevelt, who argued for "a perfectly consistent foreign policy" that would ultimately drive every European power from "every foot of American soil, including the nearest islands in both the Pacific and the Atlantic." The annexation of Hawaii was vital to American interests. As for Cuba, it was in the hands of a "weak and decadent nation." It could not be pacified by autonomy and "I earnestly hope that events will so shape themselves that we must interfere some time in the not distant future."

Earlier that winter Chanler had received a letter from one of his fellow filibusters: "Let's go to Cuba! Let's get . . . Capt. O'Brien and a few other choice spirits such as were congregated on the old *Bermuda*, and fight the beasts!" The call to action was irresistible, but filibustering didn't seem the appropriate response with war imminent. On March 11, Chanler resigned from the New York Assembly in order to raise a regiment of volunteers.

The band of Cantabrigians—Roosevelt, Hearst, Follansbee, William and Winthrop Chanler, Wood—were a remarkable group, scholars and dropouts, social lions and elephant hunters, gun-runners and entrepreneurs, soldiers and civil servants, whose paths had crossed repeatedly since the days they had walked the Harvard Yard. Most—but not all—were close friends. Some were Democrats, others Republicans. But all were expansionists who felt the country should break out of its long period of isolation, and each of them had played a role in bringing the country to the verge of a war they considered just, humanitarian, and essential to the needs of the nation. Hearst had stoked the fires of public opinion, Roosevelt had readied the navy, Wood had lobbied the president, Chanler had run guns. They would all go to Cuba—if two remaining obstacles could be hurdled: a finding by the Naval Court of Inquiry that Spain was not responsible for the *Maine* disaster, and the president's aggravating reluctance to go to war.

McKinley was, in fact, pursuing his attempt to purchase Cuba. He had consulted with his old friend Myron Herrick, the Cleveland banker who had rescued him from bankruptcy during the financial panic of 1893. They came up with the figure of $300 million. Rumor had it that the president put aides to work drafting legislation for the Congress to consider; members of the House of Representatives were discretely polled on the idea. They were not receptive. The size of the appropriation was daunting. So was the prospect of spending a vast sum for a country that might not, as Martí had put it, wish to live in the monster's lair.

Queen María Cristina, in any case, retreated from her receptive posture. On March 12, minister Stewart L. Woodford reported to Washington that "the Queen evidently lost courage." She would, colonial minister Moret told him, "prefer to abdicate her regency and return to her Austrian home rather than be the instrument of ceding or parting with any of Spain's colonies."

As the queen attempted to maintain her dynasty, the Spanish government procrastinated. The April rains—and the disease that came with them—could well dampen the American ardor for war. McKinley, too, played for time, hoping that the court-of-inquiry report would not force his hand. He suggested that Spain might pay a large cash indemnity for the loss of the *Maine* (Congress quickly pricked this trial balloon), initiated a dialogue with the Vatican on the possibility of papal arbitration between the two countries, and continued to press for Spanish concessions in Cuba.

The struggle to hold back the tide of war sentiment that washed over the country took its toll. The White House staff was concerned over the president's worn and pale appearance. Secretary Long thought he was in danger of "overdoing."

But the president still had strong support in the Republican-dominated Congress: conservative Senator John C. Spooner of Wisconsin; Eugene Hale of Maine, who now thought battleships little more than floating bombs and tried to block their construction; Orville H. Platt of Connecticut, squarely in the antiexpansionist camp; Marcus Alonzo Hanna, McKinley's campaign manager and one of his closest friends (Hanna had shoe-horned his way into John Sherman's Senate seat when McKinley appointed the befuddled legislator Secretary of State). Redfield Proctor of Vermont, another intimate of the president's, had strongly endorsed McKinley in 1896; he was considered solid and reliable, though his trip to Cuba suggested a concern for the *reconcentrados*. Even Henry Cabot Lodge did his duty by the president, doggedly striving to keep the Congress from "breaking away and acting without him."

Of all the "peace faction" in Congress, the extraordinary Thomas Brackett Reed of Kittery, Maine, the speaker of the House, was the most powerful. He was fifty-eight years old, well over six feet tall, and weighed almost three hundred pounds. (In Maine, someone remarked that he looked like "a human frigate among shallops.") Balding and clean-shaven, his round, pudgy face ballooned from his somber garb, as one observer put it, "like a Casaba melon flowering from a fat black stalk." He dominated the House with his wit, his sarcasm, his skill in debate, and the immense force of his intellect.

It was Reed who chided Roosevelt for being immune to ideas other than his own, and Reed who quipped that Lodge's soil was thin, though highly cultivated. When a garrulous representative earnestly affirmed that he would rather be right than president, Reed interrupted: "The gentleman need not be disturbed; he will never be either." Reed could be brutal and, to those skewered by his barbs, heartless and cold. Henry Adams thought him "too clever, too strong-willed, and too cynical, for a bankers' party." Even so, "Czar" Reed's command of the House had been absolute.

Roosevelt had until quite recently professed enormous admiration for Reed. In 1896 he backed his candidacy for the presidency and wrote to him: "Oh, Lord! What would I not give if only you were our standard-bearer. . . ." He considered the Speaker "in every way McKinley's superior." Lodge backed him, too, but after McKinley's nomination the two expansionists were disillusioned by Reed's firm stand against naval construction. Roosevelt wrote to Mahan in May of 1897, "I am extremely sorry to say that there is some slight appearance here of the desire to stop building up the Navy. . . . Tom Reed, to my astonishment and indignation, takes this view . . ." Lodge sparred with Reed on the same matter, comparing money spent for defense to a form of national insurance. Reed replied acidly that "insurance is a good thing but . . . an over-insured man will set fire to his house."

Reed nursed a bitterness over his principled but futile effort to achieve the Republican nomination for president in 1896. He wrote Roosevelt, when his failure became apparent, "the receding grapes seem to ooze with acid, and the whole thing is a farce." In his eyes, McKinley became "the Emperor of Expediency."

Reed considered the Cuban insurrection nothing more than a local rebellion. "Until the federation of the world comes, let each nation look out for itself." He used his authority over the House to quash resolutions recognizing the "Republic" of Cuba, its legitimacy, and its independence. Bourke Cockran, Winston Churchill's mentor in New York and Reed's equal on the podium, chastised the speaker: "On a question of morals, the American people do not divide. . . . We should insist . . . that the women and children living within 90 miles of our coast line shall not be hunted down like bulls by men without a conscience."

It became apparent to Reed, by the middle of March, that his lonely battle to keep the United States out of Cuba was doomed. Three events shortly followed to sharpen the clarity of this perception: Senator Redfield Proctor returned from his fact-finding mission to Cuba; the Naval Court of Inquiry findings were delivered to the president and reported to the Congress; and William Jennings Bryan, the standard-bearer of free silver and the Democratic party, embraced the cause of Cuba.

Proctor—not known as a firebrand—was the first to pour fuel on the fires that Reed had so desperately tried to bank. On the Thursday morning of March 17 he rose from his Senate seat and walked calmly to the podium to give his report on the situation in Cuba. As a politician, he was undistinguished, as a speaker, colorless and without passion. His colleagues expected a lengthy address in the flinty, no-nonsense style of the Vermonter, and that was what they got. Proctor spoke for more than an hour, coldly, dryly, without emotion, but what he had to say set the packed Senate chamber aflame.

He began by saying it was not true that he had decided the *Maine* had been blown up from outside. He had in fact "no opinion about it myself" and had "carefully avoided forming one." The court of inquiry was competent and would soon judge the matter. Conjecture was "unprofitable." With that, Proctor turned to the situation in Cuba which, he said bluntly, "is not peace nor is it war. It is desolation and distress, misery and starvation." The *reconcentrados*, torn from their homes and sealed inside the prisonlike towns, "with foul earth, foul air, foul water and foul food or none," were diseased or dead. "Little children are still walking about with arms and chests terribly emaciated, eyes swollen, and abdomen bloated to three times the natural size. . . . I was told by one of our consuls that they have been found dead about the markets in the morning, where they had crawled, hoping to get some stray bits of food from the early hucksters. . . ."

Proctor reported that he had gone to Cuba as an isolationist "with a strong conviction that the picture had been overdrawn. I could not believe that . . . 200,000 had died within these Spanish forts. . . ." Now he knew the case had not been overstated. Blanco's modification of Weyler's decrees had brought "no practical benefit." The suffering had to be seen to be believed, and he had seen it—"the spectacle of a million and a half of people, the entire native population of Cuba, struggling for freedom and deliverance from the worst misgovernment of which I ever had knowledge."

The Vermonter ended as quietly as he had begun. He had no solution to offer. "I merely speak of the symptoms as I saw them, but do not undertake to prescribe." The doctoring "may safely be left to an American President and the American people."

Before he spoke, there had been rumors that Proctor went to Cuba as McKinley's observer, and that the president had cleared his speech. If that were true, his report deserved an attentive, perhaps even an obedient, response. What most affected the Senate, however, was Proctor's damning indictment of the Spanish concentration camps. Senator William P. Frye of Maine remarked, "It is just as if Proctor had held up his right hand and sworn to it."

Over in the House even hard-line conservatives were calling for war. Thomas Reed tried to impute the objectivity of Proctor's report. "A war will make a large market for gravestones," he remarked caustically, referring to Proctor's marble business. It was a clever quip but served only to fan the flames of intervention in Congress, and they soon spread to the financial community. Until recently, business sentiment had crystallized against war. Now cracks appeared in the once solid front. Wall Street, which had reacted nervously to war scares, appeared willing, even eager, to get the bad news out and over with.

Worse, for McKinley and the Republican party, were indications that aroused Democrats might seize the banner of Cuba Libre and wave it lustily during the fall elections. The *Chicago Times-Herald* asked nervously, "Who can doubt that 'war for Cuban liberty' will be the . . . sign . . . held aloft and proclaimed by such magnetic orators as William Jennings Bryan [with which] they will sweep the country like a cyclone?" Lodge was alarmed by the prospect of free silver washing over the country in a tide of "Bryanism." Should the president and the Republicans in Congress fail to establish common ground on the Cuban question, he warned a friend in Massachusetts, "we shall be defeated at the polls, and your humble servant among others will go down in the wreck."

Lodge told McKinley that to threaten war for political reasons was clearly heinous, "but to sacrifice a great party & bring free silver upon the country for a wrong policy is hardly less odious." On broad questions, he added, "when right & wrong are involved I believe profoundly in the popular instinct & what that instinct is no one who goes out among the people . . . can doubt for one moment."

Bryan spoke out for Cuban independence, but he was not an expansionist and had not called for war. McKinley and his Republican leaders in Congress watched apprehensively as he straddled the fence of intervention.

Spain's replacement in Washington for Dupuy de Lôme was Luís Polo de Bernabé, an experienced diplomat. He immediately grasped the impact of Proctor's speech before the Senate and Polo cabled Madrid: "Senator Proctor yesterday made a speech which has produced great effect because of its temperate stand. . . . My impression is that the President will try to withstand the powerful public sentiment in favor of the insurrection, but any incident might hinder his purposes."

Such an incident was about to occur.

*   *   *

On Monday, February 28, the Naval Court of Inquiry re-convened in the United States Court House at Key West to take the testimony of the *Maine* survivors who had been sent back to the mainland. Marix's questions were occasionally technical in nature, but mainly focused on what they had heard and seen at the time of the disaster. Had there been one explosion or two? Had a sheet of flame or a column of water shot up beside the ship? Had the *Maine* actually lifted, or just the deck crewmen were standing on? How did they interpret the sequence of events they had experienced?

Lieutenant John Blandin did not think the *Maine*'s head-ing, pointing toward the Machina, was unusual; the ship had swung around the buoy on all points of the compass for three weeks. It was his impression there were two explosions, but he could not swear to it. There was a flare of light, but no flame that he could see, or water thrown up, and he had de-tected no upheaval of the ship.

But Lieutenant John Hood saw and felt things differently. He thought the *Maine* "was riding in a direction that I never remember having seen her ride in before." He heard what sounded like an underwater explosion, up forward, and al-most instantaneously a second explosion. At the first blast Hood "felt the whole ship just go up and tremble and vibrate all over," then saw the whole starboard side of the deck "spring up in the air." The ship heeled to port and "went down like a shot."

Marix asked if the ship had taken a sudden list at the first explosion, "as if something had struck her on either side." No, Hood replied, it was more "as though something had ex-ploded under her." He thought that the first explosion had raised the forward deck and thrown up the superstructure.

Hood was senior watch officer in charge of the powder division, and he told the court that gunnery drill had taken place on February 14 and all the magazines opened on that day. The midship magazines were the hottest, the forward magazines "comparatively cool." On the following day mag-azine temperatures were routinely taken and logged.

George Blow, who followed Hood to the stand, did think the ship's position unusual, though he had noted it once or twice before. There were two explosions. In his cabin he felt a shock that sounded like a 10-inch gun going off, "close aboard." Blow thought the *Maine* had been fired on. As he rushed through his cabin door, there was a second explosion, "much more violent." This lasted for several seconds and was "accompanied by the falling of lights, electric fittings, furniture and by a crashing and rending of metal." Immediately, the ship heeled sharply to port.

At 3:30 P.M., after several other officers testified, the court adjourned until Tuesday, March 1. There was much more to come, but by now its members must have been confused by the varying accounts of the crew. Some had heard two explosions, others only one. Several had seen a sheet of flame, others had not. No one had seen a geyser of water go up by the ship, or dead fish in the harbor, as might be expected if a mine had exploded underwater. Sigsbee had tried to explain this, saying he had heard the fish left the harbor at night. If they did not, most were probably only stunned and, recovering, had swum away. This may have struck the court as naive, but the captain's vital testimony regarding the wing passages surrounding bunker A-16 was firmly corroborated when the court convened on Tuesday.

Passed Assistant Engineer Frederick C. Bowers explained that the ship's standing orders had been to inspect the bunkers every day. A-16 contained about forty tons of Pocahontas (Virginia) coal. The escape door on the bunker was opened and the inspecting crew felt around the inside walls. The sides of A-16 could, in any case, be touched from the wing passages. Assistant Engineer John R. Morris, who followed, told the court all the bunkers had been inspected in the forenoon—between ten and eleven—on February 15. He remembered opening the escape door to A-16—"there was no heat perceptible."

To many of the crew there was no doubt the ship had dramatically lifted at 9:40 P.M. and that there had been a flash of flame. Marine Sergeant Michael Meehan, on deck duty, was "lifted clean off the gangway and fired in the water." Private Edward McKay was knocked across the deck by "a flash of fire." The ship seemed to rise "as if something lifted her up." Coal Passer Jeremiah Shea, somehow propelled up through the central wreckage, thought of himself as "an armor-piercing projectile."

Master at Arms John B. Load took a different route into the sea. Standing by the door to the armory, he saw "a red flame outside the ship. It seemed as if . . . a small boat had struck the ship at first. She seemed to tremble, and then the whole deck where I was standing seemed to open, and there was a flash of flame came up." It was as if "someone had taken a revolver and fired it close to your face." Load was a farm boy, and when the deck opened up, it sounded to him "as if a wagon with a lot of old iron had been dumped in a hole."

Load plunged down into water below him and was trapped in wreckage. There was a second explosion and this seemed to free him. The water was hot and he thought a boiler had gone up. He was suffocating—"It felt as if cotton were in our mouths"—and he and others choked down sea-water for relief. Somehow Load managed to crawl aft and up through a hatch.

Fireman William Gartrell, who was resting on a mattress in the steering-engine room in the bowels of the ship, also saw a flame—"a blue flash." The *Maine* began to shake and then there was a sound "like the whole earth had opened up."

One by one, they testified to the shock, explosions, flame, fire, and the terrible fusillade of iron and wood fragments that whipped over the ship. Many had been burned and were still bandaged. Coxswain Benjamin R. Wilbur, slammed into the water by a flash of fire—his worst fear was of sharks—also had a broken jawbone; he found it difficult to open his mouth and couldn't hear anything in his left ear. John H. Pank, a fireman, had lost two fingers.

On March 2, when all the survivors in Key West had been questioned, Marix assembled the *Maine* crew and asked them in a body whether they had "any complaint to make or fault to find with any officer or man belonging to the *Maine* as to the care and guarding of that ship in the harbor of Havana" either on the night of February 15 or previously. If so, Marix continued, "let him step to the front."

Among the rows of blue-coated sailors and officers, not a man stepped forward. Marix adjourned the court, and President Sampson ordered a two-day break before the *Mangrove* steamed back to Havana. There were clerical and administrative tasks to perform, and the first nine days of testimony could be carefully reviewed, but the break may also have been prompted by the new assignment Sampson was about to be given.

Whether or not, as Robley Evans thought, Sicard was old and sick, the medical survey board had decided he was unfit for active duty. In Washington, Evans was discussing the Spanish torpedo-boat threat with Roosevelt and Long when the secretary ordered Sicard detached and gave Sampson, promoted to commodore, command of the North Atlantic Squadron at Key West. At 3:10 P.M. on March 6, though he would remain aboard until the court of inquiry finished its investigation, Admiral Sicard's flag aboard the flagship *New York* was hauled down.

There were seventeen officers senior to Sampson on the navy list; in appointing Sampson, Long noted cryptically that "the consensus of naval opinion" considered the new commodore to have judgment, knowledge, and esteem. Roosevelt agreed. He thought Sampson "one of the best officers in our service."

Roosevelt also esteemed "Fighting Bob" Evans. He had ceaselessly lobbied Long on the importance of getting the most aggressive and capable captains off ground-pounding shore duty and onto ships. "I inflict so much advice on the Secretary," he told a naval officer, "that I fear I became *persona non grata*." But Roosevelt's persistence paid off. Long gave Evans command of Sampson's old ship, the *Iowa*. Evans was delighted. The *Iowa* was one of four new first-class battleships in the fleet, at 11,340 tons almost twice the displacement of the *Maine*.

Sampson could not immediately take over his command. The vital work of the court of inquiry had to be finished. But there was obviously more than one matter on his mind, especially when he received a long memo from Secretary Long outlining Captain Alfred Thayer Mahan's "suggestions" regarding the Spanish war plan and a blockade of Cuba.

The *Mangrove* returned to Havana on March 5, the same day the *Almirante Oquendo* arrived, and on the following day the court reconvened. The inquiry now concentrated on what divers had discovered during the court's absence. Ensign Powelson had followed their progress through the bowels of the ship, keeping watch over his charges by following the air bubbles that escaped from their helmets and popped to the surface.

Sigsbee listened to Powelson's testimony with consuming interest, but considered it "a recitation of details." He asked Powelson if he would "formulate his views as to the initial seat of the explosion, in a written report to me." The ensign agreed.

On March 9 the little *Fern* was relieved by the cruiser *Montgomery*, which entered harbor boldly, saluted Spain and Admiral Manterola, and prepared to pick up the little supply boat's mooring. A game of musical chairs ensued that would have amused everyone had it not taken place around the skeleton of the *Maine*.

Shortly after the *Fern* arrived on February 16, the Spanish had moved the *Alfonso XII* and given Commander Cowles her mooring, number 4 on chart 307, close to the Machina and to the old number 5, which had vanished when the *Maine* went down. After the *Fern* unshackled from the mooring and anchored, a Spanish launch chugged up to the *Fern* and an officer politely told Sigsbee the *Alfonso XII* would take back her original parking place. The *Montgomery* would be given mooring number 6, southwest of the *Maine* wreckage.

Sigsbee, who planned to move his quarters to the American cruiser, suddenly felt a shiver of warning. By now he was convinced the *Maine* had been blown up "from the outside," and "the situation in which I found myself was not one to inspire me with perfect trust in my fellow men." Judging that buoy number 4 was apt to be free of harbor defense mines—if any existed—he asked the Spanish officer if Admiral Manterola would consider a change of plans.

It was all swiftly arranged. The *Alfonso XII* stayed in place, the *Fern* sailed off to deliver Red Cross supplies to *reconcentrado* camps along the coast, and the *Montgomery*, under Commander George A. Converse, took the preferred mooring on arrival. Sigsbee, relieved, moved his gear to more commodious quarters aboard the cruiser, but his sense of security was short-lived. That evening a "ludicrous" but serious incident occurred aboard the *Montgomery*. She was headed eastward, into the prevailing wind. The *Vizcaya* was off her port beam, and close by. Around 8 P.M., Converse and Sigsbee decided to pay a courtesy visit to Sampson and the court of inquiry aboard the *Mangrove*. As they prepared to leave, a crew member reported that a strange tapping noise had been detected up in the forward compartments. Sigsbee and Converse investigated; they had no trouble picking up the sound. Sigsbee timed the ticking pulses and found there were 240 per minute. Any multiple of 60 suggested clockwork to him, perhaps some sort of time bomb. "That was serious."

The two officers ordered a seaman to the bow to see if the sound could be heard at the riding cable, and a boat was lowered to investigate the mooring buoy itself. The sound grew louder. Alarmed, Sigsbee ordered that a line be dropped from the bow and swept over the ship's bottom. Additional boats were lowered and put on patrol. Sigsbee angrily exclaimed that "one might as well get used to blowing up." Still, "once was enough."

Slowly, the tapping sound moved aft through the ship and, as the *Montgomery* swung southward, disappeared altogether. Sigsbee was mystified until, two days later, he spoke to Antonio Eulate about the "scare." The captain of the *Vizcaya* casually explained that if the pulse of the sound was 240 beats per second, it must have come from his dynamo or a circulating pump.

Navy photographer John C. Hemment, in Havana since February 19 to document the investigation of the *Maine* wreckage, had taken a boat out to the *Montgomery* shortly after she picked up her mooring. Admiral Manterola was just leaving the American cruiser after a courtesy visit, and Hemment was disgusted by the Spaniard's behavior. On the gangplank to his barge, the admiral took out a cigar, clipped off the end, threw fragments of tobacco on the steps, and began smoking. It was, Hemment thought, "an unpardonable breech of naval courtesy."

The photographer's stay in Havana had not been pleasant.

The Inglaterra had been full when he arrived, and he had to put up at the seedy Pasaje, where rowdy Spanish volunteer troops—they all seemed to smoke foul-smelling licorice cigarettes—were in residence. As Hemment walked the streets of Havana under "blood and gold" Spanish flags, he was jeered at and jostled; once someone spat on him from behind. He was nearly shot photographing the "antiquated ruin" of Fort Punta. But the worst moment of his trip came when, on the "twisted, mangled, charred scrap iron" of the *Maine*, they brought up the bloated body of Lieutenant Friend W. Jenkins. Hemment had known Jenkins at the navy yard in Brooklyn. He put down his heavy camera and turned aside, too affected to take a picture.

Insults from "the degenerate humanity" of Havana proliferated. The menu of a restaurant on the Plaza de Luz featured "chicken fricasse à la *Maine*." The *Montgomery* was ridiculed in a vocabulary "rich in obscenity." She would meet the same fate.

Hemment had brought with him a supply of little American flags. As Manterola's barge pulled away, he took one out and waved it proudly at the American sailors assembled on deck. They smiled and were about to cheer, he thought, when there was a cry of "silence!" from the quarterdeck. No demonstrations were allowed.

Hemment kept right on waving the little red, white, and blue banner.

Sigsbee still took the possibility of a mine seriously. He had thought it risky to send the *Montgomery* to Havana; now he recommended that she be ordered away. In that respect, he thought, it was well to "remember the *Maine*." When the *Fern* returned from her relief mission, Converse dropped the mooring that had seemed to tick and returned to Key West.

Powelson, meanwhile, refined the sketches he had made of the mangled forward sections of the *Maine*. He had little skill at perspective drawing, he told the court, yet he managed to give his renderings of the uplifted bottom plates and the inverted V of the keel some sense of dimension. A series of detailed photographs of the surface of the wreckage were also being taken under the supervision of Engineer Howell. Gradually, the pieces fell into place.

One that did not was the mooring buoy, still listed among the missing objects of the *Maine* wreckage. On March 9, diver Olsen had worked his way around the bow of the ship, above the point where the great ram thrust at an angle into the harbor bottom. He found the port anchor in the mud, but there was no sign of the mooring buoy. He was then raised up to a point where he located the scrollwork shield on the ship's bow, and the hawsehole for the mooring chain, but could not find the chain itself.

On March 11 the testimony of expert witnesses was taken. First among them was Naval Constructor John B. Hoover, who was familiar with the construction of the *Maine* and had made detailed measurements showing how parts of the ship had been displaced from their normal position. He was not asked to give an opinion on the cause of the disaster.

Hoover was followed by Commander Converse of the *Montgomery*, who had gained extensive experience with underwater explosives at the torpedo station in Newport. Converse had closely examined Powelson's sketches. He felt sure there had been two explosions. The first might have come from a mine placed well below the surface, perhaps composed of dynamite and gunpowder lashed together. Such a device could have lifted the ship "as the crest of a wave." The second explosion, he thought, was probably due to the detonation of a powder magazine.

Marix asked, "To what kind of an explosion do you attribute the force that caused this bending of plates and keel?"

A submarine mine could have done it, Converse answered.

Marix pressed him with a question that suggested the court had considered the possible effects of an internal explosion alone. Could a magazine explosion, he asked, have blown out the ship's sides, canted the bow down sharply from frame 18 and thus dragged the after section of the ship forward, forcing "the vertical keel into the condition that you see on the sketch"?

"I have never seen anything in my experience," Converse replied, "which would lead me to believe that it is possible to produce the effect indicated by any explosion within the interior of the ship in that vicinity."

Marix then asked, "Do you think, then, necessarily, there must have been an underwater mine to produce these explosions?"

Converse responded, "Indications are that an underwater explosion produced the conditions there."

That was a bit vague, but it satisfied Marix. At 5:30 P.M., the court adjourned.

On March 12, the day after Converse testified, the *New York Herald* calmly headlined, under photographs of the *Montgomery* entering Havana Harbor and of General Máximo Gómez: WRECKED BY MINE, MCKINLEY KNOWS. The story came out of the Washington bureau but may again have originated with Walter Meriwether and his navy contacts in Havana. "It is now known officially [and in] an unofficial manner by the administration," the *Herald* reported, "that the battleship *Maine* was destroyed by a mine exploded beneath her bottom. . . . It may never be known whose act or whose negligence blew up the ship."

The fruits of Meriwether's labors, including an exclusive synopsis of Ensign Powelson's testimony before the court concerning the upward thrust of the keel, had previously been published by the *Herald*. The new information received by McKinley "absolutely" confirmed Powelson's findings. "The upward force of [the] explosion under the fractured section of the hull was such that the broken keel of the vessel has assumed a position like an inverted letter V." The ship's spine had cracked and her ram bow was driven downward into the mud. The divers had been able to closely inspect part of the keel because of its position near the surface. There was some conjecture, but the *Herald*'s story was remarkably accurate.

After wrapping up the investigation, the *Mangrove* again sailed for Key West where, on March 17, the court established headquarters on the *Iowa*, Robley Evans's new command. Last-minute testimony was taken. Howell provided additional photographs. Powelson submitted a new plan of the wreck and Olsen a sketch of the broken keel. On Saturday, March 19, at 10 A.M., the court was cleared for deliberation. Sampson, Chadwick, Potter, and Marix worked on through Monday, but their conclusion was now foregone.

In Havana, Powelson prepared the written report on the disaster requested by Captain Sigsbee. He marked it, "U.S.S. *Fern*, Havana, Cuba, March 20, 1898," and wrote, "I believe the *Maine* was blown up by forces external to the ship . . . the six-inch reserve magazine could not possibly have been the seat of the initial explosion." If it had, it would have blown out the light coal bunker bulkhead and side plating, and scattered large quantities of coal to port. This had not happened. The outer bottom skin of the double keel had been blown upward, "but the inner skin has not been bulged downward." He went on, meticulously proving his point.

Sigsbee had wanted a conclusion "disconnected" from his own suspicions and prejudices. Now he was more than ever convinced that the *Maine* had been blown up from outside.

As Powelson wrote his unofficial report, the Navy Department received a confidential cable from Havana. John Long reported its contents to the president. The court of inquiry had reached a unanimous verdict. The cause of the *Maine*'s destruction had not been internal. There had to have been a mine. Blame was not fixed. Long's report of the court's finding could hardly have come as a surprise. Still, McKinley found the news depressing. George Cortelyou, his executive secretary, took note: The president "did not look well, and his eyes had a far-away, deep-set expression in them."

Roosevelt heard the news, too. The horror of the tragedy struck him with fresh intensity. On Monday, March 21, in high dudgeon, he wrote Brooks Adams: "In the name of humanity and of national self-interest alike, we should have interfered in Cuba two years ago. . . . The defective imaginations of many good people here, the limited mental horizon of others, and the craven fear and brutal selfishness of the mere money-getters, have combined to prevent us from doing our duty. . . . The blood of the Cubans . . . the blood of the murdered men of the *Maine* calls not for indemnity but for the full measure of atonement which can only come by driving the Spaniard from the New World."

It was the first day of spring, and the streets and gardens of Washington blossomed with daffodils, dogwood, and tulips; the scent of magnolia and boxwood perfumed the air. It had been a harder winter than Roosevelt cared to admit—even to himself—but now he picked up his pen and added a handwritten postscript of new hope. His wife had been very sick all winter; he hoped he would never see another like it. "At last she was put under the knife; and now, very slowly, she is crawling back to life."

In Key West on Monday, the court put finishing touches on "The Report of the Naval Court of Inquiry upon the Destruction of the United States Battleship *Maine*." "Deliberations" began at 10 A.M. aboard the *Iowa*, anchored off Key West. It was really a matter of flyspecking the few pages of the summary report to see if any last-minute changes were required.

Sampson and Marix signed for the court. The document was taken over to the *New York* for Sicard's signature. The next day, Tuesday, March 22, the admiral completed one of his last official acts at sea, writing, "The proceedings and findings of the court of inquiry in the above case are approved." He signed his name.

The report was now wrapped, sealed in a canvas mail pouch, padlocked, and given to Marix. That evening, he and several officers of the *Maine* began the long boat-and-train trip to Washington. Standing watch and watch (four hours on duty, four hours off), catching catnaps, they were besieged, at major hubs along the way, by throngs of reporters clamoring for news of the court's decision. Their train finally pulled into Washington's Pennsylvania Station at nine thirty-five on Thursday evening. Marix, who was sleeping in a corner of the compartment, was jolted awake. Lieutenant John Hood strapped on his navy revolver, picked up the pouch, and the blue-coated naval officers stepped off the railroad car onto a dimly lit station platform.

The *Maine* contingent was met only by a naval cadet who volunteered to lead them through a huge crowd to a hack stand. Hood tucked the pouch under his arm and, followed by Marix, Holman, and Blow, tried to work his way through a shouting throng of reporters and curiosity seekers. Jostled by the crowd, thinking someone had tried to grab the pouch, Hood reached for his revolver. That had the required effect. As the wall of people before them gave ground, the officers dashed through a baggage room to Sixth Street and commandeered a carriage. Pursued by reporters, they clattered off to Ebbitt House, the hotel where McKineley had stayed when he was a congressman.

In the morning Marix took the pouch to the Navy Department and delivered it to Secretary Long. After a short discussion the two men briskly walked the short distance to the Executive Mansion, where they met with McKinley and Day. The president called his Cabinet members into session at ten-thirty, and they worked through lunch into the afternoon, digesting the fine print of the report, considering new ways to pressure Spain into making concessions in Cuba. McKinley had known the gist of the report for almost a week. Now the meticulously worded opinion was in front of him, and he would have to deliver it to the Congress on Monday. In the face of the court's findings there did not seem to be much room for maneuver.

The court's unanimous conclusions, handwritten by Marix, were crisply put. At Havana all required safety procedures had been observed. No fault or negligence on the part of the crew was involved. The criminated bunker A-16, exposed on all four sides at the time of the explosion, had passed inspection on February 15. There had been two explosions "with a very short but distinct interval between them." The first, distinguished by a sharp report, had lifted the forward part of the ship, fractured the keel at frame 18, and forced it and some bottom plating up to the surface of the water in an inverted V shape. The second explosion "was more open, prolonged and of greater volume." In the opinion of the court, it was "caused by the partial explosion of two or more of the forward magazines of the *Maine*."

The upward bending of the keel and bottom plates was brought about, the court felt, by "the explosion of a mine situated under the bottom of the ship at about Frame 18 and somewhat on the port side of the ship." The explosion of the magazines had blown the forward decking and superstructure up and aft.

LONGITUDINAL SECTION

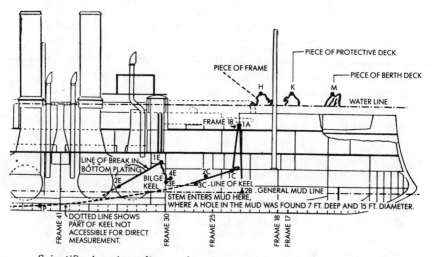

Scientific American diagram based on the court of inquiry report, shows the inverted **V** shape of the keel at frame 18. At the top, the letter H indicates a piece of bottom framing.

The court did not elaborate on the reasoning behind its decision, and did not speculate on who might have laid or detonated the mine, but it was plain to McKinley by now that most Americans would consider the Spanish guilty of "culpable negligence" even if they had not exploded the mine. As a New York newspaper put it, "If the Spanish government is unequal to the restraint of dynamite atrocities in its principal provincial anchorage . . . then it is no government at all. . . ." Clearly, it should be replaced.

McKinley still hoped to avoid using force. Negotiations with the Spanish continued. But the congressional kettle was coming to a boil. Hearst's chief "commissioner" Senator John Thurston of Nebraska, had just given a melodramatic speech to his colleagues on the horrors in Cuba. Thurston, a vase of roses on his desk, was moved to tears when he spoke of atrocities and lauded his dead wife's courage. He was there, he said, "by command of silent lips to speak once and for all on the Cuban situation. . . ." His colleague Redfield Proctor had understated the facts. As he related the plight of the re-

concentrados, his voice broke and staid senators wept. Then there was a tumult of applause.

On Saturday afternoon George Cortelyou took Marix's copy of the report and typed an original and ten copies for the president and the Cabinet. He bound them with string and put them in a safe at the White House. The safe remained locked on Sunday as McKinley worked on his message of transmittal. But McKinley's plan to make a confidential and dispassionate report on the court's findings to Congress at noon the following day, like so many of his efforts to keep the peace, came apart. There had been another leak, possibly in Havana or Key West.

On Monday morning, March 28, papers across the country blazoned an Associated Press story giving a detailed, accurate summary of the full court-of-inquiry report. The AP claimed that a staffer had gained a day-long access to the findings "despite official secrecy unparalleled in the handling of official papers." There was no doubt that he had; the AP abstract contained direct quotations from the report and its findings. An investigation was immediately conducted and the White House safe opened. Cortelyou's string-wrapped packet of copies was intact. Later that day, McKinley limply announced to the Congress and the press what they already knew from reading the morning papers.

His message of transmittal did not, in any case, say what the Congress wanted to hear. After recapitulating the events of the night of February 15, McKinley seemed to chide the more aroused interventionists in the Congress: "The appalling calamity fell upon the people of our country with crushing force, and for a brief time an intense excitement prevailed, which, in a community less just and self-controlled than ours, might have led to hasty acts of blind resentment. This spirit, however, soon gave way to the calmer processes of reason. . . ."

He went on to review the findings of the court. No evidence of an internal explosion had been found; the court felt a mine had destroyed the *Maine;* no blame had been fixed.

"I have directed," McKinley continued, "that the finding of the Court of Inquiry and the views of this Government thereon be communicated to the Government of her Majesty, the Queen Regent, and I do not permit myself to doubt that the sense of justice of the Spanish nation will dictate a course of action suggested by honor. . . . It will be the duty of the Executive to advise the Congress of the result, and in the meantime deliberate consideration is invoked."

The president's professed confidence in the Spanish sense of justice and his meek request for due consideration enraged the Congress. The *Journal* reported that congressmen "filed out with frowning faces, muttering imprecations at the President." Republican party unity crumbled. Senate resolutions for intervention in Cuba proliferated. A senator stormed into Judge Day's office at the State Department and shouted, "Day, by God! Don't your president know where the war-making power is lodged?" In the House, "Czar" Reed tried valiantly but vainly to quench the fires of belligerence that swept through the corridors.

The press was equally incensed. The *Journal* had a new war cry: "Remember the *Maine!* To hell with Spain!" The *Chicago Tribune* mocked McKinley's "desperate defiance of the popular will." If "proper amends" were not made within 48 hours, the *World* demanded, the fleet should be sent to bombard Havana. "If Spain will not punish her miscreants, we must punish Spain." The *New York Herald* had long derided the "unscrupulous propaganda" of politicians, juntas, "shameless journalists," and mercenaries, but now swung into the war camp: "It is no longer a time for debate, but for action."

Even as McKinley held back, preparations for war had gone forward. On March 24, Secretary Long ordered the resplendent white hulls of the fleet overpainted with the dull lead-gray used during the Civil War. On the twenty-sixth, as Commodore Sampson ran up his flag on the *New York*, all the officers of the *Maine* still in Havana, except for Richard Wainwright, boarded the *Olivette* bound for Key West. Fitzhugh Lee and a number of correspondents came down to the wharf to see them off. In the vessel's dining cabin, Lee made a heartfelt toast to the captain of the *Maine*. Sigsbee was deeply touched by the consul's remarks. They were good friends now, had worked together "in unison during the stress of the great disaster," shared confidences, formed a strong bond.

A correspondent stepped forward and presented the ship-less captain with a floral wreath. It was a warm but sad moment. The American colony in Havana was breaking up, and no one quite knew what would happen next. But as the diplomats and correspondents went ashore and the *Olivette* steamed slowly out of harbor, there was exhilaration as well. Cadet Cluverius and the others had endured over two months of heat and hostility, the trauma of the explosion and the funerals, the strain of the investigation. As they passed Morro Castle, the young cadet took a deep breath of fresh air. It seemed delicious to him "after having been pent up so long in those filthy waters."

Wainwright, who would wind up the wrecking operations, watched them go and reflected moodily on the corpse of the *Maine*. He approved the court's decision. It was hard for him to imagine "how an explosion from inside could throw or draw the bottom of the vessel to the surface of the water." So many had died, "hurled into eternity from their hammocks [to] a cruel hideous death." Seventy-four bodies had yet to be recovered, but clearly 260 of the 350 men on the *Maine* had died in the explosion or in Havana hospitals. He did not know what his future would bring, but he hoped there would be some way to avenge the deaths of his ship-mates.

On March 19, the mighty *Oregon*, ordered to join the North Atlantic Squadron, had left San Francisco. A week later, as she pounded her way through Pacific swells toward Callao, Peru, to take on coal, her crew noticed smoke and heat in the forward division of the ship. The smoke was traced to a coal bunker. A damage-control team dug furiously down into the bunker to expose smoldering coal and doused the fire. It had been caused by spontaneous combustion.

Even as the navy's warships were coated with battle-gray paint, Roosevelt continued to make his own preparations for war. On March 26 he again wrote to his friend William

Chanler: "Things look as if they were coming to a head. Now, can you start getting up that regiment. . . ? Do you want me as lieutenant colonel?" And, to cover a more official base, General Tillinghast was informed, on a "private" basis, that "we should soon see actual trouble with Spain."

Roosevelt was getting up a full head of steam. That evening he let some of it off in a jubilant after-dinner address to Washington's Gridiron Club. Banging his fist into his palm, he told its members that despite the peacemongers and the financiers, "we will have this war for the freedom of Cuba." The American people were for it; anyone who wanted to obstruct their will—and that included any congressmen who put financial above national interests—"was welcome to try the experiment." Then, as he turned and directly confronted millionaire Marcus Alonzo Hanna, one of the president's inner circle, his high-pitched voice crackled with glee:

"Now, Senator, may we please have war?"

On Monday, March 28, as McKinley's message on the court-of-inquiry report was delivered to the Congress, Minister Polo de Bernabé released to the State Department copies of Captain Pedro del Peral's official investigation of the "mournful catastrophe" of February 15.

The Spanish report noted the absence of a visible geyser of water at the time of the explosion, or dead fish with ruptured bladders on the surface afterward. No shock wave, it stated incorrectly, had been transmitted to nearby ships. (The captain and first mate of the English bark *Deva* had testified to the pronounced rolling of their vessel after the explosion.) The *Maine*'s plans showed her magazines to be dangerously placed next to coal bunkers. No evidence of a mine, or a wire leading to shore, had been found. Divers could not see the ship's bottom, since it was buried in the mud, but it did not appear to have suffered damage.

The report concluded that the explosion was internal, probably caused by spontaneous combustion. Captain French Ensor Chadwick was incredulous. The Spanish divers had only worked over the *Maine* for about seventeen hours, but it was hard to see how they could have failed to discover that bottom plates had been thrust four feet above the surface, and a section of keel bent up some thirty feet above its normal position. No "lurching forward" of the slowly sinking after body of the *Maine* could have done this.

When Chadwick had been appointed to the court, he suspected the explosion had been internal; the testimony given aboard the *Mangrove* had convinced him otherwise. He was doubtful the Spanish government was responsible for the detonation of "the fateful fuse," but rabid Spanish hawks, with "foolish contempt for the military power of the United States," or Cuban terrorists, "in their desire to force a war," could have destroyed the "great fortress planted in their midst."

Charles Sigsbee was more than ever certain a mine had blown up his ship. After returning to Key West, he had trained up to Washington, where Long took him to see the president. Afterward, he testified before the Senate Foreign Relations Committee. He was asked to elaborate on "possibilities"—how could the *Maine* have been blown up by a mine? Sigsbee found speculation "not pleasant"; he would rather deal in facts. Still, he swiftly outlined to the senators "a mechanical means whereby the *Maine* could have been blown up." He showed the committee two drawings.

The first diagrammed a ship swinging in a complete circle around a mooring buoy. A line bisecting the circle indicated the possible path of a lighter capable of dropping a mine. After a mine was dropped, Sigsbee explained, it was only a matter of time before the ship swung around over the position where the mine lurked. At that point in time, the mine could easily be detonated from an electrical box on shore.

The second rendering showed details of the mine-laying lighter. The mine, with a specific gravity slightly greater than that of water, was slung underneath. It was barrel-shaped and attached to an insulated wire that led aft to a reel. When the mine was released the electrical wire would pay out automatically as the lighter chugged to a nearby wharf or anchored. The device would be detonated electrically.

Sigsbee testified that he had discussed this possibility with Sampson and Converse aboard the *Montgomery*. They admitted his scenario was feasible. Moreover, Sigsbee said, "On the day of the explosion, or the day before, I caused ten

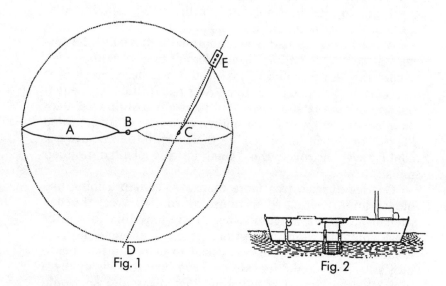

Captain Charles Sigsbee's diagram shows how a mine might have been placed so that the *Maine* would swing over it.

or twelve reports to be made to me concerning a single lighter that passed and repassed the Maine." It was not of the right type for such an operation, but it was certainly suspicious.

In short, it must have been a mine, whether planted before or after the ship's arrival in Havana. It was known in the United States, Sigsbee suggested, that mines had been set in the harbor.

Senator Frye asked him, "Who would be likely to have charge of the electric battery which exploded the mine?"

"I am unable to say that; I infer the Navy."

"An official?" Frye asked.

"I have a certain reason for believing this," Sigsbee replied, "which perhaps it would be injudicious to disclose." He did not elaborate on the source of this vital information, and the senators did not question him about it.

At the Navy Department on March 29, the assistant secretary considered the opposition to his desire for active service in the army. Everyone seemed to oppose his leaving—the president, Secretary Long, a host of friends and colleagues. Lodge told him it would end any hopes he had for a political career. Winthrop Chanler thought him mad. ("Theodore," he told his wife, "is wild to fight & hack & hew.") Even his old friend William Sturgis Bigelow tried to dissuade him.

Pensively, Roosevelt sat down at his desk to write Bigelow. Perhaps he felt the need to explain to himself that it was not simply his own impulsive nature—"my own pleasure"—that thrust him on; there was much more to it than that. "I like life very much," he told Bigelow. "I have always led a joyous life . . . and it will be very bitter to me to leave my wife and children; and while I think I could face death with dignity, I have no desire before my time has come to go out into the everlasting darkness." Death might come not from enemy fire, but from "fever in some squalid hospital. . . . So I shall not go into a war with any undue exhilaration of spirits. . . ."

His best work at the Navy Department was done, Roosevelt said. He had taken the responsibility to act on his own when Long was away; that wouldn't be possible in war time. But beyond that, "a man's usefulness depends upon his living up to his ideals. . . . One of the commonest taunts directed at men like myself is that we are armchair and parlor jingoes who wish to see others do what we only advocate doing. . . . [M]y power for good, whatever it may be, would be gone if I didn't try to live up to the doctrines I have tried to preach." And so, he concluded, he and others like him must not "stay comfortably in offices at home and let others carry on the war that we have urged."

There was still no war, of course, but it became even more likely two days later when William Jennings Bryan, the standard-bearer of the Democratic party, called a press conference. With the eloquence and political agility for which he was noted, Bryan leaped from the fence he had straddled: "the time for intervention has arrived. Humanity demands that we shall act. Cuba lies almost within sight of our shores, and the sufferings of her people cannot be ignored unless we, as a nation, have become so engrossed in money-making as to be indifferent to distress."

To some Republicans, party leadership—even party survival—was at stake. Senator William E. Chandler of New Hampshire observed with dismay the sentiment of the Democrats in the Congress. They had waffled over intervention, he wrote. Now, they "are for action. The Republicans in Congress feel that if the President will not formulate a policy it must be put forward by the Republican leaders in Senate and House."

At the State Department, Judge Day cabled Minister Woodford in Madrid: "You should know and fully appreciate that there is profound feeling in Congress . . . that a resolution for intervention may pass both branches in spite of any effort that can be made." The message was clear. If there was a diplomatic alternative to war, it had better come quickly.

VI

THE DOGS OF WAR

Both the President's message and the resolutions of Congress recognize the existence of a great wrong and express the determination to right it. In the resolution there is a strong disclaimer of any intention to profit by the acquisition of territory. We are entering upon a crusade, more practical in its objects, more lofty in its aims, than any that precede it.

—*Scientific American*, April 30, 1898

Without reason or pretext, and after the U.S. had received proofs of friendship from us, they declared war precisely when we had started to reestablish peace. . . . Perhaps, however, these American Carthaginians will now meet their Rome in this Spanish territory, which was discovered, peopled and civilized by Spain and will always be Spanish.

—GOVERNOR-GENERAL RAMÓN BLANCO

GENERAL STEWART WOODFORD—lawyer, Civil War veteran, and former congressman—had been in Madrid for almost seven months. Although he had no diplomatic training, Woodford showed spunk and persistence in his negotiations with the queen, Premier Sagasta, and various Cabinet ministers. Despite the events of the previous six weeks and the queen's rejection of McKinley's purchase proposals, he remained confident that an accommodation with Spain could be achieved.

At a remove of three thousand miles from the clamor of the Congress and the blare of jingo headlines (the *Journal* characterized his peace efforts as "twaddle"), optimism was more easily clasped than in Washington. But the American embassy was connected to the White House and the State Department by telegraph, and at the end of March the frantic clicking of the keys signaled renewed crisis.

In the days following the delivery of the court-of-inquiry report, the president, under continued siege, had tried to form his loyalists in the Congress into a defensive circle. He could not get them into line. Instead, they wheeled off to the cause of Cuba Libre. Joseph B. Foraker, from McKinley's home state, highlighted Republican disarray in the Senate when he introduced a resolution demanding that Spain withdraw from Cuba. Lodge, for the first time, admitted that "a Cuban outbreak"—and war—seemed inevitable.

The situation in the House was no better. "Czar" Reed had all but caved in to the pressure. When reporters asked him to comment on the tumult in Congress, he told them he had just received a letter from Governor Morton of New York urging him to dissuade his colleagues from war. "Dissuade them!" he snorted. "The Governor might as well ask me to step out in the middle of a Kansas waste and dissuade a cyclone!"

The president was haggard, teary, uncertain. He could not rest; sleeping potions had little effect. Jennie Hobart, wife of Vice-President Garret A. Hobart, noticed that any sound made him jump. Kindly, supportive John Long confided to his journal that his good friend had been "robbed of sleep, overworked; and I fancy I can see that his mind does not work as clearly and directly and as self-reliantly as it otherwise would."

Garret Hobart took McKinley for an afternoon carriage ride, hoping it would prove restorative. He gave the president his candid opinion on affairs in Congress. He could not hold the Senate back much longer, he said. It might declare war on its own motion.

"Say no more," the president replied sadly. He lapsed into silence, perhaps thinking of General Woodford's cautionary words in a cable of March 17: "You as a soldier know what war is, even when waged for the holiest of causes." But behind the scenes, McKinley had been stauncher than all but a few members of the Cabinet and the Congress knew.

His resolve took the form of an ultimatum cabled by Day to Woodford on March 26: "The President's desire is for peace." That acknowledged, Day's advisory stiffened: "He cannot look upon the suffering and starvation in Cuba save with horror. The concentration of men, women, and children in the fortified towns, and permitting them to starve, is unbearable to a Christian nation. . . . For your own guidance, the President suggests that if Spain will revoke the reconcentration order . . . and offer the Cubans full self-government . . . the President will gladly assist in its consummation."

Woodford was understandably confused by McKinley's demand for "self-government" in Cuba. Thinking it might refer to an expanded program of autonomy, he asked for clarification. On Sunday the twenty-seventh, the acting secretary of state replied bluntly: "Full self-government . . . would mean Cuban independence." Day also spelled out the president's other demands: immediate revocation of *reconcentrado* and an armistice until October 1. If peace terms had not been worked out by then, McKinley would be "the final arbiter" of Cuban independence.

Woodford tried valiantly to secure the concessions. On Tuesday the twenty-ninth, at a meeting in Premier Sagasta's office attended by Foreign Minister Pio Gullón and Segismundo Moret, the elderly lawyer outlined McKinley's demands. Sagasta replied that Spain was trying to help the *reconcentrados* and would welcome United States assistance. She could not offer an armistice but would accept one requested by the insurgents. He asked for time to work out further details; he would talk to the queen. They could meet again on Thursday.

With Sagasta and his ministers looking over his shoulder, Woodford drafted a cable to Washington: "I have sincere belief that arrangement will then be reached, honorable to Spain and satisfactory to the United States and just to Cuba. I beg you to withhold all action until . . . March 31." Day responded that only the president's assurance to the Congress that he would report on the peace negotiations "at a very early day, will prevent immediate action on the part of Congress."

The sense of urgency in Washington finally pricked the reluctant Spanish to act. On Thursday, Foreign Minister Gullón told Woodford that Governor-General Blanco had revoked the *reconcentrado bandos* throughout Cuba, though a full implementation of the new policy would have to wait until certain military operations were completed. In the meantime, "the Spanish Government will not . . . find it inconvenient to accept at once a suspension of hostilities asked for by the insurgents. . . ."

In Washington that evening McKinley dined with a few friends and colleagues at the White House. Mark Hanna was there, and Judge Day and Secretary of War Russell Alger. Afterward, they repaired to the Cabinet Room to await Woodford's report on the Madrid conference. A telegraph had recently been installed in a room nearby, and the group heard the keys start to click at 10:30 P.M. It was a long message, and it was early in the morning of April 1 when the machine stopped clattering and the cable was decoded.

McKinley read Woodford's dispatch with dismay. Most of the president's demands had been met, the minister reported, but not a suspension of hostilities, since it was absurd to expect that the insurgents would request a truce. Spanish pride would not permit the ministry to offer an armistice; revolution might result. It was a matter of "punctilio." War and suffering would continue. Still, "no Spanish ministry would have dared to do one month ago what this ministry has proposed to-day."

It was not enough, and McKinley knew it. The time he had stalled and fought for was running out. As Woodford desperately continued negotiations in Madrid, the president began to consider a war message to the Congress.

The next day Rear Admiral Pascual Cervera wrote Marine Minister Bermejo that, despite rough weather, he had brought elements of his squadron "safe and sound" from Cartagena through the Strait of Gibraltar to Cádiz. He had submitted supply requests for coal, lubricants, and other naval stores, but the *Colón* still did not have her heavy guns and, with the conflict fast approaching, his fears about the fleet's shortcomings were realized. He seemed to be searching for an escape route when he wrote: "... any arrangement will be good, however bad it may seem, if it can save us from lamenting a great disaster, which we may expect if we go to war with ships half armed, and only a few of them." It was unfortunate, he added, that the Vizcaya and the Oquendo were not with the fleet.

As long as two Spanish armored cruisers sat at their moorings in Havana, Governor-General Blanco was comforted by the sight of their powerful 11-inch guns, yet apprehensive they might be summoned to join Cervera's squadron. Should they leave harbor, Havana—indeed Cuba—would be virtually unprotected. Admiral Manterola had given him a candid briefing on the status of the ships under his Cuban command. Of the fifty-five vessels, thirty-two were launches. The Alfonso XII had guns but was dead in the water. The Reina Mercedes was a capable ship, but only three of her ten boilers were operating. There were three small cruisers, but only one of them could steam.

A few days later Blanco put the matter to the minister of colonies as delicately as he could: "Detention of flotilla ... leaves our coasts unprotected. You know international situation better than I under present circumstances, and will realize expediency of sending ships."

As naval experts on both sides of the Atlantic took measure of their opponent, there were significant differences of opinion on the ships of the American and Spanish navies and their crews. Ignoring the fact that a substantial part of the Spanish navy had been built in foreign yards, Hiram Maxim, inventor of the rapid-fire gun, asserted that the war would be very one-sided—Spain had no steel. The London Engineer thought otherwise, declaring that Spain had the advantage. Her ships had more firepower per minute and greater average speed than the American fleet—23.7 knots versus 19.6. "It is difficult to see," the Engineer continued, "where the usefulness of these heavily-armed floating citadels [the U.S. battleships] come in. . . . There is small chance of them even catching a glimpse of the swift and handy armored cruisers of the *Vizcaya* type. . . .

"A great deal, too, depends on the man behind the gun. The 3000 Swedish sailors [aboard] the United States vessels might be excellent material if fighting in defense of their own hearths and homes; but naval warfare of today is no pastime . . . no hirelings of an alien state are likely to come well out of such a terrible ordeal. In point of fact, we do not believe that the Yankees thoroughly understand the spirit of mischief that they seem so determined to evoke."

At a café in Havana a Spanish officer courteously touched on the matter of "mercenaries" to an American reporter, Ralph D. Paine of the *Philadelphia Press*. Paine was only a few years out of Yale but long in experience. When the *Press* refused to let him junket off on a filibustering expedition in 1896 (his editor called the request "damfoolitis"), Paine went to Hearst, who sized him up and assigned him one of his favorite projects, the delivery of a gold-encrusted, diamond-studded sword made by a Fifth Avenue jeweler to General Máximo Gómez—"the greatest living soldier." Its blade was engraved on both sides. One inscription read, "To General Máximo Gómez, Commander in Chief of the Cuban Republic from *Journal*, N.Y."; the other, "With congratulations and best wishes 'Por Cuba Libre,' May 1896."

Paine journeyed to Jacksonville and boarded the filibuster tug *Three Friends*, skippered by "Dynamite Johnny" O'Brien, who ducked the tug in and out of hiding down the Florida coast and over to Cuba. Paine was about to get into a boat, carrying the sword in its mahogany case, when a Spanish gunboat spotted them and fired several shots. The *Three Friends* steamed away only to be intercepted by another gunboat. Dynamite Johnny ordered a Hotchkiss gun to be assembled on deck and fired back. The Spanish promptly turned tail.

The upshot of it all was that Paine innocently wrote the story of the expedition ("The *Journal* sword which I am bearing to General Gómez has had a baptism of fire. . . ."), was indicted for piracy (there was not enough evidence to convict), and never managed to get the sword to Gómez.

In 1898, on his first official visit to Cuba, Paine was shocked by the sight of the *Maine*. "The ghastly tangle of twisted steel protruded above the surface of the water, all that was left of a powerful, immaculate American battle-ship—boats clustered about it and the grotesque helmets of divers searching for the shattered bodies . . . and a barge piled with waiting coffins. It bit into one's memory as though etched with acid."

This picture, and the vivid remembrance of the Spanish gunboats retreating after Dynamite Johnny's improvised salvo, may have been on his mind as he sat at the café and listened to the Spanish officer glibly explain how Spain could not lose. "If there is war, Spain will conquer your boastful United States. How? The whole thing is absurdly simple." Using the cutlery on the tablecloth to illustrate his battle plan, the officer swept aside the American fleet. Spain's navy was stronger, he said, and better manned— "You hire riff-raff of all nations." Moreover, the American army had only twenty-five thousand men, the Spanish army two hundred thousand. Once Cervera's fleet had destroyed Sampson's vessels, Spanish troops would land at Charleston and a Gulf port, roll up the American regulars, and advance without opposition on Washington and New York.

With a smile, he looked up at Paine. "More cognac, señor?"

French Ensor Chadwick, back in command of the *New York* after his tour of duty on the court of inquiry, thought the American fleet second-class at best. There were four first-class battleships now, assuming the *Oregon* made it safely through the Strait of Magellan, and two good armored cruis-ers, but the nineteen monitors in the fleet could fight effec-tively only in a smooth sea and thirteen of these were Civil War relics equipped with muzzle-loading, smooth-bore rifles. There were various other ships—a cruiser equipped with a dynamite gun, converted yachts, chartered liners, small tor-pedo boats. All in all, as British Ambassador Sir Julian Pauncefote remarked in Washington, it was "a fleet of experi-ments."

Chadwick thought the Spanish fleet imposing on paper but flawed in preparation. The *Cristóbal Colón*, built in Genoa, was an exceptional ship—fast, well-armed, and pro-tected, but apparently without her main turret. The *Vizcaya* and the *Almirante Oquendo* had both been at sea for a long stretch and would obviously be slowed by bottom growth. Other vessels were under repair or crippled by faulty boilers or deficient weapons systems. The Spanish gaggle of torpedo boats and torpedo-boat destroyers was a concern, particularly the 225-foot *Pluton,* which in calm seas could make 30 knots and outrace anything on either side of the Atlantic.

To Chadwick, as to the Spanish, the key element in the equation was crew. Cervera's ships were not fully manned. There had been no training to speak of prior to Trafalgar; there seemed to be little now. But there was something else lacking. Chadwick called it "mechanical efficiency." This was "not in [their] blood, and no education could put it there . . . it is not a race which loves the sea. . . . The courage, the self-sacrificing character of the Spanish race are beyond praise." But, he added, "on the ocean these are largely nullified by an inadaptability to the sea life. . . ."

The existence of a well-thought-out war plan also tilted the balance in favor of the American fleet. Tacticians at the Naval War College in Newport had been working on the plan since 1896, considering three basic strategies in the event of war: an attack on Spain, on the Philippines, or on Cuba and Puerto Rico. Gradually, the studies focused on Cuba. The reasoning was straightforward: "The strategic relation of Cuba to the Gulf of Mexico is so close and intimate that the value of that island to the United States in a military and naval way is incalculable."

Over the next eighteen months the plan was frequently modified. At one time a naval board proposed combining the European and Asiatic squadrons into a force capable of capturing the Canary Islands and attacking the Spanish mainland. The Philippines, hardly considered in the first plan, subsequently received strong interest. The Asiatic Squadron could lend vital support to the insurgents under Emilio Aguinaldo fighting Spanish regulars in Luzon. But in the end, Cuba again became the main target. The key to success now rested with the American fleet's ability to manhandle Cervera.

The Naval War College put a strong emphasis on war games. Tacticians, moving models around on a board showing the triangle of ocean between New York, Cádiz, and Havana, found that in general the powerful few normally won over the numerically superior but individually inferior enemy. But there were exceptions to the rule. In one scenario the battleships *Indiana, Oregon,* and *Iowa* were severely battered by a Spanish force comprised of the battleship *Pelayo* (then being outfitted at Cádiz), three cruisers, and two destroyers. The closest thing to a sure bet in the war-game derby seemed to be the contest Hearst offered his readers between the *Vizcaya* and the *Texas.* The American ship invariably won.

The gloomy scenarios envisioned by Admiral Cervera brought death and destruction to his squadron. Without a strategic plan—and there still was none—any attempt to engage the Americans would be "groping about in the dark." Like Don Quixote, his ships would sally forth "to fight windmills and come back with broken heads." Cuba was lost, but if he took his squadrons to the Canaries, at least the Spanish coast could be protected and the fleet preserved. In Madrid, Cervera felt, he could make a strong case for this option. He cabled Bermejo: "As I have no instructions, deem it expedient to go to Madrid to receive them and form plan of campaign. The Canaries trouble me; they are in dangerous situation."

On April 4, Bermejo stopped him in his tracks: "In these moments of international crisis no definite plans can be formulated."

McKinley planned to transmit his war message to the Congress on April 6. That Wednesday expectant crowds gathered outside the Capitol; inside, the Congress waited impatiently for the message. But at the White House the president had received a cable from Fitzhugh Lee warning that American correspondents, relief workers, diplomats, and businessmen in Havana would be in danger once the message was given. He urged the full evacuation of the American colony; it would take several days. Lee's advice, late as it was in coming, was sound. Moreover, there was still a shred of hope that Woodford could bring the Spanish, who had offered further concessions, around. The president told Long, Alger, and

Day, who were with him in the Cabinet Room, that he would send his message to Capitol Hill on Monday, April 11.

Long feared the expectant Congress would burst into independent action when it heard McKinley had postponed his message. To soften the impact of the delay, a delegation of congressional leaders was invited to the White House. When they appeared, outraged, bent on war, McKinley stiffened his backbone: "I will not do it," he declared. "That message shall not go to Congress as long as there is a single American life in danger in Cuba." He had bought, at severe political risk, five more days.

During the hiatus Hearst kept up the pressure. "The wires bring news of the butchery of 200 more *reconcentrados*. . . . McKinley can hardly be expected to get excited about this." And the *Journal* had not forgotten the *Maine*. On April 9 it published the results of the interviews secured from the mothers of the *Maine* dead. "How would President McKinley have felt," one wondered, "if he had a son on the *Maine* murdered as was my little boy? Would he then forget the crime and let it go unpunished while the body of his child was lying as food for the sharks in the Spanish harbor of Havana?"

In Havana, Clara Barton paid a final visit to Governor-General Blanco at the palace. They had worked together to get American relief supplies distributed to the *reconcentrados*. Blanco had been unfailingly courteous and seemed saddened by her decision to leave. He took her into an adjoining salon, pointed to eighteenth-century portraits of Spanish grandees on the wall, and remarked that during the American Revolution, "When your country was in trouble, Spain was the friend of America. Now Spain is in trouble, and America is her enemy."

Barton might have stayed, but she thought, despite rumors that an armistice was to be declared, that war was now inevitable. Red Cross policy was to go in behind the guns, not in front. There were few supplies left to distribute in any case. On Easter Sunday, April 10, J. K. Elwell made a last tour of the warehouses, closing them up, and Barton and the rest of the Red Cross mission gathered at dockside. Several correspondents were there—Scovel among them—and Fitzhugh Lee with a few remaining members of the diplomatic corps.

Ralph Paine admired the ruddy, jocund consul general. "Fitz" Lee's gritty deportment had buoyed the correspondents' morale as they faced arrest and harassment by the Spanish police. Paine remembered how, every night, "punctually at the dinner hour, he took his seat at a table in the Hotel Inglaterra, close to a long window which opened on the pavement." Lee was in full view of the hostile crowds that passed by, but he did not hurry his meal. "Suave, leisurely, he lingered to smoke a cigar and sip his wine. . . ."

The former Confederate general told the correspondents they were safe until he left, but they had better be ready to sprint when the time came. "You can stick around town until you see me grab my hat. I don't plan on getting left when the last boat pulls out, and I can move mighty spry—I learned how to retreat in good order a good many years before you-all were born."

The moment came that Sunday. Late in the day Lee and his staff, Clara Barton and her retinue, and the correspondents boarded Commander Cowles's *Fern*. She pulled away from the Havana wharves, getting up steam as they passed the corpse of the *Maine* and the jagged bits of keel and bottom plating that projected above the surface. You could *see* them, Paine thought; they had been identified by the divers and naval constructors. He could not imagine how an internal explosion could have driven the plates upward. The divers had not found all the bodies; scores were still trapped in the wreckage. Instinctively, the correspondents doffed their hats and bowed their heads in memory of the dead sailors of the *Maine*. There was a silence that lasted for several minutes.

Cowles acted as a shepherd for the last American vessels in the harbor. The *Bache* had left that morning; the flags flying from the consulate and the main truck on the *Maine* had been taken down. Even the Spanish presence had diminished. The great cruisers *Vizcaya* and *Oquendo* had sailed off to the east, possibly to San Juan, almost certainly to rendezvous at some point with Admiral Cervera's fleet.

The churches of Havana had been full that Sunday, and the tropical air rang with the sound of their bells, but now the town was quiet. The harbor had a forlorn look. Cowles was glad to go.

In Madrid, on the eve of Easter, Stewart Woodford could hardly believe the news. In the name of Christ, at the request of the pope, in the week of the Passion, the queen had agreed to declare an armistice in Cuba. Woodford's sanguine, sometimes naïve approach to the peace talks now seemed justified. Promptly, he wired the Spanish offer to the State Department, advising patience and understanding. The next day he cabled McKinley, imploring him "that nothing will now be done to humiliate Spain, as I am satisfied that the present government is going, and is loyally ready to go, as fast and far as it can. With your power of action sufficiently free, you will win the fight on your own lines."

On Easter Sunday, McKinley summoned Lodge and Senator Nelson Aldrich to the White House. Lodge disparaged the offer. It was, he thought, a "humbug armistice" since it would apparently last only as long "as he [the Spanish commanding general] may think prudent." Nor was there any reference to independence, though Woodford optimistically predicted that, too, would be offered. Had the concession come even a week earlier, something might have been done; now it was too late. The Congress, the press, and the people marched to the beat of their own drummer. McKinley's "power of action" was fettered.

The president seemed weary and resigned. There did not seem to be any way to turn back the tide of events. He said he would add the queen's armistice declaration to his message to the Congress. Otherwise, it would stand as drafted.

Monday morning Governor-General Blanco declared an armistice in Cuba. The Cuban Junta and the provisional rebel government ignored the decree. General Calixto García rejected it outright, soon ordering his troops to "go on shooting up pueblos as before and attacking any column which comes out, with greater ardor than ever. . . . Any individual who leaves our camp with the aim of conferring with the enemy on any basis except the absolute independence of Cuba will be judged with all the rigor of the law."

In Madrid and Barcelona news of the proffered armistice brought angry crowds into the streets protesting the government's capitulation. An American official wrote that "the lower classes ardently desire war. . . . The press has fed the people with all sorts of nonsense about the superior bravery of the Spanish sailor. . . . The Spanish say they have nothing to lose as they will lose Cuba anyway. At least they can destroy our navy and teach us a lesson."

It was a morning for rejection. In Washington, as clerks droned through the president's seven-thousand-word message, congressmen reacted in disbelief, thinking it ambiguous, contradictory, and indecisive. Even Long, who had seen the document at a Cabinet meeting, saw inconsistencies in the rambling message. "I suppose it is the best he can do," he wrote in his journal, placing the blame on the president's exhaustion.

McKinley began with a résumé of recent Cuban history, highlighting the suffering, destitution, and "alarming mortality" that existed on the island. Red Cross efforts had helped to relieve the situation; two hundred thousand dollars in money and supplies had been extended, thousands of lives saved. And "within a few days past the orders of General Weyler have been revoked."

The tragedy of the *Maine* was an element "of danger and disorder," McKinley related. "The destruction of that noble vessel has filled the national heart with inexpressible horror." Two hundred and sixty sailors and marines, "reposing in the fancied security of a friendly harbor, have been hurled to death. . . ." He was confident that the unanimous decision of the Naval Court of Inquiry was correct. Responsibility remained to be fixed, but "the destruction of the *Maine*, by whatever exterior cause, is a patent and impressive proof of a state of things in Cuba that is intolerable. . . . The Spanish Government cannot assure safety and security to a vessel of the American Navy in the harbor of Havana on a mission of peace and rightfully there."

The president reviewed the proposals he had made the Spanish through Minister Woodford and their "disappointing reception by Spain." Then he came to the question of what should be done. Referring to his annual report to the Congress in December, he reiterated that "annexation . . . by our code of morality, would be criminal aggression." Nor was recognition of "the so-called Cuban Republic" prudent or defensible. He rambled off on a legal tangent, citing precedents set by Presidents Jackson in 1836 and Grant in 1875.

Finally, McKinley veered back onto the track: "Recognition is not necessary in order to enable the United States to intervene and pacify the island."

The end was finally coming. "In the name of humanity, in the name of civilization, in behalf of endangered American interests . . . I ask the Congress to authorize and empower the President to take measures to secure a full and final termination of hostilities between the government of Spain and the people of Cuba, and to secure in the island the establishment of a stable government [using] the military and naval forces of the United States as may be necessary. . . .

"The issue is now with the Congress. It is a solemn responsibility. . . . Prepared to execute every obligation imposed upon me by the Constitution and the law, I await your action."

And then, almost as an afterthought, McKinley added his postscript on the peace negotiations that Long considered to be a complete non sequitur: "Yesterday . . . official information was received by me that the latest decree of the Queen Regent of Spain directs General Blanco, in order to prepare and facilitate peace, to proclaim a suspension of hostilities. . . . This fact . . . will, I am sure, have your just and careful attention in the solemn deliberations upon which you are about to enter."

In the furor that followed the reading of the president's message, the dangling postscript was hardly noticed. "Fire Alarm Joe" Foraker told a reporter, "I have no patience with the message, and you can say so." Another senator called the message "weak, impotent, imbecile and disgraceful." In the House, Joe Bailey of Texas called it "the weakest and most inconclusive speech sent out by any President."

Whether McKinley was weak or not, whether the message was imbecile or not, the president had put the issue squarely before the Congress. To some McKinley seemed to have relinquished his executive authority. Grover Cleveland wrote despondently to a friend, "I wish the President would stand fast and persist in following the lead of his own good sense and conscience; but I am afraid he intends to defer and yield to the Congress." Nevertheless, allowing that his resistance had come to an end, McKinley had asked for the power to terminate the hostilities. The Congress now set about deciding on what basis McKinley should intervene.

On Tuesday, April 12, the Senate Committee on Foreign Relations wound up its hearings on affairs in Cuba. Perhaps the most important testimony that day came from the Honorable Fitzhugh Lee, who had made a rapid journey from Florida to Washington. Lee told how he and the Red Cross workers had left Havana. Despite their efforts, the *reconcentrado* situation was dreadful; at least eighteen thousand were dying in Santiago alone. Lee reported that the Spanish had sown two rows of mines at the mouth of Havana Harbor. He did not know whether explosives had been planted before the arrival of the *Maine*, but the ship had obviously been blown up by a submarine mine. Blanco had nothing to do with this, Lee said, but he was positive the "secret" of the disaster was known by some Spanish officials in Cuba.

He paused to observe the effect of this revelation. Later he recorded, speaking of himself in the third person, "His disclosures added somewhat to the excitement already aroused." It was an understatement.

Lee planned to stay in Washington for several days before going to Richmond on Saturday. On Friday evening he dined with Lodge and Roosevelt. Lee told them new supplies sent to Havana would enable Blanco to hold out against a blockade for a month. Roosevelt, frustrated in his efforts to join up with a volunteer regiment, applied for duty on General Lee's staff, should he be given a command.

On April 13 the hawks were in full swoop on Capitol Hill. In the House there was overwhelming sentiment for recognizing the Cuban provisional republic. Representative Hugh Dinsmore of Arkansas declaimed: "We talk about liberty. Then let us give the Cubans liberty." It would be unconscionable, he said, for the United States to reserve the right to proclaim, after a Cuban government was established, "Ah, this is not a 'stable' government; we can not turn it over to you yet; we must look after this thing."

House Democrats adopted a resolution recognizing the Cuban Republic. The Republican majority turned it down. A compromise resolution was hammered out directing the president to intervene, establish peace, and secure a stable, independent government in Cuba. It was a mild resolution, almost exactly what McKinley had asked for.

But the Senate was less docile. Lodge, no longer fearing that the Congress would act on its own, now spoke out candidly: "We are face-to-face with Spain today in the fulfillment of a great movement which has run through the centuries, a greater movement than any man can hope to control. We are there because we represent the spirit of liberty and the spirit of the new time, and Spain is over against us because she is medieval, cruel, dying." Honor required action. "Ah, Mr. President, when they ask me, 'Are you your brother's keeper?' I respond, 'Yes; we are the keeper of those people in Cuba.'"

Lodge's statesmanlike appeal for intervention belied the language of the Senate Foreign Relations Committee report on affairs in Cuba, which Lodge had helped to draft. The report "arraigned the government of Spain," as a naval officer put it, "as no civilized nation ever has been in the history of the world."

The destruction of the *Maine* received top billing. It did not matter that blame had not been fixed by the court of inquiry. "The difficulty of demonstrating by conclusive proof the efficient personal cause of that sinister event was the usual one of exposing plotted and mysterious crimes. No such difficulty, however, obscures its official and responsible cause . . . with animus by Spain so plainly apparent. . . ."

In the opinion of the committee "the destruction of the *Maine* was compassed either by the official act of the Spanish authorities or was made possible by negligence on their part so willing and gross as to be equivalent in culpability to positive criminal action." The battleship was sunk by a submarine mine, the committee continued. This "contrivance is a mechanism of somewhat complicated character, not generally understood except by special manufacturers or by military or navy officers who have been instructed how to operate it." Nevertheless, "the time of the explosion must have been calculated for the moment when the *Maine* should swing within the destructive radius of the mine." The Spanish inquiry was "manifestly false." The disaster was ensured by "the duplicity, perfidy and cruelty of the Spanish character."

The report did not scant *reconcentrado*. Over 200,000 men, women, and children had been exterminated by Spain. She had "massacred sick and wounded insurgent soldiers" after they had surrendered. The "unexampled atrocities" committed by the Spanish in Cuba were "intended to depopulate . . . the island of its native people." This "colossal crime" has shocked the moral sense of the people of the United States [and has] been a disgrace to Christian civilization."

Abstention on the part of the United States would signify agreement with Spain "that the insurrection is merely a treasonable riot and not a formal and organized rebellion. . . ." Finally, the report resolved that Cubans "are, and of right ought to be, free and independent." The Spanish must withdraw immediately. The president was empowered to use the military to enforce the resolution.

That would have satisfied McKinley, but there was a tough minority report. Democrat David Turpie of Indiana introduced an amendment favoring recognition of the insurgent government. Supported by Foraker and other maverick Republicans, it passed easily in the Senate. In the House, Speaker Reed managed to corral enough Republican votes to defeat recognition.

The fangless House resolution bothered Roosevelt. On the fourteenth he told Cabot Lodge, "I have just had word that the Administration is very anxious for the House resolution, because under it they will not have to take immediate action. They regard that resolution as requiring immediate intervention, by which they understand diplomacy to be included, but not requiring them to use the Army and Navy at once. . . . We shall have more delay and more shilly-shallying."

As the House and Senate resolutions were being debated, Horatio Rubens, the lawyer for the Cuba Junta, agonized over the final wording. "I tell you, Senator," he complained to Henry M. Teller of Colorado, "they intend to steal the island of Cuba." In fact, there seemed to be little support for annexation. Most expansionists, Roosevelt included, had argued against that form of involvement. This should not be, the assistant secretary recorded, "a land-grabbing war." Many others were reluctant to assume a rebellious nation peopled with Roman Catholics and Negroes. But Rubens thought he saw loopholes in the congressional resolutions.

Teller wanted to help. He introduced an amendment disclaiming any intention on the part of the United States to exercise sovereignty, jurisdiction, or control over the island. The Senate passed it on a simple roll-call vote. After all, it merely confirmed the United States claim that it was intervening solely on moral and humanitarian grounds.

The din of patriotic debate rang out for a week on Capitol Hill. In the House congressmen interrupted their deliberations to roar out Julia Ward Howe's "Battle Hymn." Former Confederates responded vigorously with "Dixie." Everyone joined in a chorus of "Hang General Weyler from a sour-apple tree . . ." Somehow by Tuesday, April 19, they had worked out a joint resolution that did not recognize the insurgent government. McKinley had called in all his debts, mustered his remaining allies, thrown the last of his diminishing energy into the battle. The most rampant jingoes finally caved in because, as Senator Chandler reasoned, they had succeeded in forcing intervention and "we did not think it was wise to go further and delay proceedings and thus play into the hands of the peace men by continuing to insist upon specific recognition."

In the end, if there was to be war, at least it would be along McKinley's guidelines. The document of intervention was on McKinley's desk on the morning of April 20. He read it over slowly: "Joint resolution for the recognition of the independence of the people of Cuba, demanding that the Government of Spain at once relinquish its authority . . . and withdraw its land and naval forces . . . and directing the President of the United States to use the entire land and naval forces of the United States . . . to carry these resolutions into effect."

The final paragraph of the resolution incorporated the Teller Amendment: "the United States hereby disclaims any disposition or intention to exercise sovereignty, jurisdiction or control over said island, except for the pacification thereof [and will] leave the government and control of the island to its people."

At exactly 11:24 A.M., McKinley signed the Cuban Resolution. The Spanish minister, Polo de Bernabé, was immediately notified; he asked for his passports. Subsequently, the text of an ultimatum to the Spanish government was cabled to Woodford. It demanded that Spain relinquish its authority and government in Cuba by noon on April 23. Woodford delivered the ultimatum to Sagasta. The prime minister replied that the time for diplomacy was over; he interpreted the Senate resolution as a declaration of war. Despondently, Woodford prepared to leave for Paris.

The nation, save for what Roosevelt called "the peace-at-any-price theorists," was intoxicated by the news. Only a few sharp-eyed observers quibbled about the final clause. Whitelaw Reid, editor of the New York Tribune, was one of them. The specter of a second Haiti on the nation's doorstep frightened him: "I hope they [the Cubans] prove more orderly and less likely to plunge into civil strife and brigandage than has been expected." In the furor of war preparations, his caveat went almost unnoticed.

Winding up his affairs, Roosevelt allowed that the navy "is not of course in exactly the shape I should like to see it, but still it is in very good shape indeed, and will respond nobly to any demands made upon it." The army, however, was small, poorly equipped, and ill-prepared—not "one tenth as ready as the navy." But if the ground forces were inadequate, there was at least no shortage of volunteers.

Almost as McKinley signed the joint congressional resolution, William Astor Chanler placed an advertisement in several New York newspapers: "A Call Is Hereby Issued For All Able-Bodied Men between the ages of eighteen and forty-five who wish to enroll in an infantry regiment of United States volunteers. . . ." In the next few days over fifteen hundred men signed up at a recruitment office on Sixth Avenue. Chanler's enthusiasm for the cause was shortly echoed by his cousin, John Jacob Astor IV, who offered the nation a battery of artillery [to be purchased overseas] and the use of two of his railroads to transport the war matériel to Florida. In return, he hoped for an appointment on some general's staff. William Frederick Cody, better known as Buffalo Bill, offered to raise a company of cavalry scouts with 400 horses—there were about 450 broncos in Cody's western show that year. He wrote to a friend, "America is in for it, and although my heart is not in this war—I must stand by America." The services of the fifty-two-year-old ex-scout were promptly accepted by General Nelson A. Miles, who may have had in mind Cody's logistics competence. (During the showman's 1891 tour of Europe, the kaiser had studied the system Cody had worked out to transport his large company from one town to another; the German army subsequently developed rolling kitchens based on Cody's models.)

The *World* carried Cody's expertise to an extreme when it featured a story, by-lined by Buffalo Bill, with the headline: HOW I COULD DRIVE SPANIARDS FROM CUBA WITH THIRTY THOUSAND INDIAN BRAVES. Secretary of War Alger may have wondered how to handle that proposal. In any case, neither the Indians, the cavalry troupers, or the four hundred horses went to war, and financial obligations kept Cody on the home front. Somehow two of his famed broncos, Knickerbocker and Lancer, did manage to enlist.

William Randolph Hearst made the whole matter plain in a banner headline on the evening of April 20: NOW TO AVENGE THE MAINE! Vengeance should be assigned, he suggested, to a regiment of giants to include the massive Indian football player Red Water and heavyweight prizefighters James J. Corbett and Bob Fitzsimmons. As the *Journal* saw it, such "magnificent men" would "overawe any Spanish regiment by their mere appearance. They would scorn Krag-Jorgensen and Mauser bullets."

In support of the athletes, the *Journal* offered other notable "volunteers": Frank James, brother of Jesse, would lead a company of cowboys, and six hundred Sioux with tomahawks were ready and willing to hit the warpath in search of dago scalps.

In New York, five hundred Westchester businessmen, self-professed sharpshooters, volunteered en masse. New York café society also rushed to the fray. Winthrop Chanler wrote his wife excitedly from the Knickerbocker Club: "War—War—War—Extras are being shouted now under the

Club windows.... The call for volunteers and militia is
ready to be made...."

Not all of the volunteers qualified for commissions. Captain Chadwick would soon note that he was rowed by sailors
who were members of posh New York clubs. One yacht
owner joined the navy as a coal passer rather than be left
behind.

Little came of private efforts to bolster the army. Roosevelt deflated William Chanler's hopes on April 21: "Dear Willie: It looks now as though there would not be a chance for
any of us to go in a volunteer organization, because they are
only going to take the National Guard. If that is so I shall try
to get on the staff of one of the generals."

The navy strained at its anchor lines, ready to put the
Spanish war plan into effect. Decks had been cleared for action, woodwork removed, sandbags emplaced, ammunition
hoists swathed with protective chain, the last lead-gray paint
swiped on. A number of civilian vessels had been purchased
or chartered, including four ocean liners. One of them was
the *St. Paul*, of the New York–Southampton Line, which was
converted to an auxiliary cruiser. She was all Robley Evans
had expected, but Long had given him the formidable *Iowa*.
Sigsbee had hoped for a battleship "at least as large as the
Maine, as a mark of the continued confidence of the government." Instead, Long gave him the *St. Paul*.

Sigsbee took the assignment with good grace, characterizing the liner as "probably the largest man-of-war ever commanded by anybody." The *St. Paul* was certainly large—at
16,000 tons she outweighed the *Iowa* by 4,000 tons. But she
was thin-skinned, combustible, and undergunned. At least
she was fast and would be valuable as an advance scout.
Sigsbee looked forward to playing a role in the hunt for
Cervera.

Several other officers who had probed the grisly remains
of the *Maine* until the bitter end received commands. Lieutenant Commander Richard Wainwright was given the
Gloucester, born the *Corsair*, which had been purchased from
financier J. Pierpont Morgan. Long considered the little yacht
as "frail as a lady's fan," but they were putting ten guns on

her and Wainwright thought she would do. Money from the Fifty Million Bill was pouring into navy coffers and twenty-seven other yachts were procured and armed. Lieutenant Commander and Judge Advocate Adolph Marix got the *Scorpion*.

Lieutenant Commander William Cowles had long beseeched his brother-in-law for proper guns for the little "*Fern and Faithful*," or a larger command. Roosevelt popped into Long's office. He had been in the navy a year, he said, and had asked few favors, but he had one now. Would the secretary give Cowles a new ship, perhaps one of the converted cruisers? Long pointed out that the big auxiliary cruisers like the *St. Paul*, the *Yale*, and the *Harvard* were being assigned to captains and full commanders. Then he paused, threw up his hands, and told Roosevelt to see Captain Arent S. Crowninshield, chief of the Bureau of Navigation.

Roosevelt wrote Cowles triumphantly: "Crowninshield . . . said that the best thing there was without a commander was the *Topeka*, and that you should have it."

On Thursday, April 21, the Navy Department made final preparations for the conflict that was now certain. Winfield Scott Schley was promoted to commodore and given command of the Flying Squadron, based at Hampton Roads. A Northern Patrol Squadron composed of monitors and gunboats was formed to protect the coastline from Delaware to Maine. Communications were improved. Thirty-six signal stations were established along the coast and equipped with telephone, telegraph, and ninety-foot flagstaffs with signaling yards.

Commodore Sampson had earlier received a cable: "You are assigned to the command of the U.S. forces on the North Atlantic station with the rank of rear admiral immediately." He realized war was imminent and considered his fleet fit and prepared. The *Oregon* could be swiftly readied when she arrived; she had fought her way through the Strait of Magellan in a gear-busting gale and was steaming north to join his squadron.

Sampson wanted to make a quick and decisive attack on Havana the moment war was declared. Long put him on a tight leash—the ships could not be put at hazard to seize real estate until the army was ready. Even bombardment was frowned upon. Ammunition was in short supply and Cervera's fleet was the first order of business. Roosevelt wrote to Robley Evans: "As you know, I have been a heretic about the bombardment until we destroy or cripple the Spanish fleet. I think we could probably whip the dagoes even with crippled battleships, but I don't want to try. . . ."

Sampson's big ships were still anchored eight miles off Key West. Lighters and torpedo boats negotiated the tricky coral-guarded channel leading from the town to bring the fleet last-minute supplies and messages from the telegraph office. The anchorage was exposed, but at least there was a breeze offshore. In Key West itself that day, the temperature reached a sultry 103 degrees on the spacious porches of the Key West Hotel as correspondents waited anxiously for news from Washington.

Ralph Paine, the young Yale graduate reporting for the *Philadelphia Press*, watched some of the superstars in the press corps with admiration. Walter Meriwether of the *Herald* was well regarded for his reports on the wreck of the *Maine*. Frederic Remington was there for the *Journal*, and Richard Harding Davis now represented the London *Times* as well as the *New York Herald*. Davis gazed calmly out to sea at the American warships. Here was a real "war correspondent," Paine reflected. Most reporters did not aspire to this "dignity."

Paine had watched Stephen Crane at work, too. The famous novelist had journeyed from England to catch the war—it might be brief—and when not prowling the hotel porch was apt to be found playing roulette at a casino named the Eagle Bird. He bucked "the goddess of chance in contented solitude," Paine wrote, "a genius who burned the candle at both ends." With a wary smile, Crane would chant a mysterious jingle:

> "Oh, five white mice of chance,
> Shirts of wool and corduroy pants,
> Gold and wine, women and sin,
> All for you if you let me come in—
> Into the house of chance."

But no one, Paine thought, "moved with calmer assurance than the great Sylvester Scovel. Yes, you could call him that. He had won his laurels in the field with Máximo Gómez ... been imprisoned ... sentenced to be shot...." Here was a man with nerve and audacity.

But it was Walter Meriwether, with his flair for scoop, who first got the news. He was on the porch of the Key West Thursday afternoon when a messenger boy peddled excitedly up to the hotel and, in his haste, fell off his bike. He picked himself up, found Meriwether, and handed him a cable. Meriwether scanned it quickly—"Rain and Hail!" He fumbled through his pockets for the code book and quickly deciphered the cable: "War is declared, fleet ordered to sea." Davis was by his side, and Meriwether showed his fellow *Herald* correspondent the message.

"A few moments later the porch was empty," Davis reported, "and hackmen were lashing their horses down the dusty street; and at the water's edge one could see launches, gigs and cutters streaking the blue surface of the bay with flashes of white and brass; signal flags of brilliant reds and yellows were spreading and fluttering at the signal halyards; wig-waggers beat the air from the bridges, and across the water, from the decks of the monitors, came the voices of the men answering the roll: 'One, two, three, FOUR! One, two, three, FOUR!'"

On the evening of the twenty-first, Robley Evans recorded, all the commanding officers of the "outside" fleet were summoned on board the *New York*. They sat patiently, smoking cigars, listening "to the quiet words of our clear-headed commander, while the wind howled and the ship pitched and rolled in the choppy sea." It was almost midnight when a naval cadet reported a torpedo boat approaching at flank speed. A staff officer soon appeared and gave Sampson a message from the president. Sampson read it out loud. "War declared; proceed to blockade the coast of Cuba. . . ."

Evans and the other captains said a quiet good-night to the admiral and returned to their ships. When Evans boarded the *Iowa*, he told the watch in a few words what had happened. Then the signal lights of the *New York* began winking: "Be ready by daylight. . . ." Across the water he could see small boats coming out of the inner harbor, their searchlights groping in the darkness for the buoys of the difficult channel. Ralph Paine was on one of them, bound for the *New York*. He had secured permission from Sylvester Scovel to go to war aboard the *World's* press boat, the *Triton*. In exchange for Paine's passage the *World* would be allowed to use his copy. Sometime after the war message arrived, Scovel accosted Paine and told him he had a berth on Admiral Sampson's cruiser. That seemed odd to Paine. Only the Associated Press had been able to secure passage on the *New York*, and that had taken the permission of Navy Secretary Long. But he got his gear from the *Triton* and talked his way onto a launch bound for the flagship. On the way out he was impressed by the dark fleet at anchor. The ships showed no lights but their silhouettes seemed to be straining at the leash.

The officer of the deck on the *New York* had received no instructions concerning Paine; he could not bother the admiral now. In the meantime, Paine could wait in the steerage mess where the ship's naval cadets congregated. Down below, Paine found an excited group of younger officers. "Nobody could sleep or wanted to." They chewed the fat until dawn, noisily fighting the war in advance.

Before daylight on April 22 the fleet's anchor chains began rattling up through the hawse holes. As the sun rose with a flash of light and color, Davis wrote, "the leaden-painted war-ships moved heavily in two great columns, the battleships and monitors leading on the left, the cruisers moving abreast to starboard, while in their wake and on either flank the torpedo boats rolled and tossed like porpoises at play." Not long afterward, Paine was brought up to see Sampson, who was prowling the quarter deck.

The young reporter saw Sampson as "a spare erect figure in white uniform." He had a short gray beard, neatly trimmed, and a studious manner that made him seem more scholar than sailor. When Paine attempted to explain his presence on board, Sampson brought him up sharply. "Scovel told you to come aboard? Are you sure of that?" But there was no way to send the reporter back; it was too far to swim and there were more important things on the admiral's mind. He dismissed Paine.

The *Press* reporter had a ringside seat as a steamer flying the "blood and gold" flag of Spain crossed the fleet's path and the *Nashville* dashed out to capture the first prize of the war, the unsuspecting tramp steamer *Buena Ventura*. "The day passed," Paine wrote late that afternoon, "and the fleet took station off the Cuban coast, from Havana to Matanzas, grim and vigilant and wary of torpedo attack." There was gunfire on shore, as the ships closed Havana; lookouts saw no splashes. Apparently, the Spaniards were only firing off signal cannon.

The appearance of Sampson's squadron brought near panic to the streets of Havana. In the Governor's Palace, Ramón Blanco issued a call to arms and cabled to Minister of War Miguel Correa in Madrid that morale was good, "but I must not conceal from your excellency that if people should become convinced that squadron is not coming, disappointment will be great, and an unpleasant reaction is possible. Beg that your excellency will advise me whether I can give them any hope of more or less immediate arrival of squadron."

The ships so ardently desired by Blanco had left Cádiz on April 8 for St. Vincent in the Cape Verde Islands, three hundred miles off the African coast west of Dakar. Cervera still bemoaned the lack of a plan—"even on general lines"—and thought the government's intention to send the squadron to Cuba "a very risky adventure." Bermejo replied that perhaps God himself had selected Cervera "to carry out the plans which will be formulated." The *Vizcaya* and the *Oquendo* would join him at Cape Verde.

Cervera made land early on the morning of April 14, dropped anchor, and promptly complained to Bermejo that coal consumption on the voyage had been enormous—the boilers of the *Colón* and the *María Teresa* were especially inefficient. On the nineteenth the *Vizcaya* and the *Oquendo* were spotted on the horizon, temporarily buoying Cervera's spirits, but his litany of complaints and fears was soon resumed. The bow plates of two of the torpedo-boat destroyers had collapsed in heavy seas and needed reinforcing. The *Vizcaya* badly needed to be docked for a bottom scraping. Cervera worried about the vulnerable Canaries and the Phil-

ippines, but "above all I fear the possibility of a bombardment of our coast, which is not unlikely, considering the
audacity of the Yankees."

On April 20, at Bermejo's suggestion, Cervera assembled
his seven captains aboard the *Cólon* and asked them whether
the fleet "should go at once to America, or should it stay to
protect our coasts and the Canaries?" All were anxious "to
go resolutely in quest of the enemy and surrender their lives
on the altar of the mother country." But a sortie to the West
Indies would leave Spain "abandoned, insulted and trod
upon by the enemy." Cervera obliquely recommended that
the fleet retreat to the Canaries. He could leave almost immediately.

That day Bermejo advised the admiral that the United
States Congress had "approved armed intervention, declaring
Cuba free and independent." War was imminent. The following day, as diplomatic relations between Spain and the
United States were broken off, Bermejo sent a ciphered cable
to Cervera saying the Canaries "are perfectly safe." Puerto
Rico, however, was menaced. He ordered the admiral to take
the entire fleet to Puerto Rico. "The phrase *Am Going North*
will advise me that you have sailed."

Cervera cabled that his ships were still taking on coal;
loading would take at least five more days. Bermejo replied,
"The Government is inquiring constantly about your sailing
. . . go out as soon as possible." Cervera wired the minister
of marine: "Have received cipher telegram with instructions
to proceed to Puerto Rico. . . . I shall do all I can to hasten
our departure, disclaiming all responsibility for the consequences."

Even so, he still hoped for a stay of what he considered
to be execution. In a longer communication, Cervera again
insisted that the Canaries were not safe. Everyone was in
"consternation" over the orders they had received, "for nothing can be expected of this expedition except the total destruction of the fleet." Cervera's "desires" had been ignored,
and he would resign his post immediately, "without caring
a straw for being accused of cowardice, if it were not for the
fact that my retirement would produce among the squadron
the deplorable effect of a desertion of its admiral before the

enemy." He would "try to find the best way out of this direful enterprise."

Aboard Sampson's flagship off the coast of Cuba, the senior officers were intent on outguessing Cervera. He was known still to be in the Cape Verdes, 2,350 miles from San Juan, Puerto Rico. As French Ensor Chadwick saw it, he had three options: a raid on the American coastline; a swift steam to San Juan, which had coal supplies and machine shops; or a bold thrust to Havana, forcing his way into the harbor at night. It did not occur to Chadwick that the Spanish admiral might prefer to simply take a defensive posture in the Canaries. Cervera *had* to come, for the sake of honor, if nothing else.

A coastal raid would, in addition to terrorizing the seabound population, draw major American ships out of Caribbean waters and encourage potential allies in Europe to support the Spanish war effort. Forcing an entrance to Havana Harbor would have an enormously positive effect on the morale of Spanish troops and naval units in Cuba—but Chadwick did not think this likely. Later he wrote that this required "a stout heart, which he [Cervera] had, and a bold spirit of venture, which he did not." In the end, Puerto Rico seemed his most likely destination.

Sampson agreed. Denied permission to attack Havana, he proposed leaving the smaller and less seaworthy vessels at the mouth of the harbor while the battleships and cruisers of the squadron steamed east to intercept Cervera. Again, he was told not to hazard the ships at this time. No one, least of all Long and McKinley, could forget how easily the *Maine* had been lost. Aboard the *Iowa*, "Fighting Bob" Evans deplored the lack of action. For ten days, he noted, his ship rolled and pitched in trade-wind seas while his idle crew watched the Spanish army build new forts and emplace guns.

On Saturday, April 23, McKinley issued a call for 125,000 volunteers to expand the nation's small standing army. The country was fully behind him now; in a feverish burst of patriotism, more than a million Americans tried to sign up. A young Kansas editor named William Allen White wrote, "In April, everywhere over this good, fair land, flags were flying.... Everywhere it was flags: tattered, smoke-grimed flags in engine cabs; flags in button-holes; flags on proud-poles; flags fluttering everywhere...."

The real question, Secretary of War Russell Alger noted, was "how many of the thousands of men applying could be accepted." But in one particular case, that of Assistant Secretary of the Navy Theodore Roosevelt, who pounded on the secretary's door that day, there was no way to say no. Funds from the Fifty Million Bill had filtered into coastal defense units—the army had almost always assumed a defensive posture—but there was more than enough left over to equip three new cavalry regiments, to be composed of western horsemen and marksmen. The old notion that veteran cowboys would make good soldiers had taken hold at the War Department. Later, provision was made for easterners as well, but that was no concern of Roosevelt's. He qualified on either count.

McKinley wanted Leonard Wood to command one of the regiments. Alger offered a second to Roosevelt. He declined, saying his military experience did not warrant it, but cheerfully agreed to serve as second-in-command of Wood's regiment. It was done at last. He advised William Chanler, "I have just been offered a lieutenant colonelcy in a regiment of mounted riflemen ... your regiment would have to come in the second call." Roosevelt tried to soften the bad news. "If I was not limited to westerners, at least at first, in my regiment, I should feel very much like getting you ... to get a company of good horsemen and good riflemen to come with me."

Spain had interpreted the congressional Cuban Resolution and the blockade of Havana as acts of war. On April 24 she issued a formal proclamation declaring null and void all treaties between Spain and the United States. On the following morning, after meeting with the Cabinet, McKinley sent a message to the Congress recommending a declaration "that a state of war exists."

The Executive Mansion was still that afternoon. McKinley

tried to sleep as he awaited congressional action. He could not. Putting on a dressing gown, he went down the hall to the state bedchamber to talk to several friends who were staying at the White House. It was around 4 P.M. when the doorkeeper appeared with the declaration from the Capitol. Resignedly, the president read it over: "First—That War be and the same is hereby declared to exist, and that war has existed, since the 21st day of April *Anno Domini* 1898, including said day, between the United States of America and the Kingdom of Spain. . . ."

Vice-President Hobart had provided a pen for the occasion. The president used it to sign "William," and a White House pen for "McKinley." He had said early in his term, "I shall never get into a war until I am sure that God and man approve." If he was still unsure, after months of prayer, about the opinion of God, there was at least no doubt that the American people applauded his decision.

Some still felt that the president, had he been more decisive, could have solved the Cuban business without war; most Republicans now thought the task had been hopeless. As Senator John Spooner of Wisconsin put it, "the current was too strong, the demagogues too numerous, the fall elections too near."

Earlier that month an American ornithologist and entomologist named William Doherty had roamed the streets and environs of Manila taking copious notes on the city's abundant bird and insect life. He was a trained observer, and at the same time meticulously recorded the location and armament of the fortifications around Manila Bay. Doherty planned to return to the United States on a circuitous route through Hong Kong. Before leaving he hid the plans he had made in a newly laundered shirt, pinned it up in the usual fashion, and put it at the bottom of his trunk. Arriving in Hong Kong, Doherty went aboard the *Olympia* and gave his notes to Commodore George Dewey.

Roosevelt's wolfhound was straining at the leash. After receiving the assistant secretary's cable of February 25, he had put his ships in drydock to have their bottoms scraped and their topsides painted war-gray. In April, reinforcements to his flimsy fleet began to enter harbor: the little revenue cutter *McCulloch* from Singapore; the gunboat *Concord* from California; the cruiser *Raleigh* from the Mediterranean; and the formidable, 4,600-ton *Baltimore* from the Hawaiian station. On April 25, Dewey moved the squadron to Mirs Bay, a small port thirty miles from Hong Kong. The British had invoked neutrality and politely requested that Dewey leave. One of Dewey's staff officers stayed in Hong Kong to pick up messages at the cable office and bring them by chartered tug to Mirs Bay. On the twenty-fifth, at 7 P.M., after a six-hour steam on the tug, he delivered one from Long that Dewey had anticipated: "War has commenced between the United States and Spain. Proceed at once to Philippine Islands. Commence operations particularly against the Spanish fleet. You must capture vessels or destroy. Use utmost endeavor."

The leash on Roosevelt's wolfhound was officially slipped, but Dewey stayed at heel in Mirs Bay for two more days waiting for U.S. Consul Oscar F. Williams, whom he thought might have vital information on the channels leading into Manila Bay and the placement of guns and mines. On the twenty-seventh he cabled Long that the consul had arrived from Manila; the fleet would sail immediately. Williams, with his intimate knowledge of Manila Bay, found a berth aboard the *Baltimore*.

At the Hong Kong Club the British were sympathetic to Dewey's venture, but one had to scrounge around to find someone willing to bet on the Americans. English sailors had taken the measure of the Spanish navy for centuries; they tended to regard it with humorous contempt. But Manila Bay, guarded by the guns of Corregidor, by minefields, and by a Spanish squadron, was thought to be virtually impregnable. "A fine set of fellows," one British officer remarked of the American contingent, "but unhappily we shall never see them again."

Toward the end of the month, in New York, the *Maine* claimed another casualty. Julius Chien, an enterprising Russian inventor, was assembling a pyrotechnic toy he called "How the *Maine* Was Blown Up." Chien took the official view of the disaster, which his gadget graphically demonstrated. It consisted of a piece of tissue like paper imprinted with a picture of the *Maine;* beyond the battleship, on the Havana shore, a bearded Spaniard pushed a plunger, electrically detonating a mine. A miniature explosion was made possible by treating the paper with a nitrous substance leading from shore to ship. Combustion followed the trail of the chemical along the paper until it reached a "cap" of powder under the rendition of the *Maine* and exploded with a harmless, paper-ripping burst.

Perhaps Chien was working too rapidly to get his product to market; even now, the mania for *Maine* souvenirs was being overtaken by other events. At any rate, some carelessness resulted in the combustion of several pounds of powder stashed on his assembly line. The explosion blew out windows, set fire to the laboratory, and wrecked his apartment. Chien, badly injured, was taken to the hospital.

At St. Vincent, Cape Verde, Pascual Cervera continued to have technical problems of his own. The *Vizcaya* was so slow the admiral considered her "nothing more than a buoy." The after turret of the *Oquendo* did not "obey horizontal training." Ammunition was defective, the *Colón* still did not have her big guns, coal was in short supply, and heavy swells had slowed the loading.

Cervera's orders, ratified by His Majesty's government, were to proceed to endangered Puerto Rico, but he was extended "entire freedom of action as to route . . . and circumstances in which battle should be sought or eluded." On the twenty-eighth, Bermejo reported that Havana and the north coast of Cuba were still blockaded, but San Juan was clear. There had been no *golpe* in Madrid. "Quiet and harmony reigning in Spain."

Finally, on April 29, Cervera elected to see "what God has in store for us." A firm push from the Portuguese, who had declared neutrality, made the decision to depart the Cape Verdes mandatory.

Early that morning Cervera cabled Bermejo the agreed-upon signal, "Am going north," and took the fleet to sea. By 10 A.M., Captain Víctor Concas of the *Infanta María Teresa* recalled, the Portuguese islands disappeared over the horizon. The flagship led the way, followed by the *Almirante Oquendo*, the *Vizcaya*, and the *Cristóbal Colón*. All but the *Vizcaya*, already slowed by weeds and barnacles, towed a torpedo-boat destroyer, so that the smaller vessels would not have to be coaled at sea. Proper towing bridles had not been obtained. In the Atlantic swells, the destroyers rolled and yawed in the seaway. The speed of the squadron was reduced to seven knots.

It must have seemed a bad omen to Cervera, had he needed one more, that even as he left St. Vincent he was being pursued. An alert *New York Herald* correspondent, anticipating his departure, had chartered a small boat and followed the Cape Verde fleet out of the harbor, easily keeping pace with the slow-moving warships. The next day he cabled New York that Cervera was heading west, probably to Puerto Rico, and should arrive there around May 11.

It was, on the whole, an excellent piece of intelligence, but no one paid much attention to it, most especially the people Roosevelt called "seaboard cowards." The American public had yet to be disabused of the notion that ships were designed, built, and positioned at one point and another, like policemen on their beats, with the objective, as Roosevelt put it, "of protecting everything everywhere." Instead, the fleet had been massed in squadrons ready to hit the enemy wherever he appeared. And as Cervera left St. Vincent, fears fanned by the Yellow Press swept down the relatively unprotected northeast coastline.

There were hundreds of rumors. Cervera had been seen near Nova Scotia, off Maine, headed for Newport. Ocean liners bound for New York and Boston thought they spotted the Spanish cruisers following in their wake; torpedo boats were glimpsed in the fog off Long Island; Maine fishermen stowed shotguns aboard their trawlers to repel the enemy. A bombardment of the New England coast was expected, or perhaps the Gulf Coast. In Boston, businessmen moved their securities to Worcester—until safe-deposit space ran out. The governor of Massachusetts announced he would not allow the National Guard to leave the state.

In Rome the United States ambassador told a visiting American lady that their country had lost its head. "Our coast is undefended. Boston and New York will be destroyed!" Resort managers and millionaires with summer mansions pleaded for protection. Virtually every congressman with a coastline district screamed for a battleship to save his constituency. Newspapers advised their readers not to open summer cottages until Cervera had been found.

To Roosevelt, at first, it all seemed only a "fairly comic panic." The people had simply gone from unreasoning confidence to unreasoning fear. Two years earlier he had confided to his English friend Cecil Arthur Spring-Rice that "the burning of New York and a few other coastal cities would be a good object lesson on the need of an adequate system of coast defenses." But he was not amused when, in his hometown of Oyster Bay, "clauses were gravely put into leases to the effect that if the property were destroyed by the Spaniards the lease should lapse."

Roosevelt played up the importance of the antiquated Patrol Squadron and distributed a few old monitors to various cities to calm their fears. His fellow Porcellian Winthrop Chanler may have helped to relieve the tension when he remarked that if the dons landed in downtown New York, "they would all be absorbed in the population . . . and engaged in selling oranges before they got as far as 14th Street."

Scientific American thought the danger lay not to the seaboard but to a lone battleship pounding its way north off the coast of Brazil. It wondered whether the Cape Verde fleet might be strung out across the path of the *Oregon*. If Cervera intercepted Captain Charles E. Clark, the journal asserted, the *Oregon* would fight it out, despite the odds, before going to the bottom, "for it goes without saying that no American flag will be struck in the present war!"

Clark looked forward to an engagement with the Spanish cruisers. He thought he could whip them single-handedly and had worked out the tactics that would bring this about. On sighting the Spanish, he would turn 180 degrees and run away at speed. The pursuing cruisers, of varying speed potential, would become separated. Then, like a bear turning on a stretched-out pack of hounds, Clark would reverse course and hammer the Spaniards, one by one, with his 13-inch guns. Clark announced the plan to his crew; they whooped with delight. As one of his marine orderlies put it, "We all think Captain Clark is going to be a ring-tail snorter for fighting."

At Roosevelt's Sagamore Hill home in Oyster Bay, there was a similar display of patriotism. Bamie had taken Alice and young Ted to an operetta in New York, and a catchy tune had caught their fancy. Now, on the greening lawn outside the sprawling gray house, the children marched and boldly called out:

> "Unleash the dogs of war!
> The enemy will find us unrelenting.
> When our cannons roar,
> The little King of Spain
> Will be repenting."

There was enthusiasm in Madrid, too. Crowds in the streets cheered as the Queen Regent and her son Alfonso waved from a distant balcony. But a visiting French naval officer, Louis Viaud, detected an undercurrent of melancholy, perhaps even despair. There was a song they sang about the "Blood, red and gold" Spanish flag—but there was "no gold to pay for it, nor blood to sell for it." He heard another in a café:

> "They have many ships,
> We, the Right;
> They have armaments;
> And we, honor."

Viaud had served in the Far East and had written about his experiences under the name Pierre Loti. The war in Indochina was particularly bitter, rebellion widespread. He had recorded its horror in *Pêcheur d'Islande*. It may have occurred to him that Havana and Hanoi had much in common, that Cuba was the Spanish Vietnam. Perhaps it would also be a cross the Americans had to bear.

VII

WOLFHOUND AT MANILA BAY

Didn't Admiral Dewey do wonderfully well? I got him the position out there in Asia last year, and I had to beg hard to do it; and the reason I gave was that we might have to send him to Manila. And we sent him—and he went!

—THEODORE ROOSEVELT to William Wingate Sewall
May 4, 1898

[Dewey should] sail right away from that place. It will make us trouble for all time to come if he does not.

—THOMAS BRACKETT REED

AROUND 5 A.M. on Saturday morning, May 7, the phone rang at the White House. A watchman picked up the receiver. The caller identified himself as James Keeley, managing editor of the *Chicago Tribune*. "I've got news from Manila," he told the watchman, and asked him to wake the president. The watchman protested; he knew McKinley fought for sleep. You'd better, Keeley said, it's important.

The watchman went up to the second floor and woke McKinley, who put on a robe and slippers and padded apprehensively to a nearby phone. The past six days had been trying. He knew there had been a battle in Manila. Early reports were encouraging. On Monday, May 2, the *New York Herald* had reported, SPAIN'S ASIATIC FLEET DESTROYED BY DEWEY. In Madrid, however, Marine Minister Segismundo Bermejo announced total victory. Another dispatch quoted the governor-general of the Philippines, Don Basilio Augustín Dávila: "Our fleet engaged the enemy in brilliant combat, protected by the Cavite and Manila forts. They obliged the enemy with heavy loss to maneuver repeatedly. At nine o'clock the American squadron took refuge behind the foreign shipping on the east side of the bay."

Then the telegraph cable from Manila to Hong Kong had been cut. Dewey had yet to make an official report. He was well over seven thousand miles from a base of supply; with the *Oregon* around the Horn, somewhere near Rio de Janeiro, there was no way to assist the doughty commodore if things had gone badly.

Anxiously, McKinley picked up the receiver and listened to Keeley. After a few moments he put it down, sighed, and gave thanks to God.

At Mirs Bay on Wednesday, April 27, after Consul Oscar Williams arrived on the *Fame*, George Dewey had called a council of captains. They went over the charts of Manila Bay that his navigator, Lieutenant Carlos G. Calkins, had purchased in Hong Kong. Williams updated the information he had sent on mines; as far as he had been able to find out, they were not a serious problem, though one of the channels leading into Manila Bay was reportedly mined. But he had a piece of bad news. Admiral Patricio Montojo y Pasarón had taken his flagship *Reina Cristina* and the main elements of his fleet to Subic Bay, thirty-five miles up the coast of Luzon from the entrance to Manila Bay.

Subic was easily defended. The channel was narrow; if there were mines, they could be set to great advantage. The Spanish were known to have large-caliber guns, and these could enfilade the approaches to the bay with murderous fire. Montojo could entrench his fleet behind these defenses, then sally forth to cut Dewey's communications lines or attack the fleet itself.

Dewey was confident about Manila Bay. He had wired

Long earlier in the month that it could be taken in a day. After reducing the city the fleet could expect help from the insurgents who had been fighting the Spanish since 1896. Conditions in the Philippines and in Cuba were very much alike, Williams said. The rebels around Manila were armed and trained. Battles were an almost daily occurrence.

But Subic was a different matter.

At 2 P.M. on the twenty-seventh the nine ships of Dewey's squadron hauled anchors and steamed out of Mirs Bay. The *Olympia* led the way and the white-uniformed marine band played John Philip Sousa's stirring "El Capitán" as the other ships formed into line. The *Baltimore* came next, and then the *Raleigh*, the *Petrel*, the *Concord*, and the *Boston*. The little revenue cutter *McCulloch*, now transferred from the Treasury Department to the navy, escorted the steamers *Zafiro* and *Nanshan* carrying hard Welsh coal Dewey had bought in Hong Kong.

Navigator Calkins set a course southeast across the South China Sea for a point just north of Subic, 630 miles distant. The *Olympia* churned along at a slow 8 knots so the coal tenders could keep pace. Looking at the boiling wake of the flagship and the greenish-gray ships following, Calkins felt a sense of security. He did not think the Spanish would prove aggressive or bold. Rather, he expected to find them "at anchor and disposed for fighting under the protection of shore batteries, under conditions implying discouragement and anticipation of defeat."

The American ships were well supplied with coal and ammunition, the crews well trained. There were some 1,750 crewmen on board—a few Chinese stewards and mess attendants had deserted at the last moment—and two Philippine insurgent leaders who had been exiled to Hong Kong. The tonnage of the squadron was twice that of the expected defenders. The *Olympia* alone was 5,870 tons, virtually as big as the *Maine*, and double the displacement of the Spanish flagship *Reina Cristina*. She was a "protected" cruiser with steel deck plates, and 8-inch guns loomed from her fore and aft turrets. The *Baltimore* and the *Boston* also carried 8-inch guns, while Montojo's flagship had only 6.2-inch rifles.

Still, the fleet was more imposing on paper than in practice. The British thought the *Olympia* overengined and over-gunned. The turrets on the *Baltimore* were, as one observer put it, "obstructive as well as protective." As for the *Raleigh*, there was "nothing good about her but her guns." But guns, Calkins reflected, would be a key factor at Manila, along with the crew and the men who commanded them. In this department, Calkins was certain the Americans held the advantage.

George Dewey was, in many respects, unremarkable, yet the sixty-year-old commodore had a way of getting what he wanted. Born and raised in Vermont, he was considered a precocious child and, as a teenager, something of a practical jokester. After school he had wanted to go to West Point; there was no vacancy but the doors to Annapolis, then only nine years old, opened and he entered the academy in 1854. During the Civil War he served under David Farragut and assimilated the captain's "Damn the torpedoes" attitude to risk-taking.

The long, dreary postwar years followed. Promotion was slow, sea duty hard to come by. In 1887 there were fifty-nine officers available for every naval vessel, and most of these were small. Funds were in such short supply in 1889 that commanders had to log in red ink any consumption of coal—including that used in getting up steam. The following year Dewey persuaded the navy to increase appropriations for coal.

Dewey lamented the use of political patronage, yet he was not averse to asking favors of Senator Redfield Proctor, also of Vermont. In 1889, Proctor helped him secure Winfield Scott Schley's job at the Naval Bureau of Equipment, and in 1897 command of the Asiatic Squadron. Long called Dewey "this carrion of patronage"; he had not given him the courtesy rank of rear admiral on his appointment to the Far East command. Dewey pretended not to care. It was, he said, a "pin-pricking slight."

Dewey had other critics. One thought him a bit of a caricature; with his ruddy complexion, snowy-white hair and moustache, and blue uniform, he seemed to mimic the American flag. But Dewey was a popular officer, direct, determined, and decisive. Roosevelt admired this, noting, "In a crisis, the man worth his salt is the man who meets the needs of the situation in whatever way is necessary." In Washington, the assistant secretary enjoyed lunching with the commodore at the Metropolitan Club and riding with him in Rock Creek Park.

On the first day out, as the *Olympia* sliced through the calm South China Sea, her band serenaded Dewey with tunes from light operettas, favorite marches, and a new song that was sweeping the country—"There'll Be a Hot Time in the Old Town Tonight." To stir the blood Bandmaster Valifuoco switched to a medley of Civil War songs, then "Yankee Doodle," and finally "The Star-Spangled Banner." On deck fifty men picked up the words, the tenor voices of the young apprentices taking the lead, but the music plumbed all the way down to the coal passers and at the end a deep chorus of "land of the free, and the home of the brave" rolled through the entire ship.

On the *Baltimore,* Oscar Williams gave a speech to the crew, telling them what it was like to live in Manila. It was no longer safe for Americans there; they were considered a godless, insolent, impure, and cowardly race of Indian killers. The flag was insulted. The Spanish were killing and torturing Emilio Aguinaldo's insurgents, who would happily embrace the cause of America and its flag. The sailors cheered Williams and cursed the Spanish.

That Wednesday the sailors were called to musket, cutlass, and signal drills. Masts were bound with anchor chain, decks sanded, shot plugs made to stopper shell holes below the waterline, splinter nets rigged from tough manila rope, lifeboats wrapped with canvas, operating tables organized. A flotsam of lumber began to bob in the ships' wakes as polished oak and mahogany paneling and furniture were heaved overboard. Dewey advised (but did not order) the men to have their hair shingled. A short haircut would keep them cooler and ease the surgeon's work in the event of scalp wounds.

There were three correspondents with the squadron. One was Joseph Stickney of the *New York Herald.* He had been stationed in Tokyo, keeping an eye on Japanese, British, and Russian fleet movements, when James Gordon Bennett posted him to Hong Kong where Dewey gave him a berth on his flagship. Stickney was an Annapolis graduate and a Civil War veteran, but he was astonished by the level of crew training he witnessed at midnight on April 27.

The soft tropical night was suddenly shattered by the bugler blowing Quarters for Action. There were over a hundred bugle calls in the navy, so many the tars had put words to the melodies to keep them apart. Mess call began, "Soupy, soupy soup, without a single bean . . ." Taps was "Go to sleep, go to sleep . . ." But there was no mistaking the staccato insistence of the call to quarters. The men pounded up from belowdecks on the double. In the half-darkness of the moon-washed night, they hung lanterns, ran up battle flags, set the ammunition hoists, loosened the sea fastenings of the guns, uncovered the sights, and opened the magazines. Engineering officers reported to the boiler rooms, others to the bridge and the conning tower.

As the din of pounding feet diminished, Stickney heard the voice of the executive, Lieutenant Corwin P. Rees, call out, "Man the starboard battery! Pivot to starboard!" Gunners took their places as the big rifle barrels swung out over the pewter sea. There was a moment's pause, then Rees reported to Captain Charles V. Gridley, "The ship is cleared for action, sir!"

Stickney looked at his watch. It was seven minutes after midnight. For twenty minutes more, the gun crews drilled. Finally, the order to secure was given and the tired crew put their guns—and themselves—to bed.

On April 28, as the Asiatic Squadron sailed on under a squally sky, Admiral Montojo took stock of a situation that seemed at best unpromising, at worst disastrous. He had just received a wire from the Spanish consul in Hong Kong: Dewey had left Mirs Bay with his squadron the day before. The hard question Montojo faced was how best to defend Manila and the Philippines.

To protect his inferior fleet he could hide it among the innumerable inlets and islands along the coast. His vessels could then sortie to attack American ships and disrupt supply and communications lines. That meant forfeiting—at least until reinforcements arrived from Spain—the city of Manila. Governor-General Basilio Augustín Dávila made it clear this option was unacceptable. Nor did Augustín Dávila favor a second option, placing the fleet in a defensive position under the formidable gun batteries of Manila, where the city itself would inevitably become a target.

Subic Bay had long been considered the most defensible position. In 1891 a naval commission recommended the port be heavily armed. If it were not, Captain del Frigata Don Julio del Rio predicted gloomily, the squadron would end up at Cavite, six mines south of Manila. "If it is at Cavite he [the enemy admiral] attacks the arsenal and our squadron which is almost motionless suffers helplessly until its annihilation is complete."

Montojo knew that little had been done; most of the Subic defenses were not in place. Minister of Marine Bermejo had promised him seventy contact mines. According to various reports, they had not arrived, or had not been planted, or if planted hauled up by insurgents and robbed of their powder charges. On April 25, Montojo had belatedly taken his six best ships to Subic to reconnoiter the bay. The situation was worse than he had expected. For lack of cement, emplacements for 5.9-inch guns had not been built. The guns lay uselessly on the beach. Only five mines guarded the harbor entrance. Montojo was disgusted by the lack of preparation. It was a case of *Pedido queda pedido*—"Things urgent remain urgent."

Meanwhile, the wooden-hulled *Castilla* had sprung a leak in her propellor stuffing box. The housing was plugged with cement, freezing the shaft. The cruiser would have to fight from a dock or a mooring. Montojo called a council of captains. Someone pointed out that the water in the bay was well over a hundred feet deep; if a ship sank, her many country-bred seamen would have little chance of survival. The fleet, with the *Castilla* under tow, returned to Manila Bay.

As the American squadron approached the coast of Luzon, the wakes of the ships again boiled with woodwork, books, pinups, even cherished ditty boxes. Battle procedures called for the messroom tables to be hung over the sides. On the *Olympia* sailors enthusiastically heaved them into the sea. "Clearing ship for action," Calkins noted, "is a destructive yet inconclusive process which appeals to some boyish or primitive instinct of sailor-men."

Consul Williams had brought with him from Manila a fanfaronade issued by Augustín Dávila a week earlier. It was said to have been ghostwritten by the archbishop of Manila. Dewey had copies made and distributed to his captains. They were ordered to read the extraordinary proclamation to their crews before going into battle.

Charles Gridley on the *Olympia* calmly presented the document to his crew and urged them to do their best, aim carefully, make every shot count. But on the *Baltimore*, Captain Nehemiah Mayo Dyer, known throughout the navy as "Hot Foot" for his fierce temper, gave the reading a tempestuous performance. Dyer climbed onto the platform of a deck gun carriage. Immediately, an engineering officer recalled, there was an intense silence broken only by the crash of waves against the bow and the throbbing of the ship's engines. Then Dyer began to declaim: "Men of the *Baltimore*, you are about to listen to the most shameful set of lies, the most abominable falsehoods, the most horrible statements ever made against Americans. . . . Listen! This is what the Spanish Governor-General of the Philippine Islands has published." The accusations, he said, applied to everyone—"me, and you, and you, and you!—and you!"

Hardly able to contain himself, he launched into the fanfaronade. "The North American people, constituted of all social excrescences, have exhausted our patience and provoked war by their perfidious machinations, their acts of treachery, their outrages against the laws of nations. . . .

"Spain, which counts upon the sympathies of all nations, will emerge triumphant from this new test, humiliating and blasting the adventurers from those United States . . . in which appear insolence, defamation, cowardice and cynicism.

"Her squadron, manned by foreigners, possessing neither instruction nor discipline, is preparing to come to this archipelago with ruffianly intention, robbing us of all that means life, honor, and liberty, and pretending to be inspired by a courage of which they are incapable.

"American seamen undertake as an enterprise . . . the substitution of Protestantism for the Catholic religion, to treat you as tribes refractory to civilization, to take possession of your riches . . . to kidnap those persons they consider useful to man their ships. . . .

"Vain designs, ridiculous boastings!"

As Captain Dyer read, the engineer reported, "he became possessed of a mad fury that constantly augmented. His wonderful voice rolled over the deck and reached and roused every heart."

Dyer indignantly came to the end of the proclamation: "They shall not gratify lustful passions at the cost of your wives' and daughters' honor. . . . They shall not perpetrate these crimes, inspired by their wickedness and covetousness. . . . They have exterminated the natives of North America, instead of giving them civilization and progress. . . .

"Filipinos, prepare for the struggle . . . to the calls of your enemies oppose the decision of a Christian and a patriot, and cry 'Viva España!'"

The engineer watched in awe as Dyer hurled the paper to the deck, "jumped on it, cursed it—then broke into the most beautiful, though violent, statement of the soul of America, past and present.

"A wild cry went up from the hearts of the Americans before him. . . . The cry became a mighty roar. Then up went Dyer's arm: there was a perfect silence.

"'March divisions to their quarters! Pipe down!' he ordered."

On the night of Friday, April 29, the squadron made land at Cape Bolinao on the coast of Luzon. Calkins could smell the "rank tropical odor" of the island; at daybreak he spotted mangrove swamps and high rock ridges. Dewey ordered the *Boston* and the *Concord* to proceed south and reconnoiter Subic Bay; later the *Baltimore* was also dispatched. Here was the commodore's first and perhaps greatest hurdle. If the Spanish were well entrenched at Subic, his task was daunting.

Conserving coal, the rest of the squadron followed at a slow pace. By midafternoon, as they approached the bay, Calkins saw immediately that "our game was not there, and the scouting cruisers gathered like a pack of hounds at fault."

Dewey's eyes sparkled. "Now we have them," he said.

The squadron reformed and again headed south, down the Bataan Peninsula. At sunset, not far from the entrance to Manila Bay, Dewey stopped the fleet and signaled for a captains' meeting. Calkins spread out his navigation charts. Manila Bay looked a bit like an inverted ship's decanter, loosely stoppered at the southern end by the islands of Corregidor and Caballo. The city of Manila lay about twenty-five miles to the northeast. The heights of Bataan loomed over the western shore. Channels led into the bay on both sides of the high, rocky islands. Dewey chose the wider Boca Grande (the Great Mouth) passage south of Corregidor. To gain the element of surprise, the ships would enter under cover of darkness, single file, following the wake of the ship in front. A shrouded stern light was permitted, nothing else. The *Olympia* would lead the way.

Dewey's nephew, Lieutenant William Winder, had come aboard off the *Baltimore*. He gave his uncle a smart salute and proposed to take the collier *Zafiro* through the channel at the head of the fleet. If there were mines, her deep, coal-filled hull would explode them and make the passage safe for the warships following.

Dewey murmured. "Billy, I have waited 60 years for this opportunity. Mines or no mines, I am leading."

As the captains returned to their ships and the squadron formed its line, a brilliant sunset burst over the sapphire-blue sea. On the little *McCulloch*, illustrator John T. McCutcheon of the *Chicago Record* nervously eyed the sky. McCutcheon had been aboard the cutter at Singapore when she was hastily transferred to navy duty with the Asiatic Squadron. At Hong Kong he had considered Dewey's adventurous strike "like going into the jaws of a dragon," and he was quite certain, as they crossed the South China Sea, that he would be killed.

Now, as he watched the sunset, dark clouds gathered on the western horizon and formed into a spectral image—the gundeck of a warship with ominous gun barrels protruding from a turret. The dark shape was clear and unmistakable. It was a marvelous portent, McCutcheon thought, but for whom? He went below and strapped a dozen or so gold pieces to his waist in case the *McCulloch* sank and he managed to reach shore.

As the ships steamed slowly through a phosphorescent sea toward the south coast of Corregidor, a new moon rose. It was frequently obscured by billowing cumulus clouds but, when it shone through, made it difficult for the helmsmen following the *Olympia* to glimpse the hooded stern light ahead. At nine forty-five, the men were sent to their guns; they tried to sleep on the sand-strewn deck. Lighting flickered to the southwest and, at eleven o'clock a shower of rain splattered the steel topsides of the ships. Dewey welcomed the rain and clouds. He was confident his captains, who knew of his preplanned course, could follow the flagship through the twists of the Boca Grande channel.

At that moment, Admiral Patricio Montojo left a reception in Manila given by his wife, got into a carriage, and began the hour's ride back to his flagship at Cavite. A number of his officers had also gone ashore that night. Montojo knew that Dewey had left Hong Kong at 2 P.M. on the twenty-seventh. He also knew the distance to Manila and the approximate speed of Dewey's squadron. Simple long division gave him an estimated time of arrival for the commodore's squadron. In fact, his calculation had been corroborated that morning by telegraph reports from Bolinao and in the afternoon from the naval station at Subic Bay.

When Montojo reached the *Reina Cristina*, many of his officers had not yet reported to their ships.

Just before midnight the *Olympia* entered Boca Grande and glided by the little island of El Fraile to starboard. For a moment Dewey thought the fleet might pass through the sentinel islands without being seen at all. Then Calkins saw a bright white light to the north begin winking out a long message. Moments later a rocket flashed up from the heights of blacked-out Corregidor and burst with a flash of red against the dark sky. Still, they were not fired on. Calmly, Calkins ordered the course changed from east to northeast by east; the new heading would take them directly toward the mouth of the Pasig River, which divided the old city of Manila from the new.

On the *McCulloch*, still wearing the channel, John McCutcheon thought about the "dreaded Krupp guns" of the Corregidor batteries. Suddenly, to his dismay, there was a boiling roar of sound and a sheet of orange flame erupted from the single funnel of the cutter—oily soot in the stack had caught fire. To McCutcheon it looked like an infernal steel-rolling mill. He realized they were discovered. Somewhere ashore there was a shrill blast of a bugle, and then the air was split by an eerie, whistling shriek. A shell from the jagged hump of El Fraile hurtled overhead between the *Petrel* and the *Raleigh*. The *Boston* fired one of her 8-inch batteries; the *McCulloch* opened fire; two more shells from El Fraile ripped the air. Then silence. The fire was now out. Signal lanterns flashed that all was well.

The ships were now all through the channel. Dewey reduced the speed of the squadron to four knots, timing his arrival at Manila for daybreak. Shortly afterward, the moon set. Soon the officers on the bridges of the lead ships could see the lights of Manila outlining its broad avenues. On the *Olympia*, correspondent Stickney of the *Herald* recalled the words of a poem—he thought it was by Robert Southey:

> As we drifted on our path,
> There was silence deep as death,
> And the boldest held his breath,
> For a time.

The long night had exhausted the ailing captain of the flagship. Gridley suffered from a cancer, probably of the liver. Dewey tried to get him to snatch an hour of sleep and offered to excuse him from duty. Gridley would not have it. He had graduated from the Naval Academy with the class of 1864, along with Charles Sigsbee, Robley Evans, and Charles Clark, and struggled for over thirty years to make captain and command a major ship.

"Thank you, Commodore," Gridley said, "but she is my ship and I will fight her."

At 4 A.M. the mess attendants brought up steaming cans of strong coffee—the old-timers called it "bootleg"—and sticky gingerbread and butter. An hour later the tropical sun began to rise behind Manila, silhouetting the domes and spires of the city. It was already hot. A humid mist rose from the glassy surface of the bay. Pitch bubbled up from deck seams. Below, with the portholes secured, it felt to many sailors as though they were in a furnace. One, at least, was not concerned about death and the flames of the underworld. "Hell ain't no hotter than this!"

Charles Julian, an officer on the *Baltimore*, saw the Stars and Stripes break out at every masthead. In the hush on deck he clearly heard Captain Dyer's clarion voice ring out: "There it goes, men.... Let us see what we can do under the flag."

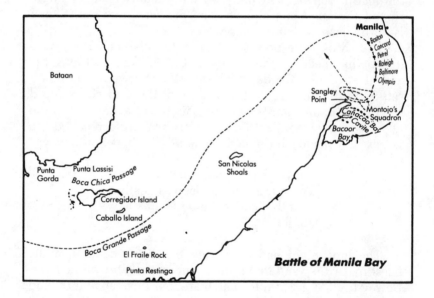

Battle of Manila Bay

Dewey slowly closed the distance to Manila, then swung the squadron to starboard along the breakwater fronting the city. Calkins picked up his binoculars and focused them on the anchorage. He saw the masts of sixteen merchant sailors, but no men-of-war. The dons must be at Cavite. The *Olympia* completed her fishhook turn past Manila and headed south.

In her wake, at four-hundred-yard intervals, steamed the *Baltimore*, the *Raleigh*, the *Petrel*, the *Concord*, and the *Boston*. The *McCulloch* and the two coal tenders had been ordered to an unfrequented area of the bay so as not to hamper the movement of the warships.

Navigator Calkins stood at his compass, taking bearings and calling out headings and ranges from a steel grating twelve feet above the conning tower. For a while Dewey joined him in the little crow's nest—there was barely room for the two of them and the compass—then moved down to the flying bridge. The commodore wore tropical whites and a golf cap; he had been unable to find his uniform cap in the jumble of his cabin.

Suddenly, they saw a puff of white smoke in Manila. In a few moments the shell from the Luneta battery exploded overhead with an ear-splitting clap. Two other batteries opened fire. Dewey declined the challenge. His objective—the target Mahan had so clearly spelled out in his naval gospels—was the enemy fleet.

It was soon sighted.

Sangley Point juts up like a curving lobster claw from the eastern shore of Manila Bay. Sangley tips the northern pincer, the Cavite peninsula forms the southern. Within the pincers are the shallow waters of Cañacao Bay. South of Cavite is another bay, much larger, called Bacoor, with shoal waters.

Calkins refocused his binoculars. He saw them now, the ships ranged in a crescent-shaped line of battle off Sangley Point, flame-colored flags flying at their mastheads, and behind them the buildings of the Cavite naval arsenal. As he watched, "a white cloud with a heart of fire rose from Sangley Point and a shell soared toward our line." It plunged into the water beyond the squadron, "describing a trajectory of more than six miles." There had been Spanish guns at Sangley Point since 1600; some of their present batteries were known to consist of ancient muzzle-loaders. Obviously, this was not one of them.

The *Olympia* drew four fathoms. Dewey wanted to make every shell count—his nearest base of resupply was San

Francisco. "Take her close along the five-fathom line, Mr. Calkins."

Joseph Stickney of the *Herald* had rejoined the navy. When Dewey's aide volunteered to help man a gun turret, the commodore impressed the newspaperman to fill his slot. From the bridge Stickney could see the curving line of Spanish ships stretching from Sangley Point on the west toward the shoal waters off Las Piñas on the coastline. At least two of them were moored, fore and aft, so as to bring their starboard broadsides to bear on an approaching fleet. The cement-plugged *Castilla* was protected by barges filled with rocks and sand. Behind them, with steam up, were the *Reina Cristina*, the *Isla de Cuba*, the *Isla de Luzon*, and several other vessels in the 1,000-ton class.

There was still desultory firing from the Manila batteries, otherwise only the throb of engines and the steady cry of a leadsman calling out soundings to Calkins as the *Olympia* headed toward Cavite at eight knots. Then, shortly after 5 A.M., Stickney saw two great jets of water burst into the air about two miles in front of the column. The mines had been detonated prematurely. He heard a petty officer remark angrily, "They ain't so good at blowing up ships that come with their fighting clothes on as they are at murdering a crew in time of peace."

When they were three miles from Cavite, Calkins saw what appeared to be "firecrackers" explode on the *Reina Cristina* and the *Castilla*. The Spanish fleet had opened fire. A shell ricocheted off the water and tumbled over the masts of the flagship with the whirr of a partridge beating its wings against the air. Dewey said nothing. "We were patient for 20 minutes," Calkins remarked. Calmly advancing, he kept the Spanish squadron just off the starboard bow of the *Olympia* as he edged along the five-fathom line.

The gun crews restrained themselves with difficulty. Stickney saw a boatswain's mate with his hand tight on the lockstring of a 5-inch gun. Suddenly, he cried out, "Boys, remember the *Maine*!" Stickney estimated that two hundred men echoed his shout.

At 5:40 A.M., fifty-five hundred yards distant, Dewey hailed the *Olympia*'s captain in the conning tower: "You may fire when you are ready, Gridley." Gridley passed the order along through a voice tube. Almost immediately, the starboard, 8-inch bow gun commenced firing ahead, hurling 250-pound shells at the Spanish.

After a few minutes Calkins turned the *Olympia* westward, parallel to the line of Spanish ships, bringing his port broadside to bear. The ships following, now at close, two-hundred yard intervals, wheeled down the line. A hail of fire, mainly directed at the *Reina Cristina*, fell over Cañacao Bay. Calkins noted with exasperation that most of the shells seemed to be hitting the water, and it was impossible to tell which guns were firing accurately. Heavy brown-powder smoke concealed the target area. But the guns kept hammering away, shuddering the flagship with their recoil.

Through the mist, Stickney spotted a forty-foot torpedo launch steaming toward the *Olympia*. He called the sighting out to Dewey. The commodore couldn't be bothered with it. "Let me know when you've finished with her," he ordered. Stickney helped to organize the quick-fire guns. A withering sheet of 6-pounder shells and small-arms fire—even marine bullets—flogged the little wooden launch and ripped up her deck. She began to sink and, as the warships following pounded her, went down bow first.

Dewey continued on past Sangley Point, turned sharply, and led the fleet back down the line, but closer, at three thousand yards. Now the starboard batteries swung into line and punished the Spanish ships and shore batteries. In Cañacao Bay several vessels were in flames. The *Reina Cristina* seemed to tremble as two shells struck home, but Montojo's flagship kept up a hot fire.

Several American ships had also been hit. Stickney noted that a hellfire of time-fuse shells burst over the fleet. Shrapnel frothed the water. The signal halyards on the *Olympia* were scythed even as Flag Lieutenant Thomas F. Brumby prepared to loft a message. A projectile "about the size of a flat-iron" clanged into the deck below Dewey's perch. Another, "with almost human intuition, came straight toward the forward bridge, but burst less than a hundred feet away."

It was worse aboard the *Baltimore*. A shell from the Cavite battery ripped through her hull, ricocheted through the ship, burst through the deck by a 6-inch gun mount, and exploded several shells. Six men and two officers were wounded. On the *Boston* two hits started fires, which were quickly extinguished. Another seared through the foremast just in front of Captain Frank Wildes on the bridge.

Dewey continued circling in deadly ellipses before the Spanish guns, firing alternately with port and starboard batteries. As the *Olympia* began her fourth pass, heading eastward down the smoke-shrouded Spanish line, the *Reina Cristina* came out of the murk and steamed bravely for the flagship. *Some dream of ramming,* Calkins thought. She took the brunt of several broadsides. At a distance of twelve hundred yards, Calkins saw shells strike home. White steam plumed up through black smoke; she seemed to be on fire in two places. Slowly, the Spanish flagship turned and limped back toward the shoal water off the Cavite arsenal, still hammered by the rear guard of the American column.

"There came upon us numberless projectiles," Montojo later reported. Shells hit the poop, the mizzen masthead (the admiral's ensign and the Spanish flag crashed to the deck), the stern ammunition room, the fire room, a starboard battery. "A fresh shell exploded in the officers' cabin, covering the hospital with blood, destroying the wounded who were being treated there." Fire and smoke boiled through the ship and, as ammunition started cooking off, Montojo flooded the magazines.

At 7:30 A.M., as the *Olympia* neared the end of her fifth pass at a range of less than two thousand yards, Dewey and Calkins saw Charles Gridley emerge from the flame-hot metal box of the conning tower. His white uniform was smudged with smoke and grease and he looked all in. Gridley shouted over the din that ammunition was low—there were only fifteen rounds left for each of the five-inch guns.

It was an anxious moment for Dewey. Resupply was an ocean away; so far as he knew, the Spanish had an ample supply of shells. He was sure they had hurt Montojo, but smoke obscured the Spanish squadron. Flags were still flying, guns still firing. He ordered the squadron to haul off so that ammunition could be redistributed.

No one wanted to tell the eager gunners they were retiring for lack of ammunition. Aide Stickney dreamed up a more palatable excuse: breakfast. That was alright, Dewey said; give anything but the real reason. The signal was sent to the squadron, and mess attendants began bringing food topside as the ships steamed slowly out into Manila Bay. "For God's sake, captain," one gunner remonstrated to Dewey's chief of staff, Commander Benjamin P. Lamberton, "don't let us stop now! To hell with breakfast!"

Nevertheless, it was welcome. Calkins noted that sardines, hardtack, and corned beef were put "on a corner of the wardroom table, still encumbered by the surgeon's ghastly gear." At least it was unbloodied. Dewey climbed down to the deck and relaxed as longboats brought his commanders to a captains meeting. A smoking hour was also declared and sailors poured out of the caldron below decks. Calkins noted that their uniforms had apparently been chosen "according to natural selection." There were golf caps and pith helmets, old pajamas, skimpy undershirts. The turret crews "were frankly primeval in their attire."

At the captains' conference, the news was all good. No casualties except on the *Baltimore*. The *Olympia* and the *Baltimore* had been hit five times, the *Boston* took four shells and the *Petrel* one, but damage was slight. Even more importantly, ammunition stocks were still ample, even on the flagship. The report Gridley received had been garbled in transmission. Actually, each 5-inch gun had fired fifteen times. The *Baltimore*, with the best shell inventory, was given the honor of leading the second attack.

The scrim of mist and smoke over Cavite had cleared. Peering through binoculars and telescopes, deck officers now witnessed a scene of carnage in Cañacao Bay. Flames burst skyward from several ships, others listed and appeared to be sinking. Admiral Montojo's flag was flying from the *Isla de Cuba*. A number of smaller vessels had retreated into Bacoor Bay, behind Cavite, and were being scuttled. Shortly after 11 A.M., the Asiatic Squadron again formed in line and stood in for Cavite, *Baltimore* in the van.

On the *McCulloch*, McCutcheon had tried to sketch and photograph the battle, but the distance was too great for him to see clearly what was happening. When the guns stopped firing, and the men were ordered to eat breakfast, he could hear Sunday cathedral bells tolling from the steeples of Manila. Beyond the city, in the hills, rising columns of smoke indicated the insurgents were putting the torch to outlying towns. There was smoke over by Cavite, too, where the Spanish fleet was anchored. Around eleven o'clock he saw the big ships form up and start past Sangley Point for the sixth time.

"The *Baltimore* now heads for Cavite," he wrote, "rushing on at full speed, and does not stop until she is almost in the shadow of the forts. There she begins to fire with her big guns, mowing masts away and tearing holes in everything in sight. The *Olympia* follows and joins in the bombardment . . . the dull muffled thunder of the cannon comes with the regularity of drumbeats. . . . The naval station is now full of burning vessels. . . . The *Reina Cristina* is now red with flames and heavy clouds of smoke roll up from her."

Closer in on the *Olympia*, Admiral's Aide Joseph Stickney saw Spanish crewmen abandoning ships to escape the flames and explosions. The little *Don Antonio de Ulloa*, which had fought gallantly all morning, returned the *Baltimore's* fire when Dyer led the new American charge, but now she lurched over and sank, colors still nailed to the mast. "Soon not one red and yellow ensign remained aloft except on a battery up the coast." At twelve-thirty a white sheet was hoisted over the Cavite arsenal.

Dewey sent the little *Petrel* into the shallow waters off Cavite to torch the ships that had been scuttled. From the nearby shore hundreds of Spanish sailors and soldiers watched as the shattered remnants of Montojo's squadron were destroyed. Dewey had executed his orders to perfection. Not a single Spanish fighting ship remained afloat.

While the *Petrel* and the smaller ships mopped up, the *Olympia* and the *Baltimore* steamed for Manila. The guns that had fired peskily earlier in the day were silent, though sometime that afternoon a revolver shot echoed across the plaza fronting the palace of the archbishop of Manila. A colonel of artillery, who considered himself disgraced, took his own life. Later his wife died and his son went insane. Carlos Calkins was saddened when he heard the story. "So much for honor," he thought.

At 2 P.M., Dewey sent a note to Augustín Dávila through the courtesy of the captain of a British ship moored at the mouth of the Pasig River. If his ships were fired on by the Manila batteries, he would destroy the city. The governor-general responded that his guns would not fire. At that moment, Dewey wrote, "the city was virtually surrendered, and I was in control of the situation. . . . I had established a base 7000 miles from home which I might occupy indefinitely."

Battle flags flew on the American ships until sunset that evening. As the hot red sun dipped toward the horizon, the *Olympia*'s band saluted the colors with "The Star-Spangled Banner." Dismayed Spaniards lining the waterfront and the city's ramparts meekly eyed the American guns, though three days later the *Diario de Manila* painted the populace in bold terms. The men had armed themselves, the paper reported, "confident that never should the enemy land at Manila unless he passed over their corpses." As for the Americans, they had shown no courage since, due to "the weakness of our batteries," they had sailed in with impunity. Only the sea now saved them from the wrath of the Spanish army. A soldier turned his eyes to heaven, saying, "If the holy Mary would turn that sea into land the Yankees would find out how we can charge in double time."

As for Montojo's sailors, "Those who fought beneath the Spanish flag bore themselves like men . . . who rather die without ships than live in ships which have surrendered. . . . To these victorious of ours we offer our congratulations; laurels for the living and prayers for the dead. . . ."

Admiral Montojo, wounded in the battle, received a commendation from the minister of marine for his valiant behavior. "Honor and glory to the Spanish fleet which fought so heroically . . ." Not long afterward, with honor but without a fleet, Montojo was called back to Spain for court-martial.

On Monday, the Spanish garrisons on Corregidor and the other islands surrendered to the *Raleigh* and the *Baltimore*. Marines slogged ashore at Cavite and took over the arsenal as a supply and repair base. John McCutcheon finally got a close look at the scene of battle. Eleven Spanish hulks still smoldered in the water. He estimated Spanish casualties at 1,000 dead and wounded. (Actually, there were 381.)

McCutcheon took a rowboat out among the wrecks. One image stuck in his mind: "The only live thing I saw was a chicken perched on a bow stanchion of the *Reina Cristina*, once the proudest of them all."

Early that evening, McCutcheon volunteered to help with one other chore on Dewey's list. The commodore had told

Augustín Dávila he would allow the Spanish to use the telegraph cable to Hong Kong if he could also transmit. When the governor-general balked, Dewey ordered the *Zafiro*, aided by the *McCulloch*, to dredge up the wire and cut it. The coal tender towed grappling hooks just off the mouth of the Pasig River and hauled the two-and-a-half-inch cable to the surface. McCutcheon watched from a long boat as a hundred-foot section was cut out. "We divided it up for souvenirs," he reported.

On the aft deck of the *Olympia*, Captain Charles Gridley penciled a letter to his mother that would go to Hong Kong on the *McCulloch:* "Well, we have won a splendid victory. . . . I am truly thankful to our Heavenly Father for His protection during our battle, and shall give him daily thanks." The *Olympia* had been hit seven or eight times, but no one had been killed. "Manila, of course, we have blockaded. We can't take the city, as we have no troops to hold it."

He signed the letter "Your loving son, Charley," without mentioning his cancer or the toll the battle had taken on his health. The searing heat in the conning tower had withered him, and sometime during the bombardment he had struck his side painfully on some obstruction. After the battle he had to be carried belowdecks. His decline thereafter was swift. In a few weeks he was ordered home on sick leave. As a gesture of respect, the officers of the *Olympia* rowed Gridley over to the *Zafiro*, bound for Japan, gripped his hand, said their last farewells. Five weeks after the battle he died aboard the passenger liner *Coptic* in Kobe, Japan, a long way from home.

In a real sense Gridley was an American fatality on that Sunday morning in Manila. As Calkins said, he made "a willing sacrifice to his country and his profession."

The three correspondents with the fleet arrived in Hong Kong aboard the *McCulloch* on Saturday afternoon, May 7, and raced by rickshaw to the telegraph office. Edwin W. Harden of the *New York World* scooped his press colleagues—and Dewey himself—by sending a bulletin at the "urgent" rate, a prohibitive $9.90 per word. It reached the paper's newsroom just after 4:30 A.M. The regular edition had been put to bed and a poker game was in progress. McCutcheon wrote that "Our man Murphy" (the *Tribune* had arranged to use the *World's* syndicated service) held a dismal hand. When the phone jangled, he threw his cards on the table and picked up the receiver. The telegraph office gave him Harden's costly bulletin. Murphy cabled it to Chicago—it was 3:40 A.M. there—and as typesetters frantically went to work, editor Jim Keeley called the president. The Navy Department was also alerted to the news.

The *Tribune's* scoop hit the newsstands at 4:30 A.M.: DIRECT NEWS FROM DEWEY! NOT ONE AMERICAN KILLED! The *World* was in on the scoop not long afterward, but the other New York papers were embarrassed. That morning, Hearst's *Journal* headlined, GREAT NERVOUSNESS IS FELT IN WASHINGTON BECAUSE NOTHING IS HEARD FROM DEWEY. The *New York Times* announced, DEWEY MAY REPORT TODAY.

At the Navy Department that rainy Saturday morning, Secretary Long waited anxiously for Dewey's report, which had been slowed in transmission as operators at relay stations toiled over the exact wording of the ciphered message. It finally arrived at 8:45 A.M. as a crowd of expectant reporters gathered outside his office. Long glanced at the gibberish in the cable and sent it off to be decoded.

Theodore Roosevelt had resigned his post the day before and had been commissioned a lieutenant colonel in the First United States Volunteer Cavalry. On April 30, as Dewey prepared to breach Manila Bay, he had wired Brooks Brothers in New York for a "blue cravenette regular Lieutenant Colonel's uniform without yellow on the collar and with leggings." The tailors were given a week to have it ready; Roosevelt was bursting "to cut a little notch on the stick that stands as a measuring rod in every family." His daughter Alice later recalled, "Poor father! He was so delighted to get into a war at last." But he had no intention of missing the scene at the Navy Department that morning.

As the clerks worked on Dewey's cipher, Roosevelt stood behind them and absorbed it. Then he went out and announced Dewey's achievement to the press. Long, meanwhile, received a copy of the report and called McKinley, who asked that certain information he considered of military significance be withheld. By the time Long, smiling broadly at the reporters, released a censored version of the report, messenger boys had dashed through the rain on their bicycles to deliver copy to newsrooms across the city.

Thus Theodore Roosevelt ended his year of service to the navy. In eight days he would be in San Antonio, Texas, in an army uniform. The secretary of the navy thought it madness. Roosevelt had been extremely useful, Long confided to his journal, "a man of unbounded energy and force, and thoroughly honest, which is the main thing." All the same, "He has lost his head to this unalterable folly of deserting his post when he is of most service and running off to ride a horse and, probably, brush mosquitoes from his neck on the Florida sands. His heart is right, and he means well, but it is one of those cases of aberration—desertion—vain glory . . . he is acting like a fool."

Long must have paused as a thought struck him. He added a postscript: "And yet, how absurd all this will sound if, by some turn of fortune, he should accomplish some great thing and strike a very high mark."

Before leaving Washington, Roosevelt cabled Dewey: "Every American is in your debt." He was replaced by Charles H. Allen, who had served with Long in Congress. The secretary considered Allen agreeable and competent, less inclined "to disorder and rush, tempestuousness and over-conversation." But, Long added, neither did he have Roosevelt's "tremendous energy."

Following the terrible events in Havana on February 15, the country was flooded with souvenirs and bric-a-brac exhorting citizens to "Remember the *Maine*." The slogan appeared on candies, matchboxes, paperweights, flimsies, hats, and cutlery. Now that there was a heart-stirring victory to temper the disaster, it was Dewey's turn. An anonymous lyricist was one of the first to wed the tragedy and the triumph:

> Dewey! Dewey! Dewey!
> Is the hero of the Day!
> And the *Maine* has been remembered
> In the good old fashioned way—

O. H. Cole in Minnesota weighed in with "Yankee Dewey," sung to the tune of "Yankee Doodle." Enterprising composers also offered up, to less memorable melodies, "Dewey's Duty Done" and "How Did Dewey Do It?"

The advertising community stirred. Executives at Pear's Soap began a far-reaching campaign. One of their spreads pictured Commodore Dewey standing over a wash basin gazing serenely out a porthole, a bar of Pear's at the ready. The copy explained, "The first step towards lightening THE WHITE MAN'S BURDEN is through teaching the virtues of cleanliness. *Pear's Soap* is a potent factor in brightening the dark corners of the earth as civilization advances. . . ." A cartouche in a corner of the spread showed a garbed missionary handing a cake of soap to a dark native in loincloth.

For several years Americans had toasted Cuban independence with the Cuba libre, a straightforward cooler blending rum and cola. Now they also had the Dewey cocktail, as formidable, some thought, as the guns of the Asiatic Squadron. It was an insidious concoction laced with Scotch, brandy, and Benedictine smoothed over with a bit of syrup and a dash of bitters. "One of them," the *New York Herald* reported, "will make you feel like a true American; two will cause you to wonder why you are not fighting for your country; and five or six will make you believe yourself to be as big a man as Dewey."

Hearst was not long in jumping aboard the bandwagon. Scooped by the *World* on the Manila story, he emblazoned the American eagle across the front page and, under its outspread wings, trumpeted, VICTORY, COMPLETE! . . . GLORIOUS! . . . THE MAINE IS AVENGED. The affluent publisher gave one of his more spectacular extravaganzas in celebration of the triumph, an explosive affair in Union Square with bands, fireworks, and a hundred thousand guests.

Scores of babies born on May 1 were named Dewey. So were racehorses, pets, cigars, and yachts. Children stroked Dewey rabbits' feet and sank their teeth into "Dewey Chewies." A laxative featuring Dewey on the package was christened "the Salt of Salts." At several Dewey hotels, diners ate ice cream frozen into the shape of the cruiser *Olympia*. A creative chef at the Metropolitan Club dreamed up Poulet Sauté à la Dewey, a far more elegant bird than the Chicken

Fricasse à la Maine disdained by photographer Hemment on the Plaza de Luz in Havana.

Finley Peter Dunne wrote Irish dialect stories for the *Chicago Journal* featuring the engaging Martin Dooley, who enjoyed nothing more than cutting heroes down to size. Dooley referred to Roosevelt as "Tiddy Rosenfelt" and remarked that "he has to stay up at night steerin' the stars straight." Dewey was an obvious target for Dunne's Dooley who, when the news from Manila arrived, turned the commodore into an instant cousin: "Dewey or Dooley, 'tis all the same. We dhrop a letter here and there . . . but we're th' same breed iv fightin' men. . . . Georgy has th' thraits iv th' family. 'Surrinder,' he says. 'Niver,' says th' Dago. 'Well,' says Cousin George, 'I'll just have to push ye ar-round,' he says."

Senator Redfield Proctor reminded the president that he had earnestly requested Dewey's appointment. Secretary Long now wrote in his journal that the commodore's selection "was entirely my own." Congress appropriated ten thousand dollars for a Dewey sword and commissioned Fifth Avenue jeweler Tiffany's to make it sparkle. There was talk of making May 1 Dewey Day.

But perhaps the most valued token of the nation's gratitude was expressed in a wire from Secretary Long to the commodore: "You are assigned . . . the rank of Rear Admiral. Hoist the flag of a rear admiral immediately."

The *McCulloch* stayed in Hong Kong only long enough to send and pick up cable messages, then steamed back to Manila. On May 10, Stickney reported, the broad blue flag bearing the two white stars of a rear admiral was hoisted to the masthead of the *Olympia* as warships in the bay fired thirteen-gun salutes. When that excitement was over, the Asiatic Squadron continued to blockade Manila. Long had advised that the president was sending reinforcements; he did not say how they were to be used. On the admiral's flagship, the officers sat on the poop in the blazing heat and humidity, swatting mosquitoes, and wondered what would happen next.

In Washington no one knew. Dewey's objective had been achieved in a week; the consequences of instant and total victory had hardly been considered. A newspaper posed a troubling riddle to its readers: Why was Uncle Sam like a woman heaving a stone? Answer: Because he aimed at Cuba and hit the Philippines.

McKinley firmly opposed annexation in Cuba, but postponed a decision on the Philippines. Not long after the battle he wrote a note to himself: "While we are conducting war and until its conclusion, we must keep all we can get. When the war is over, we must keep what we want." He was warned against committing ground forces. A friend wrote, "I fear we will not be able afterwards to withdraw our troops without turning over the islands to anarchy and slaughter." Lodge felt that "the American flag is up and it must stay." At the time, he considered the importance of the Philippines to the nation "almost beyond imagination."

The president decided to reinforce Dewey's precarious position with the cruiser *Charleston* and five thousand troops the admiral thought adequate to protect his land flanks at Cavite and make his position secure. The Manila expedition would be led by General Wesley Merritt, commanding the Army Department of the East. Even then, however, the army was revising the figures upward. Merritt, who had the president's ear, thought it probable he would have to fight "the so-called insurgents" as well as the Spanish. He felt he could take the entire Philippine archipelago with fourteen thousand men. The figure soon escalated to twenty thousand. Meanwhile, the Spanish were said to be assembling a relief squadron.

To McKinley, the Philippine islands were *terra incognita*. Soon after the Battle of Manila, he pored over a small schoolbook map trying to find the little points of Luzon and Mindanao. An officer of the Coast and Geodetic Survey arrived at the White House and was taken to see the president. He gave McKinley proper maps and talked briefly of distances and tactical considerations. McKinley was grateful. "It is evident," he said, "that I must learn a great deal of geography in this war. . . ."

Later, according to a friend of the president's, McKinley regretted the whole sorry business. "If old Dewey had just sailed away when he smashed that Spanish fleet, what a lot of trouble he would have saved us."

VIII

HIDE
AND
GO
SEEK

Now is in progress a huge game, with wide and lonely
stretches of ocean as the board, and with great steel ships as
counters. . . . The Spaniard made his first move. He played
his fleet plump in the middle of the board, and he watches
eagerly to see if our next move is a blunder. . . ."

—STEPHEN CRANE

According to information brought by exchanged prisoners,
arrival our squadron at Santiago de Cuba has caused sensa-
tion. United States and their admirals are being charged with
lack of ability.

—GOVERNOR-GENERAL RAMÓN BLANCO to Minister of War
Miguel Correa

I
N THE PACIFIC, Dewey unfettered had struck at Manila
with glorious success. In the South Atlantic, Sampson's
North Atlantic Squadron was still muzzled by Secretary
Long's orders to dodge a fight, unless the antagonist was
Cervera. In time of war, Long wrote, naval commanders must
act on their own responsibility, but "the Department does not
wish the vessels of your squadron to be exposed to the fire
of the batteries at Havana, Santiago de Cuba, or other strongly
fortified ports. . . ." Cruising slowly on blockade off Havana,

French Chadwick, Robley Evans, and the other fleet captains watched in frustration as fresh scars on the heights commanding the harbor marked the construction of new Spanish gun emplacements.

Frederic Remington, still writing and illustrating for Hearst, had secured a berth on Evans's *Iowa*—"an iron island floating on the sea." He found little to engage his pencils and paints—sailors wigwagging signals, the searchlights around Morro Castle. Several American ships, including the flagship *New York*, had taken valuable prizes; the *Iowa* claimed only a Cuban fishing smack. It had run out of ice and the catch was "high." The unhappy fishermen were told to take their "cargo of odors" out to sea and dump it.

The "sea-going plainsman," as Roosevelt now addressed Remington, was developing a visceral dislike for ships and their hot, heaving environment. When the wind blew and the seas kicked up, Remington "nearly had the breakfast shaken out of me." When it was calm, the tropical sun blazed down—"the iron plate of the *Iowa* is like a griddle, the sky is more red than blue, and a mosquito's wings would create a hurricane in the air." He longed for his western haunts: "I wanted to hear a 'shave tail' bawl; I wanted to get some dust in my throat; I wanted to kick the dewy grass, to see a sentry pass in the moonlight. . . ."

One day Remington went below to examine the bowels of the battleship. "Through mile after mile of underground passages I crawled and scrambled and climbed amid wheels going this way and rods plunging that. . . . I believe they fairly worshipped that throbbing mass of mysterious iron; I believe they loved this bewildering power. . . ."

"'Jackie,'" he said, "the prevailing thing on a man-o-war, I fail to comprehend fully. He is a strong-visaged, unlicked cub, who grumbles and bawls and fights. He is simple, handy, humorous and kind to strangers. . . . His hope is for a bang-up sea fight. . . ." And if the *Iowa* were to get into a brawl, Remington noted, at least there was a motive for it. Inside each of the ship's six turrets someone had painted, "Remember the *Maine*!"

"Fighting Bob" Evans agreed with Sampson that the thing to do, after hostilities commenced, was "to strike quickly and strike hard." Havana might well have been bombarded and captured by now. It was true, as Remington pointed out, that "the blessed old United States Army is not ready yet," and certainly unwise to risk crippling the fleet before Cervera was found and destroyed. Even so, the endless hot days of passive blockade palled. Evans sometimes stalked the deck on his gimpy legs but more often, as Remington observed, perched on the bridge staring balefully at the enemy shoreline.

Toward the end of April, Remington jumped aboard the torpedo boat *Winslow* and transferred to the *New York*. One of the first people he ran into was his old colleague from Havana, Richard Harding Davis, who grinned and told him about the "good sport" they had had shelling Matanzas on the twenty-seventh. Remington was "stiff with jealousy." All he could think was that "it takes more than one fight to make a war—so here's hoping." Remington was soon relieved of his onerous sea duty—"dumped ashore" by Navy Department orders in a sweeping cutback of correspondents allowed on warships—but his dream would come true on a bullet-speckled hillside near Santiago.

Davis had finalized his break with Hearst and the *Journal* after the embarrassment of the *Olivette* incident by publicly apologizing to his readers in Pulitzer's *World:* "For the benefit of people with unruly imaginations, of whom there seem, to be a larger proportion in this country than I had supposed, I will state again that the search of these women was conducted by women and not by men. . . ."

Roosevelt knew Davis and admired his work. Before leaving Washington, the newly commissioned lieutenant colonel secured permission for the correspondent to sail with Sampson and Chadwick aboard the *New York*. Davis, now working for the *Herald* and *Scribner's Magazine*, arrived in Key West too late to clear his credentials and get aboard the *New York* for her dash to Cuba on April 22, but managed to rendezvous with the squadron four days later. He found the flagship, with its elegant officer's mess and excellent band, "like a luxurious yacht, with none of the ennui of a yacht." His view from the *Herald*'s press boat had been limited—"like reporting the burning of the Waldorf Astoria from the Brooklyn Bridge." Now he was at the center of the blockade, and the very day after he got aboard, Admiral Sampson gave him something to scribble about.

Sampson's theater of operations extended from Bahia Honda west of Havana to Cárdenas on the east. On April 27 he decided to reconnoiter Matanzas, fifty-two miles east of Havana, where the Spanish were reported to be erecting shore batteries. Arriving shortly before 1 P.M., he found the cruiser *Cincinnati* and the monitor *Puritan* blockading the port. Sampson steamed past them toward the heights guarding the harbor. Suddenly, French Chadwick saw a puff of smoke rise from a point on the western shore. He turned to Sampson.

"They're firing at us. Can't I open on them, sir?"

A shell whined through the air and fell short of the *New York*.

Sampson nodded. Chadwick gave the order and a naval cadet lofted an 8-inch shell toward the fortification. Several artillery pieces returned the fire and the *New York* responded with its big guns. As the shelling intensified, the *Puritan* and the *Cincinnati* frantically ran up flags requesting permission to join in. Again, Sampson assented.

Davis, standing on the flagship's superstructure, tried to keep track of the number of shots fired, "but soon it was like counting falling bricks. The guns seemed to be ripping out the steel sides of the ship. . . . The thick deck of the superstructure jumped with the concussions, and vibrated like a suspension-bridge when an express train thunders across it. . . . Your eardrums tingled and strained and seemed to crack. The noise was physical, like a blow from a baseball bat. . . ." Amid the smoke, heat, and flame of the bombardment, Davis heard a gunnery officer cry out, "Oh, *will* you take your damned smoke out of my way!"

One by one, the shore batteries were silenced. The cannonade was over in nineteen minutes. There were no American casualties. Governor-General Ramón Blanco shortly reported from Havana that one Spanish *mula*—later dubbed the "Matanzas Mule"—had been killed in action. Ralph Paine, now known aboard as "the burglar who crawled in through a hawse-hole," knew he could not write with the panache for which Davis was celebrated, but he had a scoop, too, and he set to work.

Not long afterward, an alert *New York Herald* press boat chugged up to the *New York*. Paine watched in dismay as

Davis, who had written his story in fifteen minutes, tossed his copy down to the deck in a weighted envelope. The *Herald* boat would not take Paine's story.

On April 29, the day Pascual Cervera took his squadron to sea from Cape Verde, Sampson prowled the Cuban coastline to the west of Havana. He took a look at Mariel, saw nothing of interest, and moved on to Cabañas. Around 6 P.M., as the flagship's band serenaded the officers at dinner, sailors on deck heard the sound of rifle shots from the shore. A troop of Spanish cavalry had ridden into a clearing, dismounted, and aimed several volleys at the distant *New York.* Associated Press staffer William Goode noted that "the novelty of attacking an armored cruiser with Mauser bullets at two miles range appealed to all on board."

As the bandmaster played on, Davis saw a hatch pop open on the nearby torpedo boat *Porter.* The grimy head of a coal passer emerged. He took a pipe from his mouth, had a look at the shore—and laughed.

Stephen Crane, also aboard, heard a boatswain roar, in "a voice like the watery snuffle of a swimming horse . . . 'Man the port battery!'" A 4-inch gun was readied and pumped off several shells toward the cavalry. Bluejackets and marines crowded around as Chadwick himself aimed the last shot and pulled the lanyard. "As each shell struck home," Davis wrote, "they whispered and chuckled as though they were seated in the gallery at a play. . . . Meanwhile from below came the strains of the string band playing for the officers' mess, and the music of Scheur's 'Dream of Spring' mingled with the belching of the four-inch gun . . . when the smoke had cleared there was no cavalry troop. . . . The horsemen were riding madly in 50 directions, like men at polo. . . ."

End-of-the-century war, Davis concluded, was civilized.

On May 1, the day Dewey pummeled Cavite, Sampson sailed for Key West for coal and messages. He knew now that the Cape Verde Squadron was at sea, probable course west, possible destinations San Juan, Havana, or one of the two major ports on the south coast of Cuba, Cienfuegos and Santiago.

Long advised that the Grand Fleet might also try to intercept the *Oregon*, then in port at Rio de Janeiro. It was also possible Cervera might assault the U.S. coastline. New England was still in a state of near panic and the Flying Squadron under Commodore Schley was held on a tight rein at Hampton Roads, ready to steam north or south once Cervera was spotted. Evans called the Flying Squadron a "sop to the quaking laymen."

Sampson's mission was clear: find the Spanish cruisers and destroyers and bring them to bay. At the same time, he could not risk letting them slip by his squadron and sweep aside the old monitors and gunboats still blockading Havana, or worse yet, bombard Key West and sneak through the Florida Strait into the Gulf of Mexico. He threw out fast scouts—the *St. Paul*, the *St. Louis*, the *Yale*, and the *Harvard*—to guard the sea-lanes converging on the Windward Passage dividing Cuba from Haiti, and to probe the Antilles. The cruiser *Marblehead* and two smaller vessels had been sent around Cape San Antonio at the western tip of Cuba to patrol the southern coastline and scout the harbor at Cienfuegos. The ocean was large, but Cervera's range was limited and he had to cross certain known shipping lanes to reach port. Most of these were now patrolled.

Sampson bet that the Spanish fleet was headed for San Juan, where, Long wired, it was expected on May 8. On May 2 the battleships *Iowa* and *Indiana* steamed into the anchorage at Key West and began coaling. The round trip to San Juan and back was over two thousand miles; they would need full bunkers. These were filled by May 4, and additional coal was stored in bags on the decks of the ships. Sampson ran up the signal, "Steer east by south, speed 11 knots," and the fleet fell into line.

There were problems almost immediately. The *Indiana* had a valve failure and kept falling out of line. Two monitors with limited cruising range were under tow and, in the choppy seas, proved skittish. Sampson slowed to eight knots and tried to keep his ships on station.

The lights of San Juan were finally sighted at 3:30 A.M. on May 12. There was a hidden gunboat anchorage at the Puerto Rican port, but no place for a cruiser to hide. At dawn the telescopes and binoculars of the fleet focused on the harbor.

Cervera's ships were not there. Sampson, who had hoped to battle him that day, transferred his flag to the *Iowa* and—despite Long's injunction not to risk crippling his ships—ordered a bombardment. First, the *Detroit* was sent in to within eight hundred yards of shore to mark a shoal. The Spanish guns targeted her and began firing. On the *Iowa*, Robley Evans admired the way Captain Dayton fought his ship. "Her crew was making her five-inch rapid-fire guns roar and blaze. She was simply magnificent, a veritable spitfire."

Lieutenant Carl Jungen, a *Maine* veteran, took the armored tug *Wompatuck* in at the western end of the harbor and moored a rowboat to mark the point where the fleet would turn and pass across the harbor mouth. Then Evans led the *Iowa* down the firing line at five knots. The bugler sounded "Commence Firing" and her 11-inch guns boomed.

Associated Press correspondent W.A.M. "Chappie" Goode saw that the Spanish were firing back furiously and accurately. A shell ricocheted off the surface of the water "like a monster flying fish." Goode wiped saltpeter from his eyes and tried to follow the bombardment.

Miraculously, the *Detroit* was not hit, but as the *Iowa* completed her second pass across the harbor mouth, a Krupp armor-piercing shell hit the upper deck, passed through a steel beam, and exploded under the ships' boats. When the smoke cleared, Evans saw that a number of sailors had their caps blown off by the explosion—"they were laughing and joking while they brushed the dust from their clothes . . . not a man was even scratched." A small American flag had blown out of a box on a sailing launch. Evans had it retrieved; it would make a memorable souvenir for President McKinley.

It was not a laughing matter, however, when two more shells hit the superstructure and several men were wounded. On the *New York* a sailor was killed by shrapnel. Evans counted nine fires on shore, but damage to the port's fortifications did not seem substantial. He persuaded Sampson to call off the attack: "You have no force of occupation. . . . You may have to meet the Spanish fleet this evening."

Evans thought it all good practice. The young jackies now knew "that every shell fired was not going to kill each individual man who heard it screaming over his head." Even so, he sensed danger. With the squadron at San Juan, Cervera might slip through the Windward Passage, relieve Havana, and threaten Key West. He advised Sampson "to get to the westward with all possible despatch."

Sampson ordered the signal raised, "Form column heading west."

Alfred Thayer Mahan, reviewing the San Juan expedition in Washington, found it "an eccentric movement." Secretary Long, perusing damage reports, considered it a failure. Even French Chadwick thought San Juan should not have been engaged. "The admiral's fighting instincts," he explained, "were too strong for him."

As Pascual Cervera left the Cape Verdes on the morning of April 29, pursued by the *New York Herald* correspondent, he set his course for Martinique—not for Puerto Rico as Marine Minister Bermejo had directed. Unknowingly, he avoided a confrontation with Sampson at San Juan.

There were seven ships in his squadron, four armored cruisers and three torpedo-boat destroyers. All the cruisers save the barnacle-bottomed *Vizcaya* towed a destroyer. As the choppy seas calmed, Cervera was able to increase the fleet's speed to eight knots.

On May 8, still four days out of Martinique, Cervera explained his decision to Bermejo: "After mature consideration, and in view of the wide scope of the instructions received . . . I formed a plan (which I did not announce until after we had left) of shaping my course for Fort-de-France, Martinique, there to obtain information, and, if possible, coal and provisions. . . ." The letter was given to Captain Fernando Villaamil, commanding the destroyer division, and on May 9 the *Terror* and the *Furor* were sent off to Martinique. They sped ahead at eighteen knots for several hours; then three of the four boilers of the *Terror* broke down. Villaamil paused while one of them was repaired, then went ahead in the *Furor*, knowing the fleet would soon pick up the stricken destroyer. There was nothing else he could do.

On arrival at Fort-de-France on May 11, Villaamil first sought intelligence on American ship movements from the Spanish consular agent, a Frenchman. Unaccountably, he

had left for the country. Villaamil cabled Cervera's messages
to Bermejo and managed to pick up some information from
local newspapers—an American squadron was said to be approaching San Juan. He found that a promised English coal
collier had not arrived, and was told by the governor of Martinique that none was available at Fort-de-France. In fact, the
governor said, the *Furor* would not be allowed to leave since
a United States warship, the *Harvard*, had just left a nearby
port. Neutrality regulations required that he wait twenty-four
hours after her departure.

Showing enterprise, Villaamil made a swift exit under
cover of darkness, picking up channel buoys with the help
of lights on boats off the *Alicante*, a Spanish hospital ship in
port. At flank speed he dashed back over the dark Atlantic
searching for Cervera's flagship. At 2 A.M. on the twelfth, Captain Víctor Concas, commanding the *María Teresa*, saw a
bright light on the horizon. It was "the signal agreed upon
thrown upon the clouds by the searchlights of the *Furor*."

Within an hour Villaamil had rendezvoused with the
flagship. His news was all bad. War had, in fact, been declared; there had been a "disaster" at Manila on May 1. A
powerful American squadron was near San Juan. The *Harvard* was somewhere in the vicinity and may have spotted
him shortly after he left Fort-de-France. Even if that were not
so, Concas said later, "we felt sure that the telegraph had already announced our arrival."

That assumption was not then true, but soon would be.

The *Harvard* had not, in fact, left Martinique on May 11.
That morning she had entered the port of Saint-Pierre. U.S.
Consul George L. Darte had heard that Cervera was in Fort-
de-France, sixteen miles to the south. He considered it im-
prudent to use the telegraph to confirm the Spanish fleet's
presumed location. There was a primitive road over rough
country to the capital, but Darte proposed to Marine Lieutenant Theodore P. Kane of the *Harvard* that they go by boat. A
large canoe was chartered and four native oarsmen paddled
them down the coast. The canoe nearly foundered in a sudden rainstorm; Darte and Kane were soaked and exhausted
when they reached Fort-de-France around midnight. Finding

no signs of the Spanish in the harbor, they repaired to a hotel to rest and dry out.

At dawn on Thursday, May 12, they went down to the beach. There was a mist over the water and at first they could see nothing unusual. But a few minutes later a warship took form in the mist, and then five more. A destroyer, the *Terror*, limped into harbor. The Spanish squadron was at Martinique.

Darte and Kane returned to Saint-Pierre. The consul wired his findings to the State Department and Captain Charles S. Cotton of the *Harvard* cabled the Navy Department. Cervera's fleet, which had vanished in the Atlantic Ocean for two weeks, was found. With the exception of the wounded destroyer, it apparently would not enter port, but the Flying Squadron could now be unshackled from its defensive position at Hampton Roads and the navy could tighten the net around the Spanish squadron.

Cervera promptly disappeared again for seventeen days. His second vanishing act caused consternation in Washington and dissension and back-biting in naval circles.

On May 13, Commodore Winfield Scott Schley took his "Quaker-hued" flagship *Brooklyn* out of Hampton Roads, followed by the battleships *Massachusetts* and *Texas*, and the supporting vessels of the Flying Squadron. They were stripped for action—there was not even a band on the flagship, though the mess stewards of the mandolin and guitar club played catchy tunes while the officers dined. Afterward, they saved scraps for the ship's mascot, a goat named Old Billy.

The *Brooklyn* put into Charleston for messages, then steamed on uneventfully for Key West. At 11 P.M. on the sixteenth, alarm bells sounded over the ship. Associated Press correspondent George E. Graham strapped a revolver over his pajamas and went to investigate. It turned out to be a fire in a coal bunker adjacent to a magazine. The ammunition was quickly run out of the magazine on dollies and steam was spewed into the bunker to extinguish the fire.

The automatic annunciators had worked perfectly.

*   *   *

Marine Minister Bermejo, with the destruction of Montojo's fleet in mind, had wired Martinique on May 12: "Situation changed since your departure. Your instructions amplified so that if you do not believe that your squadron can operate there successfully may return to Peninsula, choosing route and destination, preferably Cádiz. Acknowledge receipt and indicate decision."

It was the message Cervera had long hoped for, but when it was sent, he had bypassed Martinique and was steaming south by west for Curaçao, one of the ABC islands off the coast of Venezuela, desperately hoping to find the English coal promised by Bermejo before he left the Cape Verdes. The cable never caught up with him.

Cervera reached Curaçao with six ships—the Terror was left at Fort-de-France for repairs—early on the morning of May 14. The English collier was not there, he cabled Bermejo, "and I have not been able to obtain here the coal I need. . . . Only two ships have been allowed to enter, and their stay has been limited to 48 hours."

Bermejo's reply must have depressed Cervera: "In view of your going to Martinique, steamer sent to Curaçao was ordered to go to Martinique. Do not know whether latter has arrived."

Dutch authorities allowed the María Teresa and the Vizcaya to enter St. Ann Bay to coal around 2 P.M. Captain Concas reported that they spent an anxious night interpreting "every noise we heard as an attack upon our comrades, and we could not even go to their assistance, for the harbor of Curaçao, which is closed by a bridge, is completely cut off from the outside at sunset."

The next day was no better. It was a Sunday and "everything was strictly closed up, so that we could not even buy postage stamps for our letters." That evening a crewman off the Plutón fell overboard and delayed the fleet's departure. The squadron finally left at dark, steering for Santiago, some seven hundred miles to the northwest, "at an economical speed." The ships were unlighted save for screened lamps at the stern.

On the night of May 18, off Jamaica, they saw in the darkness two transatlantic steamers, possibly auxiliary cruisers. One of them used a searchlight but did not pick up the Spanish flotilla. Concas suspected they might have to fight their way into Santiago; certainly, the situation must have seemed more serious than the lack of postage stamps at Curaçao. Santiago was an odd choice of destination, but Concas defended his admiral's decision. San Juan, Havana, Cienfuegos, and Santiago were the only places where the squadron could effectively support the Spanish war effort. San Juan was out—Sampson's fleet was apparently already there. Havana was also blockaded (though thinly) and was perilously close to the American naval base at Key West. Cienfuegos Harbor was, he thought, "a veritable rat trap, very easy to blockade, and from which escape is more difficult than from any other harbor of the island." Moreover, it was poorly fortified. There remained only Santiago, the eastern capital of Cuba, which was thought to be well supplied and defended.

But Santiago, Concas failed to note, was also a poor choice for a number of reasons. The channel in was tortuous and shallow. There was no rail connection with Havana, and insurgents often closed off the roads connecting it with the population centers to the west.

But Cervera's curious choice of refuge had one unexpected advantage. Commodore Winfield Scott Schley could not believe the Spanish would go there.

At dawn on May 19, Cervera's squadron approached the entrance to Santiago Harbor. The *St. Louis* had just left the area on a cable-cutting mission at Guantánamo. There was not an American ship in sight.

Schley reached Key West just before Admiral Sampson led elements of his San Juan expedition into harbor at 4 P.M. on May 18. Sampson had known since the fifteenth, when the *Porter* delivered a dispatch from Long, that Cervera was in the vicinity of Curaçao. The next day he had stopped off at Puerto Plata, Santo Domingo, to pick up additional messages. A cable from the U.S. consul in Curaçao confirmed Long's intelligence: "*María Teresa* and *Vizcaya* in harbor coaling. . . . Only two admitted at time. Short of coal and provisions, dirty bottoms; and leave 15th at 6 P.M. Destination unknown."

"It now seemed probable," Sampson wrote, "that Cervera's objective was either Santiago or San Juan."

Early on the evening of the eighteenth, Commodore Schley boarded the *New York* to confer with Sampson. The two-star admiral's flag flying over the flagship might well have given him pause. Schley had been eight numbers ahead of Sampson on the navy list. His promotion to commodore was dated February 6, while Sampson's leapfrog orders to commodore and "acting admiral" did not arrive in Key West until April 21. Some naval officers thought Long's order illegal since the Senate had yet to advise and consent, as was usual, on the promotion. Sampson was still being paid as a captain, Schley as a commodore. The Flying Squadron, moreover, had not been put under Sampson's command, though Long had written a confidential letter to Schley stating that if his command and Sampson's came together, Sampson would command the whole.

The careers of the two officers had followed roughly the same path, but by nature they were as unlike as Roosevelt and Long. Schley, with his thinning hair combed delicately over a bald spot, his upswept moustache and wispy Parisian imperial, looked a bit of a dandy. He was a raconteur with a high sense of the dramatic and a taste for public relations and Washington politics. His wit, charm, and vitality were universally acknowledged. Even so, boarding the *Brooklyn* in Hampton Roads, reporter George Graham had expected to encounter a martinet. Not at all. "Summer sun never dispelled morning fog more quickly than Schley's smile and handshake dispelled that illusion." In the navy, however, many considered him vain, self-centered, and boastful.

If so, Schley had certifiable bragging rights. An Annapolis graduate of 1860, he had fought under Farragut with distinction in the Civil War. In 1884 he commanded the Arctic relief expedition that saved the lives of explorer Adolphus Greely and a few of his men. But there was one blot on his record—at least Robley Evans thought so. In 1891, as commander of the *Baltimore*, Schley anchored off the tense city of Valparaiso, Chile, just after a revolution against the government had taken place. Grog was abolished in the navy in

1862, and the crew had not had a drink for over three months. Schley nevertheless gave shore liberty to over a hundred thirsty sailors. Some time after they hit the waterfront, they were attacked by a mob of over two thousand. Twenty jackies were knifed in the back; two of them died.

Shortly afterward, Evans, commanding the little gunboat *Yorktown*, relieved the *Baltimore* at Valparaiso and managed to restore order. Schley always claimed the sailors were sober when attacked. Evans found that hard to believe. He thought them "probably" and "properly" drunk on Chilean rum. Evans's coolness and firmness in a tense period earned him the sobriquet "Fighting Bob" (a misnomer, he thought, since he had kept the peace), while many in the navy questioned Schley's judgment.

Sampson was the antithesis of the hale and hearty commodore—reserved, modest, dispassionate, generous, selfless. His staff work was superb—he was in great demand as an aide—and his judgment was rarely questioned. He was a man of few words and, as Mahan said, "lacked the tricks of the popularity hunter"; many in the navy appreciated him all the more for that. After Civil War service he worked his way diligently through the peacetime doldrums: head of the Physics Department, and later superintendent, of the Naval Academy; chief of the Bureau of Ordnance; captain of the *Iowa;* president of the *Maine* court of inquiry; commander of the North Atlantic Squadron.

Sampson was often described as scholarly and intellectual. Reporter Ralph Paine described his "precise and studious manner [and] superior intelligence." The "spare erect figure in white uniform" seemed more scholar than sailor. Commodore Dewey thought him not only brilliant and efficient, but "one of the handsomest men I have ever seen." To Richard Harding Davis he seemed a "professor of mathematics . . . an intellectual fighter, a man who impresses you as one who would fight and win entirely with his head."

Scholar or not, he was no-nonsense. Stephen Crane, on the *New York* for a few days before the Navy Department severely reduced the number of shipboard reporters, called him "the Dewey of the Atlantic." "Men thought of glory, and he considered the management of ships. . . . No bunting, no arches, no fireworks; nothing but the perfect management of a big fleet. . . . Just plain, pure unsauced accomplishment."

Critics faulted him on two counts. Although the ship on which he served in the Civil War, the *Patapsco*, was blown up by a mine, he had never been in a real fight. That charge was flimsy; Sampson had, in fact, shown conspicuous bravery under fire at Charleston. The second charge, that his health was failing, was more serious. Yeoman Fred Buenzle considered Sampson "the most thoughtful and considerate" officer he had ever worked for, but saw immediately when he reported to the *Iowa* at the end of 1897 that Sampson was stooped and ill. Photographs taken over the past six months showed that his dark hair was fast graying, and his gray beard had turned white. He was frail—his stiff navy collars fit loosely—and often seemed apathetic. Sometimes he got words, and even the names of ships, mixed up. The court of inquiry and the expedition to San Juan had exhausted him. Buenzle wondered "how the old man's enfeebled physique could stand such a strain."

When Schley reached the admiral's spacious cabin on the *New York*, Sampson and Chadwick were waiting for him. He entered, paused, and saluted. Chadwick immediately sensed the import of the gesture—Schley had acknowledged his subordinate status. Then Schley made the point verbally. He would be "loyal in all his conduct." The commodore thought Sampson looked "worn and anxious; in fact, his appearance was that of a sick man."

Sampson told Schley he had received a cable from Long twenty-four hours earlier. The Spanish had ammunition and supplies for Havana. They were heading for Cienfuegos, with its railroad connection to the capital. Schley, with the *Brooklyn*, the *Massachusetts*, and the *Texas*, was to reconnoiter the key port which, the Navy Department now felt, best suited Cervera's requirements. Sampson should add a "suitable armored ship" to the Flying Squadron for this vital mission. The *St. Paul*, also at Key West, was ordered east to Cap-Haïtien to guard the Windward Passage and keep an eye on Santiago. Sampson's other vessels were to maintain the blockade of Havana.

Long's orders had explicitly stated, "Sampson to have choice the command of Havana or at Cienfuegos." The admiral could have superseded Schley as commander of the expedition to Cienfuegos, now the most likely scene of glory. Perhaps out of gratitude for the salute, and to express his confidence in the commodore, he did not. It was a decision he would soon rue.

Evans came in with the *Iowa* after sundown on the eighteenth and Sampson assigned the battleship to Schley's squadron. Evans immediately began coaling—"all night long my willing men shovelled away and stowed bread and powder." They were still filling bunkers when Schley took the Flying Squadron out at eight the following morning, shaping a southwest course for Cape San Antonio. The scout cruisers were assigned their patrol routes. And at the very moment Schley left, Cervera entered Santiago Harbor and dropped anchor. That evening the *Oregon*, which had put into Barbados the previous day for coal, steamed out of the roadstead and headed for Jupiter Inlet, Florida.

It was all the beginning of an intricate game of nautical musical chairs in which, for ten days, the American ships circled and probed, backed and filled, stood constant watch day and night—and somehow failed to notice that Admiral Cervera had occupied an empty seat at Santiago.

Safely in Santiago, Pascual Cervera counted his blessings and cabled Governor-General Ramón Blanco in Havana: "Have cast anchor to-day in this harbor, whence whole squadron sends you greeting, desirous of cooperating in the defense of the country." Another cable went to the new minister of marine, Captain Ramón Auñón y Villalón, in Madrid saying that the squadron would have to stay in Santiago for several days for boiler cleaning and repair.

Bermejo was out, and the rest of the Spanish Cabinet with him. The news of Dewey's victory had brought demonstrations and riots to Spain. Premier Sagasta feared revolution or a coup. A spokesman for pretender Don Carlos gave a fiery speech in the Cortes, citing Ecclesiastes to make the point that countries ruled by women and children are miserable. But Carlos, Weyler, and other opposition groups were not prepared to intervene. Sagasta and his new Cabinet rode out the storm.

Auñón cabled the government's new naval policy via the

Terror, just completing boiler repairs in Martinique. Retreat was no longer acceptable—"government cancels telegram as to return to Spain." Since Cervera had not received Bermejo's cable approving a return, the new order was meaningless. It did not matter in any case. Cervera did not have enough coal to sail back to Spain.

Later on the nineteenth, Cervera's messages were received in Havana by cable operator Domingo Villaverde. After giving the wires to a messenger, he waited until his colleagues had gone out to eat and surreptitiously tapped out the news to Key West. (By mutual agreement of Spain and the United States, the cable had been kept open.)

Villaverde was an agent in an intelligence network organized by the Western Union Telegraph Company with the Army Signal Corps. In the past the Cuban's intelligence had been quite accurate. But the existence of the network was little known, and when the news reached the Navy Department, Long did not know what to make of it.

Long was soon let in on the secret, however, and there were additional reports that Cervera had come to roost at Santiago. One was an Associated Press story from Madrid that the Cape Verde Squadron was at Santiago. And there was news from Kingston, Jamaica, that the merchant ship *Adula* had seen seven vessels steaming north toward Santiago on the night of the eighteenth.

On the morning of the twentieth, Sampson received a cable from Long: "The report of the Spanish fleet being at Santiago de Cuba might very well be correct, so the Department strongly advises that you send word immediately by the *Iowa* to Schley to proceed at once off Santiago de Cuba with his whole command, leaving one small vessel off Cienfuegos. . . ." Long now believed the intelligence from Havana. He even had a notice tacked to the Navy Department's press bulletin board advising reporters that reliable information placed Cervera at Santiago.

Sampson and Chadwick were puzzled by the message, particularly the uncertain qualifier, "might very well be correct." No source was given for Long's conclusion. If Cervera was bringing supplies for Havana, as Washington had suggested, it still seemed more likely he would head for Cienfuegos. Sampson cabled Long: "I have decided to follow the plan already adopted, to hold position at Cienfuegos. . . ."

Last photo of the *Maine*, riding to mooring buoy No. 5 at Havana Harbor, was taken at 4 P.M. on February 15, 1898. COURTESY OF THE MARINERS MUSEUM, NEWPORT NEWS, VIRGINIA

Captain Charles Dwight Sigsbee of the *Maine* posed for a formal portrait in Washington on April 2, 1898. U.S. NAVAL HISTORICAL CENTER

Assistant Secretary of the Navy Theodore Roosevelt addressed navy brass at the Naval War College in Newport, Rhode Island, in June 1897: "It is through strife, or the readiness for strife, that a nation must win greatness." NAVAL INSTITUTE PHOTO COLLECTION

Fitzhugh Lee, consul general at Havana. U.S. NAVAL HISTORICAL CENTER

Admiral Pascual Cervera y Topete

Frederic Remington sketched Spanish irregulars bringing in captured *pacíficos*, probably for "reconcentration."

Cuban insurgent general Máximo Gómez.   U.S. NAVAL HISTORICAL CENTER

Valeriano Weyler, governor-general of Cuba; William Randolph Hearst called him "the Butcher."
LIBRARY OF CONGRESS

The *Maine* is launched in Brooklyn, New York, on November 18, 1890. Secretary of the Navy Benjamin Tracy, in top hat, watches as his granddaughter christens the ship with California champagne.
LIBRARY OF CONGRESS

The *Maine* on February 16, 1898. Pieces of decking and bottom plating nick the water's surface at left.

Harvard dropout William Randolph Hearst, "proprietor" of the New York *Journal*.   CULVER PICTURES

Spanish contact mines. U.S. NAVAL HISTORICAL CENTER

Spanish Dons prepare to blow up the *Maine* in a fanciful newspaper "solution" to the tragedy.   LIBRARY OF CONGRESS

A SOLUTION TO THE MAINE EXPLOSION.

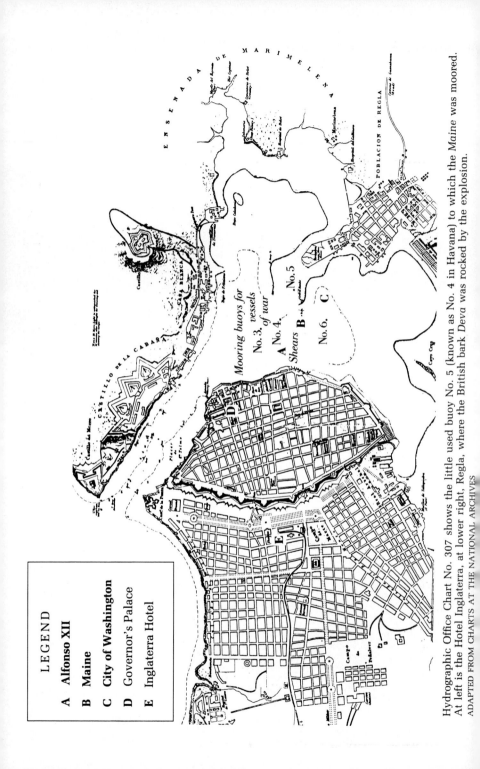

LEGEND

A Alfonso XII
B Maine
C City of Washington
D Governor's Palace
E Inglaterra Hotel

Hydrographic Office Chart No. 307 shows the little used buoy No. 5 (known as No. 4 in Havana) to which the *Maine* was moored. At left is the Hotel Inglaterra, at lower right, Regla, where the British bark *Deva* was rocked by the explosion.
ADAPTED FROM CHARTS AT THE NATIONAL ARCHIVES

Navy (later Hearst) photographer John Hemment frames dignitaries at the first burial of *Maine* victims in the Cristóbal Colón Cemetery. At right, in clerical collar, is Chaplain John Chidwick. To his right are Fitzhugh Lee, Charles Sigsbee (with head bared) and, at center, Clara Barton.

Members of the court of inquiry pose on the fantail of the *Mangrove*. From left to right, Lieutenant Commander William Potter, Captain French Chadwick, Captain William Sampson, and Lieutenant Commander and Judge Advocate Adolph Marix.

President William McKinley, in the White House Cabinet room, shows the strain of trying to slow the nation's rush to war.
LIBRARY OF CONGRESS

BELOW LEFT: Hearst's *Journal* headlines congressional unrest on April 4, 1898. Even the formidable "Czar" of the House, Thomas Reed (right) could not quell the outbreak.

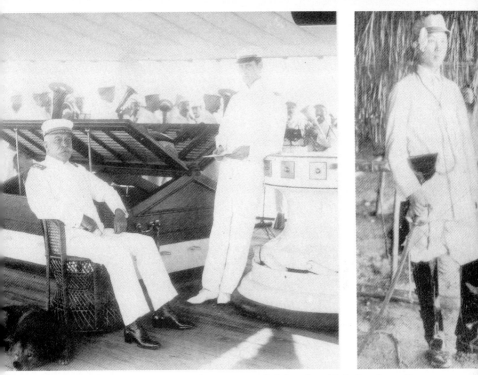

Commodore George Dewey being serenaded by the ship's band on the *Olympia*. Dewey perceived that his dog, Bob, knew as much about politics as he did.   LIBRARY OF CONGRESS

Dewey considered the Philippine insurgent leader Emilio Aguinaldo (above right) an "unimpressive little man."

The *Olympia* charges down the Spanish line off Sangley Point in Manila Bay.   U.S. NAVAL HISTORICAL CENTER

The "dilatory" Commodore Winfield Scott Schley (left) and the ailing Admiral William Sampson (right). U.S. NAVAL HISTORICAL CENTER

Lieutenant Colonel Theodore Roosevelt with correspondent Richard Harding Davis. LIBRARY OF CONGRESS

General "Fighting Joe" Wheeler in Tampa; Colonel Leonard Wood and Roosevelt are on his left. CULVER PICTURES

Despite his three-hundred-pound weight, gouty foot, and a nagging fever, General Rufus Shafter, togged in a white pith helmet and gauntlets, boarded a horse in Cuba.

American troops make a precarious landing on the dock at Daiquirí.

Frederic Remington sketched away as Captain George Grimes spurred his artillery battery up El Pozo Hill.

In *Shrapnel Coming Up the Road*, Remington portrayed American troops taking casualties as they advanced on Santiago.

Roosevelt, *Maine* revolver on hip, with his Rough Riders after the battle for the San Juan Heights.
LIBRARY OF CONGRESS

Judge Magazine indicted Spain for atrocities as well as the *Maine* deaths. The "mutilated" American dead were actually savaged by land crabs and vultures.
LIBRARY OF CONGRESS

The *Almirante Oquendo* (left) and *Infanta Maria Teresa* burn furiously off the beach near Santiago on July 3, 1898.   U.S. NAVAL HISTORICAL CENTER

The charred wreck of the *Vizcaya*. Though wracked by fire and magazine explosions, the Spanish cruisers did not suffer keel and hull damage comparable to that on the *Maine*.   U.S. NAVAL HISTORICAL CENTER

Turret gunners on the *Oregon* focus on the *Cristóbal Colón* near Point Turquino.

The Spanish cruiser, choking on Cuban coal of poor quality, labors to escape the *Brooklyn* (right) and the *Oregon* as they fire ranging shells.

A 1911 photograph of the unwatered *Maine* shows mast toward stern and, in foreground, mangled superstructure blown out to starboard. Eighteen feet of water have been pumped out of the surrounding cofferdam.

With Old Glory flying bravely from a jury-rigged pole, the *Maine* slides to her final resting place four miles off Havana on March 16, 1912.

The *St. Paul* and other scouts could determine whether
Cervera had in fact holed up at Santiago. "Plans may be
changed when it becomes certain that Spanish ships are at
Santiago."

Sampson put a message—letter No. 7—to Schley aboard
the *Iowa*, which had finished coaling, advising the commodore of ship movements and enclosing a copy of Long's telegram. He told Schley there would be no change in plans:
". . . you should hold your squadron off Cienfuegos. If the
Spanish ships have put into Santiago, they must come either
to Havana or Cienfuegos to deliver the munitions of war
which they are said to bring. . . ."

The *Iowa* left Key West at 11 A.M. on the twentieth and
the *Dupont*, carrying a copy of the letter, half an hour later.
At almost that moment Captain James Allen of the Army Signal Corps in Key West ran into Lieutenant Sidney A. Staunton, Chadwick's assistant chief of staff. Allen told Staunton
that he had top-secret information from Havana. A cable had
arrived on the evening of the nineteenth reporting Cervera at
Santiago. Staunton immediately took a launch out to the *New
York* and gave the news to Sampson. The admiral now knew
the reason behind Long's order to send Schley to Santiago.

Before dawn on the morning of May 21, the *Marblehead*
took Sampson's letter No. 8 to Schley at Cienfuegos. Long's
order to blockade Santiago was now confirmed—with one
proviso: "Spanish squadron probably at Santiago de Cuba—
four ships and three torpedo boat destroyers. If you are satisfied that they are not at Cienfuegos, proceed with all despatch, but cautiously, to Santiago de Cuba, and, if the enemy
is there, blockade him in port." Local fishermen, Sampson
advised, might prove helpful, since the harbor was concealed.

The admiral then wired Long: "Schley has been ordered
to Santiago."

An hour after the *Marblehead* left, the *New York* led what
was left of the North Atlantic Squadron south to Havana. A
motley flotilla of clumsy monitors, antiquated cruisers, thin-
skinned torpedo boats, makeshift gunboats, and press tugs
milled around the harbor entrance. Casting a professional eye

at the eclectic fleet, Sampson noted wryly to Chadwick, "We are pretty weak at this end of the line. I am afraid we have been too kind to Schley."

In terms of ship speed and armament, the Flying Squadron was in fact now superior to the North Atlantic Squadron. For a number of reasons, however, it was in the wrong place. Long's cable to Sampson ordering Schley to Santiago had been ambiguous (the Navy Department's messages lacked a certain crispness following Roosevelt's departure). As a result, Sampson had not ordered Schley to Santiago until the twenty-first, and then used the qualifier, "If you are satisfied . . ." Moreover, the scouts patrolling the Windward Passage and the Caribbean waters off Santiago seemed to have put on blinders. And the chain of communication (as well as of command) had weak links. Long's cables reached Sampson swiftly—when he was in Key West. But it took even the speedy but frail torpedo boats almost two days to cover the 520 nautical miles of lumpy seas from Key West to Cienfuegos. By the time Schley had Sampson's messages, Washington was operating under a new set of circumstances.

To make matters worse, Schley had decided on his own that Cervera, almost certainly, was at Cienfuegos.

On the morning of May 19, only thirty miles west of Sand Key Light, Schley had encountered the *Marblehead* and the *Eagle* returning to Key West for coal. They had been on patrol duty off Cienfuegos until the sixteenth. The *Eagle* communicated that Cuban insurgents in a boat offshore reported the only vessels in Cienfuegos Harbor were a torpedo boat and two gunboats. The insurgents had "perfect knowledge" of ships in the harbor.

Schley steamed on, giving Cape San Antonio a wide berth so that his ships would not be seen from shore. At 4:20 P.M. on May 21, forty miles southwest of Cienfuegos, an officer on the flagship's bridge picked up a pen and recorded in the log that he had "heard the report of two great guns" from the direction of Cienfuegos. Schley heard them, too, six or seven shots, fired at intervals, "with the cadence of a salute." He pictured the Cape Verde Squadron entering harbor. At midnight, still twelve miles from Cienfuegos, he brought the Flying Squadron to a halt. They would go in at daybreak.

The fleet's screws began to turn again at 5:07 on May 22 and Schley took the *Brooklyn* within four thousand yards of the shoreline. Mines were being laid across the harbor entrance. There was a lighthouse on Point Sabanilla on the west side of the channel, which led in almost due north for some distance before veering to the east. It appeared to be about six hundred feet wide. Beyond the channel Schley's charts showed a large bay extending northwest for some five miles. From the deck no warships were seen, but lookouts on the *Brooklyn's* fighting tops spotted ships' masts beyond the high land to the west of the harbor entrance; and smoke drifted up from the vessels.

Schley—unlike many of his officers—assumed the mast tops were the tip of a naval iceberg; Cervera's ships were hiding in the screened northwest sector of the big bay. He withdrew the fleet to a safe distance and began the blockade.

That morning, the *Dupont* steamed up and delivered a copy of Sampson's letter No. 7 instructing the commodore to hold his position at Cienfuegos. Schley readily complied. He was on the scene, after all, in a position to make a more informed judgment than naval strategists in Washington. He advised Sampson: "Cannot say whether Spanish fleet in port or not. The anchorage not visible from entrance . . . expect difficulty here will be to coal from colliers in the constant heavy swell. . . ."

On May 23, Schley intercepted the British steamer *Adula* on her way from Kingston to Cienfuegos to pick up British nationals. Captain William Walker related his sighting of the seven ships heading due north toward Santiago. But, Walker added, he had heard in Kingston that Cervera had put into Santiago, but left on the twentieth. The steaming distance from Santiago to Cienfuegos was 315 miles. At a comfortable ten knots, Cervera could have made port at Cienfuegos just as the Flying Squadron heard the cadenced artillery reports on the afternoon of the twenty-first. Schley allowed the *Adula* to enter harbor after Walker promised he would bring her out the next day and confirm Cervera's presence.

The commodore wrote Sampson, "I think I have them here almost to a certainty."

That night the watch on the *Brooklyn* spotted three white

lights in a line on the shore. They appeared to be a signal, but no one on the flagship could decipher it. On the *Iowa*, however, Robley Evans knew exactly what the lights meant: the insurgents wanted to communicate. He assumed Schley did, too: "I, of course, took it for granted that the commodore understood this signal as well as I did, otherwise I should have informed him of its significance. It appeared afterwards that he did not; and thus much valuable time was lost."

Schley later responded, "The only officer who professed to know the significance of these signals did not think them important enough at the time to communicate them."

The mystery was cleared up on the twenty-fourth when the *Marblehead* under Commander Bowman McCalla joined the squadron. McCalla had arranged the signal with the insurgents on his earlier patrol off Cienfuegos: three lights in a horizontal line by night; three horses in a row by day. The information had not been relayed off Key West, but McCalla did give French Chadwick a full verbal report on the signal system. Since the *Marblehead* was due to return to Cienfuegos as soon as she coaled, Chadwick did not feel any special action was required: ". . . in the tremendous rush of business it soon passed out of [my] mind, though it was evidently mentioned to Captain Evans of the *Iowa*."

With or without the signal system, Schley had made no effort to contact the Cubans.

When McCalla boarded the *Brooklyn,* bringing Sampson's letter No. 8, he found that Schley had already received a copy of the orders to Santiago the day before via the swift *Hawk.* Indeed, Schley had already sent off his response: "Sir: . . . In reply to your letter No. 8, I would state that I am by no means satisfied that the Spanish squadron is not at Cienfuegos." He had seen a large amount of smoke in the harbor, and "under such circumstances it would seem to be extremely unwise to chase up a probability at Santiago de Cuba, reported via Havana, no doubt as a ruse." He had sent the *Scorpion* to Santiago to contact the scouts, but was convinced the Spanish were in Cienfuegos. "I shall therefore remain at this port."

Captain Francis A. Cook of the *Brooklyn* overheard the conversation between Schley and McCalla.

"We have had three lights," the commodore observed,

"one ahead of the other here, that we cannot make out; and I believe it is something in connection with the Spanish fleet."

McCalla gave a start and threw up his hands: "Why commodore, that is the signal from the insurgent camp. They want to communicate with you."

Schley was furious, Graham observed, grinding his heels into the deck and nervously twitching his wispy imperial. He told McCalla to go to the insurgent rendezvous point and find out what the Cubans wanted. McCalla returned around 4 P.M. The Cubans were certain, he said, that Cervera was not at Cienfuegos.

"We will move to Santiago," Schley announced.

That day, Secretary Long formally placed the Flying Squadron under Admiral Sampson's command.

As the gray ships of Schley's flotilla headed eastward on the evening of the twenty-fourth, the weather worsened. Squalls, rain, and rough seas made it heavy going, especially for the smaller vessels.

The next day, it blew like stink.

Aboard the press tug *Sommers N. Smith*, laboring through angry seas off the northeast coast of Cuba, it seemed worse than that. Sylvester Scovel said "the wind blew half a hurricane." One of his shipmates, fellow *World* correspondent Stephen Crane, suddenly found his latest venture "ultra-hazardous, almost suicidal."

The *Sommers N. Smith*, jointly chartered by the *New York World* and the *Herald*, was making a circumnavigation of the island of Cuba in search of Cervera. If the navy couldn't find the Spanish admiral, perhaps they could. Crane was now a veteran of several nautical expeditions. On an earlier venture, aboard Johnny O'Brien's old filibuster, the *Three Friends*, a budding novelist named Frank Norris working for *McClure's Magazine* had admired Crane's nonchalant approach to journalism: "The Young Personage was wearing a pair of duck trousers grimed and fouled with all manner of pitch and grease and oil. His shirt was guiltless of collar. . . . His hair hung in ragged fringes over his eyes. . . . Between his heels he held a bottle of beer against the rolling of the boat, and when he drank was royally independent of a glass."

Crane found news dispatches drudgery, even when far-fetched. Reflecting on the slop yellow journalism that had washed over the American public since the beginning of the war, he confessed: "We lulled them. We told them this and we told them that, and I warrant you our screaming sounded like the noise of a lot of sea birds settling for the night among the black crags."

As the *Sommers N. Smith* bucked through the angry waters around Cape Maisi, on the easternmost tip of Cuba, and shaped a course toward Santiago, she was on the verge of a discovery the navy had yet to make. Crane, Sylvester Scovel, and Jimmy Hare, a *Collier's* photographer who had mapped the Cuban coastline with Scovel on a mission for Sampson, were sitting under an awning on the stern of the tug, dressed in pajamas, when the captain announced offhandedly that they were being chased by a warship. As stokers shoveled on the coal and the tug leapt through the water toward Jamaica, Crane speculated on the consequences of capture by the Spanish—garroting was certainly a possibility.

The tug could only do 11 knots; flight was useless. Crane took Hare's binoculars and focused on the big bow wave of the warship: "On swept the pursuing steamer—inexorable . . . a terrible water sphinx in her silence." The silence was broken when a gun fired and a shell wailed over the *Sommers N. Smith;* the tug quickly hove to.

The cruiser turned out to be the *St. Paul.* One of the reporters shouted that Cervera was in Santiago. "Your information is wrong." Charles Sigsbee hailed over a megaphone, but "I advise you to make yourself scarce, as Cervera might show up at any minute. You are in a very dangerous position."

The *Sommers N. Smith* steamed off to the west, blithely passing Santiago. When Crane and Scovel reached Key West on June 2, they found they had narrowly missed one of the war's greatest scoops. It was all just an "onion," as Crane called a failed venture.

After entering the well-screened harbor at Santiago, Pascual Cervera had dispatched several additional cables. On May 21 he wired Ramón Auñón: "Congratulate your excellency on elevation to ministry, of which we hope great results." After performing that obligatory bow, he turned immediately to the reality of the situation at Santiago as he perceived it. The city was "very short of provisions, and if it does not receive any it must succumb." Coal was also scarce, and as his squadron was "greatly inferior" to the American fleet, he could not "accept decisive battle, which would mean certain defeat." If blockaded, "we shall succumb with the city."

Auñón could only put him on notice: "Her majesty charges me to congratulate your excellency in her name on your skill and sends greetings to crews of squadron, whose movements she follows with interest."

Cervera knew he was wanted in Havana—at least by Blanco. In Santiago, however, his arrival was not marked by the usual jubilation. The poorer classes in the city, Víctor Concas noted, were already hungry. Spanish merchants, anticipating defeat, had ceased placing orders. Credit was almost nonexistent—the Spanish Bank had only four thousand silver dollars in its vaults—and inflation was out of control. Concas wrote: "To do honor to Admiral Cervera, who had not eaten bread for two weeks, I bought for him from a Spaniard a small barrel containing 50 pounds of flour and had to pay for it $42 in gold."

In Havana, Governor-General Blanco made his own disappointment clear. Cervera had gone to a distant harbor with limited facilities where he was in imminent danger of being blockaded. And, Blanco complained to the new minister of war, Miguel Correa, Cervera "has brought no transports with coal and provisions which would have helped so much, nor weapons and ammunition."

At a banquet one night, as Concas reflected moodily on the squadron's shortcomings, the archbishop of Santiago rose and proposed a toast "to our assault upon the Capitol of Washington. This toast was received with feverish enthusiasm by some and with profound sorrow by us who knew that our fate was already decided and that we were irredeemably lost."

Coaling, watering, and repair facilities at Santiago proved inadequate to the squadron's needs. On May 23, Cervera strongly considered making a break for San Juan—the city Bermejo had ordered him to a month earlier—where they might find better dockyards. Early the next day he called a council of captains. Concas, Eulate, Villaamil, and the others were unanimously opposed. The *Vizcaya*—the "boil" on the fleet's bottom—could only make 14 knots, and American scouts had been sighted in the vicinity of Santiago. No one saw an opportunity. Cervera cabled Auñón: ". . . certain danger of sortie greater than advantages gained by reaching San Juan. . . . Shall await more favorable opportunity."

Later that day Blanco cabled General Arsenio Linares, commanding the Spanish army forces in Santiago: "If [Cervera] does not go out, [he] may be closed in."

Then the sea began to kick up.

Beating his way east toward Santiago on the morning of the twenty-fifth, Schley had problems of his own. As the gale intensified, green water foamed over the ships' decks. On the *Marblehead*, the lower port boom was unshipped and carried away. A heavy sea broke over the forecastle of the *Vixen* and washed a petty officer down to the main deck, leaving him with a severe flesh wound in the thigh. The collier *Merrimac* reported engine problems and the fleet slowed to let her keep up.

As Schley had foreseen, coaling was a dangerous operation in the grumpy waters off the south coast of Cuba. Even off Key West, under the best of circumstances, it was a tough, dirty job. In the hold of the collier, stokers filled canvas bags with up to half a ton of "black diamonds." The bags were attached to "whips," swung up on deck, and derricked over to the ship that was coaling. There the coal was dumped into long chutes leading down to the hold where the engineer force smoothly stowed it in bunkers. Afterward, crew members swabbed themselves down, hosed the superstructure, and holystoned the decks.

Schley had just one small collier for his squadron, the ailing *Merrimac*. The *Texas* was especially short of coal and the commodore kept signaling her, "Can you coal?" Captain Jack Philip would answer, "I will try." Then the collier would sidle up in the lee of the battleship. In the steep southeast swell the two ships would grind and crash together as the *Merrimac*'s derrick tried to time the transfer of coal bags.

Wooden fenders were shredded to pulp and the protruding gun sponsons of the *Texas* hammered down on the deck railing of the wallowing collier.

The Flying Squadron made slow progress toward Santiago.

The *St. Paul* had made her first inspection of Santiago early on the morning of the twenty-first. She was soon joined by the *Yale*, Captain William Wise commanding, and the next day the two scouts closely reconnoitered the entrance to the harbor. Its narrow entrance—the channel there was only about 190 feet wide—was flanked by sloping hills to the west and a steep cliff to the east. Another Morro Castle dominated this height. Just inside the entrance the channel ducked eastward and was partially hidden behind the craggy headland. Then it curved back to the north and again became visible. After passing two inlets on the eastern shore, and Smith Cay to port, it veered to the right around Punta Gorda and vanished. The city, where Cervera's ships would logically be moored, was four miles beyond the point.

Wise and Sigsbee could see only a torpedo boat or a small gunboat off Smith Cay. The next day, joined by the *Harvard* and the *Minneapolis*, they cast their scouting net to the east and west of the city.

Early on the morning of May 25, the *Cristóbal Colón* left her position in the inner harbor and proceeded south to a position off Punta Gorda where her guns could control the channel entrance. Her log recorded: "Anchored at 7 A.M. At this time the vessels of the enemy were discovered off the mouth of the harbor. Morro made signal to begin firing; but . . . an English steamer was about to enter the harbor."

The *Restormel* had triangulated the rim of the Caribbean from San Juan to Curaçao to Cuba trying to deliver her three thousand tons of Cardiff coal to the Spanish fleet. She was within a few miles of Santiago, laboring through heavy seas at seven knots, when sighted by the *St. Paul*, which chased her down just outside the harbor entrance. The captain of the *Restormel* expected—and was delighted—to be captured.

Sigsbee put a prize crew on board and dispatched her to Key West via the Yucatan Channel.

The *Cristóbal Colón* had steam up and could have gone out to attack the unarmored *St. Paul*. But the weather was foul and, as Concas observed dolefully, what would that have proved since "the collier would have been sunk and nothing would have resulted but the loss of the coal which we so much needed."

On the *St. Paul*, preoccupied with the chase, nobody observed the *Cristóbal Colón*.

There was less wind on the twenty-sixth, but the sea was still nasty as Schley's squadron gingerly approached Santiago. Spotting ships about thirty miles south of the harbor entrance, the commodore ordered general quarters. They turned out to be three scouts, including the *St. Paul*. At 6:20 P.M., Sigsbee came up the gangway of the *Brooklyn* to report to Schley. He was greeted by the commodore and the two strolled to the quarterdeck. Newsman George Graham was within earshot.

"Have we got them, Sigsbee?" Schley asked.

"No, they are not here."

"Are you sure they are not in there?"

Sigsbee replied that he had been in the area for a week and had been "very close to the harbor entrance two or three times." So had Captain Cotton of the *Harvard*. "They are not there."

Sigsbee brought with him a Cuban coastal pilot, Eduardo Núñez, who had worked for the Spanish navy. The former commander of the *Maine* told Schley that Núñez thought the Spanish cruisers too large to enter the twisty, narrow, unmarked channel—the Spanish had removed the navigational buoys.

It might have been done with tugs at the bow and stern, when the water was calm, Núñez interjected.

Sigsbee thought that unlikely. He simply hadn't left Santiago long enough for Cervera to enter.

The forward elements of the squadron steamed to within about fifteen miles of the harbor entrance.

*   *   *

That morning Cervera had called yet another captain's meeting in his cabin aboard the *María Teresa*. Santiago had proved a disappointing choice of harbors. It was a simple case of "bad luck." The fleet's fires were banked, but there was not a single American ship off the harbor that morning, and the foul weather might help to screen their departure.

A week after entering Santiago, the officers unanimously decided to leave for San Juan. Coal passers began spreading the coal under the ships' boilers. But at 2 P.M., Cervera reported, "the semaphore signaled the presence of three hostile ships." The wind had died down, but a heavy swell still surged into the harbor entrance. The pilot who had brought the admiral's flagship into harbor was summoned. He felt that the *Colón*, with a draft of almost twenty-five feet, might bang on a flat rock off Socapa Point at the harbor entrance. the *Colón* had entered without difficulty. Now it seemed she could not get out.

All but two officers—Víctor Concas and Joaquín Bustamente—were now against the sortie. Cervera put his decision on the record: ". . . in hopes that the sea will calm down and that another opportunity will present itself, the sortie is deferred." The fires under the squadron's boilers were extinguished.

Commodore Schley's distant reconnaissance of Santiago Harbor had turned up nothing. The scouts said Cervera was not there. The sound of the measured cannon-firing at Cienfuegos still rang in his ears, he could see the smoke rising, he needed coal, and he still had a gut hunch the dons were at Cienfuegos. The *Adula*, which could have confirmed his guess, had not come out of Cienfuegos Harbor; she must have been seized by Cervera.

Toward dusk on the evening of May 26, the red and white signal lights on the *Brooklyn* winked out a startling message: "Destination Key West via south side Cuba and Yucatan channel, as soon as collier is ready; speed nine knots." On the *Iowa*, Robley Evans, who had anticipated an order to advance on Santiago, hailed Jack Philip on the nearby *Texas*.

"Say, Jack, what the devil does it mean?"

"Beats me," Philip replied. "What do you think?"

"Damned if I know," Evans said, "but I know one thing—I'm the most disgusted man afloat."

The *Yale* took the *Merrimac* in tow (she had broken down repeatedly and was now unable to turn a prop) and the fleet dutifully headed westward.

Forty miles southwest of Santiago, Schley, beset by doubts, brought the fleet to a halt. On Friday morning, May 27, in calming seas, the *Texas* and the *Marblehead* eased up to opposite sides of the *Merrimac* and began coaling. At 8:30 A.M. the *Harvard* overtook the stuttering squadron, bringing a cable from the Navy Department she had picked up in Haiti: "All department's information indicates Spanish division still at Santiago. The department looks to you to ascertain facts, and that the enemy if therein, does not leave without a decisive action." Long indicated there were landing places where insurgents could be contacted about six miles west of the harbor entrance and noted that from the heights around Santiago one "can see every vessel in port. . . ."

Schley posted the *Harvard* to Kingston, Jamaica, with his astonishing reply: "Much to be regretted, can not obey orders of the department. Have striven earnestly; forced to proceed for coal to Key West, by way of Yucatan passage; can not ascertain anything positive respecting enemy."

Around noon the squadron continued fitfully westward. On Saturday morning the fleet again stopped while the *Vixen* coaled. The warships then drifted around for several hours until 1:12 P.M., when Schley suddenly signaled them to steer back to the east. With coal in his ships' bellies, he seemed to have stoked his own resolve. He may also have reflected that he had now three times ignored Navy Department orders.

Evans on the *Iowa* found the constant stopping and starting bewildering, the steaming toward Cienfuegos an "unexpected retreat." In Santiago, Concas, who assumed the blockade had been established on the twenty-sixth, described the maneuvers of Schley's squadron as "incomprehensible to us. It would not explain matters if we were to describe the coming and going of the hostile ships. . . ."

Spanish reaction paled beside that of Long and the president on the twenty-eighth when Schley's cable advising that he could not obey orders arrived from Kingston. Apparently, the Cape Verde cat was to be let out of the bag. Long remembered that Saturday as "the most anxious day in the naval history of the war and was the only instance in which the Department had to whistle to keep its courage up. . . ." The thought that Cervera might again vanish, head north through the Windward Passage, and "appear at any time on the coast of the United States, was depressing beyond measure."

It was all "plain as a pikestaff" to Long. He considered relieving Schley of command, even ordering a court-martial. The commodore had shown "indecision and indications of inefficiency. . . . This, coupled with the fact that he was not able to tell us whether the Spanish fleet was inside the harbor or not, was very irritating."

Long sent Schley "a rather sharp telegram that he must find out that fact."

On May 27, Sampson's North Atlantic Squadron stalked the Cuban coastline near Frances Cay, guarding the sea routes to Havana and the Florida coast. Now sure that Cervera was at Santiago, Sampson wanted to make certain the neck of the bottle was corked.

A conference of commanding officers was called in the admiral's cabin. Sampson broached an old Civil War blockading ploy. The Spanish fleet could be sealed in port by sinking a hulk—perhaps a captured Spanish ship filled with granite blocks—in the narrow channel. French Chadwick observed that Schley had one cripple in his squadron, the *Merrimac*. The troublesome collier could be run into the channel and scuttled, effectively sealing the harbor.

Sampson promptly dictated a message to Schley ordering him to use the collier for this purpose. Then he turned the squadron back to Key West for coal so that he might have full bunkers for his planned rendezvous with Schley at Santiago.

The *New York* arrived at Key West early the next morning. As she approached Sand Key Light, a great gray shape loomed on the horizon. Even in the morning mist there was no mistaking the formidable *Oregon*. Unbelievably, she had logged fifteen thousand nautical miles on her journey from San Francisco to Key West in just sixty-seven days. In the battleship's fifty-eight days at sea, her average speed was almost 12 knots; during that time, except during target practice, her engines never stopped or slowed.

At eleven o'clock that night the *Oregon* steamed off to join up with Commodore John C. Watson's skeleton fleet blockading Havana. She arrived on Sunday morning, Captain Charles Clark noted, and "all hands in the fleet were dressed for inspection. Our decks were still piled with coal, and everybody black with its dust. I was not permitted to report on board the flagship, however, before we had passed the length of the entire line, the crews cheering themselves hoarse as we went by, and the *Indiana*'s band playing 'The New Bully.' Truly, we felt as some one aptly described the Highlanders, 'Proud and dirty.'"

Watching from the press boat *Three Friends*, Ralph Paine felt a stab of exaltation as the fleet's bulldog steamed down the line at speed, showing off a little bit, "her flag hoists gay with fluttering bunting, the bluejackets massed on deck and some of them wearing cap ribbons of their own devising, "'Remember the *Maine*.'"

An hour after the *Oregon* left Key West, Sampson received an alarming message from Secretary Long concerning Schley's decision to return to Florida: ". . . he goes to Key West with his squadron for coal, though he has 4000 tons of coal with him in a broken-down collier."

Sampson was incredulous, but later messages confirmed the news and asked how soon Sampson could leave and how long he could blockade. Sampson replied that he would like to start immediately. "I can blockade indefinitely."

Long cabled, "Go if you wish." Sampson took the *New York* out at 11 P.M. on Sunday, May 29, to rendezvous with the *Oregon* and other elements of the fleet near Havana. They would then head east for Santiago by way of the Windward Passage.

*   *   *

On the night of May 28, Commodore Winfield Scott
Schley had brought his squadron to a halt about ten miles
south of Santiago. At dawn on Sunday morning his ships at
last closed on the harbor fortifications guarding the channel
entrance. "The morning sun showed us Cuba," Schley observed, "green with verdure, the white surf breaking along
the coral reefs, and the picturesque old Morro in its coat of
dirty yellow plaster standing grim guard over the entrance. . . ."

They were about five miles off the Morro when signal
lights on the *Marblehead* blinked urgently: "Just caught view
of Spanish warship in harbor entrance. . . ."

At almost the same moment, aboard the *Iowa*, Lieutenant
Commander Raymond P. Rodgers shielded his binoculars
from the bright rising sun and aimed them down the channel
toward Punta Gorda. He had been a naval attaché in Madrid
and was familiar with the unusual configuration of the *Cristóbal Colón*. Built in Genoa, she had a tall military mast between her two funnels. Suddenly, he cried out: "Captain,
there's the *Cristóbal Colón!*"

Evans focused his glasses; there she was, her big black
form outlined against the rich green heights of Punta Gorda,
"in a position to command the channel." Then he saw another Spanish warship to port of Smith Cay and a torpedo
boat. The information was signaled to the *Brooklyn*.

Schley replied, "I understand."

It may have been the morning light, but suddenly everybody could see the Spanish. George Graham, from the *Brooklyn's* crow's nest, clearly made out the ominous nose of the
black-hulled ship. And at eight-thirty, belatedly, Captain
Sigsbee's *St. Paul* dashed up flying the signal, "Can see a
strange vessel in the harbor."

Schley ordered the squadron to form in a distant semicircle around the harbor entrance. "We've got them now," he
said. "They'll never go home."

The navy's net had finally closed. The army, such as it
was, could now embark.

IX

"CHILDREN OF THE DRAGON'S BLOOD"

> Seventy million people in the United States went to bed last night knowing that American guns were thundering at the gates of Santiago, that American men were fighting and dying in the sweltering and fetid thickets of Cuba that a new nation might be born and the cause of human liberty make yet another forward stride.
>
> —*New York Journal*, July 2, 1898

> We never think of Cuba in our progress: it is for revenge on a people for cowardly blowing up our boys in Havana harbor.
>
> —CORPORAL JAMES M. DEAN, Rough Rider

LIEUTENANT COLONEL THEODORE ROOSEVELT remained unimpressed by the army's state of readiness and its top leadership. He wrote in his little pocket diary that the commanding general of the army, Nelson Appleton Miles, was "a brave peacock," while Secretary of War Russell Alger "has no force whatsoever." It appeared to him that America "has pranced into war without making any preparation for it."

Roosevelt spent his last week in Washington ensuring his own preparedness. Before he could win the war, he had to be able to see it. Roosevelt ordered a dozen pairs of steel-rimmed eyeglasses and had several sewn into his new uniform and campaign hat. Gifts of spurs, a watch, and a traveling medicine chest were received and acknowledged, navy relations cemented with a heartfelt good-bye to Secretary Long: "I hate to leave you more than I can say. . . ." He packed a navy revolver salvaged from the *Maine* and helped Leonard Wood overcome army reluctance to provide the regiment with modern Krag-Jorgenson carbines using smokeless powder. (Conventional army wisdom had it that smoke powder concealed troops from the enemy.) Finally, he entreated Fitzhugh Lee, now a major general, "Do for heaven's sake get our regiment with you when you go to Cuba." His greatest fear was that the First Volunteer Cavalry would not make it to Cuba before the navy secured a decisive victory.

Roosevelt left Washington on the evening of May 12 after writing his sister Corinne Robinson that he had "about 25 'gentlemen rankers' going with me—five from the Knickerbocker Club and a dozen clean-cut, stalwart young fellows from Harvard; such fine boys." When they reached the railroad station at San Antonio, seeking directions to Camp Wood two miles outside of town, they found instead a sign declaring, THIS WAY TO CAMP OF ROOSEVELT'S ROUGH RIDERS. A Madrid newspaper accorded him even greater stature, informing its readers that "Ted" Roosevelt was "Commander-in-Chief of the American Army" and was usually accompanied by "rough rioters."

The press had given the regiment its monicker after launching a number of alliterative trial balloons: "Teddy's Texas Tarantulas," "Roosevelt's Rustler Regiment," "Teddy's Terrors," "Teddy's Gilded Gang," and "Teddy's Riotous Rounders." Roosevelt had never liked the nickname Teddy and let it be known. "Roosevelt's Rough Riders" became the favored sobriquet. "Wood's Wild Westerners" never had a chance. The commanding officer of the First Volunteer Cavalry later admitted that if the war were to drag on, he "would be kicked upstairs to make room for Roosevelt."

The Rough Riders already mustered in San Antonio were mostly from the west—cowboys, plainsmen, blacksmiths, farmers, mountain men. About a thousand recruits had been culled from twenty thousand volunteers. They were picked, in accord with army directives, from men who were "young, sound, good shots and good riders." More than half of them came from Texas and the New Mexico and Indian territories. Their skills ranged from broncobusting and buffalo-hunting to Indian-tracking, and they did not quite know what to make of the Ivy Leaguers arriving by trolley and carriage at the camp grounds outside of town, some with golf clubs, walking sticks, and leather trunks, or the toothy, bespectacled officer with a high-pitched voice who accompanied them.

The eastern volunteers, while perhaps best known for their social credentials, were not without skills. Bob Wrenn was the United States tennis champion. Almost everyone considered the legendary Dudley Dean to be Harvard's greatest quarterback, and Joseph Sampson Stevens, son of a French duchess, the world's finest polo player. Craig Wadsworth was a superb cross-country rider. Woodbury Kane, a classmate of Roosevelt's at Harvard and a cousin of Jack Astor's, was a world-class yachtsman. Hamilton Fish, Jr., grandson of President Grant's secretary of state, had captained the Columbia crew. Even the regimental chaplain, Roosevelt observed, was "a Methodist Minister who played three years on the Wesleyan football team."

Roosevelt, with his penchant for cataloguing and analyzing, wrote Henry Cabot Lodge about the unusual composition of the regiment. It was recruited, he noted, "largely from among classes who putting it mildly, do not look at life in the spirit of decorum and conventionality that obtains in the East." Nevertheless, he observed, they were fine men. "You would be amused to see three Knickerbocker Club men cooking and washing dishes for one of the New Mexico companies."

"The Fifth Avenue Boys," as the cowboys called the eastern contingent, soon asserted themselves in the dust and heat of San Antonio. They were better at drilling, one observer remarked, because they had spent so much time in ballroom dancing. The bandy-legged cowboys, who had spent most of their life in the saddle, were more adept at riding than walking. A trooper from Oklahoma announced "he was pretty sure he could keep step on horseback."

Many of the Ivy Leaguers could ride as well as march and dance. One day Craig Wadsworth volunteered to tame a wild Texas mustang with a particularly malevolent eye. The cowboys could barely conceal their glee as the elegant dude, still dressed in city clothes, approached the tense horse. Wadsworth calmly swung into the saddle. As the animal trembled and prepared to bolt, the noted equestrian reined up its head and lightly heeled its flanks. The mustang calmly cantered off as Wadsworth tipped his hat to the astonished broncobusters.

The Rough Riders considered Leonard Wood, who devoted himself to organization, administration, and horse-training, a bit stiff and called him "Old Poker Face," or "Old Icebox." Roosevelt, who took over most of the drill work, was more apt to be regarded as "Laughing Horse," a monicker fixed on him by the Indians of the Dakotas. The enlisted men, at first perplexed by his strange accent and shrilly articulated "Hahs!" soon admired him for his informality and drive.

Roosevelt's casual approach to army discipline occasionally got him in trouble. Wood had to chew him out for offering to buy beer for the dehydrated troopers he had drilled in the hot Texas sun. (Apologizing, Roosevelt classified himself as "the damndest ass within ten miles of this camp.") A more significant breach of discipline took place on May 24 at a concert provided the Rough Riders by the San Antonio city fathers in Riverside Park. Professor Carl Beck, said to be the best bandmaster in Texas, offered as his *pièce de résistance* "Cavalry Charge: A Descriptive Fantasy."

The score called, in the manner of Tchaikovsky's "1812 Overture," for saluting cannon to fire off blank charges at appropriate moments. As Beck's baton triggered the first salvo, and an impressive report tore through the balmy evening air, the Rough Riders decided to embellish Beck's fantasy charge with their pistols. Someone later reckoned that two thousand shots were fired as the whooping troopers charged beer stands, cut electrical wires and, under cover of darkness, dashed into San Antonio for a bit of merrymaking.

Roosevelt, in a letter urging McKinley to put the regiment into Cuba "with the very first troops," informed the president that the Rough Riders were, to his surprise, "very orderly." Lodge was also assured that "the men are as quiet and straight as possible," though "now and then a small squad goes to town and proceeds to paint things red, and then we get hold of them and put them into the guardhouse...."

Later, in a more candid mood, he called them "children of the dragon's blood."

Despite the occasional fracas, the regiment was, by the end of May, honed to a fighting edge. Mob scenes on the drill field had been replaced by orderly formations and awesome charges at full gallop. The ornery Texas broncos had been broken and trained. Thanks to Wood's clout and Roosevelt's persistence in Washington, the troopers were supplied with smokeless-powder, six-shot, .30-caliber carbines. (They were the only volunteer regiment so equipped.) Everyone wore slouch hats and lightweight brown fatigue trousers, trimmed in cavalry yellow. They appeared to have been tailored with an ax, and gave off a nauseating smell of dye, but they were a vast improvement over the heavy blue flannel uniforms designed for western winters provided the rest of the army.

Finally, the mascots were readied—an eagle named Teddy, a dog named Cuba, and a young pink-nosed mountain lion named Josephine. Early on the morning of May 30, the mascots, along with their lieutenant colonel, more than a thousand troopers and over twelve hundred horses and mules, entrained for Tampa, Florida. Roosevelt was now sublimely confident that the regiment could have whipped Caesar's legendary Tenth Legion.

But he was increasingly irritated by the blunders of the War Department, and he was right to be; the army was still in total disarray.

As Roosevelt began his training in San Antonio, McKinley's secretary George Cortelyou remarked on the chief executive's appearance: "The President is again looking careworn, the color having faded from his cheeks and the rings being once more noticeable about his eyes. The strain upon him is terrible." One concern, Cortelyou noted, was Admiral Cervera's disappearing act, but even more disturbing were the "differences and bickerings among the officers of the army and the navy, which in certain high quarters are altogether too apparent."

John Long had, in fact, uncharacteristically squabbled with Russell Alger over what he called the army's "striking lack of preparation and promptness." On May 2 the secretary of the navy and Admiral Sicard, now on the Naval War Board, had met with Alger and General Miles. Alger had casually bragged to the president and others that he could put an army of forty thousand in the field on ten days' notice. Long thought that number, or perhaps a few more, would be enough to take Havana. He advocated a prompt invasion of Cuba. While he left most detail work to his bureau chiefs, he well knew the sailor's hurricane doggerel:

> June, too soon,
> In July, stand by.
> August, look out you must.
> September, remember,
> October, all over.

Miles observed that the army was unprepared for an immediate invasion and cited the threat of yellow fever in the rainy season, but in the end the joint chiefs decided that a sizable expeditionary force should embark within a few weeks for the north coast of Cuba and take Mariel, twenty-six miles west of Havana. An attack on the capital city could be launched from this beachhead.

On May 6, however, Sicard informed Long that the Naval War Board considered the army ill prepared to fulfill its commitments to the operation. The secretary, fearing delay would reflect unfavorably on the navy's readiness, wrote Alger an imperative letter urging him to act swiftly—and presented it to him at the Cabinet meeting that day. The ailing sixty-two-year-old secretary of war fired back in anger, telling Long to mind navy business, not the army's. Afterward, he complained to McKinley of Long's meddling. The president indicated that this kind of talk was "unwise."

Stung by the president's cold response, annoyed by Long's superior attitude, plagued by his own commanding general's derogatory remarks on the army's state of preparedness, Alger promptly issued a command that he knew could not be carried out, ordering Miles to take seventy thousand troops and immediately capture Havana.

Miles, an ambitious man (he aspired to the presidency) with important political connections in Washington, saw the jaws of a trap opening up. On May 8 he put in his own appearance at the White House and counseled the president against the expedition. The fever-breeding rains fell in torrents in June. The army was short of ammunition. Havana was well defended. McKinley, who had been thrust along by cries in the Congress and the press to move swiftly "On to Havana!" now agreed the invasion should be postponed. Plans for the less ambitious landing at Mariel were revived.

Miles's intrigue confounded both Long and Alger, but the decorated veteran of the Civil and Indian wars seemed the only figure in authority in touch with reality. Long had somehow forgotten that Pascual Cervera was loose in the South Atlantic and that nothing could move by sea until the fast, well-armored Spanish cruisers had been found and destroyed or bottled up. Alger, for his part, knew the army was short not only of ammunition, but of guns, uniforms, tent canvas, canteens, mess gear, and rations suited to the tropics. It had only begun to enlist civilian troop transports, and they were in scarce supply since the navy had already commandeered the best vessels for auxiliary cruisers and scouts. Most of all, it was short of men.

A million men had responded to McKinley's call for 125,000 volunteers, but recruits were only beginning to trickle into training camps across the country. When war began, there were just 28,183 officers and men in the regular army and General Wesley A. Merritt, assigned to the Department of the Pacific, had requested 5,000 of them to help cement Admiral Dewey's tenuous grip on Cavite. Estimates put the strength of the Spanish army at almost half a million men. Some 278,000 were thought to be in Cuba, and half of these were in the Havana area.

When Cervera was sighted off Martinique, then lost again, the invasion was postponed indefinitely. Alger may have appreciated, even relished, the delay. This was the navy's inadequacy. Long had touted the navy's readiness, but all those ships scattered across the Caribbean had not pinned down the Spanish fleet. While it was still footloose, the army's recruits could be trained and supplied.

Some organization was at last achieved. As Commodore Schley bobbed ineffectually along the south coast of Cuba, the army, with the regulars as a nucleus, was divided into seven corps, each led by a major general. Fitzhugh Lee was given the Seventh Corps and his old confederate Joseph "Fighting Joe" Wheeler the cavalry.

Wheeler was a spidery little man, barely over five feet tall, a Democratic congressman from Alabama who had vigorously supported the Fifty Million Bill. When it was introduced in the House on March 8, he hootled a triumphant Rebel yell and spoke emotionally for its passage. "Mr. Speaker," he told Thomas Reed, "20,000,000 brave and true hearts that dwell in that beautiful land south of yon river [the Potomac] join me in most earnest support of this resolution. . . . For a century American mothers have taught their sons that an ounce of glory earned in battle was worth more than a million pounds of gold. . . ." There was loud applause as Reed's gavel fell.

The sixty-two-year-old Wheeler, summoned to the White House, told McKinley he had thought his fighting days were over, but courteously agreed to serve once more; he had no qualms about putting on a Union uniform. If he had to face Robert E. Lee at the gates of heaven dressed in blue, so be it.

It was in large measure a political appointment; McKinley wanted the Rebs and the Yankees to fight together in this war. But he also recognized the spunk and tactical skills of the frail-looking man who had achieved the rank of lieutenant general in the Confederate Army at the age of twenty-eight.

Major General William Rufus Shafter, assigned the Fifth Corps then mustering at Tampa, was, at three hundred pounds, more than twice the size of Wheeler. People called him monstrously fat, a floating tent, a balloon, a lumbering bear, perhaps the most corpulent man in the entire army. Newsmen liked to write that he weighed a sixth of a ton and cartoonists caricatured his obesity. He was not a West Pointer, he was sixty-three years old, and he had gout, hardly a recommendation for service in the tropics.

But Shafter had credentials, too. Like Miles, he had won the Medal of Honor in the Civil War and distinguished himself in the Indian fighting. He had soldiered in every grade from private on up; he was professional, blunt, hard-boiled, honest, and apolitical. As the days passed, he struggled to impose some order on the chaos at Tampa, now designated the main port of embarkation for the American expeditionary force.

In the army's distress, the Astors and the Chanlers were not the only citizens to volunteer their services and war matériel. William Randolph Hearst wrote McKinley offering, entirely at his own expense, a completely equipped regiment of cavalry. Hearst, a skilled horseman, asked to go along, though only as "a man in the ranks" since he had no special qualifications to lead the charge. McKinley politely declined. The specter of Hearst galloping through Cuba in pursuit of "the *Journal*'s war" may have put him off.

Hearst accepted the rejection gracefully, but soon made the president another offer: "Sir: I beg to offer the United States, as a gift, without any conditions whatever, my steam yacht *Buccaneer* . . . fully equipped, armed and manned." He asked McKinley to appoint him either "commander or second in command" of the vessel. The letter was forwarded to the Navy Department; Acting Secretary Charles Allen gratefully accepted the offer of the *Buccaneer* and told Hearst a naval board would consider his qualifications for a commission. As it turned out, the wheels of navy bureaucracy ground exceedingly slowly when it came to making Hearst a line officer.

There was also a rescue mission the *Journal*'s publisher felt duty-bound to undertake, and in this instance he felt no obligation to inform the president. A report had reached Hearst that a Spanish relief fleet mustering at Cádiz under the command of Admiral Manuel de la Cámara would sail for the Philippines by way of the Suez Canal. Cámara's squadron included the French-built battleship *Pelayo* and the armored cruiser *Carlos V*. They were both over 9,000 tons and superior to anything in the Asiatic Squadron.

Hearst promptly cabled correspondent James Creelman, then in London, and told him that if the Spanish fleet actually sailed he should buy "some big English steamer at the eastern end of the Mediterranean" and block the Suez Canal by sinking her in an appropriate place.

Creelman discreetly began working on the secret project. He considered it "a piece of heartfelt, practical patriotism."

It was also a clear breach of international law, but under the circumstances, Creelman later observed, "the whole country must have acknowledged the service rendered by the despised yellow journalism."

On May 30, the day after Commodore Schley finally discovered elements of Cervera's squadron at Santiago, the *New Orleans* steamed up to Santiago and delivered Sampson's directive about sinking the *Merrimac* in the channel as a blockship. Sampson ordered "the promptest and most efficient use of every means" to bottle up the Spanish fleet, but Schley was reluctant to take action. The collier still held valuable coal in her bunkers. Moreover, he felt that Cervera should not be sealed into the harbor, where his ships could prove invaluable defending Santiago, but rather lured out to his destruction.

After consideration, Schley postponed the *Merrimac* venture until he could discuss the matter with Sampson. The next day, however, he ordered a long-range bombardment of the harbor entrance. Little damage was done by the fleet's big guns, firing at ranges up to six miles. A Spanish officer on the *Cristóbal Colón*, still anchored near the harbor entrance, recorded in her log: "Our shot falling short on account of the enemy keeping at too great distance. . . ." Shrapnel did hit the ship; several china bowls were broken.

Robley Evans was incensed by the timidity of the attack. The extreme elevation required for long-range fire had severely strained the *Iowa*'s gun carriages. Schley thought the bombardment a useful reconnaissance. Several Spanish batteries had been located. So, apparently, had the Cape Verde Squadron. Schley wrote to Secretary Long, "Quite satisfied the Spanish fleet is here."

Sampson, now doubting Schley's subordination, pressed on with his plans for the *Merrimac*. Before leaving Key West for Santiago, he had summoned Lieutenant Richmond Pearson Hobson to his cabin and told the twenty-seven-year-old naval constructor, who at the age of eighteen had graduated first in his class at the Naval Academy, that he wanted to scuttle the Merrimac in the channel leading out of Santiago. Hobson began working out the technical details.

The New York, the Oregon, and two smaller vessels arrived at Santiago shortly after dawn on June 1, and Sampson immediately conferred with Schley, who had still done nothing about the Merrimac operation. Sampson immediately ordered the collier stripped of useful gear and prepared for her mission. Ten 8-inch copper "torpedoes," each containing eighty pounds of brown powder, were coated with pitch, lashed at intervals below the port waterline of the Merrimac, and connected by electrical wires to the bridge; anchors rigged fore and aft so that they could be instantly dropped; sea-cock valves greased. Before dawn, on a flood tide, a skeleton crew would take the collier in and sink her in a bend of the narrow channel off Estrella Point.

It was, Sampson realized, a suicide mission. Batteries on the heights of Morro and Socapa would have a clear field of fire as the Merrimac approached the harbor entrance. The channel was mined and torpedoes were a threat. But when Sampson issued a call for volunteers, nearly everyone in the fleet stepped forward. "Fighting Bob" Evans signaled: "My entire crew has volunteered." Captain Jack Philip on the Texas offered 250 men. A report had it that the bandmaster of the flagship begged to go, with several of his musicians, so they could play "The Star-Spangled Banner" as the ship went down.

Hobson, not a line officer, was officially ineligible to command at sea, but earnestly pleaded that he be allowed to take the collier in, arguing that he was most qualified to ensure the detonation of the explosive devices. Commander James M. Miller of the Merrimac protested. She was his ship. He knew her best. He had brought her to Cuba and coped admirably with the ship's foibles during the hazardous coaling of the Flying Squadron. And he had over thirty years of experience. There were tears in his eyes when Sampson gave the command to Hobson.

At three o'clock on the morning of June 3, with the tide flooding and the cloud-shrouded moon in its last hour, the Merrimac, with Hobson and seven in crew, began her dash for glory. Press vessels had been herded out to sea by a torpedo boat, but AP reporter "Chappie" Goode on the New

York had a ringside seat. He peered anxiously toward the dark shoreline. For a long time nothing happened, but suddenly "the flash of a gun streamed out from Morro. Then came another, and in a few seconds the mouth of Santiago Harbor was livid with flames that shot viciously from both banks. . . . The dull sound of the cannonade and its fiery light were unmistakable evidences of the fierce attack that was being waged upon Hobson's gallant crew. . . ."

Aboard the *Merrimac*, Hobson observed that they were within about two thousand yards of the harbor entrance when the moon came out from behind a cloud. He ordered full speed ahead, only about 9 knots on the patched-up collier. As the ship responded, he noticed that the flukes of the fore and aft anchors, hung just at water level, were throwing up foamy white spray. Then two bright flashes of gunfire pricked his eye. Both shots missed. Peering through binoculars, he made out a picketboat firing rapid-fire guns. Then a battery on Socapa opened up. A shell impact clanged somewhere near the bridge.

Hobson had only to take the *Merrimac* a short distance past the point below Morro Castle, stop engines, coast in with the tide, swing the ship hard to starboard so the stern would drift athwart the channel, drop the anchors, fire the explosives, and open the sea cocks. The sequence went smoothly until he tried to broadside the ship—and nothing happened. Apparently, the steering gear had been shot away, and with it the stern anchor. The bow anchor dropped but failed to hold the careening ship. The electrical circuits to the powder charges were activated. Only two exploded.

The Spanish finished her off. A hail of small-arms fire—a "downpour of iron at pistol range," Víctor Concas noted—flogged the decks of the *Merrimac*. A mine burst underneath her. The *Plutón* and the *Reina Mercedes*, lurking behind Socapa Point, fired torpedoes. Two struck home. The barrage continued for fifteen minutes as the mortally wounded collier slowly drifted in with the tide. Miraculously, not a man aboard had been killed. As the ship went down—the bow suddenly plunged like a stone—Hobson ordered his sailors onto a raft with twin sponsons that had floated off the deck.

Admiral Pascual Cervera was stunned by the audacity of

the little *Merrimac*'s attempt to breach the harbor. As the firing gradually ceased, he ordered his steam launch readied and personally joined the search for survivors. Shortly after dawn he heard a voice calling out near the shore. His marines cocked and pointed their rifles, but the admiral ordered them to lower their guns. A man in underclothes waded out, swam the last yards to the launch, and grabbed the gunwale. Cervera gazed with admiration into a coal-blackened face.

"¡*Valiente!*" he exclaimed. Then the admiral assisted Lieutenant Richmond Hobson into his launch.

That afternoon Captain Joaquín Bustamente, Cervera's chief of staff, steamed out of Santiago on the tug *Colón* under a flag of truce and reported that while the *Merrimac* had sunk, the entire crew had survived. The prisoners had been lodged in Morro Castle. Sampson knew the ship was down; looking past Morro Point, he could see the masts of the ship and about ten feet of funnel sticking out of the water on the west side of the channel. It appeared that she had passed the desired point of sinking and did not block it.

In Havana, Blanco received appalling news from Correa in Madrid. The war minister cabled: "Very serious situation in Philippines compels us to send there ships and reinforcements of troops as early as possible." Only two warships were ready to go, and one might be too large to get through the Suez Canal. "The only thing we can do is to send all the ships of Cervera's squadron that can get out of Santiago." Before a final decision was made, the governor-general's opinion was sought.

Blanco no longer bothered to put a sanguine face on matters. He replied bluntly: ". . . departure of Cervera's squadron at this time would be of fatal effect on public opinion. . . . Volunteers already much exercised over inadequacy Cervera's squadron. . . . Would rise in body upon learning that instead of reinforcements the few ships here are withdrawing. The repression would necessarily be bloody. . . . Loss of island certain, in view of horrible conflagration it would kindle here."

*   *   *

As the Merrimac made its bold approach to Santiago Harbor, the last contingent of Rough Riders reached Tampa. It was, Roosevelt observed, "a perfect welter of confusion." Some fifteen thousand troops had already arrived over the two single-track railroad lines running into the town, but freight cars carrying uniforms, tents, cooking gear, food, and other supplies were backed up all the way to South Carolina, and without proper bills of lading, no one knew what was in them. If there should be another war, Roosevelt wrote, "I would earnestly advise the men of every volunteer organization always to proceed upon the belief that their supplies will not turn up. . . ."

Tampa was a two-faced city. To the troops camped on its outskirts, it was an unhappy aggregate of swamp, scrub pine and palmetto, sand, mosquitoes, and grotesque land crabs. Tampa Heights, a soldier from New York remarked, "were about 15 feet higher than Tampa itself—a veritable hill! We dug new latrines, and the area of palmetto scrub was so barren of habitation that they did not need to be screened."

But seventy-nine-year-old entrepreneur Henry Bradley Plant had seen the possibilities of a port at Tampa Bay, nine miles to the south. The Plant System operated hotels, railroads, and steamships. His vessels, including the indefatigable *Olivette*, plied the Gulf Coast from Mobile, Tampa, Fort Myers, and Key West to Havana and Jamaica. He had built a mile-long wharf at Port Tampa, a railroad connecting it to the city, an amusement park, and a trolley line.

But the brightest jewel in Plant's diadem was the Tampa Bay Hotel, built in opulent Moorish style. The hotel's five stories and five hundred rooms sprawled over six acres, and its silver-tipped towers and minarets shimmered over the Florida desert like a gaudy mirage. Plant had provided it with a casino, a peacock park, a golf course, a German pipe organ, and broad verandas. A cavalry general remarked, "Only God knows why Plant built a hotel here, but thank God he did."

Two floors of the hotel were reserved for officers—including Shafter and his staff—and their wives. Regimental bands played waltzes and marches under strings of incandescent lights on the veranda. The press corps, more than a hundred strong, shopped the dance floor for stories. Former Hearst artist and *Maine* medal designer Charles Johnson Post, now a private in the Seventy-first New York Volunteer Regiment, envied the newspapermen the steaks, ice cream, and Scotch whisky "highballs" available at the Tampa Bay. "To us doughboys," he wrote, "it [the Scotch] tasted like creosote. We were very common folk. Richard Harding Davis was busy conning his Social Register on the cool hotel porch, until he knew the elite of the Rough Riders from Teddy on up or down, and keeping himself and his silk undies in perfect condition for the rigors of the upcoming campaign."

Clara Barton, organizing a hospital ship for the Red Cross and perhaps recalling her experience with the victims of the *Maine,* found the Tampa scene ominous. She wrote with foreboding of "the great ships gathered in the waters; the monitors, grim and terrible, seemed striving to hide their heads among the surging waves.... It seemed a strange thing, this gathering for war."

Naval Academy Cadet Daniel Mannix, who had been ordered to report to the battleship *Indiana* at Key West, observed: "This place is like a Western mining camp in the days of Jesse James. There are ... some of the famous Rough Riders wandering around brandishing loaded revolvers. As the Duke of Wellington said about some newly-arrived troops, 'I don't know what effect they will have on the enemy but by God they frighten me.' ... The camp is supposedly under the command of General William Shafter but there seems to be no discipline whatsoever. I caught a glimpse of the general. He is an enormous man and must weigh over 300 pounds. I can't imagine him leading troops in the tropical jungles of Cuba."

Roosevelt usually pitched his tent with the troopers, but when Edith came down for a few days, he spent evenings at the Tampa Bay. On June 6, Roosevelt took a moment to write his children: "Blessed Bunnies, It has been a real holiday to have darling mother here. Yesterday I brought her out to the camp, and she saw it all—the men drilling, the tents in long company streets, the horses being taken to water, my little horse Texas, the colonel and the majors, and finally the mountain lion and the jolly little dog Cuba, who had several fights while she looked on. The mountain lion is not much more than a kitten yet, but it is very cross and treacherous. . . .

"Mother stays at a big hotel about a mile from camp. There are nearly thirty thousand troops here now, besides the sailors from the war-ships in the bay. At night the corridors and piazzas are thronged with officers of the army and navy; the older ones fought in the great Civil War. . . . Most of them are in blue, but our rough-riders are in brown. . . . It is very hot, indeed, but there are no mosquitoes. . . ."

That day, as Richard Harding Davis escorted Edith Roosevelt to yet another cavalry exercise, two columns of American warships, led by Sampson on the *New York* and Schley on the *Brooklyn*, approached the entrance to the channel into Santiago and, at a close distance of two thousand yards, peeled to the right and left and began a heavy bombardment of the city's coastal defenses and the harbor inside. Spanish artillery captain Severo Gómez Núñez announced afterward that 100 guns had fired 2,000 shots in 175 minutes.

In his Morro Castle cell, Naval Constructor Richmond Hobson dove under a table, but only a few errant rounds struck the old fortification. The battery on the Socapa Heights, however, was pummeled. Shells passed over Punta Gorda and landed in the inside harbor close aboard the flagship *María Teresa*. The *Vizcaya* was hit twice, the *Furor* once. Nearer the harbor entrance, the *Reina Mercedes* was riddled. "A hostile shell of large caliber," Núñez reported, hit Commander Emilio Acosta y Eyermann, the ship's executive officer. His right leg and hand were torn off. The dying Acosta grimaced through the pain and said, "*Esta no es nada* [This is nothing]. ¡Viva España!"

The gunners of the Socapa battery, for the most part unable to see the American fleet through the smoke, fired forty-seven shells. The military mast of the *Massachusetts* was hit, and there was a shrapnel casualty aboard the little *Suwanee*. Sampson, now convinced the shore batteries did not pose a serious threat, envisioned an amphibious attack on the fortifications guarding the harbor entrance. He cabled Long: "If 10,000 men were here, city and fleet would be ours within

48 hours. Every consideration demands immediate army movement. If delayed, city will be defended more strongly by guns taken from the fleet."

After maneuvers on the morning of the sixth, Wood and Roosevelt heard there was room on board the thirty-two transports the army had cobbled up for just eight of their twelve cavalry troops. And only senior officers could take their horses. It was tough telling the cowboys their horses could not go, even harder telling so many of the men they could not. "To the great bulk of them," Roosevelt thought, "I think it will be a lifelong sorrow. I saw more than one . . . burst into tears. . . ."

The bowlegged Rough Riders were soon dubbed "Wood's Weary Walkers." Roosevelt thought it was something Washington should know about. He wrote Cabot Lodge: "They send us dismounted but we should be glad to go on all fours rather than not to go at all. It will be an outrage though if they do not send the horses after. . . . If not too much trouble I wish you would see the Secretary [Alger] and have him keep us in mind. . . ."

Russell Alger had a more pressing matter in mind—Sampson's cable of June 6 to Long urging the immediate dispatch of an army expeditionary force. He conferred immediately with McKinley. Around 6 P.M. the following evening, as Shafter relaxed over coffee in the rotunda of the Tampa Bay Hotel, he was summoned to the telegraph office. A cable arrived from the War Room at the White House: "You will sail immediately as you are needed at destination at once." Shafter replied that he would go the next morning—"Steam cannot be gotten up earlier." As he well knew, it was impossible to do anything "immediately" at Tampa.

But "the rocking-chair period," as Davis called it, was clearly over. At the Tampa Bay Hotel, William Dinwiddie of the *New York Herald* wrote, "the corridors and lobbies were jammed with men and luggage. . . . It was a motley assembly which scurried through the hotel, in canvas hunting suits, in white ducks . . . even in immaculate white shirt fronts and patent leathers. Six-shooters, machetes, and belts full of ammunition circulated through the halls. . . ."

At the camps around Tampa, acres of white canvas floated to the ground as the dog tents came down. Baggage wagons were loaded, the men formed up, and it all went smoothly until it came time to train-lift some seventeen thousand troops and two thousand animals—all the transports could take—the nine miles to Port Tampa on the single-track railroad.

The Rough Riders waited all night for their train to appear. At 6 A.M. some coal cars came by, running in the wrong direction. "These were seized," Roosevelt noted. The locomotive went into reverse and headed back to Port Tampa. Private Post, settled in a freight car on a spur track, watched it go by just after daybreak: "Then there came a waving and halloing far up the track . . . in the open door of a boxcar was Teddy, Colonel Theodore Roosevelt, grinning as his car passed our lines of flatcars. . . . He wore the polka-dot blue bandanna that was the hallmark of the Rough Riders. The rest of our army wore red bandannas."

At Plant's mile-long wharf thousands of troops milled around—"A good deal of higglety-pigglety," Roosevelt observed. No one seemed to know which troopship the Rough Riders were supposed to board. Wood and Roosevelt finally located the quartermaster general, who told them to take any ship they could, perhaps the *Yucatán*, though other troops had already been assigned to it. While Wood commandeered a rowboat and went out to bring in the transport, Roosevelt double-quicked his men down the wharf to the *Yucatán*'s allotted berth and posted a heavy guard at the gangplank. "I was determined that we should not be among the men left off." Officers of the Second Regulars and the Seventy-first Volunteers, units assigned to the *Yucatán*, pushed through the swarm of Rough Riders to protest. Roosevelt stalled for time—"I was under the orders of my superior and of a ranking officer—to my great regret, etc. etc.—could not give way as they desired." The transport finally docked and Roosevelt hurried his men on board. "There was a good deal of expostulation, but we had possession."

Before nightfall the Rough Riders had loaded baggage, guns, stores, and what horses they could take. Other ships, loaded to the gunwales, had taken on over sixteen thousand troops. William Shafter climbed laboriously aboard his headquarters ship *Segurança* and ordered her to take the van of the transport fleet. A number of ships had already headed for the entrance to the Gulf.

Then a last-minute cable to Shafter from Secretary Alger was delivered by tug. "Wait until you get further orders before you sail. Answer quick." The flotilla sorted itself out and straggled back to its anchorage. Ashore, Shafter discovered that the navy's *Eagle* had sighted a Spanish armored cruiser and a destroyer in the Nicholas Channel off Cuba's north coast—smack on the rhumb line to Santiago.

The "naval problem," as General Miles called it, remained unsolved for six days. The horses, which perversely began to die in the inferno below decks, were taken ashore; the troops, for the most part, were not. Roosevelt was incensed. The *Yucatán* was parked in a backwater of sewage flowing out from Port Tampa, the drinking water was brackish, the tinned beef "embalmed" (it turned out to be a meatpacker's experiment), and many of his men were "in the lower hold, which is unpleasantly suggestive of the Black Hole of Calcutta." As he wrote angrily to Lodge, "They won't even let us put out into the bay, where we should all swim in spite of the sharks, and we stay crowded in this fetid ditch. . . ." He did not, however, ignore the world picture, advising Lodge: "You must get Manila and Hawaii; you must prevent any talk of peace until we get Porto Rico and the Philippines as well as secure the independence of Cuba."

Some of the Second Regulars had managed to fight their way on board and their band made life more bearable. The favorite tune was "Animal Fair":

> The monkey he got drunk
> And sat on the elephant's trunk.
> The elephant sneezed and fell on his knees
> And what became of the monk, the monk?

The Rough Riders took a childish delight in whooping out the chorus—"de monk, de monk!"—banging on their mess tins and boot-stomping the decks of the *Yucatán* as though there were rattlers underfoot. The rackety clamor swelled across the anchorage. Tampa Bay was not a quiet place.

*   *   *

While the army's stumpy coastal steamers boiled in the sun and the navy again searched for a phantom Spanish fleet, the marines took the initiative in Cuba.

Captain Charles Sigsbee had proposed that the navy seize Guantánamo Bay, about forty miles east of Santiago, as a coaling station and hurricane hole. The surrounding land was "much lower than elsewhere, and therefore does not offer the usual facilities of the region for a plunging fire on vessels and troops from surrounding hills." The Naval War Board thought the idea had merit and on June 7, as Commander Bowman McCalla's *Marblehead* entered the outer harbor and pounded shore fortifications, the First Marine Battalion, then training at Key West, embarked for Cuba on the *Panther*. The "leather-necks," as the bluejackets called them, had enlisted only in April. They were young and green. Most had never heard a shot fired in anger.

Under cover of their ship's guns, marine detachments from the *Oregon* and the *Marblehead* hit the beach on the east side of the outer bay on the morning of Friday, June 10. The *Panther* arrived several hours later and her 650 marines landed. They were followed by a gaggle of correspondents off the press boats *Sommers N. Smith* and *Three Friends*, including Ralph Paine and Stephen Crane. There was little resistance. Paine observed that most of the marines, who had taken up positions on a high point called Crest Heights (soon renamed Camp McCalla), did not bother to dig trenches on the red gravel hill.

There was little firing the first night. Crane thought the situation "rather comic." But on Saturday, a corps of three thousand crack Spanish riflemen launched an attack on the marine battalion that lasted for thirteen continuous hours, paused, and began again. The fighting continued for three days. It was, Crane reported, "no longer comic."

Crane described the sounds of the Spanish rifles. "The Mauser says 'Pop!'—plainly and frankly pop, like a soda water bottle being opened close to the ear." As the bullet ripped through the air, there was a "sneering" sound, then a hot hiss. The marines fired back with the "prut-prut" of their carbines, trying to spot targets in the beams of searchlights on the ships offshore.

Sunday night was as bad as it got. Crane had gotten to know Assistant Surgeon John Blair Gibbs, who had given him quinine for a bout of fever. In the long fire fight Gibbs was shot through the head. Crane, in a shallow trench nearby, heard somebody "dying near me. He was dying hard. Hard. It took him a long time to die. He breathed as all noble machinery breathes when it is making its gallant strife against breaking, breaking . . . this breathing, the noise of a heroic pump which strives to subdue a mud which comes upon it in tons . . . I thought this man would never die."

But Gibbs did die, sometime after midnight, as the Spanish attack intensified. The marines, Crane wrote, longed for dawn, craved the sun, were ravenous for light. When it finally came, Crane was "furious with this wretched sunrise. I thought I could have walked around the world in the time required for the old thing to get up above the horizon."

Paine and other reporters had gone off on the *Three Friends* to Jamaica to file invasion stories when it had seemed there would be no serious fighting. On return, they saw the slumped figure of Crane on the beach raggedly waving his hat. They got him on board and poured coffee into him. He had not slept for two days and "was dirty and heavy-eyed and enormously hungry and thirsty." But his "weary young eyes brightened when he told us how it had fared with the battalion of marines. And as he went on, he used words as though they were colors to be laid on a canvas with a vigorous and daring brush."

Crane was back in action on June 14 when Lieutenant Colonel Robert W. Huntington ordered an attack in force on the Spanish outpost at Cuzco, five miles distant. In the woods beyond Camp McCalla they could hear the Spanish signaling to each other by crooning in the voice of doves. Crane thought he had "never heard such a horrible sound as the beautiful cooing of the wood-dove when I was certain that it came from the yellow throat of a gueriila." Then the Spanish were flushed from their thickets by shells from the *Dolphin*, and as they ran, it was like a quail shoot; brass shell casings cascaded from the marine rifles. "Sometimes we could see a whole covey vanish miraculously after the volley. . . . Everybody on our side stood up. It was vastly exciting. 'There they go! See 'em! See 'em!' "

Though the fighting went on sporadically, it was clear that the marines meant to hold a large piece of real estate in Cuba. The starred and striped banner waving over Guantá-namo Bay became a permanent fixture.

On June 13 the navy firmly established the presence of the Cape Verde Squadron at Santiago. The day before, Lieutenant Victor Blue of the *Suwanee* had gone ashore near Aserra-deros, west of the harbor, and linked up with Cuban insur-gents who guided him to the top of a hill overlooking the harbor. Through binoculars Blue made a positive identifica-tion of four cruisers, two torpedo-boat destroyers, and the battered *Reina Mercedes*. (The *Terror*, after repairs at Marti-nique, had made her way unopposed to San Juan.)

The next day Blue's sightings were cabled to the Navy Department. They confirmed Sampson's suspicion that the *Eagle*'s "ghost squadron" had been composed of American ships. The Fifth Army Corps could sail. On the afternoon of June 14, to little fanfare, it finally did.

Cadet Daniel Mannix found the *Indiana* in the Sand Key Light anchorage off Key West and reported to Captain Henry C. Taylor. In the crowded junior officers' mess, he found about twenty officers. "Some have bunks, some swing in hammocks, some sleep on the transoms and two are on the table." Mannix preferred a hammock "as the roaches crawl over anything stationary." But what bothered him most was the heat. "When we wake in the mornings the sheets are dripping wet with perspiration and, as the water has a tem-perature of 100, there is no relief in taking a bath."

On June 16 the *Indiana* and nine other warships rendez-voused with Shafter's lumbering "prison hulks" (as the troops called them) off the Dry Tortugas, and the convoy headed south across the Gulf Stream, turned east past Ha-vana, and headed down the Nicholas Channel.

The fifty-odd vessels, Mannix observed, "are of all ages and every known type of architecture. One old paddle-wheel ferry boat loaded with mules is waddling along like a duck about a mile to port of her proper position." Water barges and landing scows under tow slowed the convoy which compressed and flexed out like an accordion as it wheezed uncertainly along the Cuban coastline.

Richard Harding Davis, comfortably berthed on Shafter's *Seguança*, deplored the disorder in the convoy: "We rolled along at our own pace, with the lights the navy had told us to extinguish blazing defiantly to the stars, with bands banging out rag-time music, and with the foremost vessels separated sometimes for half a day at a time from the laggards at the rear." He wondered how the Spanish torpedo boats could resist such a "happy-go-lucky" target.

The sea kicked up and Frederic Remington, also on the *Seguança*, again made plain his views on ships: "I hate a ship in a compound, triple-expansion, forced draft way. . . . [M]ake me a feather in a sick chicken's tail on shore and I will thank you."

Private Post on the *Vigilancia* was bothered by the wind, which made it difficult to play poker on deck. On the *Yucatán*, "Old Icebox" Leonard Wood was entranced by the tropical scene. "Painted ships on a painted ocean," he wrote his wife. "Imagine three great lines of transports . . . steaming . . . over a sea of indigo blue, real deep blue, such as I have never seen before."

Although Roosevelt did not know it, the House of Representatives had overwhelmingly passed a resolution providing for the annexation of Hawaii on June 15, the day after the *Yucatán* left Tampa. Even so, he clearly saw the direction in which the convoy and the nation were headed. That day he wrote his sister Corinne, "It is a great historical expedition, and I thrill to feel that I am part of it . . . if we are allowed to succeed (for we certainly shall succeed if allowed) we have scored the first great triumph in what will be a world movement."

On Sunday, June 19 the armada rounded Cape Maisí at the eastern end of Cuba and straggled through the Windward Passage. The trade wind had been "blowing steadily in our faces," Roosevelt noted after church services that day, but on the new southwest course it was "on our quarter, and we all knew that our destination was Santiago." Monday morning, as they cruised past Guantánamo, the lofty blue-tinted peaks of the Sierra Maestra came into view. Some of the cowboys were reminded of the Rockies.

Short of Santiago, the convoy halted and French Ensor Chadwick boarded the *Segurança* from Richard Wainwright's *Gloucester*. After a brief consultation the army headquarters ship continued on toward Santiago, picked up Sampson off the *New York*, and steamed to Aserraderos, where longboats took a small party ashore—Sampson, Shafter, staff officers, Davis, Remington, and a few others—to confer with General Calixto García, commanding the insurgent Cubans in Oriente Province.

Shafter was understandably nervous about the expedition. Spanish troops were known to be in the vicinity, and the major general's gout and inertia precluded rapid withdrawal. He was provided with a small but stouthearted mule for the short trip from the beach to the rendezvous with García. A Cuban officer recorded, "One had to have compassion for the poor mule, upon contemplating it giving profound groans (*pugidos*) of anguish during its ascension, because of the cargo with which it had been punished that summer morning!"

To this point, Sampson believed that the army had come to help the navy breach the entrance to Santiago Bay and destroy Cervera's squadron, thereby freeing elements of the squadron to reinforce Dewey or attack the Spanish coast. He could not sweep the mines from the channel, or direct accurate fire on the Spanish ships, without commanding the thinly defended heights of Socapa and Morro. Soldiers and marines could storm the heights under the fleet's guns. Once a foothold was established, the army could follow up in force.

At first, Sampson reported to the Navy Department, Shafter gave "cordial assent to this plan. But Shafter had seen the ominous fortifications guarding the harbor; he did not relish a frontal assault on stone bastions perched on high cliffs, perhaps guarded by more Spaniards than Sampson thought. In his mind, at some point, the objective changed from Cervera's fleet to Santiago itself. Shafter peremptorily advised Sampson that he meant to go ashore at Daiquirí, sixteen miles east of Santiago, and then at Siboney, almost halfway to the harbor entrance. From Siboney he would move northwest, away from the immediate protection of the fleet's guns, toward El Caney and the city of Santiago. He asked Sampson to provide steam cutters and pulling boats to ferry his men ashore, and invited García to attack the Spaniards from the rear.

Sampson, confused by Shafter's proposal to thrust inland, still expected the army would move on the heights guarding the harbor entrance. The prime target was Cervera's squadron, not the city of Santiago. Shafter had been ordered to cooperate "most earnestly" with Sampson to this end; nevertheless, he had the authority to map out his own plan of campaign, and he did.

Spanish Navy Lieutenant José Müller, charged with port defense, wrote later, "If the enemy had taken possession of them [the heights], it would have been easy to remove the torpedoes and force the bay, and then the city and its defenders would necessarily have had to surrender."

It was raining now, heavily at times, and the invading army, camping in the field, would begin taking casualties from malaria and yellow fever. If the Spanish troops could hold out long enough, the Americans might be forced to withdraw.

On the evening of Tuesday the twenty-first, the troops aboard the transports got the news that they would land before dawn the next day at Daiquirí. After two weeks on the dreary tramp steamers, with stomach-turning food and foul water, the Rough Riders were jubilant, none more so than Roosevelt. One hand on hip, the other waving his campaign hat, "Teethadore," as the New York Press called him, broke into a lively song-and-dance he had learned out west:

> "Shout hurrah for Erin go Bragh
> And all the Yankee Nation!"

Bugles jolted them up at 3:30 A.M., but the naval bombardment, extending for miles down the coast, did not begin until after sunrise. On the Indiana, which engaged the Morro batteries, Cadet Mannix learned a lesson. The first Spanish shell went over the battleship only a few feet high, and a few minutes later "there was a tremendous shock, as if a locomotive had run into the ship; a shell had struck our armor belt just below the port sheet anchor." Thrown across the room, his knee banged painfully into a projecting steel shelf. "It is all nonsense about their not being able to shoot," he wrote. "Any ship that tried to run the channel between the forts would have been instantly sunk."

At Daiquirí the *New Orleans* and four other ships bombarded what Roosevelt called "a squalid little village" before the troops began to disembark. "We did the landing as we had done everything else—that is, in a scramble. . . ." It was, in fact, a scramble for survival. The army had not paid marine insurance on the civilian transports, and their masters hesitated to bring them into the uncharted waters off Daiquirí. Some anchored a mile and a half off the beach. There were not enough boats, barges, and scows to bring the troopers and their horses and guns ashore. The surf was high. There was only one pier of substance at the village, and that so far above the water two men drowned when they fell trying to get out of their boat. (In full uniform, encumbered by horse-collar blanket rolls, bulging haversacks, canteens, rifles, and a hundred rounds of ammunition, they sank like human anchors.)

General Arsenio Linares, commanding the defense of Santiago, had left only a token force at Daiquirí. The Spanish dug a few trenches, emplaced several cannon, neglected to destroy the pier, and all but disappeared when the bombardment began. It was fortunate, Leonard Wood had written his wife, to have "struck a broken-down power, for we should surely have had a deuced hard time with any other." It embarrassed him that foreign observers were watching the amateurish operation.

It was fortunate for Wood when the converted yacht *Vixen*, commanded by a formal naval aide of Roosevelt's, appeared. The *Vixen* put a Cuban pilot aboard the *Yucatán* who guided the ship to within a few hundred yards of the beach. Even so, the landing was difficult. Roosevelt's kit disappeared, including the medicine chest with soap, razor, and brandy; he carried only a light poncho and, in his pockets, a toothbrush, some food, and extra pairs of spectacles.

He lost a horse, too. It was swim or sink for them and, as Roosevelt watched, Rain-in-the-Face was put in a belly sling, boomed over the side, and lowered toward the water. A wave broke over the rig, dragged the horse under, and drowned it. Roosevelt, a motion-picture cameraman recorded, "snorting like a bull, split the air with one blasphemy after another." The terrified crewmen took exquisite care with the second horse, Texas, treating it with "the supreme deliberateness of an *accoucheur* delivering an heir apparent." The operation took so long Roosevelt roared out, "Stop that goddamned animal torture!" Finally, in a lull between waves, the horse was dropped into the sea and swam ashore.

Frederic Remington, finally leaving the *Segurança* that afternoon—Shafter had ordered that only troops go in the first landings—faced an agonizing dilemma: whether to carry his beloved silver pocket flask ashore. Already encumbered by artist's paraphernalia, three-days' provisions, poncho, camera, and six-shooter, he sadly hefted the heavy, spirit-filled container—and jammed it into a pocket of his tropical jacket.

New York Journal correspondent Edward Marshall on the *Olivette* circumvented Shafter's press dictum by flagging down one of the little boats in Hearst's fleet and hitching a ride ashore. He took along an American flag which, he felt, should be raised on Cuban soil in honor of the *Journal*. That morning he had spotted just the place, a flagpole standing next to a Spanish blockhouse atop a peak just to the east of Daiquirí. Cuban soldiers signaled that the blockhouse had been abandoned, and Marshall began to climb.

Several Rough Riders also set off up the hill toting an elegant silk flag presented the regiment by the Women's Relief Corps of Phoenix, Arizona. At the summit Marshall agreed, with as much grace as he could muster, that the Phoenix flag took precedence over the *Journal*'s, but there was no flag halyard and none of the cowboys were able to climb up the tall pole. Finally, a sailor off one of the transports appeared and, to everyone's admiration, deftly shinnied up and affixed the Stars and Stripes to the flagstaff.

Far below, the sailors and soldiers of the American armada saw the flag unfurl in the stiff breeze and began to shout. Then a pandemonium of steam whistles and foghorns, of trumpets and drum rolls and tumultuous cheering, erupted from the ships. On the *Olivette*, Malcolm McDowell of the *Chicago Record* noted that it went on for fifteen minutes.

"Then the noise ceased, and out of it came the strains of 'The Star-Spangled Banner' from the regimental band on the *Mattewan*. The soldiers ashore and the soldiers afloat were quiet until the brasses became silent, and then three full-lunged hurrahs crashed against the hill. . . ."

Daiquirí had been taken and, in spite of the chaos, six thousand men put ashore, without a rifle shot being fired. It was hard for Roosevelt to understand: "Five hundred resolute men could have prevented the disembarkation at very little cost to themselves." He managed to find his horse Texas and helped Wood to establish a camp.

The night was peaceful, dry and cool. "A breeze came from the sea," Stephen Crane wrote, "while overhead lay a splendid summer night sky, a-flash with great tranquil stars. . . . The light of the transports blinked on the murmuring plain in front of the village."

On Thursday the twenty-third, after unloading artillery and supplies from the transports, the Rough Riders were ordered to Siboney, which Brigadier General Henry W. Lawton's Second Infantry Division had occupied earlier in the day. It was a hard, hot trek over rough coral for the cavalrymen. Roosevelt insisted on walking the eight miles with them rather than ride.

That afternoon, and on into the evening, troopships off Siboney disgorged men and matériel. Davis found the operation "weird and remarkable. . . . An army was being landed on an enemy's coast at the dead of night, but with somewhat more of cheers and shrieks and laughter than rise from the bathers in the surf at Coney Island on a hot Sunday."

The exhausted Rough Riders arrived late that night in a torrential downpour, pitched camp north of Siboney, and managed to fry up some hard tack as Wood went off to confer with Joe Wheeler and Brigadier General Samuel B. M. Young, commanding the Second Brigade of the cavalry division. Shafter still had his headquarters on the *Segurança*, and until he came ashore, Wheeler was in full command of the cavalry. The ex-Confederate had arrived at Siboney that afternoon and personally scouted the valley road leading north toward Las Guásimas—some ranch buildings, a blockhouse—at the junction of a wagon trail and a hillside footpath about four miles to the north.

There had been a short fight there that day between insurgents and Spanish troops retreating from Siboney; the Cubans had hit and run, leaving the field to the Spanish. Wheeler was determined to push them out of the critical road junction. He had yet to receive Shafter's order from the *Seguran-ça*: "The commanding general begs to say it is impossible to advance on Santiago until movements to supply troops can be arranged. Take up strong positions. . . ." It was not, in any case, the kind of order a cavalry general—"a man with a fighting edge," as Roosevelt put it—was apt to favor.

Wheeler jumped them off at sunrise. Young, with eight troops of the First and Tenth Regular Cavalry regiments, also dismounted, went up the grandly titled Camino Real (Royal Road). Wood led eight troops of Rough Riders along the ridge trail to the west. The two forces would rendezvous at Las Guásimas where the two trails came together. The expedition numbered less than a thousand men, including correspondents Davis, Crane, and Marshall; the Spanish force was reported to be more substantial.

The Rough Rider volunteers started out, in column of fours, toward the high hill looming over Siboney. Nearby, a regular army major could not contain himself.

"Goddamn it—they haven't even got a point out!"

It was tough going. As Davis pointed out, the men had been on the transports for two weeks, made a difficult landing, unloaded supplies, marched most of the night, slept a few hours on wet ground, and were then launched "under a cruelly hot sun, right into action." It was easier when they reached the top of the ridge, though Colonel Wood continued to push them hard, hoping to keep pace with Young's troops on the main road. Even the tireless Roosevelt grumbled a bit—"to myself"—about the pace Wood was setting.

As the trail narrowed and led into the jungle,. the veteran Apache fighter did establish points: first, two Cuban scouts; behind them five trailers under Sergeant Hamilton Fish; then Captain Allyn K. Capron's troop of sixty men. But it was impossible to put out flankers, Davis wrote, "for the reason that the dense undergrowth and the tangle of vines that stretched from the branches of the trees to the bushes below made it a physical impossibility for man or beast to move forward except along the beaten trail."

Stephen Crane had gotten a late start and was at the tail of the line of troopers, now advancing single file, "babbling joyously," Crane said, "arguing, recounting, laughing, making more noise than a train going through a tunnel." He knew from Guantánamo that the Spanish had adopted Cuban guerrilla tactics, and all the talk and laughter worried him. And then he heard "from hillock to hillock the beautiful coo of the Cuban wood-dove—ah, the wood-dove! the Spanish guerrilla wood-dove which had presaged the death of gallant marines." Alarmed, he remarked on the cooing to some of the men around him; the Spanish did not use the signal, he was told. The troopers rout-stepped on.

After an hour and a half, at a place where the trail narrowed and pitched steeply downward, Wood stopped his column. After conferring with Capron, he ordered Roosevelt, "Pass the word back to keep silence in the ranks." Crane heard it coming down the line: "'Stop talkin', can't ye, ——— it,' bawled a sergeant. 'Ah say, can't ye stop talkin'?' howled another."

Roosevelt paused to wipe off his glasses with a corner of his blue bandanna. A barbed-wire fence ran along the left side of the trail, where the foliage was less dense than on the right, and the ex-rancher picked up a strand that had been cut. The end of the wire was bright and shiny. "My God!" he exclaimed to Edward Marshall. "This wire has been cut today." Then, as troops began to deploy to both sides of the trail on Wood's orders, the terrible fusillade began, a continuous popping of soda corks and then, as the steel passed overhead, what Marshall described as "a long z-z-z-z-eu" or, as Roosevelt heard it, "a noise like the humming of telephone wires." And finally, when a bullet hit someone and he spun like a top, there was simply a *chug*. But nothing could be seen behind the curtain of forest before them. The Mausers were absolutely smokeless.

The Rough Riders had wanted first blood, and they got it. The point men went first. Sergeant Hamilton Fish, a giant of a man, scion of an old New York family, former captain of the Columbia crew, was hit by a slug that entered his left side, tore out the right, and slammed into the chest of Private

Ed Culver, a half-breed Cherokee. Fish had only time to gasp, "That bullet hit both of us," before he died. Private Tom Isbell, another Cherokee on point, thought he saw a Spaniard and fired at him. His shot triggered a staggering volley from the underbrush. Isbell was shredded by seven bullets, three in the neck. He began crawling to the rear.

On Wood's orders, Roosevelt had deployed three troops into the jungle on the east side of the trail. "I was told if possible to connect with the regulars who were on the right. In theory this was excellent, but as the jungle was very dense the first troop that deployed to the right vanished forthwith, and I never saw it again until the fight was over—having a frightful feeling meanwhile that I might be court-martialed for losing it." Roosevelt managed to hang on to the last platoon entering the forest and—in some semblance of order—position it on what he thought was the firing line.

Davis ran after Roosevelt. "It was like forcing the walls of a maze," he reported. "At one moment the underbrush seemed swarming with troopers and the next, except that you heard the twigs breaking, and the heavy breathing of the men, or a crash as a vine pulled someone down, there was not a sign of a human being anywhere."

Roosevelt finally came out "on a kind of shoulder, jutting over a ravine." Beyond that was a ridge, separating them from the regulars coming up the valley road. Probably the Spanish were entrenched on the ridge, but he still could not see them. Then Davis crawled up on his stomach and scanned his binoculars across the ravine. Suddenly, he spotted the distinctive conical hats of the Spanish troops.

"There they are, Colonel, look over there!" He gestured off to the right across the valley.

Roosevelt pointed them out to the men around him, got more troopers up on the firing line, and ordered quick-firing. The Spaniards flushed from their cover and retreated into the jungle. Apparently, they were hurt. The Rough Riders went after them, Davis reported, "in quick, desperate rushes— sometimes the ground gained was no more than a man covers in sliding for a base. . . . At all times the movement was without rest, breathless and fierce . . . every man had stripped as though for a wrestling match, throwing off all his impedimenta but his cartridge belt and canteen."

The Rough Riders were being hurt, too. Edward Marshall, back on the jungle trail with Wood, saw several troopers fall. "Every one went down in a lump without cries, without jumping up in the air, without throwing up hands." It was strange—"They just went down like clods in the grass. . . ."

Moments later Marshall heard a chug and "fell into the long grass, as much like a lump as had the other fellows."

Davis came again to the trail as troopers edged to the left seeking a better field of fire. A dressing station had been set up at the point where the cavalry column had first stopped. Davis saw "a tall, gaunt young man with a cross on his arm approaching . . . carrying a wounded man much heavier than himself across his shoulders." He realized he had seen the doctor before at "another time of excitement and rush and heat."

Hearst had paid Davis richly to cover the Yale-Princeton football game in 1895, and suddenly Davis remembered: "He had been covered with blood and dirt and perspiration as he was now, only then he wore a canvas jacket and the man he carried on his shoulders was trying to hold him back from a whitewashed line. And I recognized the young doctor with the blood bathing his breeches as "'Bob' Church, of Princeton."

A soldier passing Stephen Crane told him, "There's a correspondent up there all shot to hell." He led Crane to the spot where his friend and rival, Edward Marshall of the *Journal*, was lying. Marshall had been shot through the spine and was paralyzed. "Hello, Crane!" he said.

"Hello, Marshall! In hard luck old man?"

"Yes, I'm done for." He asked if Crane would file his dispatches, not ahead of his own, "but just file 'em if you find it handy."

Crane got some soldiers to carry Marshall back to the dressing station. Later the *World* reporter walked down to Siboney and sent the dispatches to William Randolph Hearst's *Journal*. The act of insubordination would cost him his job at the *World*.

To Davis, it sounded as though the firing had moved half a mile forward; the Spaniards had been driven back. He trotted quickly down the trail toward the front, despondently noting the horrors of war. "The rocks on either side were splattered with blood and the rank grass was matted with it. Blankets, haversacks, carbines, and canteens had been abandoned as though a retreating army had fled along it. . . ." Among the whistling of bullets he heard "the clatter of the land-crabs, those hideous orchid-colored monsters that haunt the places of the dead. . . ." They had come out to feed; later he would see the body of a dead trooper with his eyes torn out and his lips ripped off.

He passed the still form of Captain Allyn Capron; Roosevelt thought him perhaps the best soldier in the regiment. There was a big black spot on his chest. Another trooper was breathing with a "hoarse, inhuman rattle." And then he came across the body of Hamilton Fish, not shrunken like most dead bodies, but as large in death as it had been in life. The motto on the watch in his blouse, Davis observed, read, "God gives."

Davis went on, his boots cobbling over loose stones and thousands of Mauser shell casings. The country was more open now and he saw Roosevelt urging the troops up a hill toward red-tiled ranch houses on top of a hill. Roosevelt had taken cover behind a large palm and, just as he stuck his head out to scan the terrain, a Mauser bullet exploded through the tree driving dust and wood splinters into his left eye and ear.

You could tell, Davis observed, "which men were used to hunting big game in the West and which were not, by the way they made [their] rushes. The Eastern men broke at the word, and ran for the cover they were directed to take like men trying to get out of the rain . . . while the Western trappers and hunters slipped and wriggled through the grass like Indians. . . ."

Roosevelt picked up a carbine and fired a few shots at the Spanish. It seemed a far more satisfactory weapon than his sword, which had swung between his legs and tripped him up in the jungle all day. Wood was out of touch, so Roosevelt checked his men and told them to fire vigorously into the ranch buildings. "Then we heard cheering on the right, and I supposed this meant a charge on the part of Wood's men, so I sprang up and ordered the men to rush the buildings ahead of us. They came forward with a will."

Davis watched the exhausted Rough Riders charge in

amazement and admiration. "It was called 'Wood's bluff' afterward," he wrote, "for he had nothing to back it up with. . . . The Spaniards naturally could not believe that this thin line which . . . came cheering out into the hot sunlight in full view, was the entire fighting force against it. . . . As we knew it was only a bluff, the first cheer was wavering, but the sound of our own voices was so comforting that the second cheer was a howl of triumph."

The Spanish fired a few volleys and then, also under attack by Young's troops on their left flank, broke and ran. Unthinkingly, Joe Wheeler broke into a cry he had not delivered in more than thirty years: "Come on, boys, we've got the damn Yankees on the run!"

"When we arrived at the buildings," Roosevelt recalled, "panting and out of breath, they contained nothing but heaps of empty cartridge-shells and two dead Spaniards, shot through the head." The Rough Riders had spearheaded the army's first victory of the war.

Most of that morning it had not seemed like a victory at all. As the Rough Riders fell and thrashed in the grass, Crane wrote, "the heroic rumor arose, soared, screamed above the bush. Everybody was wounded. Everybody was dead. There was nobody. Gradually there was somebody. There was the wounded. . . . And the dead."

At the field dressing station, the badly wounded Rough Riders were being prepared for the trip back to Siboney. Edward Marshall, still conscious, heard a man quietly singing:

> "My country 'tis of thee,
> Sweet land of liberty . . ."

Soon most of the men joined in. Marshall remembered that "the quivering, quavering chorus, punctuated by groans and made spasmodic by pain, trembled up from that little group of wounded Americans in the midst of the Cuban solitude. . . ."

Eight Rough Riders were dead, and thirty-four had been wounded: Young's troopers had suffered a similar casualty rate. Stephen Crane's dispatch for the *New York World* attributed the losses to "a gallant blunder." Other accounts reported the Rough Riders had walked into a trap. Davis, who had thought the prospect of battle remote as they strolled down the jungle trail, first wrote to his family, "We were caught in a clear case of ambush," but later explained: "There is a vast difference between blundering into an ambuscade and setting out with the full knowledge that you will find the enemy in ambush. . . ." Roosevelt asserted that "there was no surprise; we struck the Spaniards exactly where we had expected." As to Wheeler's precipitate advance, he observed trenchantly that "war means fighting; and the soldier's cardinal sin is timidity."

Ambushed or not, the Rough Riders had shown extraordinary courage in dispersing and inflicting heavy casualties on a superior enemy force, later variously estimated at from twelve hundred to four thousand men, well entrenched, hidden from view in the jungle, and commanding the ridges above the trail. A Spanish soldier later reported, "The Americans were beaten, but persisted in fighting." Another, asked how the Americans had fought, replied, "They tried to catch us with their hands."

Two days later, as the bloodied Rough Riders camped near the little town of Sevilla, past the crossroads of Las Guásimas, Admiral Sampson anxiously wrote Long, "essential not to reduce this force too much for some few days, in view of the fact that the weather may compel me to coal at Guantánamo. Channel was not obstructed by the Merrimac and we must be prepared to meet the Spanish fleet if they attempt to escape."

A week earlier Long had informed Sampson that three of his best ships—the Iowa, the Oregon, and the Brooklyn—and four other vessels might soon be assigned to an Eastern Squadron under Commodore John C. Watson: "They will be sent to coast of Spain in the event of Cádiz division passing Suez, Egypt." The admiral's responsibilities were multiplying. He already had on his hands the blockades of Santiago, Havana, the north coast of Cuba, and San Juan, the convoying of army troopships, and their protection off Siboney, Daiquirí, and Guantánamo. Now Long wanted to strip him of important armor.

Two monitors had been ordered to reinforce Dewey at

Manila, and the auxiliary cruiser *Charleston* was also on its way with three troop transports, but Dewey had no armored ships and Long had to take the threat of the Cádiz squadron seriously. He hoped that a feint at the Spanish coast would force Cámara's recall.

Admiral Cámara had received his orders from Marine Minister Auñón on June 15: Take the battleship *Pelayo*, the armored cruiser *Carlos V*, two troop transports, and a posse of supporting vessels through the Strait of Gibraltar, proceed through the Mediterranean to Port Said, Egypt, pass through the Suez Canal, take on board "such Arabic personnel as you may deem necessary to lighten the arduous work of the firemen in the Red Sea," and continue eastward to the Philippines.

Cámara took the convoy out on the sixteenth—and was spotted passing Ceuta, the little Spanish enclave at the northeastern tip of Morocco. Dewey heard the news two days later. "With a superior squadron of the enemy coming," he wrote, the latter days of June were full of care. . . . In every cable from Washington we looked for fresh news about Cámara and hoped for decisive action by our troops and our squadron at Santiago. . . ."

One thing was now clear. Cámara would not be penned up in the Mediterranean by William Randolph Hearst. James Creelman, Hearst's correspondent-emissary in London, had failed in his effort to procure a merchant vessel to scuttle in the Suez Canal.

Long still dragged his feet on the matter of Hearst's naval commission, so the publisher turned his inventive mind to another pet project, a *Journal* beachhead in Cuba onto which he personally would lead a platoon of reporters and photographers. Ships were hard to find, but he managed to charter a steamer from the Baltimore Fruit Company and equipped it with modern, fast-shutter cameras, a darkroom, a huge supply of ice to chill developing chemicals, and a printing press to put out the Cuban *Journal-Examiner*. James Creelman, back from London, came aboard along with Jack Follansbee and photographer John Hemment.

Hemment wisely packed a formidable array of nostrums to counter the perils of the Cuban climate: quinine and belladonna for fever, Vaseline for sunburn, cholera drops for diarrhea, rhubarb pills for bowel complaints, and stout leggings for cacti—the so-called "Spanish bayonets." Hearst had everything he needed except horses, so the *Sylvia* first put in at Kingston, Jamaica. Hearst and Follansbee visited the local racetrack, bought some polo ponies, and stowed them aboard the *Sylvia*.

On June 18 they left for Santiago, where Hearst interviewed Sampson on the *New York* and, when the army arrived, Shafter aboard the *Segurança*. The austere admiral, perhaps recalling the *Journal's* melodramatic coverage of the *Maine* explosion, put on, Hearst thought, a "stiff, severe" front. But Shafter's very bulk awed Hearst. Shafter was, if not the model of a modern major general, at least "massive as to body—a sort of human fortress in blue coat and flannel shirt." Hemment was less favorably impressed: ". . . as I saw the general, stripped to his trousers and a light blue shirt, he seemed physically unfit for an arduous campaign."

Hearst finally hit the beach at Siboney, where the printing press was set up at the *Journal's* improvised headquarters. After interviewing General García, who presented him with a bullet-holed flag ("Its colors are faded, but it is the best thing the Cuban Republic can offer its best friend"), Hearst wrote that "he is a splendid old hero in spotless white linen from head to foot." Probably he did not know, at the time, that eight hundred of García's men, who were supposed to savage the Spanish rear at Las Guásimas, had given the cavalry lackadaisical support. And, as Roosevelt wrote to Lodge, "our Cuban scouts and guides ran like sheep at the first fire."

On June 27, Hearst climbed the steep hill above Siboney and made some notes in his new role as correspondent in chief of the *Journal*: ". . . from the top of a rough green ridge where I write this, we can see dimly on the sea the monstrous forms of Sampson's fleet lying in a semicircle in front of the entrance to Santiago harbor, while here at our feet masses of American soldiers are pouring from the beach into the scorching valley, where . . . vultures that have already fed on the corpses of slain Spaniards wheel lazily above the thorny, poisonous jungle of Santiago."

Hemment went to Las Guásimas, photographed the mass grave where seven Rough Riders had been interred, and reverently placed one of his little American flags on top. Then he made a point of visiting his colleague Edward Marshall, who had been taken aboard the *Olivette*, converted to a hospital ship. Creelman gave him a note for Marshall: "Cheer up, old man! . . . I trust you have passed the worst. . . . Keep up a good heart, and reserve the cot next to yours for me, as I may be with you before long."

Hearst wrote his mother that he had provided the hospital ship "with ice and delicacies which they lacked."

Frederic Remington had missed out on the fracas at Las Guásimas and he was determined to get to the front and stay there. With John Fox, Jr., of *Harper's Weekly*, Remington headed up what he called the Via del Rey toward Sevilla. The heat was overwhelming, and the folly of the army quartermaster corps was everywhere evident: "The sides of [the road] were blue with cast-off uniforms. . . . Men will not carry what they can do without. . . . In the tropics, mid-day marching under heavy knits kills more men than damp sleeping at night."

That evening Remington and Fox camped out near the front. The troopers were on half-rations, he noted, there was no tobacco, his flask had disappeared (probably into an insurgent's knapsack) "and it rained, rained, rained. We were very miserable." At least the troopers had dog tents, he and Fox only their ponchos. They put them down in "good, soft, soggy mud [and] turned into our wallow."

On Sunday the twenty-sixth, as Shafter completed the disembarkation of his forces at Siboney, the forward elements of his army were ordered to move westward along the Camino Real toward Santiago. There was no resistance as they trudged forward. Several miles along the muddy path, on the south side of the road, there was a high hill called El Pozo. Climbing the hill, Richard Harding Davis looked "across the basin that lay in the great valley which leads to Santiago. The left of the valley was the hills which hide the sea. The right of the valley was the hills in which nestle the village of El Caney. Below El Pozo, in the basin, the dense green forest stretched a mile and a half to the hills of San Juan. These hills looked so quiet and sunny and well kept that they reminded one of a New England orchard."

But Davis had also seen blockhouses on the San Juan Heights, and on Monday "a long yellow pit opened in the hillside ... and in it we could see straw sombreros rising and bobbing up and down ..." As the days passed, and the trenches grew in size and length, no artillery was brought up to shell the entrenchments, and no reconnaissance was allowed beyond El Pozo. Then Davis began to look upon the dense jungle between the Rough Riders and the San Juan Heights with foreboding. It looked, he thought, like a place where men could be "driven as cattle are chased into the chutes of the Chicago cattle-pen."

Brigadier General Adna R. Chaffee, who commanded a brigade in Henry Lawton's Second Infantry Division, joined Davis on the hill. Scanning the rough jungle road toward Santiago, he thought he saw a second trail branching off to the left that also debouched onto the brush-covered plain fronting the San Juan Heights. He explained to Davis what would happen if the army took this approach to Santiago: "Of course, the enemy knows where those two trails leave the wood; they have their guns trained on the openings. If our men leave the cover and reach the plain from those trails alone they will be piled up so high that they will block the road." He hoped that additional trails would be cut through the jungle to the plain, and also a path along the forest's edge. But Shafter's engineers were busy improving roads and building pontoon bridges from Siboney to Sevilla so that supplies could be brought up. The trails were not opened.

General Shafter appeared at El Pozo on the pleasant Thursday morning of June 30 and surveyed the triangle of jungle and plain between El Pozo, San Juan Hill, capped by its blockhouse and, to the north, El Caney, guarded by six wooden blockhouses, a stone fort, and a loopholed stone church where Cortez was said to have prayed before leaving to conquer Mexico. It seemed to him the army could not advance on the heights with this threatening fortification on its right flank.

Around noon, back at his headquarters between Sevilla and La Redonda, Shafter outlined a three-pronged attack to his generals. Lawton would take his infantry division and an artillery battery down the Camino Real, branch off to the north toward El Caney, camp for the night, and assault the town at daybreak on Friday. El Caney was thought to be lightly defended; Lawton could take it in two or three hours, then wheel southwest toward the Spanish left flank on the heights.

At the same time, a regiment of the newly landed Michigan troops would wind westward down the coast from Siboney and feint at Aguadores, pinning down troops General Arsenio Linares might otherwise bring up from the coast to reinforce the San Juan Heights. General Jacob F. Kent's First Infantry Division, with Joe Wheeler's cavalry on the right wing, would frontally assault the hills. But Wheeler was down with fever, and so was Sam Young. General Samuel S. Sumner was given temporary command of the cavalry and Wood that of Young's brigade. As a result, Roosevelt observed with delight, "I got my regiment."

Shafter's strategy, by his own admission, was not subtle. His blunt thrust toward Santiago over the San Juan Heights was pretty much a matter of "going straight for them." Time was an increasingly important factor. Shafter had spent a week unloading supplies and reinforcements. It rained now, every afternoon, heavily, as towering clouds billowed across the mountains. There was nothing like it in the United States, one officer remarked. "It was like standing under a barrel full of water and having the bottom knocked out." And the Cubans reported a Spanish relief column nearing the city. Shafter wanted to get there first.

He thought his light artillery adequate to soften up the rifle pits and blockhouses on the heights and did not ask the navy for a bombardment. French Chadwick always wondered why. "Day and night from the easy distance of 8000 yards half a hundred guns could have dropped a continuous shower of shell upon the position, making it absolutely untenable." It may have been, as critics later suggested, that Shafter did not want to share the glory of a victory with Sampson and the navy.

Timing seemed critical to Lawton. Around three P.M., when the meeting was over, he turned to Shafter's adjutant, Lieutenant Colonel Edward J. McClernand, who would be orchestrating the attack, and said: "McClernand, do not order the other divisions to attack until I get up. Give me time to reduce El Caney."

But once the chaotic assault began, not Shafter, well behind the lines, or McClernand, perched on El Pozo, could leash the "patriotic insanity," as Crane called it, that burst from the American army.

It seemed to Davis that all the elements of the army received orders to move out down the Camino Real at four P.M. that Thursday. "It was as though 15 regiments were encamped along the sidewalks of Fifth Avenue and were all ordered at the same moment to move into it and march down town. If Fifth Avenue were ten feet wide, you can imagine the confusion. . . .

"Twelve thousand men . . . treading on each other's heels in three inches of mud, move slowly. . . . The lines passed until the moon rose. . . . Midnight came, and they were still slipping forward." Finally, they came to their bivouac points near El Pozo and "along the trails to El Caney, waiting to march on it and eat it up before breakfast."

Captain George S. Grimes had been ordered to emplace his battery of light artillery on El Pozo by dawn on Friday, and as the sun rose he had just reached the hill. From a vantage point above him, Frederic Remington, lamenting the loss of his flask, sketched away as Grimes's battery, red guidons flashing, galloped their guns and caissons up the steep slope under whip and spur. Then they reached an escarpment and the charge came to a halt. In some embarrassment—the foreign military attachés were watching—the drivers dismounted and zigzagged their guns up the slope and into position. Grimes ranged them on the San Juan Heights, twenty-five hundred yards to the west, and waited for the attack on El Caney to begin.

Leonard Wood was not happy with the site chosen for the gun emplacements, remarking to Roosevelt that "he wished our brigade could be moved somewhere else, for we were directly in line of any return fire aimed by the Spaniards at the battery."

About 6:30 A.M., up the road to the north, there was a sudden crump as Captain Allyn Capron's artillery opened up on the defenses at El Caney. Only a few days earlier he had paid his respects at the Siboney gravesite of his son Allyn, killed

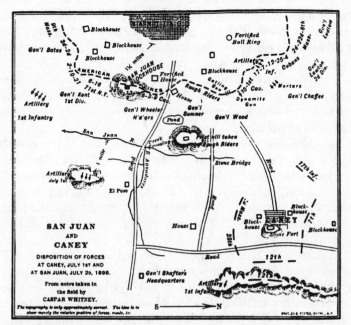

Caspar Whitney of *Harper's Weekly* mapped the defenses at Santiago. Note that north is to the right.

at Las Guásimas. Now he banged away with a vengeance, but his obsolete 3.2-inch field guns, armed with black powder charges, seemed to have little effect on the Spanish fortifications.

Chaffee, on Lawton's right flank, realized "there was not sufficient artillery there to demoralize the garrison." His troops began working their way up the hillside. First from the cover of thickets and rifle pits, then from blockhouses, the stone fortifications, and the towers of the church, the Spanish returned the fire. There were thought to be fewer than six hundred defenders at El Caney; if so, they were outnumbered more than ten to one. Lawton's confident troops made their first approach furtively, fearing the Spanish would run at the sight of their numbers. Later, a correspondent wrote, "we began to wonder if they were ever going to run."

On El Pozo, McClernand could hear the continuous popping of the Mausers. It was clear the Spaniards were putting up more resistance than expected. Shafter, light-headed from fever, his gouty foot swathed in burlap, exhausted by his trip to the front, had taken refuge in his headquarters tent. Sumner, Wheeler's replacement as commander of the cavalry, was anxious to get his troopers on the road. Around 8 A.M. he came up to Shafter's adjutant and asked impatiently, "Well, when are we going to begin this thing?" McClernand advised him of Lawton's injunction not to advance until the right wing was secure.

But McClernand could not wait all day. The Spanish might reinforce El Caney if the heights were not threatened. And just possibly, the vicious clamor of rifle fire across the valley meant that Lawton was closing in on his objective. He ordered Sumner and Kent to begin deploying along the jungle road; they could advance after the heights had been softened up by Grimes's artillery.

At 8:20 A.M., Grimes opened fire with his four guns. The first shot was short, the second long, but the third crashed through the red tile roof of the small blockhouse on San Juan Hill, blasting a satisfying cloud of stone, cement, and red tile dust into the air. With the range pinpointed, Grimes's continued a heavy fire. There was no response from the Spanish lines though, as Stephen Crane noted, clouds of billowing white smoke from the "old-fashioned powder . . . clearly defined [the battery] as though it had been the Chicago fire."

A Swedish military attaché, puzzled by the one-sided barrage, remarked: "I should think they would tire of receiving these. Have they, then, no artillery?"

Almost as he posed the question, Roosevelt heard "a peculiar whistling, singing sound in the air, and immediately afterward the noise of something exploding over our heads. . . . We sprung to our feet and leaped on our horses." A second shell burst overhead and a piece of shrapnel chunked off Roosevelt's wrist, "hardly breaking the skin, but raising a bump about as big as a hickory-nut." A third shell burst among the hacienda buildings where a troop of Cuban insurgents had bivouacked, scattering them "like guinea hens."

The rout was general, Remington observed, after the first shell spattered the hillside with chunks of steel. "Some as gallant soldiers and some as daring correspondents . . . did their legs proud there. The tall form of Major John Jacob Astor moved in my front in jack-rabbit bounds. . . . Directly came the warning scream of No. 2., and we dropped and hugged the ground like star-fish. Bang! Right over us it exploded."

Despite the Spanish shells, Grimes kept up his fire for about thirty minutes. Meanwhile, Sumner and then Kent started their divisions along the Camino Real toward the forest fronting the heights. The troops started out in column of fours but, as the muddy path narrowed, went into double file. From time to time, as the snaking tail of the column collapsed upon its head, bugles blew the order to halt.

During one pause that morning Private Charles Post looked up to see a large man in black civilian clothes seated on a small horse, his long legs dangling. He wore white socks, a crimson tie, and, on his straw hat, a matching crimson hatband. "It was William Randolph Hearst, who had fanned the flames of emotion in his New York *Journal* with tales of a beauteous maiden helpless in a cruel Spanish dungeon. . . ." In the hot Cuban jungle, it seemed wildly improbable to Post that he had once, on Hearst's instructions, designed *Maine* medals "for something or other."

Hearst was a New York man, known by sight to them all, and the infantrymen casually hailed him—"Hey, Willie!"

Then the bugle blew "Forward" and the column moved off. Hearst, poker-faced, took off his boater and waved it: "Good luck! Boys, good luck be with you."

A few hundred yards farther on, Post and the New York volunteers entered the jungle and began to hear the firecracker popping of the Mausers, and an occasional buzz as a bullet hit a tree. They were under fire at last. "I felt a tenseness in my throat, a dryness that was not a thirst, and little chilly surges in my stomach. . . ." They went on, lugging their heavy 1873 vintage, .45-caliber Springfield rifles which, Post observed, could "knock down two men, the one it hit and the one who fired it. For the kick was tremendous . . . and . . . there burst forth a cloud of white smoke somewhat the size of a cow."

The Spanish were familiar with the geography of the muddy trail that paralleled the Aguadores River until it met the San Juan, flowing from north to south down the basin fronting the San Juan Heights. Volley-firing, they concentrated a murderous fire on its sinuous course through the jungle, especially on those points where it crossed the streams. To make the passage even less pleasant, Spanish sharpshooters in forest-green uniforms had taken cover in the tops of the royal palms and behind mango trees on both sides of the jungle trail. They fired at everything in blue whether alive, wounded, or dead, at horses, at Red Cross workers, army surgeons—and correspondents. Crane thought "the gentry who contributed from the trees to the terror of this road" should be hung by the neck. He felt almost as strongly about the Signal Corps troops who had inflated a gas observation balloon—"huge, fat, yellow, quivering"—and dragged it down the trail by a heavy guy rope directly over the main body of troops. It made a perfect target for Spanish artillery and rifle fire and sheets of lead fell like Cuban rain on the troops beneath it.

Roosevelt was incensed, too. McClernand had personally given him orders (which he considered vague) to move forward, ford the San Juan River, hook to the right, "and then halt and await further orders; and I promptly hurried my men across, for the fire was getting hot, and the captive balloon, to the horror of everybody, was coming down to the ford."

Remington wormed his way down the trail on a mare he had acquired from a wounded colonel, calling out, "Gangway, please . . . gangway." The popping sound of the Mausers disconcerted him. "I could hear what sounded like a Fourth of July morning, when the boys are setting off their crackers." Someone had jumped the gun; it was only July the first.

He came out of the darkness of the jungle into a little clearing where troops were fording the San Juan, and someone shouted out, "Get down, old man; you'll catch one!" As he leaped off the mare, "A man came, stooping over, with his arms drawn up, and hands flapping downward at the wrists. That is the way with all people when they are shot through the body, because they want to hold the torso steady, because if they don't it hurts."

He forded the river and, as horses and mules fell bleeding and dead around him, abandoned his mare.

When First Lieutenant John J. Pershing of the Negro Tenth Cavalry (known to his devoted troops as "Black Jack") reached the ford—Bloody Ford, the troops called it—the bullet-shredded pongee-silk balloon had collapsed into the tops of trees nearby. "We were posted for a time in the bed of the stream to the right, directly under the balloon, and stood in water to our waists awaiting orders to deploy." A withering hail of shrapnel and Mauser fire frothed the water. Most of the officers had dismounted, but General Wheeler sat his horse in the middle of the stream. Hearing the shooting that morning, he had risen groggily from his sickbed and ridden to the front.

As Pershing lifted his hat in salute, a large chunk of shrapnel crashed between them and a sheet of water soaked them both. Wheeler returned the salute. "The shelling seems quite lively," he observed.

As the Seventy-first New York pressed forward, Private Post's foot slipped and he looked down. "The trail underfoot was slippery with mud. It was mud made by the blood of the dead and the wounded, for there had been no showers that day. The trail on either side was lined with the feet of fallen men. . . . Over four hundred men were killed or wounded in that trail and at that ford" by the fire converging on the accursed Signal Corps balloon.

The observers in the bobbling inflatable had performed one useful service, confirming the existence of a second trail through the jungle crossing the San Juan River about four hundred yards downstream. General Kent had found the path opening and ordered the Seventy-first New York off the main road, which was jammed with troops approaching the grass-covered plain fronting the heights. Even so, the neck of the Camino Real bottle was plugged by a mass of densely packed troops who had halted when they reached the edge of the forest.

"The situation was desperate," Davis thought. "Military blunders had brought 7000 American soldiers into a chute of death. . . ." Then, for an hour, as they waited in the steaming jungle, "Men gasped on their backs, like fishes in the bottom of a boat . . . with faces aflame, and their tongues sticking out, and their eyes rolling. All through this the volleys from the rifle-pits sputtered and rattled, and the bullets sang continuously like the wind through the rigging in a gale . . . and still no order came from General Shafter."

Roosevelt had led his exhausted regiment across the river into open, grass-covered forest land. He was on the right flank of the army's thrust toward the Santiago heights. Now he could see the trail leading up toward the city over a cut between two fortified hills—San Juan on the left, and on the right, closer, a height that would be called Kettle Hill after the huge iron sugar-refining pot that dominated its crest. His men were under a withering fire: "Mauser bullets drove in sheets through the trees and the tall jungle grass . . . man after man in our ranks fell dead or wounded. . . ." Roosevelt sent one messenger after another to Sumner and Wood asking permission to advance. Finally, around 1 P.M. an officer rode up "through the storm of bullets with the welcome command 'to move forward and support the regulars in the assault on the hills in front.'" His specific objective was the red-tiled ranch house on top of Kettle Hill. Roosevelt sprang into the saddle of Texas. His "crowded hour" had begun.

Slowly, at first—"Always when men have been lying down under cover for some time, and are required to advance, there is a little hesitation"—Roosevelt got the regiment moving forward. Soon they came across the hunkered-down bodies of regular infantry. Roosevelt thought it "silly" for them to stay where they were—"the thing to do was to try to rush the entrenchments"—but the regulars had not received orders to assault the kettle-topped height. The lieutenant colonel announced that as the ranking officer he would give the order—it was the kind of unplanned battle, he wrote later, where everyone had to act on their own responsibility. An elderly captain of the regulars was reluctant to accept the order.

"Then let my men through, sir," Roosevelt commanded, and spurred Texas on through the lines of regulars followed by his grinning troopers. That proved too much for the veterans; they jumped up and followed, "all being delighted at the chance," as Roosevelt waved his hat with the blue polka-dot bandanna fixed to its aft brim and ordered the charge.

Independently, on the left and the right, Roosevelt saw that "the whole line, tired of waiting, and eager to close with the enemy . . . slipped the leash at almost the same moment. . . . By this time we were all in the spirit of the thing and greatly excited by the charge, the men cheering and running forward between shots. . . ."

Elements of three regiments staggered and scrabbled up the hillside toward the Spanish entrenchments several hundred yards away. Someone was shouting, "Dress on the colors, boys, dress on the colors!" You could see no smoke from the line, Crane marveled, and no men, but you could hear "a noise like a million champagne corks." A military attaché, appalled by the thin blue line on the hillside, turned to Crane: "It's plucky, you know! By Gawd it is plucky! But *they can't do it!*"

Davis, appointed an honorary captain of the Rough Riders after Las Guásimas, watched from a point near Bloody Ford. He could hardly believe what he saw. *There were so few of them!* "One's instinct was to call to them to come back. You felt that someone had blundered and that these few men were blindly following out some madman's mad order . . . the folly of such a sacrifice was what held you."

Over on the left General Hamilton S. Hawkins began leading Kent's regulars up San Juan. Crane wrote: "Then suddenly someone yelled, 'By God, there go our boys up the hill' . . .

"Yes, they were going up the hill, up the hill. It was the best moment of anybody's life."

On Texas, Roosevelt galloped ahead of his men toward the ranch buildings on the crest of Kettle Hill. Rumor had it he was being boomed back in New York for the governorship. If he wanted to be a governor, one of his men observed, "it must have been in Hades, for no one courted death more." Another, who had thought the dude in spectacles foppish back in San Antonio, now "wouldn't undertake to harness him with a pitchfork."

Forty yards from the crest Texas ran into a wire fence. The horse had been bloodied twice by bullets, one of which nicked Roosevelt in the elbow. Roosevelt jumped off and ran on up the hill with his orderly, Henry Bardshar, a tough Arizona miner. The Spanish defenders were abandoning the ranch houses now, running westward toward Santiago. And then flag bearers of the various cavalry units rushed the crest of Kettle Hill and proudly rammed the staffs of their yellow guidons into the bloody earth.

Frederic Remington, who had nearly been killed by a sniper and had now lost his sketchbook as well as his flask, struggled on behind the Rough Riders. He did not think the hills could be taken, but after a while he looked up from where he was hugging the ground and saw American soldiers on the hilltop. The rain of Mauser bullets slackened. A flag was broken out, and there was a cheer. "'Cheer' is the word for that sound. You have got to hear it once when it means so much, and ever after you will grin when Americans make that noise."

Roosevelt had a fine view of Hawkins's charge up San Juan from a sheltered point near the bulbous iron kettle on top of the hill. He organized volley fire to support the charge. Suddenly, above the rattle of rifle fire, there was a fierce drumming roar off to the left. A trooper yelled, "The Spanish machine guns!"

Roosevelt listened intently, then slapped his thigh and shouted exultantly: "It's the Gatlings men, our Gatlings!"

The Rough Riders had brought four of the rapid-fire guns. Each had ten barrels rotating around a central axis and could fire sixty shots per second. A stream of lead scythed over the Spanish rifle pits. The Rough Riders cheered.

When General Sumner rode up behind the First Cavalry banner, Roosevelt asked permission to lead an attack on a northern extension of the San Juan Heights. Sumner assented and fragments of several regiments charged across a valley past a small lake fronting the Spanish entrenchments. As he chugged along toward the trench line, outstripped by some of the "long-legged men," Roosevelt could see Spanish regulars in their blue and white pin-striped "pajamas" running to the rear. But two soldiers leaped up and, at a distance of ten yards, fired at Roosevelt and Bardshar.

"I closed in and fired twice, missing the first and killing the second. My revolver was from the sunken battleship *Maine*, and had been given me by my brother-in-law, Captain W. S. Cowles of the Navy." Reaching the trenches, Roosevelt found them filled with corpses. "Most of the fallen had little holes in their heads from which their brains were oozing. . . ." Under heavy fire the exhausted cavalry troopers were ordered by Sumner to regroup and dig in on the heights they had taken. A counterattack was expected, and while reinforcements poured up the hillside, the line was very thin.

Over on the right, at El Caney, the sound of firing finally slackened around 3 P.M. as Chaffee's brigade took the stone fort of El Viso anchoring the Spanish defense of the town. James Creelman, a firm believer in Hearst's "journalism of action," was in the van of the charge, trying to capture the Spanish flag for the *Journal*. "The *Journal* had provoked the war, and it was only fair that the *Journal* should have the first flag captured. . . ." He found it outside El Viso, attached to a shell-shattered flagstaff, but a few minutes later, inside the fort, he felt a stinging pain as a Mauser bullet slammed into his left shoulder. As he was carried outside on a Spanish hammock to a dressing station, the troops cheered him and one placed the flag over him.

He lay in the hot sun for some time. A black soldier nearby addressed a vulture: "Wastin' yo' time, suh." Then "some one knelt in the grass beside me and put his hand on my fevered head. Opening my eyes, I saw Mr. Hearst . . . a straw hat with a bright ribbon on his head, a revolver at his belt . . .

"'I'm sorry you're hurt, but'—and his face was radiant with enthusiasm—'wasn't it a splendid fight? We must beat every paper in the world. . . .'"

Creelman began dictating to the proprietor of the *Journal* his account of the battle at El Caney.

Shortly afterward, Stephen Crane and some of the other correspondents—Davis, Remington, Fox, Jimmy Hare of *Collier's*—reached the top of the San Juan Heights. Mauser fire from the outskirts of Santiago still swept overhead, and the men were crouched down behind the crest of the hill. Crane, however, garbed in a shiny white rubber raincoat, smoking a pipe, strolled leisurely down the parapet in full view of the Spanish. No one knew why. He might have been thinking about courage and cowardice, themes he had explored in *The Red Badge of Courage*.

Wood, lying almost at his feet, shouted at him to get down. "You're drawing fire on these men!"

Crane did not, or pretended not, to hear him. As the firing intensified, he kept staring at the Spanish lines. Hare yelled out, too, suggesting that Crane wanted to get wounded to boost Pulitzer's circulation. Still, nothing happened.

Then Richard Harding Davis got to him. He knew that Crane disdained "anything that savored of a pose." He called out, "You're not impressing anyone by doing that, Crane." Crane dropped to his knees and crawled over to Davis, grinning.

The situation, as Davis saw it, was still desperate. The army had taken the heights, but at great cost, and the troops were hot, thirsty, hungry, wet, without tobacco, and short of ammunition. "They were seldom more than a company at any one spot, and there were bare spaces from 100 to 200 yards apart held by only a dozen men." Lawton's troops, held up by new resistance southwest of El Caney, had not yet connected with their exposed right flank. "The position," Davis wrote, "was painfully suggestive of Humpty-Dumpty on the wall."

Remote as they were from the main body of the army, rumors began to circulate: Lawton's casualties were severe; the Spanish relief column had arrived in Santiago; Shafter was considering withdrawing the thin line of vulnerable blue coats from the heights they had won.

Roosevelt, who had dined on captured salted flying fish, did not think there was any truth to the rumor they might be ordered to fall back. He was wrong. That night, General Wheeler told the acting colonel to have his troops ready to retreat. Roosevelt allowed that they might not obey such an order—"If we have to move out of here at all I should be inclined to make the rush in the right direction."

Wheeler looked feverish and frail in the moonlight. He paused a moment, then vigorously nodded assent. "He was a gamecock if ever there was one," Roosevelt thought.

X

LAMBS TO SLAUGHTER

We Spanish are very proud of the disaster of Trafalgar on account of the heroism which our navy showed on that occasion, when they placed honor above everything else, though our ships were buried in the sea. The battle of Santiago de Cuba is much more glorious even than that of 1805.

—Lieutenant José Müller y Tejeiro

The work begun by General Simon Bolívar in expelling the Spanish from Venezuela, in 1822, was completed on July 3, 1898, at Santiago de Cuba, when Cuba was rescued from the Spanish yoke.

—Commodore Winfield Scott Schley

T HAT FRIDAY NIGHT, as a damp chill fell over the battlefield and the firing subsided, Crane, Davis, Remington, and some of the other correspondents and photographers straggled back toward El Pozo. Crane thought the bloody jungle trail even more dreadful in the darkness. "The wounded men, stumbling along in the mud, a miasmic mist from the swampish ground filling their nostrils, heard often in the air the whiplash sound of a bullet that was meant for them by the lurking guerillas." After they had gone a mile or so, passing dark forms of dead men and horses, hearing anxious cries of "Litter bearer!" they came to "great populous hospitals" where army surgeons operated by the faint light of the moon and by flickering candlelight. Frederic Remington found the trail hard to describe. "The rear of a battle. All the broken spirits, bloody bodies, hopeless, helpless suffering . . . men out of their minds from sunstroke, dead men, and men dying." He had been calm during the fight but now found his nerves unsettled. The artist told his colleagues that he "would in the future paint set pieces for dining-rooms. . . . The novelist allowed that he would be forced to go home and complete 'The Romance of a Quart Bottle.' The explorer declared that his treatise on the 'Flora of Bar Harbor' was promised to his publishers."

As Davis staggered past the carnage (he suffered from sciatica and Crane had to help him along), he reflected that the men on the San Juan Heights clung to the crest only "by their teeth and fingernails, and it seemed as though at any moment their hold would relax and they would fall." "Another such victory," Davis thought, "and our troops must retreat."

On Sampson's flagship Captain French Chadwick again considered the consequences of army hubris. San Juan Hill was only about four and a half miles from the ring of steel around the harbor entrance. The fleet had sixty-four big guns, ranging in size from 8 to 13 inches, that could lob shells over five miles. They could have unrolled a devastating carpet of fire across the fortifications guarding Santiago; "the Spanish forces would have become so demoralized that the American troops could have entered the city at once with little or no difficulty."

Instead, Shafter was stalled and the fleet continued its endless patrol around the Morro bastion. The blockade was now in its thirty-fifth day, and the strain was beginning to tell. A seaman named R. Cross aboard the Oregon had recorded in his personal log for June 3, "Nothing doing but laying off hear [sic] and watching what looks like to me a big hole in the grond. same thing the 4th and 5th." Toward the end of the month Cross summed up, "there is nothing doing but laying around hear like a lot of sharks watching for a fish." When Commodore Schley began the blockade on June 29, he directed his ships to pace back and forth, five to ten miles off the Morro, ready to steam directly at the harbor entrance should Cervera attempt to break out. It was a workable tactic, but wasteful of coal, hazardous at night, and too loose. Shortly after Sampson arrived and took command two days later, he established a close-in, "immobile" blockade, positioning the ships in a six-mile semicircle around the harbor mouth with enough steam up to hold place against wind and tide. It would take the fleet at least ten minutes to achieve speed, but Cervera could only come out in slow single file through the twisty, narrow channel, and that would give the American ships time to fire up their boilers.

On June 12 the blockading crescent around the Morro was reduced to about three miles by day, and two by night. The newer battleships were equipped with 100,000-candlepower searchlights, and Sampson ordered them trained on the harbor entrance when the moon, full on June 1, was not strong enough to provide illumination. The duty was taken, in turn, by the *Massachusetts*, the *Oregon*, and the *Iowa*, and all found it daunting. Even "Fighting Bob" Evans thought it risky to go in within a mile or so of shore in front of "two of the fastest torpedo boats in the world." Captain Charles Clark of the *Oregon* worried about the Spanish batteries on the Socapa and the Morro. Night after night, Clark observed, as the searchlight pinpointed his ship's location like a fixed star, "I used to look at the dark forms of my crew sleeping on deck, for the heat made anything else impossible, and think what havoc in their ranks a well-directed fire would make." No one could imagine what kept the Spanish from shooting at the searchlights.

They kept the tedious vigil, Ed ("Guncotton") Murphy of the *Oregon* thought, like cats around a rat hole. Almost no one expected the rats to come out. That would mean destruction to no end. Better to stay holed up, defend the city with their guns and marines, hope that malaria and yellow fever would afflict the exposed American troops, pray for a hurricane, and scuttle if all else failed.

Shortly after the gray dawn of Saturday, July 2, a drizzle began to pock the slush of the Camino Real. In his headquarters tent near Sevilla, General William Rufus Shafter sprawled uncomfortably on a cot and nervously considered his options. Heat, gout, fever—and the desperate struggle for El Caney and the San Juan Heights—had taken the fight out of him. His troops had outnumbered the Spanish defenders, yet had been brought to their knees, in shaky defensive positions, on the crest of bleak wet hills they might not be able to hold. (In Santiago that morning naval lieutenant José Müller y Tejeiro, assigned to the city's port defenses, marveled at Shafter's naïveté. "Did they think . . . all they had to do was to attack our soldiers en masse and put them to flight?")

Shafter knew casualties were high, but had yet to grasp the severity of the army's losses. When the body counts were tallied, they recorded almost 1,200 wounded and over 200 dead—virtually 10 percent of Shafter's effective force. It seemed to him the army had done its duty; clearly, it was time for the navy to make a similar sacrifice. He sent a message to Sampson: "Terrible fight yesterday. . . . I urge that you make effort immediately to force the entrance, to avoid future losses among my men, which are already very heavy. You can now operate with less loss of life than I can."

Sampson read the message with consternation. In his view, Shafter had chosen the wrong point of attack, then failed to coordinate it with naval firepower. The stack of the Merrimac poked out of the water off Estrella Point, a grim reminder of what mines could do. Not that one was needed. The first ship on which Sampson had served, the Patapsco, had been blown out of the water during the Civil War while removing mines, with the loss of sixty men. The admiral had seen with his own eyes what a mine had done to the Maine in Havana Harbor. If his lead ships were sunk, the others, jamming up behind, would be at the mercy of Cervera's guns and those of the shore batteries.

And Shafter ignored the main point. Men could be replaced, but ships could not. There was not a single battleship being built in the United States that could take to the water in fighting trim for at least six months. Sampson promptly sent a reply to Shafter: "Impossible to force entrance until we can clear channel of mines—a work of some time after forts are taken possession of by your troops."

Shafter replied, rather petulantly, that he did not know when—or even if—the forts could be taken. That would mean additional, heavy casualties. "I am at a loss to see why the Navy can not work under a destructive fire as well as the Army."

Sampson replied sharply: ships, not personnel casualties, were his primary concern. They were needed for the Philippines, for the investment of the Spanish coastline, for the invasion of Puerto Rico. He would make an attempt to force the entrance, if the general desired it, but added that "our position and yours would be made more difficult if, as is possible, we fail in our attempt."

Sampson added that he had begun countermining operations and proposed a meeting the following morning to coordinate land-sea operations, perhaps an army assault on the Morro while marines from Guantánamo hit the beaches near the Socapa batteries. Since Shafter was unable to get down to Siboney ("I am prostrate in body and mind," he told one of the attachés), the meeting would have to take place near Sevilla.

Shafter, meanwhile, left Washington in the dark. On Friday night he had cabled that after "a very heavy engagement" his troops had taken the Spanish outer works. "There is now about three-quarters of a mile of open country between my lines and the city." Press reports in New York and Washington were generally sanguine. The *Journal* announced, MORRO CASTLE OURS, and declared that Sampson's ships would momentarily enter the harbor. This did little to cheer McKinley and Alger, who waited nervously all Saturday for news from the front.

Despondent, dazed by heat and fever, unable even to leave his tent, frustrated by Sampson's lucid replies to his plaintive entreaties, Shafter seemed unable to cope with the bleak situation he faced. But on Saturday evening he managed to rise from his cot and, perhaps in the elegant, single-seated buckboard transported to Cuba for his comfort, rode to a 7 P.M. meeting with his generals at El Pozo.

Reclining on a door liberated from one of the farmhouses, Shafter outlined the army's unpromising position. The Spanish were about to be reinforced by the relief column from Manzanillo. A Spanish counterattack might sweep away the thin line of troops holding the heights. The long supply line leading back to Siboney—what was left of it after the rains that day—could be enfiladed. Malarial fevers had begun to afflict the army. Many had counseled retreat, warning that the alternative was "utter defeat."

The four division commanders—Wheeler, Kent, Lawton, and John C. Bates—chewed it over for almost two hours. Shortly before nine Shafter called for a vote. Kent cast his for withdrawal, the others against. Shafter announced that for the time being the troops would hold their positions. The meeting was over.

Still, Shafter did not cable the secretary of war. At one o'clock on Sunday morning, Alger cabled Shafter: "We are awaiting with intense anxiety tidings of yesterday." Three hours later, still without word from Shafter, McKinley went to bed.

In all this, Shafter seemed hardly to consider that the Spanish might also have problems. They, too, had taken heavy losses at El Caney and San Juan. Over 200 were killed, including 22 officers. General Vara del Rey, leading the gallant defense of El Caney, was hit in both legs and killed, along with his two sons, as he was being carried to the rear. General Arsenio Linares, commander-in-chief of the Fourth Army Corps of Santiago, was seriously wounded near San Juan Hill. General José Torál y Velásquez took his place.

More than a thousand seamen, led by Cervera's chief of staff, Joaquín Bustamente, took positions behind the troops defending the heights. Bustamente took a bullet in the abdomen and was carried to a hospital in the city. Wounded soldiers were fighting in the trenches. Colonel Federico Escario's relief column was within a few miles of the city on Saturday afternoon, but he had lost more than 10 percent of his force on the grueling 160-mile march from Manzanillo to Cuban bullets, disease, and desertion. Only about 3,300 men, exhausted by their nine-day forced march over the mountains, virtually without provisions, would straggle into the city. Ammunition was in short supply, the civilian population was starving and disease-ridden, and the water supply had been cut off. Worst of all, Admiral Pascual Cervera was preparing to abandon the city.

To the very end Cervera resisted making a sortie, but the decision had been taken out of his hands on June 24 when Marine Minister Ramón Auñón reminded the admiral that he operated under the overall command of Governor-General Blanco. Cervera was relieved that he would not have to take, on his own responsibility, "extreme measures of the utmost importance."

The next day Cervera sent off the first of a series of woeful messages to Blanco in Havana listing, once again, the deficiencies of the squadron in ammunition, guns, training, speed, coal, and, with so many men sent ashore to aid in the defense of Santiago, crew. In case Blanco missed the point, he concluded, "it is absolutely impossible for squadron to escape under these circumstances."

As Segismundo Bermejo had once tried to thrust Cervera into a more active and optimistic posture, so now did Ramón Blanco. Since the fleet was more important than the beleaguered city, he urged Cervera (through General Linares, who was becoming an intermediary in the increasingly bitter correspondence) to leave Santiago as soon as possible. The moral effect of losing the squadron without a fight would be severe. Surely it was possible to go—a number of ships had recently run the blockade of Havana at night.

Cervera responded that the squadron had been doomed since it sailed from Cape Verde. That "mistake" was not his; what happened now was not his responsibility. In any case, Havana and Santiago harbors were not similar. A single-file departure from his anchorage could only ensure the destruction of the ships and the death of their crews. Why sacrifice them to vanity? If the fleet had to be destroyed, at least let it contribute to the defense of the city. "I, who am a man without ambitions, without mad passions . . . state most emphatically that I shall never be the one to decree the horrible and useless hecatomb which will be the only possible result of the sortie. . . ."

On June 26, Blanco replied cautiously: "It seems to me you somewhat exaggerate difficulties of sortie. It is not a question of fighting, but of escaping from that prison in which the squadron is unfortunately shut in. . . ." The sortie could be made "in dark night and bad weather," or "while part of enemy's ships are withdrawn." He warned bluntly: "The eyes of every nation are at present fixed on your squadron, on which the honor of our country depends, as I am sure your excellency realizes."

Cervera seemed to understand that. The next day he replied: "I construe your excellency's telegram as an order to go out, and therefore ask General Linares for reembarkation of forces which were landed at your excellency's suggestion. I beg that you will confirm the order of sortie, because it is not explicit. . . ."

If "the fall of Santiago is believed near," Blanco responded, "the squadron will go out immediately, as best it can." But it was not until after the battle of Friday, July 1, that Blanco ordered Cervera to get the thousand-odd sailors back on board and leave at the earliest possible moment. Cervera ordered fires lighted under the boilers of his ships and began working out the logistics of a Saturday afternoon sortie. The acting commander of the Fourth Corps, José Torál, was ordered by Blanco to maintain the defense of the city at any price until the squadron left. "Main thing is that squadron go out at once, for if Americans take possession of it Spain will be morally defeated and must ask for peace at mercy of enemy. A city lost can be recovered; the loss of the squadron . . . can not. . . ."

Captain Víctor Concas, who had taken the post of chief of staff in Bustamente's absence, went ashore at 7 A.M. on Saturday to meet with Torál and arrange the reembarkation of the squadron's sailors. At the same time, Cervera sent an aide carrying a thick file of secret dispatches scurrying to the archbishop of Santiago. He had no intention of letting the "hecatomb" be laid at his doorstep. In Spain the admiral had sent his cousin Juan Spottorno copies of official correspondence "in defense of my memory." Now, Concas reported, Cervera wisely put "in the hands of the archbishop all the original documents of the tragedy." In the event that the María Teresa went down, at least their honor would be salvaged.

Most of the seamen ashore were swiftly embarked, but the sailors of the Vizcaya, in positions north of the city, did not arrive at the loading docks until 4 P.M., after a long march. It took two and a half hours to get them aboard. Captain Antonio Eulate ordered the battle flag hoisted and reminded his officers of the heroic deeds of their ancestors. After a prayer they knelt and were given a benediction by the ship's chaplain. But no orders came from the flagship. Cervera, never one to move hastily, had decided to let the weary crews rest until Sunday morning.

The order of battle was established and pilots were taken aboard the cruisers to guide them through the narrow channel. Lookouts on the Morro reported that three American ships, the *New Orleans*, the *Newark*, and the *Suwanee*, had steamed off the blockading ring headed east, presumably to Guantánamo to coal. That would at least reduce the odds. Cervera asked Concas to reconnoiter the harbor entrance at dawn; last-minute adjustments in their plans might be required. Obscured by fitful rain and low clouds, smoke wisped from the stacks of the squadron as coal passers fired up the boilers.

At sunset that evening, on the bridge of the *Iowa*, Lieutenant F. K. Hill, the officer of the deck, called Captain Evans's attention to columns of smoke pluming up beyond the entrance to the harbor. Evans did not consider the sighting unusual. The Spanish often moved their vessels around. But his signal quartermaster was taking no chances. He bent Signal 250—"Enemy's ships escaping"—to the mast and had it ready to hoist.

On the *Brooklyn* that afternoon Schley, wearing a white rubber coat for protection from the heavy rains, had noticed a little Spanish gunboat puffing around the harbor entrance. Possibly, it was fussing with the channel mines. He also saw the plumes of smoke. The commodore sent the news over to the *New York* via the *Vixen*. The little armed yacht returned with a message from the flagship: Watch carefully.

Sampson, Chief Yeoman Fred Buenzle noted, looked tired and worn. For more than a month, night and day, he had coped with the endless details of the blockade. Now the army had gotten itself in a bind and the navy had somehow to ease the pressure. That night Buenzle worked until after midnight with Sampson and French Chadwick as they devised new battle orders, then retired.

As the clock tolled five bells—2:30 A.M.—"there was a knock on the door of the little office in which I had my bunk, and when I pulled aside the drapes I saw the admiral . . . in striped pajamas, his wide, staring eyes dry and hot for want of sleep." The admiral carefully explained some changes he wanted made in a message concerning the meeting with Shafter in the morning. Buenzle took the cable and retyped it, wondering if the admiral ever slept. "Yes, he did, for when I took the finished message into the cabin for his approval he was sitting at his table, his head down on his arms, an untouched cup of tea alongside him. What a pity I had to awaken him!"

Shortly after Sampson finally turned in for a few hours' sleep, the *Massachusetts* left to coal at Guantánamo. At noon on July 2, there had been fourteen ships in the blockading ring around Santiago. Now only ten remained.

At 7 A.M. the Spanish gunboat *Alvarado* cautiously poked its bow through the morning mist near the harbor entrance. The haze soon burned off and Víctor Concas scanned the arc of defense in front of Santiago with his binoculars. The big ships, from left to right, were the *Indiana*, the *New York*, the *Oregon*, the *Iowa*, the *Texas*, and the *Brooklyn*. Four auxiliaries filled in gaps in the line. The *Massachusetts* was absent—that was a pleasant surprise—and the *Brooklyn* was out of position; even from his crow's nest perch forty feet above the water, Concas could barely make her out. He put down the binoculars and picked up a stadimeter with a maximum range of 7,656 yards. The *Brooklyn* was beyond the grasp of its optics. He estimated she was five and a half miles from the harbor entrance, well past her normal three-mile daytime patrol distance, and closer to the *Texas* than was normal. Only a small yacht guarded the space between the cruiser and the shore.

The *Brooklyn* was considered the swiftest ship in the American squadron. At a captain's meeting the day before Cervera had ordered that the *Infanta María Teresa* would lead the charge out of the channel and try to ram Schley's cruiser. The fleet Spanish cruisers and destroyers would follow in column, turn inside the flagship and try to escape westward to Cienfuegos or Havana.

"The words of the admiral," Concas recalled, "were received with enthusiasm, and we all clasped hands fervently, as soldiers who knew how to meet death and destruction, from which no power could save us."

Concas's pessimism was, to a degree, well founded. The eleven-hundred-yard channel leading out from Smith Cay was very narrow. There was a shoal, El Diamante—Diamond Bank—off Socapa where it debouched into the Caribbean. This squeezed the mouth of the channel to a width of about seventy-five yards. The ships would have to come out in slow single-file, drop their pilots, and give the shoal a wide enough berth to avoid running aground. The sunken *Merrimac* would also act as a brake on their speed. Concas estimated that, in turning past the old collier, the screws of the Spanish cruisers would come within three or four yards of the wreck. As the ships sortied, one by one, some five minutes apart, they would meet the concentrated fire of the entire American fleet.

Still, they would have the element of surprise, would be under forced draft, the Morro and Socapa batteries would provide covering fire—and the American line looked thin to the west. With luck, some ships might escape; if they did not, honor, at least, would have been served.

Concas returned to the flagship to make his report. Cervera, sipping a cup of hot chocolate, ordered the signal *Zafarando de combate* (Clearing for action) run up. The ships of the squadron weighed anchor and the signal for the sortie was hoisted: *"¡Viva España!"* The crews, and the soldiers stationed along the high banks of the harbor, began to cheer.

Almost everyone remarked on the weather that morning. Saturday's rains had washed the sky clean. Concas had thought it a bit foggy at first light, but when the sun came up, it was clear as a bell. "The sun does not rise, in Cuba," AP correspondent George Graham observed on the *Brooklyn*. "It jumps above the horizon . . . and extinguishes the stars." Cadet Mannix on the *Indiana* was dazzled by the sudden brightness—"not a cloud in the sky, the atmosphere clear as gin, visibility absolutely perfect." The surface of the sea was like polished glass, though a heavy surf broke on the rocky beaches.

On the *Brooklyn*, Schley rose early and put on white ducks, white shoes, white summer hat without insignia of rank, and, Graham thought, a rather shabby blue coat. With some annoyance Schley noted that the *Massachusetts* had left station; Sampson had not bothered to inform him that the battleship was to coal.

After breakfast he surveyed the blockading fleet. The *New York*, on the eastern quarter of the crescent around Santiago, was perhaps five miles distant. The diameter of the arc, from the little *Vixen* off to port, to the *Gloucester* east of the Morro, was about eight miles. Then, at about eight-fifty, he saw the *New York* circle and head eastward, signaling, "Disregard movements of commander in chief." The torpedo boat *Ericsson* and the armed yacht *Hist* steamed after the flagship. That was odd. It seemed to him later that Sampson should have gone in the *Gloucester*, leaving the fast, formidable *New York* on line. One thing at least was clear. The commodore would shortly be the senior officer of the blockading squadron. But his command—if it was a command—had dwindled. Now, of the fourteen ships blockading on Saturday noon, only seven remained, and two of them were armed yachts.

Cervera had gotten lucky.

On the *Indiana*, Cadet Mannix noted, everyone on board prepared for Call to Quarters by putting on the freshest white uniform they could muster. "It was the first Sunday of the month and in accordance with Navy custom, we expected to have Captain's Inspection followed by Divine Service and the reading of the Articles of War." All over the fleet, signalmen took the Blue Cross—the only pennant ever flown above the national colors—from their flag chests and prepared to hoist.

As the *New York* settled into an easy gait for Siboney, William Sampson, dressed in a fatigue uniform, strapped on leggings and spurs for his ride from Siboney to Sevilla. George Strollom, his steward, had three sandwiches made up in the galley and Sampson stuck them in his pocket. On the bridge, he called for Buenzle and began dictating a memorandum listing the points he wanted to make at the meeting with Shafter.

At almost that same moment, at the military hospital in Santiago, Lieutenant Müller paid his respects to Captain Joaquín Bustamente. The wounded chief of staff seemed alright physically, but despondent. Müller, who had convinced himself that a Spanish relief squadron was on its way, asked Bustamente, "Is it known when the other fleet will arrive?"

"What other fleet?"

"The one that is supposed to come from Spain . . ."

"Don't be simple. There is no other fleet. The ships are going out and that is all there is to it."

"Today?" Müller asked.

"I thought he was going even now."

Müller was speechless; without additional ships it would be a suicidal—if heroic—sortie. A cannon report froze him in place. He kept staring at Bustamente "like an imbecile." Neither said a word. Suddenly, a thunderous cannonade rocked the building. Müller dashed out, jumped on his horse and galloped down the hill toward the port captain's office.

At 9:30 A.M., "Fighting Bob" Evans smoked an after-breakfast cigar in the captain's cabin with his son Franck, who had come aboard the *Iowa* at daylight when his ship, the *Massachusetts*, left station for Guantánamo. Dressed in clean white uniforms, the captain and the cadet chatted and waited for the call to inspection. Already, the sweet sound of bugles drifted across the water presaging divine services.

The battleship was positioned almost due south of the channel entrance, with the *Texas* to port and the imposing *Oregon* to starboard. From the bridge, the view up the channel toward the sunken *Merrimac* was excellent. Lieutenant Hill, again officer of the deck, glanced toward the harbor entrance and stiffened. The big, black, gold-crested prow of a Spanish cruiser was charging past Punta Gorda, white water hunched at her bows. Hill ran to a nearby 6-pounder and let off a shot. Signal 250 rattled up the mast.

Down below, Franck Evans leaped to his feet. "Papa,

they're coming out!" As a tumult of brassy gongs and bugle calls sounded General Quarters, Evans hurtled up to the bridge as his son ran to a temporary duty station. The engines had already been set full speed ahead, and the guns of the starboard battery swiveled to the north.

Five miles from her blockading post, and seven miles from the *Iowa*, the *New York* approached Siboney. A lookout on the bridge turned at the sound of Hill's cannon shot and spotted signal flags fluttering toward the top of the fleet's masts. "The fleet's coming out!" he shouted. Sampson picked up a telescope and focused on the *Iowa*, then the harbor entrance. He had not heard the cannon, Chadwick realized, because "he had been somewhat deafened a few days before by the firing of an eight-inch gun under the bridge." But looking westward, away from the sun, he could easily see the smoke and the flags.

Sampson put down the telescope. "Yes," he said evenly, "they're coming out. Hoist 250." He had endured the burden of the blockade for thirty-three days and nights. Now, at the whim of a fat, gouty general who had ignored his plan for the assault on Santiago, he was caught off post. Worse, Commodore Schley, whom the admiral thought dilatory and insubordinate, was on the scene. There was one hope; if Cervera turned east the *New York* would be directly in his path.

As General Quarters sounded and the helm was put sharply to port, the *New York* wheeled smartly to starboard and raced back toward Santiago. AP correspondent "Chappie" Goode heard someone cry out, "Steam! More steam!" He looked at the weary, frail figure of the admiral and suddenly thought that Sampson might commit suicide if the Spanish escaped.

"Let us get on after the fleet," Sampson said. "Not one must get away." Then, motioning to Buenzle, he fished in his pocket and brought out the paper-wrapped package of sandwiches. "Please give this to George," he said. "I won't need them today."

Shafter would have to lunch alone.

Pilot Miguel López conned the *Infanta María Teresa* as she accelerated past Smith Cay toward the wreck of the *Mer-*

rimac. All of the electrical mines in the channel had been removed. The Vizcaya followed in her wake, over five hundred yards behind, and then came the Cristóbal Colón, the Almirante Oquendo, and the destroyers. Nearby, the admiral, his son and flag lieutenant Ángel Cervera, and Víctor Concas, wearing dress blues and gold-banded caps with tortoiseshell peaks, scanned the American fleet on the horizon. A few minutes later, off Estrella Point, a cannon sounded on the Iowa; they had been seen. Concas was under no illusion about what that meant, but this time there was no turning back.

As the María Teresa came under fire approaching Diamond Bank, Cervera calmly asked López, "Pilot, when can we shift the helm?"

"I will advise you, Admiral," López replied. They went on past the Socapa and Morro heights where the motto of the old seventeenth-century, smooth-bore cannon read "Ultima Ratio Regnum"—"The Last Argument of Kings." After a few moments more, López said, "Admiral, the helm may be shifted now."

"To starboard," Cervera ordered. The ship heeled sharply as it made a fast turn around the shoals. As the port broadside began to bear on the American ships at the eastern end of the blockading arc, Concas asked Cervera's permission to fire.

"Fire!" the admiral ordered. Then he turned to López. "Good-bye, pilot; go now; go and be sure you let them pay you, because you have earned it well." As bugles echoed the order to commence firing, López was lowered over the side into a pilot boat. Sailors quickly cast off and López headed swiftly back to Estrella Cove. A hail of lead flogged the cruiser. Smoke rose from the decks. Even now, López thought, the María Teresa seemed to be on fire.

As the bugles sounded, a roar of approval burst from the crew of the flagship. It was magnificent, Concas thought, but his seamen "did not know that those warlike echoes were the signal which hurled their country at the feet of the victor. . . . The sound of my bugles was the last echo of those which history tells us were sounded at the capture of Granada. It was the signal that the history of four centuries of grandeur was at an end. . . ."

Go for the Brooklyn, Cervera ordered. Concas adjusted the

helm. The fast cruiser was closer in than she had been at dawn, but still well outside the blockading arc. They might be able to ram her, allowing the ships behind to pass inside and escape to the west.

Concas turned to Cervera and murmured, "¡*Pobre España!*" The admiral said nothing, but gave "an expressive motion, as though to say that he had done everything possible to avoid it, and that his conscience was clear."

Aboard the *Indiana*, Captain Henry Taylor had already begun his inspection on the quarterdeck when the cannon fired aboard the *Iowa*. For a few seconds, Mannix reported, there was dead silence—the discharge might have been accidental. Then Taylor called quietly to his bugler, "Sound General Quarters."

Mannix took his post topside, turned to the harbor entrance, "and for the first time saw Cervera's squadron. The *María Teresa*, his flagship, was already clear of the entrance. The brilliant sun shone full on her . . . black smoke poured from her funnels and she was rushing forward with a 'bone in her teeth.' At her masthead was the red-and-gold banner of Spain and, as she swung westward, she fired every gun that could bear. We could see the flickering light of their discharge against the shiny black of her side."

It took Taylor only moments to reach the bridge. "Get to your guns, lads," he called, "our chance has come at last." As battle hatches clanged shut, he urged them on, shouting, "They will all get away; two of them are outside the Morro already!" The men, Taylor observed, "simply 'fell below,' throwing themselves down the steep ladder in their eagerness to reach their posts, until the ammunition deck was swarming with bruised and bleeding men, staggering to their feet, and limping to their stations."

On the bridge of the *Iowa*, Evans called for steam and pointed the battleship directly at the harbor entrance. His sailor's spirit was stirred by the sight of the *María Teresa's* glorious dash for freedom. The rays of the rising sun shimmered on her dew-glistened black flanks and yellow upper works, on multicolored flags and bright polished brass. The rusty-gray American ships rushing toward her seemed to Evans drab in comparison. The *María Teresa* and then the *Vizcaya* accelerated to 12 knots as they charged around Diamond Shoal and began firing. "My God," he thought, "they come at us like mad bulls."

At first, he planned to ram or torpedo Cervera's flagship, but the *Iowa* was only beginning to get "way" and, seeing the *María Teresa* rush westward, he swung off to port and gave her a starboard broadside.

The *Oregon*, about a mile to starboard of the *Iowa*, had fires spread in all her boilers and moved quickly for the harbor entrance in accordance with Sampson's instructions to close in. But there was more to it than that, Captain Charles Clark remembered. "I am sure every commander was obeying his natural impulse rather than any order, when the forward movement began."

On the *Texas*, muster and inspection had been canceled to allow the crew extra rest, and no services were planned since the chaplain was ill. That was a disappointment to Captain Jack Philip, one of the most devout sailors in the fleet. The Sabbath was a day for worship, not for battle. History demonstrates, he had told Sampson, that the person firing the first shot on the Sabbath is defeated.

The *Texas* was in fighting trim that morning, with good steam up. As electric gongs sounded the alarm and the officer of the deck shouted down the speaking tube to the engine room, "For God's sake, give us all the steam you can!" the near sister of the *Maine* charged for the harbor entrance. Philip saw gouts of black smoke billowing up from the harbor. Then the Spanish ships came into view, brightly colored and flag-bedecked. They seemed to Philip to come down the aisle of the channel "as gaily as brides to the altar."

The *María Teresa* fired and a shell exploded a column of water between the *Texas* and the *Iowa*. Almost immediately, a 6-inch gun on the *Texas* retorted. Philip was fighting on a Sunday.

On the bridge of the *Brooklyn*, lazing nearly five miles off Socapa, navigator Albon C. Hodgson had been scouting the harbor entrance through binoculars; he had a clear view in past the Morro to Estrella Point. First he saw the smoke, then a form took shape. Just as a signal cannon fired on the *Iowa*, he wheeled and shouted: "Afterbridge, there! Report to the commodore and the captain that the enemy's ships are coming out!" A voice on the bridge shouted, "Clear ship for action!"

Commodore Schley was relaxing on the afterdeck, his feet on a hatch coaming, when the alarm bells clanged. He and Captain Francis Cook, who was reaching for a clean white jacket in his cabin, ran to the little platform carpenters had hammered together outside the conning tower. Schley got there first, followed by George Graham. The AP correspondent heard him say, "Come on my boys, we'll give it to the them now."

Forty-five minutes earlier Schley had watched the *New York* slowly get up way and steam toward Siboney. The commodore's first thought was to clarify his command responsibilities—with Sampson conning the fleet, and Cook commanding the *Brooklyn*, Schley had actually exercised little authority during the long days of the blockade. Graham heard him hail the bridge: "Can you see the flagship?"

"No, sir. The *New York* is out of sight," a quartermaster answered.

"Then it's our fight," Schley announced.

Lieutenant Hodgson called out, "Commodore, they are coming right at us!"

"Well," Schley replied, "go right for them!" The *Brooklyn* charged in, accelerating.

As French Chadwick, commanding the *New York*, later observed, signals can be difficult to perceive looking against the sun at a distance of a mile or less. Looking "down the sun," however, they can be spotted many miles away. From the bridge of the flagship, he and the commander in chief could clearly see Cervera's cruisers burst into view as they ducked out from behind the Morro. And, Chadwick further noted, the *Gloucester* and the *Indiana* were actually closer to the flagship than they were to the *Brooklyn*.

The question of who commanded at Santiago would be argued bitterly for years to come. And what Schley did in only a few more minutes brought him inevitably to a court of inquiry.

As the *María Teresa* passed Diamond Bank at nine thirty-five, Victor Concas put her bow directly at the *Brooklyn*. To

Concas it seemed as though the *Teresa* "was entirely alone for ten minutes" before the *Vizcaya* steamed out. It was less than that, but long enough for the flagship to come under the fire of four American battleships as well as the *Brooklyn*. The *María Teresa* fired back with her port broadside and turret guns, but the ship staggered as, Cervera recorded, "one of the first projectiles burst an auxiliary steam pipe . . . which made us lose the speed on which we counted." It could have come from anywhere—several ships later took the credit—but Concas thought it was a 12-inch shell from the *Iowa*, only twenty-six hundred yards off the *María Teresa*'s stern.

As the *Vizcaya* came out, Evans went right for her, but she crossed the *Iowa*'s bow. Evans ported and dispatched another broadside at nineteen hundred yards. Then at nine-fifty the *Cristóbal Colón*, one of the finest armored ships in the world, rushed out. She had never received the 10-inch guns for her main turrets, but had an excellent battery of 6-inch guns. Rushing into the clouds of smoke left by the first two Spanish ships, she fired twice at the *Iowa*—"two as beautiful shots as I ever saw," Evans thought.

The first hit forward of the bridge on the starboard side of the ship, exploded in the berth deck, and demolished the dispensary. On the bridge, even with acrid niter smoke from the guns billowing past, Evans could smell the sharp pungence of medicines. The second shell ripped an eighteen-inch gash just above the waterline about eight feet farther forward, without exploding. Evans had always wondered whether the ship's cellulose flotation, which was designed to swell up and keep the hull watertight if holed, would function under stress. It did not. He watched anxiously as it "washed out and floated astern in a broad, brown streak."

As the crew re-secured bulkhead doors, water poured in and slowed the *Iowa*. There was no time to think about it. In only a few minutes the *Oquendo* burst through the clouds of smoke at the harbor mouth; the *Iowa* and several other ships raked her with fire.

On the *Texas*, Jack Philip had sensed only a few minutes after the *María Teresa* came out that all the Spanish ships would head westward. As they wheeled to the right to fight in wing formation, he turned his ship toward the Morro and closed in. Through heavy smoke he glimpsed the *Brooklyn* off his port quarter. She "was plowing up the water at a great rate in a course almost due north, direct for the oncoming Spanish ships, and nearly a mile from the *Texas*." Shortly before ten, as Philip anticipated a chase and veered westward, his ship was shrouded by heavy smoke. "We might as well have had a blanket tied over our heads," Philip said.

The *Brooklyn* and the *María Teresa* charged toward each other, headed almost bow-to-bow, at a combined speed of over 20 knots. Schley realized that in a few moments they would be within the thousand-yard range of the Spanish Bustamente torpedoes; the *María Teresa* seemed intent on ramming. Cook observed that they would soon pass into the zone of crossfire between the American and Spanish ships. Yes, Schley acknowledged.

Graham sensed the tension on the bridge, then heard Schley order, "Put your helm hard aport, Cook."

Cook had anticipated the order. "It is hard aport, sir."

At speed the *Brooklyn* veered to starboard in a great fishhook turn that would take her east toward Siboney and then south, *away* from the battle, before she could complete her loop and head back westward. Almost at the same time, the *María Teresa*, fearing she might be rammed by the oncoming *Texas* (Concas did not know Philip's ship was not designed to ram) sheered to the west. Concas was astonished by the *Brooklyn*'s turn to starboard—"it would seem more reasonable for it to have [been] made to port." As the *Brooklyn* sped away from the *María Teresa* and past the oncoming *Vizcaya*, she spoke her port battery of 8-inch guns. The ships came so close that Schley could see sailors on the *Vizcaya*—"I observed daylight between their legs as they ran."

Navigator Hodgson was less concerned about the *Vizcaya* than he was about the *Texas*, which appeared to have swung west just before Schley made his surprising loop. A tighter turn seemed to him an imperative safety measure.

Graham heard him ask the commodore: "Hadn't we better back on our starboard engine?"

"No, we'll lose headway. We must get around quickly."

Hodgson heard the answer differently. By his later account, Schley responded, "Damn the *Texas*! She must look after herself!"

It was about 10 A.M. "Then occurred," as Jack Philip put

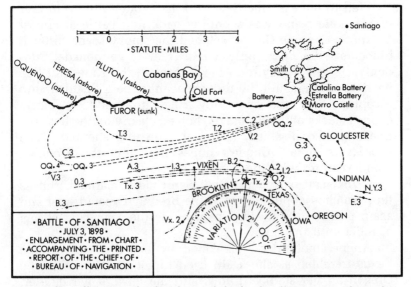

Navy chart illustrates the first hour of the battle off Santiago. Above the compass rose, the *Brooklyn* "loops" into the path of the oncoming *Texas*.

it, "the incident which caused me for a moment more alarm than anything Cervera did that day."

A puff of wind momentarily cleared away the pall of smoke before the onrushing *Texas*. Philip gasped. "There, bearing toward us and across our bows, turning on her port helm, with big waves curling over her bows and great clouds of black smoke pouring from her funnels, was the *Brooklyn* . . . so near that it took our breath away.

"'Back both engines hard!' went down the tube to the astonished engineers, and in a twinkling the old ship was racing against herself." As the screws reversed and bit into the foamy green water, the shuddering *Texas* slowed and wallowed in the turbulence of her own wake. Then, "as the big cruiser glided past, all of us on the bridge gave a sigh of relief. Had the *Brooklyn* struck us then, it would probably have been an end to the *Texas*. . . . Had the *Texas* rammed the *Brooklyn*, it would have been equally disastrous, for the *Texas* was not built for ramming, and she would have doubled up like a hoop."

Well to the east, the *New York* had gotten fire up in four of her boilers and was scudding back into battle at almost 12 knots. Chappie Goode watched the smoky scene through binoculars; he heard only a faint roar of cannonade. Suddenly, he saw a gray form break through the American line heading to the south; he thought it must be a Spanish ship escaping—then the three towering, hundred-foot, black-capped stacks of the *Brooklyn* showed clearly on the horizon. She appeared disabled. A man beside him shouted, "The *Brooklyn's* gone!" Goode's hopes fell; only the *Brooklyn* could keep up with the Spanish cruisers.

"What can be the matter?" Sampson exclaimed. But as they watched apprehensively, the *Brooklyn* veered west and again pursued the fleeing Spanish. On the *New York* cheers of relief split the sky.

Almost motionless, blanketed by her own smoke, the *Texas* trembled as she again tried to get up way. With the *Oregon* off her starboard bow, and the *Iowa* at her quarter, she was now at the focus of the Spanish fire. Philip was almost blinded by the smoke, but he could hear the shells screaming by all too plainly. He decided to take his staff on the exposed flying bridge to the lower bridge around the conning tower. As they climbed down the ladder, a shell struck the door of the pilothouse and burst inside. Moments later another shell exploded over the forward superstructure. The concussion was tremendous. Philip remembered "pitching up in the air, with my coat-tails flying out behind me, as if I had been thrown by one of Roosevelt's broncos." A naval cadet threw a hand to his head as an eardrum split.

Now the second consequence of Schley's unexpected loop to the south came close to putting half the American fleet out of action.

When the Spanish came out, chief engineer Robert W. Milligan of the *Oregon* had fires in all four main boilers; they were quickly spread. In a short time the 10,000-ton battleship worked up a 14-knot speed. Charles Clark saw immediately, as Philip had, that the Spanish were all going westward. He turned to port past the *Iowa*, still heading in to ram the *Vizcaya*, and sped in pursuit. At about 10:10 AM the curtain of dense smoke parted to starboard. Clark saw the *Iowa*, only a ship's length away.

"Hard a-starboard!" Clark ordered the helmsman. The *Oregon* wheeled to port and, moving faster than Evans's ship, seemed to clear her bows. "Just then," Clark reported, "some one near me shouted, 'Look out for the *Texas!*' and I turned to see her looming through the smoke clouds on our port bow. For one intense moment it seemed as if three of our ships might be put out of action then and there. . . ."

There was only one thing to do. Clark veered back to starboard "with the hope that we might clear the *Texas* and that the *Iowa*, seeing that we must either cross her bows or run her down, would sheer sharply to starboard. Captains Philip and Evans . . . must have instantly grasped the situation and acted on it, for we did pass between them, but by so narrow a margin that I felt that coming to close quarters with the Spaniards would be infinitely preferable to repeating that experience."

Much later Schley would say that Cook had ordered the "retrograde turn," as it came to be called. "I did not." However, Schley, added, he would have given the order if Cook had not. He felt "that the original plan [Sampson's] had failed; and that the Spanish fleet in order . . . had succeeded in passing the battle-ship line." A new plan was needed, one that would give the *Brooklyn* needed sea room. "During the turn Mr. Hodgson very properly made some allusion to look out, perhaps for the *Texas*." But that ship was never closer than six hundred yards, "so distant that she never entered my head as a menace or danger."

Whatever Schley's motive for turning away from the Spanish line and across the bows of the three battleships turning westward, two near-collisions resulted and the American pursuit was slowed. French Chadwick estimated the *Texas* lost three miles in the chase. Schley, too, lost vital ground. When he and Concas began their turns, they were beam on; when the *Brooklyn* completed her loop, Schley admitted, the *María Teresa* was off the starboard bow; the *Vizcaya*, too, was a little ahead. He turned to Cook: "We must stay with this crowd."

Looking aft, he saw no support in sight. The *Oquendo* had passed Socapa around ten, and it seemed to Schley that all four Spanish cruisers were single-mindedly bent on destroying his high-sided ship. They carried bigger guns, were just as fast, and did not appear to be damaged. The battleships behind him could not, he thought, keep up with the Spanish cruisers. The commodore felt uneasy and alone. He distinctly remembered seeing "jets of water ahead and astern; and over and short; and the roar of the projectiles was one of the things that can be heard once in a lifetime." As his 8-inch guns banged off shells at the *Vizcaya*, Schley shouted to Cook, "Tell your bullies they're doing great work!"

Chief Yeoman George H. Ellis was standing about ten feet from Schley calmly taking ranges with a stadimeter. Ellis was a devout twenty-five-year-old from Brooklyn. Since there was no chaplain on the cruiser, he made a point of distributing religious literature, and the men appreciated his zeal. Suddenly, Graham wrote, "Plainly distinguishable from the hum and buzz of the Spanish shells ... there came a dull, sickening thud, and the warm blood and brains spattering in our faces and on our clothes gave warning of a fatality. ..." A naval officer recorded, "His head was severed completely from his body, very much as one might snip off the head of an insect with the finger." The head flew overboard; the body, for an instant, remained perfectly erect, the hands still holding the stadimeter, then slowly toppled.

Schley pulled out a handkerchief and wiped off his face and jacket. As seamen rushed up to throw Ellis's body overboard, standard procedure in battle, the commodore stopped them. "Take it below," he ordered, "and we'll give it a Christian burial."

Those ten or fifteen minutes after he completed the loop were, Schley thought, the most furious part of the battle. But he suddenly realized they were no longer alone. Some four hundred yards off his starboard quarter the *Oregon* burst out of the smoke "with a tremendous bone in her mouth." Cook shouted, "God bless the *Oregon*!" Schley signaled, "Follow the flag."

Clark was equally pleased to find a comrade-in-arms nearby. After shooting the gap between the *Texas* and the *Iowa*, the *Oregon* had sped down the Spanish wing, hammering each ship in turn. Now here was an old friend; Francis Cook had been at Annapolis with him. Clark turned to someone on the bridge and said emotionally, "My old roommate is in command of that ship."

Then Schley saw the *María Teresa* "wabbling like a bird wounded." Smoke poured from her superstructure and she slowed. "We have got one," Schley said. "Keep the boys below informed of all the movements. They can't see and they want to know." A few moments later, even over the tumult of gunfire, he heard a cheer ring out below decks.

The first ship out and the farthest offshore after her dash at the Brooklyn, the *María Teresa* was hit repeatedly. After the flagship took the hit to her steam pipe, a shell burst one of the fire mains and other projectiles set fire to Cervera's cabin, where ammunition was stored, the after deck, and the chart house. Without water, the fires could not be fought and Cervera ordered the after magazines flooded. Crewmen were unable to make their way through the smoke-and-steam-filled access passages.

Topside, the decks ran with blood. A medic attending the chief boatswain counted fourteen wounds. A forward gun crew was blown into the water. On the unprotected bridge, Concas heard what he thought was the explosion of a magazine—and fell severely wounded. Two staff officers went down with him. As they were carried off to the sick bay, Cervera took direct command of the ship.

The admiral convened a few remaining officers in the conning tower and asked them whether the battle could be continued. They answered that the ship was defenseless. As fire, fanned by the ship's forward motion, swept down the length of the *María Teresa*, he turned the flagship to starboard and headed for a small beach west of Cabrera Point, just six miles from the Santiago Harbor entrance. The engines stopped as the ship staggered onto a sandbar near shore and flames burst skyward. In the engine and boiler rooms sailors were suffocated by smoke, scalded by steam, roasted by fire. On deck, survivors began helping the wounded overboard.

It was worse on the *Almirante Oquendo*, the last Spanish cruiser to leave harbor, which was taking hits from at least three American battleships. On the *Iowa*, only sixteen hundred yards off her bow, Evans saw that "she rolled and staggered like a drunken thing. . . . I could see the shot holes come in her sides and our shells explode inside of her, but she pluckily held on her course and fairly smothered us with a shower of shells and machine-gun shots."

Fire broke out in the after torpedo and magazine rooms of the *Oquendo*. Ammunition hoists broke down. At one 5.5-inch gun station a breech block burst, killing or wounding its crew. The ship's red-hot side plates bulged out from heat and pressure. A shell cut the executive officer in two, the third officer was blown up by an ammunition explosion, and three others were mowed down. Another projectile clanged into the forward 11-inch gun turret between the gun and the gun port; the explosion inside killed six men. The head of the captain of the turret, torn off by the blast, rolled onto the deck through an opening.

Damage-control teams managed to flood forward compartments but could not reach aft areas because of the inferno on the poop. Captain Juan B. Lazaga ordered his flag lowered, but before sailors could reach the mast, the halyard burned and the flag fell into the flames. Lazaga sheered toward the beach and ran his ship onto a coral outcropping about a mile west of the *María Teresa*. A chain was let down at the bow and sailors began sliding down. The ship's yawl was launched but sank. Men jumped over the side. As flames burst up higher than his ship's military tops, Lazaga refused to abandon her. Suddenly, his hands clutched his breast and he fell to the deck, apparently dead of a heart attack. Crewmen covered him with a flag.

On the *Texas*, closely following, sailors saw a huge explosion wrack the Spanish cruiser and gave a cheer. Philip would not have it. "Don't cheer, boys," he shouted. "Those poor devils are dying!"

At ten-fifty, when the burning *Oquendo* headed for the beach, an officer on the bridge of the *Oregon* turned to Clark and observed, "Captain, that vessel could be destroyed now."

"No," Clark replied, "that's a dead cock in the pit. The others can attend to her. We'll push on for the two ahead." The *Oregon* surged on after the *Vizcaya* and the *Colón*, which had shot the gap between the *María Teresa* and shore and pulled ahead.

Shortly after ten, well behind the *Oquendo*, the *Furor* and the *Plutón*—"the dreaded vipers of the Spanish squadron,"

John Long called them—had raced out of the channel entrance with a full head of steam. Evans saw "black smoke and long white streaks on the water." The *Iowa* began firing on "the little gamecocks." So did the *Texas*, the *Indiana*, and the *Oregon*. But it was the frail *Gloucester*, purchased from J. P. Morgan and converted to a gunboat, that stole the honors.

"We sent a signal to the *Gloucester*," Cadet Mannix remembered. "'Destroyers coming out.' This signal was misunderstood [perhaps purposely]. . . . She headed for the Spaniards at full speed running directly into our zone of fire and, before 'Cease firing' could be transmitted to the secondary battery, we barely missed sinking her."

The *Gloucester* was commanded by Lieutenant Commander Richard Wainwright, the former executive officer of the *Maine*. A navy yard had equipped her with four 6-pounders and a few smaller guns, but she was unprotected. A good shot from a 1-pounder could have disabled the little message-carrying vessel. Her log entries had, to this point, been unremarkable: "Dropped a few shells along the shore"; "Coal passer put in double irons for leaving his station without permission."

Early that Sunday morning the *Gloucester* had anchored the eastern end of the blockading arc, just three thousand yards southeast of the Morro. When the Spanish cruisers came out of harbor, Wainwright held position. There was nothing he could do about them. He waited patiently for the destroyers. They had become his obsession, his "plain duty."

When they finally came out, about fifteen hundred yards behind the *Oquendo*, Wainwright dashed in, quickly getting up to 17 knots. The destroyers' Maxim one-pounders opened up and geysers of water walked their way up to the gunboat—then inexplicably stopped.

"From the very first," Lieutenant Commander Diego Carlier of the *Furor* reported, "we received an enormous amount of fire . . . and were struck by shells of every caliber. We soon commenced to have casualties from the galling fire and many injuries to the ship. . . ." Captain Fernando Villaamil, commanding the destroyer flotilla, was wounded by a shell that hit the bridge. Steam pipes and boilers burst, the engines were damaged, fires broke out, and a magazine exploded. Finally, the servomotor controlling the rudder was put out of commission. The Furor began circling erratically. The Gloucester raked her with deadly automatic fire at a range of six hundred yards.

The Plutón, following, was also greeted with a hail of projectiles. A large-caliber shell penetrated the orlop deck, pitching the ship forward; another burst in the ammunition-filled cabin of Lieutenant Commander Pedro Vásquez, starting a fire. The forward boilers burst. The destroyer limped on, taking water at the bow but still fighting.

Seaman Cross, on the Oregon, admired the way the Spanish fought back. One destroyer gunner in particular caught his eye. "I do think he was one of the bravest men I ever had the pleasure to look upon. That man must have known he was going to a shure Deth, he stud on Deck and cep firing at us all the time, and the last time I seen him he was Just going up in the air."

As the Furor circled helplessly, the Plutón turned toward shore and ran onto the rocks four miles west of the Morro. A large section of her weak bows tore off as the impact threw her back, then she surged again onto the rocks. Surf crashed over her decks. A few survivors swam or rowed ashore. A few moments later an explosion rocked the ship and she settled to her deck line in the water.

The engines on the circling Furor gave out and she staggered to a stop, ablaze from stem to stern. A white flag was hoisted and sailors jumped over the side or took to the boats. Minutes after they sheered off, a boiler burst and, as the destroyer sank almost vertically, a geyser of steam and coal dust erupted from her stack. Boats from the Gloucester picked up survivors. Wainwright hoisted, "Enemy's vessels destroyed." He considered his personal score settled, the Maine avenged.

Around 10:40 A.M. just before the Furor sank, the New York stormed onto the scene and fired three shots from her 4-inch guns. Chadwick waved his cap and led the crew in cheers for "the plucky little Gloucester." As the flagship steamed westward at the tail end of the chase after the Vizcaya and the Colón, she swept through the flotsam of battle—ammunition boxes, rigging, bodies. Goode saw a sailor—"a black-headed, fine, swarthy Spaniard"—in front of the flagship. The New York changed course to avoid him and "as we flew past him he threw up one arm and cried despair-

ingly, '¡Amerigo! ¡Amerigo! ¡Amerigo! ¡Auxilio! ¡Auxilio!'
Some of the crew standing near me laughed at this 'lingo.'
'Damn you, shut up!' came in strident tones from an officer
that overheard the jeers, and there was silence. A life buoy
almost hit the swimmer. . . ."

As the *Indiana* surged westward, Mannix saw more ominous shapes in the translucent Caribbean water—"several
torpedoes floating vertically . . . their propellors clear of the
surface. . . . They must have been fired by the Spanish destroyers. . . ." As they approached the burning hulks of the
María Teresa and the *Oquendo*, the *Indiana* launched three
rescue boats. Mannix conned one of them in. They passed
about twenty dead bodies drifting out to sea with the ebbing
tide. One body, with a "tremendously expanded" chest, reminded him of a Mathew Brady Civil War photograph.

Then, to his horror, Mannix saw that some of the bodies
were "twitching restlessly. . . . They were being attacked by
sharks or other fish."

Fred Buenzle on the *New York* saw the sharks, too, and
heard a floundering Spanish sailor shriek, "¡Madre de Dios!"
Buenzle looked around and saw the chaplain's wooden pul-
pit, ready for Sunday services, still covered with an altar
cloth. It seemed a heaven-sent life preserver. He and several
other sailors hoisted it up and dropped it over the side. Coxswain Billy Plummer, Buenzle remarked, "who stammered
when he was excited, and was blasphemous at all times,
cried out: 'Cling to the c-cross, you s-s-spiggoty, c-cling to the
c-cross!'"

Now the *Vizcaya* was in peril. During the second hour of
the battle she was closely chased by the *Brooklyn*, the *Oregon*, the *Texas*, and the *Iowa*. The *Oregon* took a particular
delight in pounding her. As Gunner Murphy put it, "We had
it in for the Vizcaya because she had pointed her guns arro-
gantly at New York." Murphy was standing outside an 8-inch
wing turret, handling a hose used to cool off the breeches of
the guns. When the ship's range finders were knocked out by
concussion, an officer cried out, "Murphy, climb to the top
of the turret." Murphy clambered up and tried to observe the
effects of the *Oregon*'s salvos.

Every ship Murphy could see from his perch was firing—it was just like a picture book on naval battle: "The sea was covered with dense rolls of black smoke from the guns and funnels. Blinding flashes cut the murk." The noise was terrific; he wondered why his eardrums didn't split. But everyone seemed calm, even the fifteen-year-old apprentice boys who "held their hands over their heads and yelled 'High Ball!' as the singing shells flew above them."

The Spanish cruiser should have been able to outrun the *Oregon*, but her bottom was foul and shell concussions had burst a steam pipe, exploded a boiler, and destroyed fire mains. A conflagration on the aft deck burned furiously. She fought back bravely, handicapped by deficiencies in her guns and ammunition. Breeches jammed, firing pins failed, and one gun crew tried seven shells before they found one that fired.

From her main truck she proudly flew a huge silk flag presented to the *Vizcaya* by the historical society of the province after which she was named. Captain Antonio Eulate ordered the precious banner lowered and burned so that it would not become a United States trophy; a replacement was hoisted. Shortly before eleven, Eulate, wounded in the head and shoulder, unable to return fire, turned for the shore.

Aboard the little *Vixen*, which had darted out of the path of the oncoming Spanish cruisers before turning west in parallel pursuit, an officer recorded that explosions on the *Vizcaya* "resembled huge chrysanthemums with ribbons of smoke, as burning powder grains fell from the end of the petals." "Fighting Bob" Evans could only reflect that "God and the gunners had their day." Charles Clark was saddened by the sight: "As this last battletorn wreck of what had once been a proud and splendid ship fled to the shore like some sick and wounded thing, seeking a place to die, I could feel none of that exultation that is supposed to come with victory."

Eulate, faint from loss of blood, charged his ship toward the beach at Aserraderos, sixteen miles west of Santiago. Like her sister ships, the *María Teresa* and the *Oquendo*, she was a chariot of fire and smoke. On the poop the mast burst into flames and toppled over, whipping the replacement flag into the holocaust on deck. The red-hot ship shuddered onto a reef several hundred yards from shore and Eulate ordered her abandoned.

As the *New York* rushed onto the scene, Buenzle saw the *Vizcaya* roll drunkenly. "Fires had broken out on all her decks, black smoke shot up from her hatches, bursts of flame came through her ports and licked up her starboard side. Naked men hung over the rails to escape the blistering heat; some of them were clinging to her anchor cables near the waterline, and others with hair afire jumped into the sea."

As the flagship passed down the line, Sampson sorted out the elements of his fleet and signaled new assignments. The *Gloucester*, the *Hist*, and the *Ericsson* were ordered not to chase; they began picking up survivors from the destroyers and the *María Teresa* and the *Oquendo*. The *Indiana* went off to investigate the report of a Spanish warship approaching from the east. Intercepted near Guantánamo, she proved to be an Austrian battleship flying a look-alike flag—red and white rather than red and yellow—and ironically named the *Infanta Maria Teresa*.

The *Iowa* had been seventeen months in the water without a bottom scraping, and she was further slowed by the gash in her side. Sampson ordered Evans to rescue duty, and then to resume the blockade in case the *Reina Mercedes* should come out to harass the transports at Siboney. Then he dashed on in pursuit of the only Spanish ship still afloat, the swift *Cristóbal Colón*.

The *Colón* had turned inside *Vizcaya* and *María Teresa* and, as Schley's loop slowed the fleet, put on a marvelous burst of speed. When the *Vizcaya* beached at Aserraderos, almost six miles of open water separated the *Colón* from the nearest pursuing ship. Looking aft, Commodore José de Paredes thought he had escaped. Both the *Brooklyn* and the *Oregon* seemed to be falling back. He was confident he could outrun them to Cape Cruz, jutting into the Caribbean about a hundred miles west of Santiago, and then shape a course for Cienfuegos. Still, he hugged the sinuous coastline in case he had to run ashore.

On the *Brooklyn*, Schley munched on a cracker and drank coffee. Graham observed that his lips were cracked, his eyes bloodshot, and there were little red spots on his face where flecks of saltpeter had burned his skin. Schley tried to signal the *Texas*, which he thought too slow for pursuit, to pick up survivors from the *Vizcaya*, but the flag halyards had been shot away and apparently Philip couldn't make out the signalman's wigwag message.

"Never mind," Schley said, "Philip is always sensible; he needs no instructions about such things."

Schley called for more steam. Only two of his four engines were engaged—to couple the others meant stopping the ship, waiting for the shafts to stop rotating and throwing in cumbersome clutches. The operation took at least twenty minutes; they would lose another four miles in the chase. But she could still make perhaps 17 knots. By noon, when the last boilers came on line, she was doing over 14. Now the dim shape of the fleeing Spanish cruiser seemed to grow larger.

Paredes's confidence had been misplaced, not in the ship he commanded but in the coal she carried. Sometime after noon an engineer appeared topside to report that his good hard coal was exhausted; they were down to the inferior Santiago supply. Boiler pressure was down; propellor revolutions were slowing. Paredes began to wonder whether he would make it past Turquino Point, fifty miles down the coast from Santiago.

Coal was no problem on the *Oregon*. Chief Engineer Milligan thought each chunk precious, especially the sought-after, high-grade Welsh coal loaded on the West Coast. Milligan still had a few hundred tons of the prized fuel in a padlocked battle bunker. He babied the ship's four "Scotch" boilers, too. They were never filled with corrosive salt water. That meant reduced drinking and bathing water for the crew, but they willingly cut back.

Once the *Oregon's* crew had been green. On the West Coast, the story went, a new seaman emerged from below decks and announced with disbelief, "The fat man in the cellar wants me to sleep in a bag!" But Clark had honed his crew and his ship into a cohesive fighting machine. The Spanish called her "the Yankee Devil." Murphy thought of

the *Oregon* as "the Irish Boat *O'Regan*" because there were
seven Murphys and three Kellys on board. Built as much for
coastal defense as war at sea, the heavily armed and armored
ship was known as "the bulldog" of the fleet.

But on this day, unleashed by Milligan's black gang, pow-
ered by the "dusky diamonds" of Cardiff, she became a grey-
hound.

Milligan watched happily as the needle of the steam-
pressure gauge shivered past the standard 160-pound reading; the temperature soared to 150 degrees. Firemen, dripping
with coal-blackened sweat, collapsed and were carried topside. Revived, they fought to get back to the furnaces. At
Clark's order, a stream of messenger boys carried cold beer
below from the officers' quarters refrigerator.

Standing on his turret, "Guncotton" Murphy was awed by
the ship's furious charge through the water: "Our two stacks
were pillars of red fire." White water boiled over the jack
staff, surged across the deck, and crashed against the forward
turret. Her propellors thrashed the green water of her wake
into white froth more than a mile long. The *Oregon's* maximum design speed was 15.5 knots. Now, even with the
growth of two oceans on her bottom, she was doing 16 and
still accelerating. The *Brooklyn* was coming abeam.

But the *Colón* was still beyond the range of the *Oregon's*
big guns. While some men went below to grab a quick bite,
others came on deck to smoke a pipe. Bandsmen came topside—those who could be spared from other duties—and
played "Darling Nellie Grey" and "There'll Be a Hot Time,
in the Old Town, Tonight." The jackies cheered.

On the *Brooklyn*, now four hundred yards abeam of the
Oregon, a marine shinnied up the signal mast and reeved a
new flag halyard through the block. Schley felt more cheerful. The *Oregon* seemed to have a cruiser's speed, and the
Texas was not far behind. The commodore shaped a course
west by south for Turquino Point; the Spanish cruiser still
hugged the shoreline—she would have to cross his bows to
get around the promontory.

On the *Oregon* Clark sent up a familiar signal: "Remember
the *Maine!*" He watched as answering pennants fluttered up
the signal mast of the *Brooklyn*: "We have!"

The *Colón* was now discernibly closer. When the range

had closed to about ninety-five hundred yards, Schley asked Clark to try one of his "railroad trains"—the 1100-pound shells of the 13-inch guns. Clark consulted with Lieutenant (jg) Edward W. Eberle in the forward turret to see if the gunnery officer thought the elevation required for the long-range shot would strain the gun mounts. They decided to lob one off. It fell short, but the thunder of the discharge cheered the black gang in the pressure cooker below decks. Engineer Milligan appeared topside and told Clark, "Our men down below are nearly played out, but if they can only hear the guns, they will brace up again."

Clark ordered Eberle to increase the range for the next shot.

Commodore Paredes could not return the Oregon's fire with his after turret—the Colón's 30-ton rifle was still in Genoa. Boiler pressure was still going down and he appeared to have dug himself into a hole by hugging the shoreline. A column of smoke directly astern—probably the New York—cut off any chance of his "doubling." Stretching in an arc seaward, the Texas, the Oregon, and the Brooklyn had virtually closed his escape route around Cape Cruz. When the watery explosion of a shell from the Oregon soaked the Colón's fantail, he doubted the wisdom of fighting on. As Concas rationalized later, "a commander cannot in cold blood give an order which will send 500 men to their death, though it may be considered a very natural act by the great admirals around the tables of the café."

Admiral Cervera had set the example of running his flagship ashore. His battle plan—like Montojo's at Manila—eschewed deep-water operations. Paredes took one more look at the ominous plumes of black smoke behind him. Suddenly, the Brooklyn opened up with her 8-inch guns. Another 13-inch shell exploded a huge geyser of water off the Colón's starboard bow. It was time. "In order to obviate being captured," he reported, "I decided to run ashore and lose the ship rather than sacrifice in vain the lives of all these men. . . ." He ordered the helmsman to turn the ship to starboard. At 13 knots, the Colón charged directly at the mouth of the Turquino River.

*   *   *

On the *Brooklyn*, Graham saw the Spanish strike their colors. Navigator Hodgson looked at his watch. It was exactly one-fifteen. Guns on the Spanish cruiser began firing to leeward. Schley asked the meaning of the salvo and was told it was a signal of capitulation. "It's a good thing we didn't lose," Schley said, "for I wouldn't have known how to surrender." He ordered, "Cease firing."

The *Colón* found her last resting place at 1:20 P.M. on a sandbar just off the Turquino River, under the majestic green heights of the sixty-six-hundred-foot Turquino Peak. On the *Oregon* the band, after playing the "Star-Spangled Banner," struck up a funeral march. On the *Texas*, closing up, Captain Jack Philip called all hands to the aft quarterdeck. Standing sole-deep in the ashy-white grit of saltpeter, he took off his cap and began speaking to the crew in a voice full of emotion: "Men, I have always had implicit confidence in the *Texas*, my officers and my crew, but my greatest confidence is in almighty God . . . and I ask every man of you to uncover his head with me, that is, if you have no religious scruples, and silently thank God for our deliverance and for the victory he has given us."

"There they stood," said the ship's chaplain, "stripped to the waist, blood streaming from their strained muscles, their bodies stained from the powder, the coal dust and smoke of the fire-room; but from the heart of every one of us that beautiful Sabbath morning went up the most fervent prayer that ever left the heart of man."

Forty-five miles to the east, rescue operations had been underway since 10:30 A.M. Admiral Pascual Cervera had swum ashore, aided by two seamen and his son Ángel. Lieutenant George H. Norman, Jr., of the *Gloucester* found them on the beach and formally received the surrender of the commander in chief of the Spanish squadron. He took the Cerveras and other officers out to the *Gloucester*, just offshore.

Wainwright questioned Cervera's tactics, but not his courage. As best he could, he drew his crew up to receive the admiral. There was no ship's bugler to sound the proper flourishes, and no boatswain's mates were on the vessel to pipe the admiral aboard. Wainwright could only meet Cervera at the top of the gangway, shake his hand, congratulate him on a brave fight, and offer him his cabin. Concas came on board, too, and the ship's surgeon attended to his wounds. Executive officer Harry P. Huse gave Concas his room.

Shortly, a lunch was served in the converted yacht's small messroom in two sittings. Huse, who spoke French, took the first. He turned to Ángel Cervera and said, sympathetically, *"Nous avons remporté la victoire, mais la gloire c'est à vous."* The admiral's son got his father's attention and repeated Huse's remark.

Pascual Cervera nodded approvingly, *"C'est très bien."* He seemed in high spirits. He had obeyed orders, done his duty, made the sacrifice called for by the government in Madrid and Havana. The day was lost, but honor gained. Down the table, however, Huse's gentle words shattered the composure of an exhausted Spanish officer. He put his hands to his face as tears rolled down his cheeks.

By the order of Captain Robley Evans, Cervera and a few other ranking officers were taken to the *Iowa*, which had been rescuing seamen from the explosion-wracked *Vizcaya*. Evans recalled that "the ship had grounded about 400 yards from the beach, and between her and the shore was a sand-spit on which many had taken refuge, the water being about up to their armpits. The Cuban insurgents had opened fire on them from the shore, and with a glass I could see plainly the bullets snipping the water up among them. The sharks, made ravenous by the blood of the wounded, were attacking them from the outside."

The *Hist* and the *Ericsson* were sent in close to pick up survivors and bring them out to the battleship. "Our boats soon began to arrive, filled with horribly mangled men," Evans reported. "The beautiful white quarter-deck of the *Iowa* was soon stained with the blood dripping from the wet clothing of the wounded, and she looked as if she had been used as a slaughter pen."

Evans watched as Captain Antonio Eulate was brought up to the *Iowa* in a leaky longboat. He was "covered with blood from three wounds, with a blood-stained handkerchief about his bare head. . . . In the bottom of the boat . . . was a foot or so of blood-stained water and the body of a dead Spanish sailor which rolled from side to side as the water swashed about."

A chair was lowered and Eulate winched up to the deck. Sailors carried the *Vizcaya's* captain to the quarterdeck. Eulate shakily rose to his feet, "unbuckled his sword belt, kissed the hilt of his sword, and, bowing low, gracefully presented it to me as a token of surrender. I never felt so sorry for a man in all my life."

As Evans gravely gave the sword back to Eulate as a token of respect, his crew gave a cheer of appreciation. Then Evans helped the Spanish captain toward his cabin. As they reached the hatchway stairs, Eulate stopped, and "drawing himself up to his full height, with his right arm extended above his head, exclaimed, '¡Adios Vizcaya!' Just as the words passed his lips the forward magazine of his late command, as if arranged for the purpose, exploded with magnificent effect."

In his cabin Evans offered the Spaniard a Key West cigar—the best he had. Eulate accepted it gratefully, turned it in his hand, stared intently at it, reached into a pocket of his drenched uniform coat and brought out "a beautiful but very wet Havana cigar. He bowed and handed it to me with the remark, 'Captain, I left 15,000 aboard the *Vizcaya.*'"

That afternoon they began burying the Spanish dead. With the colors half-masted, the padre of the *Vizcaya* read the service. As officers and men uncovered, and a marine guard presented arms, the first bodies of Pascual Cervera's "hecatomb" were committed to the deep.

Less than an hour after the *Colón* turned for shore, the unlucky *New York* rushed by the *Vixen* at 17 knots and hove to near the *Brooklyn*. During the battle the American ships had fired some ten thousand shells at the Spanish; Sampson's flagship had spoke just three of them. Schley underscored Sampson's absence, signaling: "A glorious victory has been achieved. Details later."

On the *New York*, Chappie Goode thought this a bit presumptuous. Sampson had, after all, organized and maintained the difficult blockade, repositioned ships of different speed and armament when they scattered after the Spanish fleet, and, though far from the Morro at the start of the fight, added his ship to the chase.

Schley waited anxiously for an answer. When there was none, he hoisted, "This is a great day for our country." Sampson's response was a curt directive: "Report your casualties."

Graham saw a pained expression flicker over Schley's face. "'Report your casualties,' repeated Schley, turning on his heel and walking over to the other side of the bridge . . . and up to our signal masts went the flags, 'One dead and two wounded.'"

Captain Cook finally got his white jacket on and took his gig to the *Colón* to collect high-ranking prisoners for a formal surrender. He found the decks awash in half-empty brandy bottles (the Spanish sailors had been without food for thirty-six hours, an officer of the prize crew reported, and "to make up for this, they were liberally dosed with brandy to brace them up"). Down below, however, he found Commodore Paredes and Captain Emilio Díaz Moreu commiserating over a bowl of soup. As Cook brought his prisoners back to the *Brooklyn,* they passed the *Oregon* and the Spanish saluted the salt-splotched battleship: "*¡Bravo Blanco Diablo!*"

There was a tremor in Schley's voice, Graham recalled, as he hailed the *New York:* "I request the honor of the surrender of the *Cristóbal Colón.*" The message was apparently garbled and reported to Sampson as, "Schley claims the honor of the capture of the *Cristóbal Colón.*" Whatever Schley said, the only reply he got was an order to Cook to report aboard the flagship with his prisoners. Shortly afterward, Schley was also ordered to report.

He received a frosty reception. Then, as the admiral and the commodore discussed the victory announcement that should go to Washington, the *Resolute* steamed up in a panic with the news that a Spanish battleship, the *Pelayo,* was bearing down on them. Sampson doubted the report. Taylor on the *Indiana,* in any case, had gone off to verify it hours before. Sampson nevertheless ordered Schley to "go after it."

It was curious, Graham thought, that the *New York* did not go. The *Brooklyn* and her crew were battle-worn and weary, her starboard batteries barely operable. She had been hit perhaps thirty times by Spanish shells and—no one quite knew why—had taken on water at the stern. Reluctantly, Schley returned to his ship and again ordered up steam. At dusk, when he found and aggressively approached the *María Teresa*, the Austrian captain lofted a string of international signals and outlined them with his searchlight: "This ship flies the Austrian flag. Please don't fire."

Schley returned to his blockading position. It was well after midnight on July 4 when he finally retired, "weary with fatigue, and with the mucous membrane of throat and nose sore from ammonia gas released in the powder smoke of battle. . . ." Reflecting on that day, he thought Santiago a more decisive battle than Trafalgar, and his action in making the loop comparable to that of Horatio Nelson at St. Vincent when he "wore ship" away from the Spanish fleet. The *Brooklyn* had won a renown that could never be impugned, yet Sampson had not extended congratulations. That would have meant so much to the men.

It took him some time to fall asleep.

At 2 A.M., as Schley nodded off, Sampson's victory message to Washington was delivered to the telegraph operator at Siboney by his assistant chief of staff, Sidney Staunton. But Schley had made one last effort to present the victory under his signature, dispatching his flag lieutenant, James H. Sears, to Siboney with his own message of "annihilation." Staunton told Sears, who had arrived almost at the same moment, that regulations precluded its being sent. All communications to the secretary of the navy had to go through Sampson, the senior officer present. Sears capitulated.

Consciously or not, Staunton had drafted Sampson's message in the manner of William Tecumseh Sherman offering Abraham Lincoln Savannah as a Christmas present. The clatter of the telegraph machine drowned out the crackling noise of the land crabs outside the shack: "The fleet under my command offers the nation as a Fourth of July present the whole of Cervera's fleet . . ."

The Spanish fleet was dead and burning on the coast of Cuba, but the acrimonious battle over who won the day at Santiago would rage on in the press, the navy, and even the White House for years to come.

Early on the Sunday morning of the battle, as Shafter awaited Sampson's arrival at his headquarters, he had finally broken his mysterious silence by cabling Alger: "We have town well invested on the north and east, but with a very thin line." The Spanish defenses, on the other hand, were "so strong it will be impossible to carry it by storm with my present force and I am seriously considering withdrawing about five miles and taking up a new position. . . . I have been unable to be out during the heat of the day for four days, but am retaining the command."

Gloom pervaded the trenches that beautiful Sunday. Richard Harding Davis reported that "the situation in the rifle pits on the morning of the 3rd was really most critical. One smelt disaster in the air. The alarmists were out in strong force and were in the majority."

For once, Theodore Roosevelt was among them. Somehow he managed to scribble off a long letter to Henry Cabot Lodge: "Tell the President for Heaven's sake to send us every regiment and above all every battery possible. We have won so far at a heavy cost; but the Spaniards fight very hard and charging these intrenchments [sic] against modern rifles is terrible. We are within measureable distance of a terrible military disaster; we must have help. . . . Our General is poor; he is too unwieldy to get to the front . . . how I have escaped I know not. . . ."

Colonel Edward McClernand had dispatched Shafter's wire. Afterward, he suddenly recalled a notion Shafter had advanced on the Segurança. He would surround Santiago and demand its surrender. McClernand strode back to Shafter's tent. The general was still sprawled on his cot, obviously ill, depressed. "General," the aide said, "let us make a demand on them to surrender." There was no answer. "He looked at me for perhaps a full minute and I thought he was going to offer a rebuke, for my persistence . . . but finally he said: 'Well, try it.'"

McClernand sat under the tent fly that shaded his field desk and, at 8:30 A.M., wrote a dispatch advising the commanding general of the Spanish forces in Santiago that unless he surrendered, the city would be shelled. Signed by Shafter, the message was delivered under a flag of truce. Sampson, of course, never arrived for their meeting. Shafter could hear the cannonading—someone later reported it was audible two hundred miles away—but as the roar of guns trailed off to the west, the general decided that the Spanish squadron had broken through the admiral's blockade. That evening, he cabled Washington ambiguously that "Cervera had come out and had escaped and that he [Sampson] was in pursuit."

In Washington that Sunday, Shafter's defeatist messages spawned gloom and consternation in the War Room at the White House. On receipt of Shafter's message of retreat, Alger consulted with McKinley and cabled that Shafter could, of course, best judge the situation on the battlefield. "If, however, you can hold your present position, especially San Juan heights, the effect upon the country would be much better than falling back." Shafter's response—that he had demanded that the Spanish surrender—differed so markedly from his earlier messages that it was hard to credit. The hours dragged on.

Finally, near midnight, Shafter cabled: "I shall hold my present position." Another message reported Cervera's squadron defeated. Euphoria replaced despondency. At 2 A.M. on July 4 Alger walked home with a light step. He could hear newsboys hawking an early edition. "Spanish fleet destroyed!"

Perhaps the only person the news did not entirely please was Stephen Crane. Early Sunday morning he had steamed off from Siboney to Jamaica on a press boat. Returning, he saw that nothing had changed. Sampson's fleet still formed a blockading arc around the harbor mouth. But then a gunboat hailed that Cervera had taken his ships out; they were all sunk. "The squadron hadn't changed a button," Crane wrote ruefully. "There it sat without even a smile on the face of the tiger. And it had eaten four armoured cruisers and two torpedo-boat destroyers while my back was turned for a moment."

XI

THE COST OF CONQUEST

> The son and heir was coming fast, blue-shirted, sunburned, burdened with glistening cartridges. He was sweeping before him the last traces of a fallen Empire; the sons of the young Republic were tearing down the royal crowns . . . and raising the flag of the new Empire over the land of the sugar-cane and the palm.
>
> —RICHARD HARDING DAVIS

> . . . the interests of the country were forgotten, even by the members of the Government who were not willing to recognize that, just as military men must give their lives in a holocaust for the country, political men should also make some sacrifice for it, and take at least a little risk before they permit the Crown of Spain to lose 10,000,000 of its subjects.
>
> —CAPTAIN VÍCTOR M. CONCAS

EARLY ON THE morning of the Fourth of July, William Randolph Hearst's Sylvia worked in close to the smoldering Vizcaya. Hearst, Jack Follansbee, and photographer John Hemment got into a launch and went over to the wreck. Climbing up the sea ladder, Hemment noted it was still hot to the touch. As they reached the deck line, he saw that the woodwork had burned off and the supporting girders were twisted into grotesque shapes. The foremast had somehow been uprooted and thrown across a turret. The bodies of crewmen, charred to a deep black, were strewn about the deck.

Hearst, immaculate in blue flannels and a yachting cap, was astonished by the destruction. "Great heavens!" he wrote, "Is this rent and ruined hull, black and battered, blistered and burned . . . the noble boat . . . from which Captain Eulate trained his guns on the tall buildings of New York?" He picked up a warm lump of fused Spanish silver money— it would make a good paperweight—and they went back down the ladder and headed for the *Oquendo*. As they approached, Hearst was shocked by the sight of dead bodies floating in the water, "stripped to the waist as they had stood to man their guns. We steered nervously among the bodies, feeling much pity, and some satisfaction, too, that the *Maine* had been again so well remembered."

Even in the flush of victory, sides were drawn for battles still to come. Schley's adherents tried to position their favorite as the commander at Santiago, while Sampson's partisans accused the commodore of dilatory tactics in establishing the blockade and poor judgment—if not cowardice—in looping the *Brooklyn* away from the battle. Sampson advised Long that he was reluctant to recommend Schley for advancement. Recalling Schley's fuddled behavior between Cienfuegos and Santiago, he stated: "This reprehensible conduct I cannot separate from his subsequent conduct. . . ." Hearst's *Journal* announced in favor of Schley—"as much the hero of Santiago as Dewey is of Manila." Sampson was mocked as a "teagoing admiral—a rear admiral, always in the rear."

Speaker of the House Thomas Reed allowed that he could not make out "what the row between these two naval heroes is about. As far as I can see one of them wasn't in the fight at all and the other was doing his damnedest to get out of it."

Shafter chided Sampson for not forcing the harbor entrance. Alfred Thayer Mahan dressed down Secretary of War Russell Alger in front of the president for his woeful ignorance of the purpose of seapower—"It was a very pretty scrimmage," Long remarked. And virtually everybody took Shafter and his ubiquitous, high-ranking colleagues—"Gen-

eral Mismanagement and General Neglect," as Hemment
called them—to task.

Rather more plausibly, the Spanish squabbled in defeat.
On the day after the battle, Sampson allowed Cervera to cable
Blanco in Havana, and the admiral immediately established
the ground he would hold at his court martial: "In compli-
ance with your excellency's orders, I went out from Santiago
yesterday morning with the whole squadron, and after an unequal battle against forces more than three times as large as
mine my whole squadron was destroyed. . . . Gallantry of all
the crews has earned most enthusiastic congratulations of enemy." In his full report on the battle he emphasized that he
had foreseen the appalling disaster and disclaimed responsibility: "Our country has been defended with honor, and the
satisfaction of duty well done leaves our consciences
clear. . . ."

Blanco tipped his hat to Cervera in a manifesto to the inhabitants of Cuba: "Fortune does not always favor the brave.
The Spanish squadron, under the command of Rear-Admiral
Cervera, has just performed the greatest deed of heroism that
is perhaps recorded in the annals of the navy in the present
century, fighting American forces three times as large. It succumbed gloriously. . . ." But as he sorted out the sad affair,
and established the actual odds Cervera faced, Blanco could
not refrain from commenting, "Perhaps if another time had
been chosen for sortie result would have been different.
Sampson states in his report he sustained only three casualties. Is that possible?"

Cervera replied testily, "Am deeply grieved that all my
actions meet with your excellency's censure. . . . The sortie
at night would not have obviated loss of squadron. . . ."

Blanco answered that he accepted full responsibility for
the sortie, but Cervera would not let it go at that. He had been
right from the beginning; the squadron was doomed from the
moment it left for the West Indies; his honor had been "spotted." He warned Blanco that he planned to publish "my
whole correspondence. . . . If anything personal should result
from this . . . it will not be my fault."

Shafter cabled Washington that he had been able to watch
the battle for the heights from his distant headquarters, but

he was hard put to defend himself from the volleys of abuse that fell on him from his own ranks. A soldier in the Sixteenth Infantry put it plainly: "General Shafter is a fool and I believe should be shot." Roosevelt invoked, in a letter to Lodge on July 5, the specter of a greedy, inept Roman general: "Not since the campaign of Crassus against the Parthians has there been so criminally incompetent a General as Shafter. . . . Shafter never came within three miles of the line, and never has come; the confusion is incredible."

Shafter finally did manage, rather painfully, to at least approach the front. Private Post saw him inspect "his line of trenches in a Maine buckboard that sagged under his weight and was pulled by an artillery horse." (Shafter later explained that he had a gunny sack on his gouty foot and could not mount his horse without a platform.)

Shafter's press relations, poor in Tampa, had worsened when he refused to let correspondents land with the troops at Daiquirí. Davis, who held a special grudge (Shafter had disparaged his credentials as a historian), thought he should have removed himself from command. "His self-complacency was so great that in spite of blunder after blunder, folly upon folly, and mistake upon mistake, he still believed himself infallible, still bullied his inferior officers, and still cursed from his cot."

Battered but unbowed, Shafter doggedly pursued the course proposed by his aide, Colonel McClernand, to squeeze a surrender from General José Torál in Santiago. There was a considerable element of bluff involved. The positions Shafter had taken at such heavy cost were thinly held, the troops tired, hungry, and wet, the muddy supply line from Siboney clogged with hospital wagons full of wounded soldiers. For want of lighters, desperately needed siege guns, ammunition, food, and medicine sat uselessly in the holds of the transports offshore.

In Santiago, however, the situation was equally grim. Artillery Captain Severo Gómez Núñez reported virtually no ammunition left for the Krupp cannon. A million Mauser cartridges were on hand, but he estimated these sufficient only to repel two attacks. Food and water were in short supply; the soldiers existed on rice, sugar, coffee, and brandy. A large number of officers had been killed or wounded in the defense of the city. Hospitals held 1,700 sick and wounded.

Even so, Torál quickly rejected Shafter's surrender demand. On the evening of July 3, he responded with a curt note: "It is my duty to say to you that this city will not surrender. . . ." He would, however, inform "the foreign consuls and inhabitants" that Shafter had threatened to shell Santiago.

When the extent of Cervera's defeat became apparent, Shafter postponed the bombardment scheduled for July 4 and tried again: "To save needless effusion of blood and the distress of many people, you may reconsider your determination of yesterday." Torál responded that he had not changed his mind—"this place will not be surrendered."

That Monday Alger cabled impatiently: ". . . you will use your own judgment as to how and when you will take the city of Santiago, but, for manifest reasons, it should be accomplished as speedily as possible." Shafter had no more stomach for a frontal assault on the Santiago fortifications, with or without promised reinforcements. If it had to be done quickly, let the navy force the issue. He sent another imperative message to Sampson, knowing that the admiral could not act upon it without the approval of Long and McKinley: "Now, if you will force your way into that harbor the town will surrender without any further sacrifice of life. My present position has cost me 1,000 men, and I do not want to lose any more." Sampson, seeking guidance from Washington, was told ambiguously to cooperate with the army but "not to risk the loss of any armored vessels by submarine mines."

As Shafter pursued his surrender initiatives, the soldiers on the heights took umbrage at the annoying white flags of truce that passed with increasing regularity between the Spanish and American lines. "To the men in the pits," Davis reported, "who knew nothing of the exigencies of diplomacy, these virgin flags were as offensive as those of red are to the bull . . . when they saw crawling across the valley below the long white flag of truce, their watchfulness seemed wasted, their vigilance became a farce, and they mocked and scoffed at the white flag bitterly."

A Rough Rider, Davis recalled, expressed the idea "in

professional phraseology: 'Now that we got those Mexicans coralled,' he said, 'why don't we brand them?'"

Washington found the protracted negotiations alarming. The feeling grew that Shafter was infirm, that Torál was tricking out the negotiations until tropical disease wasted the American army's capacity to mount an assault.

And that is what happened. A devastating surge of fever began with the rains, and with the release of Santiago refugees—women, children, old men, and invalids—into the American lines.

On the evening of July 4, as Shafter pressed his surrender demands, the sky darkened and lightning flashed over Santiago. Clara Barton, recently arrived in Cuba on the Red Cross ship *State of Texas,* thought it "one of the most fearful storms which I have ever seen."

From then on, it stormed virtually every day. The soldiers were chilled in the early morning, baked in the midday sun, and soaked in the afternoon. Their ponchos shredded and leaked. The dog tents gave little protection from sun or rain. Davis, who spent almost two weeks in the rifle pits after the naval battle, described how "the water ran down the hills in broad streams, overflowing the tent-trenches and leaping merrily over the bodies of the men. It was not at all an unusual experience to sleep through the greater part of the night with the head lifted just clear of the water and . . . the body down in it." If Davis had read the *Army and Navy Journal* for April 23, he must now have recalled the medical advice provided by a Cuban doctor: "When sleeping, soldiers must be kept off the ground and out of the rain. . . . Never put on stockings that are damp."

Field hospitals were drenched, campfires extinguished. Streams overflowed their banks and the rotting bodies of men and horses washed out of shallow graves. The Camino Real became a morass all the way to Siboney. Cavalrymen had to swim their horses across fords. On the coast angry seas and high surf made landings and departures from the transports perilous.

Everyone thought the storms reached a climax—if not an ending—on Monday the eleventh. Even Roosevelt was distraught. At midnight his tent blew over. "I had for the first time in a fortnight undressed myself completely, and I felt punished for my love of luxury when I jumped out into the driving downpour of tropic rain, and groped blindly in the darkness for my clothes as they lay in the liquid mud." The storm was immortalized by the troops as "the night it rained."

As the rains increased (August would be worse, the troops were told), lice thrived. Private Post, turning entomologist, classified them in three distinct species. There was the familiar grayback of Civil War fame. A newer variety, which made its home in the hairs of the head, was named the "Rough Rider." Finally, there was *Phthirius pubis*, the scourge of armies since ancient times, which inhabited more private regions. The lousy soldiers of the New York Seventy-first were overjoyed when they received little cubes of potent yellow soap to discourage the insects. But the lice hung grimly on and, perhaps spurred to action by the sting of the fatty acids, multiplied.

Food was always in short supply. Spoiled turnips and hard beans occasionally made it to the front, but there were no stew pans to boil them in. The soldiers ate them raw. Coffee beans were green and had to be "ground" with a pistol butt or a rock. Orders not to eat the local mangoes were ignored and, as Post wrote, "latrines began to be flecked with blood." If the result was painful, at least the fruit had food value.

Most of the troops were still unable to choke down the nauseous, slimy tinned beef the army had issued. For the most part, they existed on moldy hardtack, sometimes sugared, sometimes fried in the grease of rancid sowbelly. Roosevelt called it a "Klondike" ration. Whatever it was, it was not suited to the tropics, and after the storm on July 11, when the supply line broke down, even hardtack was hard to find. Roosevelt put it simply: "We were threatened with famine."

As the soldiers with gaunt faces and swollen bellies scavenged for food, malaria swept through the fetid campgrounds. Little was known about the various tropical fevers, not even that they were transmitted by mosquitoes. They were lumped under the general heading of "calenture," which George Kennan of the Red Cross, traveling with Clara Barton, classified as "Cuban malarial fever." The symptoms were chills, delirium, temperatures ranging up to 106 degrees, back pains, flushed and swollen faces, and fierce headaches. Army doctors called it "the Five-day Fever." Usually, after several days, the symptoms abated, but the patient was left with "languor and prostration." Often, the fever returned. Treatments included quinine, calomel, and sulphate of magnesia.

The troops put their own name to the fevers: "head exhaustion." Most managed to go about their duties, but severe cases were incapacitating. A soldier wrote home: "For three alternate days I lay groveling on the ground hour after hour, just praying God to let me die. . . . It was as if I were put in crematory while alive and the heat turned on . . . and it appeared as if my spine had been broken. I tell you, it was terrible."

From time to time, soldiers heard the melancholy strains of Taps not at the end of the day, but after reveille, marking a burial. Then, five days after some 20,000 civilian refugees came out of Santiago, the first cases of yellow fever, or "jack," were reported at Siboney. The dreaded yellow fever was known to be infectious and more apt to be fatal than malaria. When General Nelson Appleton Miles arrived in Cuba, he had the baker's dozen disease-ridden shacks in the town burned to the ground, an action Shafter had resisted taking. But as men died, the repulsive red, yellow, and black land crabs foraged by night, and the bloody-necked vultures by day.

The commanding general of the army had set foot on Cuban soil on July 11 with an ambiguous portfolio. Alger had instructed him not to supersede Shafter unless he was not "able for duty," and the Fifth Corps commander protested that he was fit. Miles had some thirty-five hundred volunteers with him aboard the *Yale* and the *Columbia*, the nucleus of the force assembling for the long-delayed Puerto Rico campaign, but he had yet to receive final approval from Washington. He considered an assault on the fortifications guarding the harbor of Santiago, but after conferring with Shafter and determining the extent of the fever problem, Miles quarantined most of his men aboard their ships and gave his support to the surrender negotiations.

In the meantime, General Torál had been advised that a

naval bombardment of Santiago would begin at noon on Saturday July 9 unless he capitulated. Again, white flags passed back and forth between the trenches. Torál replied that he would surrender the city if allowed to march his army north to Holguín. Shafter first advised Washington that the naval bombardment should bring about unconditional surrender. Then, noting that cases of yellow fever had been diagnosed at Siboney, he did an about-face, cabling Alger that Torál's conditions should be met.

McKinley's response, through army channels, was virtually a reprimand. Shafter was brusquely ordered to accept only unconditional surrender: "Your message recommending that Spanish troops be permitted to evacuate . . . is a great surprise, and is not approved."

The truce ended on the Sunday afternoon of July 10 as the *Indiana* and the *Brooklyn* took position south of Aguadores. Cadet Mannix watched as the *Indiana*'s heavy 13-inch gun turrets were swung seaward so as to give the ship a heavy list to starboard, thus raising the elevation of the port 8-inch batteries so that they could arc shells over the hills guarding Santiago. The range was set for nine thousand yards; a gun barrel wavered, then stilled; almost immediately there was an ear-splitting crack. "As the shell passed out of sight over the summit of the hills," Mannix wrote, "it awoke a series of wails and howls that no banshee in Ireland could have equalled. . . ."

There was a long pause until a signal corpsman on shore wigwagged, "Low and to the right." Range and deflection were adjusted. Another shot was fired, further adjustments made. Observers on the heights saw shells, now fired at two-minute intervals, walk their way through the nearly empty city. The bombardment continued until Sunday evening, paused, and resumed on Monday morning. Finally, at 1 P.M., "Cease firing" was ordered.

As the navy bombarded the city, Secretary Alger presented McKinley with a suggestion that he felt might save Spanish face and break the deadlocked surrender negotiations. He proposed that should Torál surrender unconditionally, those of his soldiers who wished to return to Spain would be repatriated "at the expense of the United States Government." The cost, Alger maintained, would be no more than that of establishing a prisoner-of-war camp in the United States. The danger of tropical fevers invading the mainland would also be reduced.

McKinley approved. Shafter was notified and conveyed the proposal to Torál. Alger's compromise proved the key to settlement, though negotiations dragged on as Torál sought instructions from Havana and Madrid and Shafter showed further willingness to settle for something less than unconditional surrender—what Roosevelt called "tacking and veering." In Washington, Shafter's friend and confidant, Adjutant General Henry Clark Corbin, was finally compelled to put it bluntly: "The President and Secretary of War are becoming impatient with parley. . . . The way to surrender is to surrender. . . ."

On Thursday, July 14, Miles and Shafter met with Torál between the lines, and the Spaniard reported he had authorization to surrender "on the basis of repatriation." Torál wondered if that would include his whole command; he also had troops at Guantánamo, Holguín, and San Luis. Certainly, Shafter replied, all were included. Torál agreed, and Shafter "was simply thunderstruck that, of their own free will, they should give me 12,000 men that were absolutely beyond my reach."

In the next two days the protocol of surrender was hammered out. The Spanish would remove mines and other obstructions at the harbor mouth. Troops would be transported home at U.S. government expense. The protocol would employ the word "capitulation" rather than "surrender." The ceremony was scheduled for Sunday, July 17.

On Saturday, asked by a correspondent whether the press would be given permission to enter the city, Shafter replied with characteristic acerbity, "No sir, you will not." That ill-considered refusal set the stage for his final skirmish in Cuba.

The church bells of Santiago began to peal at ten o'clock on Sunday, a bright and clear morning, as chaplains led their regiments in services of thanksgiving for the end of hostilities. General Torál with a company of a hundred men from various regiments rode out of Santiago to a field about two hundred yards in front of the American lines and was met by Shafter, astride a huge bay horse, escorted by mounted cavalry. Shafter's gouty foot was wedged in a stirrup and a white pith helmet crowned his formidable head. Spanish buglers blew a salute; afterward, the American buglers added their own. "It was an odd medley of blaring notes," a correspondent noted, "but extremely thrilling. . . ."

Shafter presented Torál with the sword and spurs of General Vara del Rey, killed at El Caney. Torál saluted. Shafter stretched out his hand, gave Torál's a firm shake, and commended the Spanish general on his gallant defense. Then the Spanish, followed by the Americans, marched into Santiago.

On the way in, everyone noticed the impressive Spanish defenses—artillery redoubts, ammunition depots, thick-walled buildings with firing loopholes bashed in their sides, barbed-wire entanglements, piles of paving stones and sand-filled barrels, networks of flanking and enfilading trenches. On one point, at least, Shafter had been right. A frontal assault on the city would have been enormously costly.

At noon there were formal ceremonies in the central plaza of Santiago, ringed by the Café Venus (soon to be touted for its horsemeat and onion stew), the cathedral, and the Governor's Palace. Hundreds of troops massed in the square. On the roof of the palace, three officers prepared to raise General Wheeler's headquarters flag over the oldest Spanish city in the new world. A military band readied its instruments.

At that solemn moment a shabby-looking man in a black coat and a battered derby hat appeared on the palace roof and strode aggressively up to the flagpole. Ralph Paine of the *Philadelphia Press*, who had infiltrated the city with several other correspondents, knew immediately who it was. On the roof "there appeared the active, compact figure of the incomparable Sylvester Scovel, Special Commissioner of the New York *World*."

Scoval had been in Cuba on and off since 1895, had fought with Gómez, reported the *Maine* tragedy in Havana, and performed intelligence operations for Sampson. This was a moment he had long waited for, and he seized it—and the flag halyards—firmly. Shafter glared at him, then roared out orders to haul the correspondent down.

In the square, according to Paine, Scovel protested his enforced departure from the palace roof. Shafter told him "to shut up or be locked up," and brushed him aside. Scovel thought the fat, florid general had insulted him. He took a swing at Shafter. "It was a flurried blow," Paine said, "without much science behind it, and Scovel's first glanced off the general's double chin, but it left a mark there, a red scratch visible for some days."

Scovel was promptly put under arrest. As he was hauled away to a lock-up, the cathedral clock bell began to ring out the hour of noon, the Stars and Stripes rose over the square, the troops presented arms, and the band of the Sixth Cavalry blared into the national anthem, then "Hail, Columbia." When the band stopped, Shafter began to read a message from President McKinley: "Your splendid command has . . . triumphed over obstacles which would have overcome men less brave and determined. . . ." As he went on, a small band of Hearst correspondents roamed the city plastering walls with posters emblazoned with REMEMBER THE MAINE, and underneath, BUY THE JOURNAL.

Santiago had been a strategic objective only because Pascual Cervera had entered harbor there. After the destruction of his squadron, the navy was free to move on to the coast of Spain, the Philippines, and Puerto Rico.

As plans for these operations continued, Spain realized that her globe-circling ring of colonial dominoes were in free fall. Dewey had taken Manila Bay and Cavite on May 1. Guam had meekly surrendered to the cruiser *Charleston*, on her way to reinforce Dewey, on June 20. On July 7, McKinley signed a joint congressional resolution to annex Hawaii. It was, the president said, "manifest destiny." Ten days later, Santiago fell.

Spain's hopes to command the sea and defend its colonies had been dashed by Sampson's victory over Cervera. Admiral Cámara, who had taken his squadron through the Suez Canal into the Red Sea on July 6, was recalled the next day to meet the threat of Commodore John C. Watson's Eastern Squadron. Cámara was to proceed swiftly to Cartagena, then sail through the Strait of Gibraltar to Cádiz, keeping close to shore so that the nervous seaboard population might see the Spanish flag.

Torál had surrendered Santiago, vast quantities of arms, and the entire Fourth Army Corps—some 23,500 soldiers. Havana and its impressive defenses had yet to be tested, but Ramón Blanco was now checkmated by a reinforced blockading squadron. He knew, in any case, that Spain had no further zest for war in Cuba. Minister of War Correa had written that he could not fathom his "tenacity in maintaining our position in so ungrateful a territory. . . ." And at Manila, Dewey had been reinforced by thirty-six hundred troops under the command of Brigadier General Francis Greene. Clearly, if the Philippines were to remain Spanish, they were more apt to be held at the conference table than in the trenches.

On Monday, July 18, Spain asked France to represent her interests to the United States government. On the twenty-sixth, the French ambassador to Washington, Jules Cambon, met at the White House with McKinley and Secretary of State William Day. Cambon delivered a note from Madrid in which Spain admitted she had been "worsted." She believed "the time has now come when she can properly ask the cooperation of the United States in terminating the war." Cambon expressed the hope that McKinley would be "humanely Christian and generous." He tried to focus the discussion on Cuba, which Spain was now willing to relinquish, if her other territories could be retained.

A day earlier the army had finally reached Puerto Rico on what Mr. Dooley would call "Gin'ral Miles' gran' picnic an' moonlight excursion in Porther Ricky." Miles had finally secured permission for the invasion on the day after Torál surrendered Santiago. A planned assault on fortress Havana could be postponed until the rainy season was over. Miles sailed east with his thirty-five hundred quarantined troops while twelve thousand more hastily assembled at Tampa, Charleston, and Newport News. Before leaving, he had nagged Sampson for an armored escort. The admiral's responsibilities already included the transatlantic foray and the

Cuban blockade, and several of his battle-worn ships needed drydocking, but he reluctantly pieced together a convoy that sailed from Guantánamo on July 21.

Miles's bold little expedition, spearheaded by the battleship *Massachusetts*, was explicitly directed to land at Fajardo on the northeast coast of Puerto Rico. Within a week, with his reinforcements, he would march on San Juan, only forty miles away. There were no fortifications of substance at Fajardo, and a troop concentration there was unlikely. The Spanish were thought to have dispersed their limited forces (some eight thousand regulars and nine thousand volunteers) to various parts of the island, leaving a hard core at San Juan where naval bombardment could soften resistance.

But as the convoy passed through the Windward Passage and began to traverse the north coast of Haiti, Miles told Captain Francis Higginson of the *Massachusetts* that the Spanish probably knew of his plan to land at Fajardo; to achieve the element of surprise, he wanted his troops put ashore at Guánica, on the southwest coast. Higginson remonstrated. The reefs along the south shore were "imperfectly charted" and at least three of his ships would be unable to enter the shallow harbor at Guánica. Coaling and communications would be far more difficult than at Fajardo, just thirty miles from St. Thomas. And, as French Ensor Chadwick would emphasize, "the change put between the American forces and the main Spanish position a much greater distance, and a mountain range which a determined enemy might have made impassable."

Higginson had no authority to deny Miles his newly chosen landing site. "All right, Guánica it is," he told the army general. Alfred Thayer Mahan, when it was all over, labeled Miles's decision "a military stupidity so great" that he could explain it only in terms of an "obsession to vanity."

On Tuesday July 26, Russell Alger was astonished to read an Associated Press dispatch announcing Miles's landing at Guánica the previous day. At first, he did not credit it, but Miles was known in the War Department for harebrained schemes and Alger feared it might be true.

Later that day, when a cable arrived from Miles via St. Thomas, he knew it was. Miles reported that he had "deemed it advisable to take first the harbor of Guánica, 15 miles west of Ponce, which was successfully accomplished . . . Spaniards surprised.

"The *Gloucester*, Commander Wainwright, first entered the harbor . . ."

Alger's first task was to notify the supporting troop convoys that there was nothing to reinforce at Fajardo.

The feisty *Gloucester* had taken Guánica single-handedly. Lieutenant Harry Huse brought a landing party of twenty-nine ashore unopposed, took over the waterfront, hauled down the Spanish flag, and raised the Stars and Stripes. The Spanish took umbrage and began firing on the sailors, who built a little stone *trocha* across the town's single street, named it Fort Wainwright, and called in fire from their armed yacht. Richard Harding Davis, one of a handful of correspondents with the expedition, reported that the Spanish fled "before the hideous bombardment of the *Gloucester's* three-pounder."

Miles had been told to raise the flag, but as Alger digested the news from Puerto Rico and the president met with Cambon, the commanding general issued a proclamation to the Portoriqueños that seemed to establish policy: ". . . in the cause of liberty, justice and humanity [United States] military forces have come to occupy the island of Porto Rico. They come bearing the banners of freedom, inspired by noble purposes, to seek the enemies of our Government and yours and to destroy or capture all in armed resistance . . . it is hoped that this will be followed by the cheerful acceptance of the United States Government . . . and give the people of your beautiful island the largest measure of liberty consistent with military occupation."

Miles announced that his troops had been received with "wild enthusiasm," and this was not far off the mark, but some Puerto Ricans may have wondered whether the Americans could improve upon the concessions already granted by Spain. At the end of 1897, as Sagasta liberalized colonial policy, Puerto Rico was granted home rule with an elected parliament and a cabinet with significant power over domestic and foreign affairs. The powers of the Spanish governor-general were severely curtailed. Shortly before the American invasion, Luis Muñoz Rivera, the island's most prominent political figure, declared loyally, "We are Spaniards, and wrapped in the Spanish flag we will die."

As Miles proclaimed the "blessings of enlightened civilization," Brigadier General Guy V. Henry, who had arrived on Charles Sigsbee's *St. Paul,* moved his troops eastward toward Yauco while Miles sailed down the coast to Ponce. Yauco was captured after a brief engagement. The channel into the harbor at Ponce proved to be unmined, unfortified, and undefended. Several of the smaller American warships entered. The transport *Columbia* did not. Embarrassingly, she was stuck on an uncharted reef for more than a day.

It did not matter. Ponce, by most accounts, surrendered at least four times. "It was possessed of the surrender habit," Davis wrote, "in a most aggravated form. Indeed, for anyone in uniform it was most unsafe to enter the town at any time, unless he came prepared to accept its unconditional surrender." Commander Charles H. Davis of the *Dixie* was given the official credit, "But, as a matter of fact," Davis recalled, "the town first surrendered to Ensign Curtin of the *Wasp,* then to three officers who strayed into it by mistake, then to Commander Davis, and finally to General Miles."

Miles came ashore with Davis, several officers of his staff, and four army regulars. One of them waved a flag vigorously as the launch approached the town docks and a crowd of thousands of Puerto Ricans yelled *vivas.* Nearing shore, Davis reported, a soldier who spoke Spanish announced that General Miles's arrival "brought them liberty, fraternity, peace, happiness, and wealth. He promised them no taxes, freedom of speech, thought, and conscience, 'three acres and a cow,' plurality of wives, 'one man, one vote,' and to every citizen a political office and a pension for life."

"So General Miles landed in triumph," Davis concluded. And as news of the general's easy victories filtered back to Washington, even Alger became resigned to Miles's circuitous approach to San Juan.

With the arrival of his reinforcements, Miles devised a four-pronged thrust on the island's major centers; the pincers would eventually close on San Juan. It took a week to plan the operation and unload supplies, but when the army columns finally moved out, they made swift progress. On August 9 there was a sharp skirmish at Coamo, up the military road toward San Juan, where the Puerto Ricans were less welcoming than they had been at Ponce. But when the Spaniards were flushed out, Davis reported, the Puerto Ricans turned "their backs on the men who had ruled them for a hundred years." As an army band marched briskly down the main street and broke into the jubilant cadence of a Sousa march, there were wild shouts of "¡Viva!"

Stephen Crane, Davis admitted, played a small role in the sweep of history. Hearst's new recruit (Pulitzer's *World* had released him for filing Edward Marshall's *Journal* dispatch after Las Guásimas) still had a gaunt and fragile look from his bout with malaria, but he returned to the fray early in August freshened by a sojourn in Virginia. In Ponce on the night of August 2, he and Davis decided to move at dawn on Juana Díaz, nine miles to the east. They flipped a coin to see who would wake the other. "I won the toss," Davis recalled. "But I lost the town." Crane did not wake him up.

"While I slumbered," Davis wrote, "Crane crept forward between our advance posts and fell upon the doomed garrison." The *alcade* (mayor) promptly surrendered and Crane, rather than shooting prisoners and looting the town, "organized a joint celebration of conquerors and conquered."

It was not always that easy. There were towns, as Crane pointed out, where Americanism was elective. And at Aibonito the Puerto Rican "picnic" finally took a serious turn. Here, where the road to San Juan snaked into the mountains, the Spanish had elected to fight. An officer sent out to reconnoiter on August 12 reported there was "a deep gorge on one side and a perpendicular wall on the other." Above the "wall" a thirteen-hundred-man Spanish force had dug rifle trenches along an eighteen-hundred-foot height. Machine guns and artillery pieces were emplaced above them. The army was bloodied a bit—Davis reported "a terrific fire of shrapnel, common shell, and Mauser bullets [that] did much damage to our infantry"—and Mayor General James H. Wilson postponed a major assault until Saturday, August 13.

That morning, Davis recalled, as an artilleryman put a shell in his gun and took aim, a Signal Corps officer "galloped upon the scene, shrieking, 'Cease firing, peace has been declared!' Whereat the men swore." "The campaign," Davis observed, "was nipped by peace. . . ."

Probably it was just as well. The rugged terrain at Aibonito and beyond was more ominous than the heights before Santiago. And the navy had underscored the ill-advised nature of Miles's march through the mountains six days earlier when twenty-eight sailors and marines landed at Fajardo, without opposition, and captured the lighthouse. Still, Miles could rightly claim that his misplaced beachhead in Puerto Rico had increased pressure on the Spanish to come to terms.

McKinley had discussed Cambon's peace overtures on behalf of Spain with his Cabinet. There was little disagreement that Spain should cede Cuba, an island in the Ladrones (now the Marianas), probably Guam, and Puerto Rico. On the Philippines, however, the Cabinet split down the middle. Judge Day favored keeping only a naval base—"a hitching post," as McKinley thought of it. It seemed to the secretary of state unwise and unprincipled to annex an archipelago whose "eight or nine millions of absolutely ignorant and many degraded people" would be unable to govern themselves. The flag should be planted only where the Constitution could take root. Secretary of Agriculture James H. Wilson, on the other hand, favored retaining all the islands so that the natives might be evangelized. McKinley smiled. "Yes, you Scotch favor keeping everything including the Sabbath."

The president had not made up his own mind about the Philippines, but he had a substantial number of troops there and Dewey was certain Manila would soon fall—probably without a fight. In his inaugural address McKinley had warned against territorial aggression; war against Spain had been declared for humanitarian purposes—Cuba Libre. But it now seemed politic to take what he could get; final disposition of the islands could be made when a peace protocol was in place. Adroitly, he guided the Cabinet to this view. The peace terms, as finally drafted and presented to Cambon, required Spain to relinquish sovereignty over Cuba, Puerto Rico, and an island in the Ladrones. The United States was also entitled to "hold the city, bay and harbor of Manila pending the conclusion of a treaty of peace."

Cambon found the terms severe and asked for changes. McKinley would not compromise. He warned that unless they were accepted conditions might become harsher. Cambon, like so many others, had thought McKinley weak. Now he observed that the president was "as firm as a rock."

Madrid protested, but won concessions only on minor points. Premier Sagasta canvassed senior army officers and politicians; he found little support for continuing the war. On August 11 he accepted the American terms. Cambon worked out last-minute details: peace commissioners appointed by both governments would meet in Paris no later than October 1 to negotiate and conclude a treaty of peace; hostilities would be suspended the moment the protocol was signed.

At 4:23 P.M. on August 12, as a violent thunderstorm rumbled over Washington, Secretary of State Day, representing the United States, and Ambassador Cambon, representing Spain, signed the peace protocol in the Cabinet Room of the White House. McKinley immediately proclaimed a suspension of hostilities. In Puerto Rico the shooting stopped just as Spanish resistance stiffened. In Manila Bay, where the telegraph cable to Hong Kong was still severed, the news would take four days to arrive. And in Cuba, while conventional war came to a halt, the armistice had no effect on the fevers that had now all but destroyed the Fifth Army Corps as a fighting unit.

At Santiago, as Miles sailed for Guánica, the situation had worsened. Roosevelt, now promoted to full colonel, reported that less than 50 percent of his men were fit for duty. "The lithe college athletes had lost their spring; the tall, gaunt hunters and cow-punchers lounged listlessly in their dog-tents, which were steaming morasses during the torrential rains, and then ovens when the sun blazed down. . . ." On July 28, 4,270 men of the Fifth Corps were reported ill; of these, 3,406 had fever. Burials were no longer announced, Private Post wrote. "Volleys and taps had been stopped by official order from headquarters lest their frequency might demoralize us!" Feverish buglers continued to blow retreat and reveille, but their quavering notes "seemed the ghastly echo of a thinning and dying army corps."

Shafter waffled on the appalling import of the sick lists.

On July 25 he cabled the War Department that the fever cases were mild and the situation "somewhat improving." But, prodded by Roosevelt ("the whole command is so weakened and shattered as to be ripe for dying like rotten sheep") and his generals, alarmed by surgeons' reports, fearful of catastrophe, he advised Washington that his was "an army of convalescents" that would suffer grievously if not immediately transported to the United States. "If it is not done, I believe the death rate will be appalling."

On August 4, Alger wired Shafter: "Load ships that can be supplied with medicine. . . ."

At last, some troops were going home, to a detention center at Montauk Point on the eastern tip of Long Island.

When Private Post heard the news, he devoted an entire paragraph to one word: *Home.* There was more good news. *Scientific American* hinted at it early in July when it announced that lightweight uniforms had been shown by a New York clothier. The brown duck outfits were woven of a "special" preshrunk yarn suitable for the tropics and styled in the fashion of the English army in Egypt. The handsome new uniforms reached the Seventy-first New York just as they were about to leave the tropics. Post stroked the khaki—"It felt like silk!" Not until September, when the brisk sea winds at Montauk chilled the troops, did they long for the heavy blue shirts in which they had sweltered in Cuba.

Before embarking for Montauk, Roosevelt celebrated with a tour of the Morro, finding in the dungeons "hideous rusty instruments of torture. . . . Afterward I had a swim, not trusting much to the shark stories." Lieutenant John Greenway, asked to go along, nervously complied. As they paddled out to the *Merrimac,* which Roosevelt wanted to inspect, they were convoyed by a fish Greenway thought perhaps twelve feet long. Roosevelt told Greenway not to worry. He had studied sharks all his life. All that business about them biting swimmers was "poppy cock."

On that afternoon, at least, he was right.

The *Miami* arrived off Montauk on the evening of August 14, anchored for the night, and docked at a pier in Fort Pond Bay shortly after 11 A.M. the next day. Roosevelt stood on the bridge of the ship with "Fighting Joe" Wheeler, waving his campaign hat and scanning the cheering crowd at the wharf through binoculars. In a lull, someone cried out, asking if he was well. Roosevelt, one of a handful of Rough Riders who had not succumbed to fever, had lost twenty pounds, but felt all the better for it. His high-pitched voice cut through the noise of the crowd: "I am feeling disgracefully well!" After a moment he added, "I've had a bully time and a bully fight! I feel as big and as strong as a bull moose!"

As they disembarked, a band played "Rally Round the Flag" and "Home, Sweet Home." Wheeler went first, then Roosevelt, his *Maine* revolver strapped to his waist, and finally the troopers, led by their officers and the little dog named Cuba. Some limped down the gangplank, others, suffering from malaria and dysentery, were carried on stretchers. The *New York Sun* called them "a worn and tired lot," but thought fresh air and good food would bring them around.

The *Journal's* war came to a glorious end on Saturday, August 20, when Sampson paraded the North Atlantic Squadron up the Hudson River from the Statue of Liberty to Grant's Tomb. Hearst had nobly called upon Mayor Robert A. Van Wyck to proclaim "a complete holiday, abandoning all business save that of cheering the Navy." The mayor responded that he had no legal authority to declare the holiday, but did ask New Yorkers to forgo as much business as possible. Hearst brushed aside the mayor's disclaimer: JOURNAL'S PLAN FOR FULL HOLIDAY ADOPTED.

It was a beautiful summer day. Hearst launched what he called a "war balloon" from which showers of purple, green, red, white, and blue confetti would signal the progress of the fleet up the Hudson. Hundreds of vessels of all descriptions joined the naval procession, which was led, no doubt to Sampson's surprise, by the former Hearst yacht and press boat *Anita*, swathed in *Journal* banners.

For all the commercialism, it was a heart-stopping sight as the patched-up greyhounds of Santiago steamed majestically up the river. The *Times* ("It does not soil the breakfast cloth" was then its slogan) reported that every pier, boat, and rooftop between the Narrows and Riverside Drive "held a mass of well-nigh frantic men and women, who cheered until they were hoarse, and then screamed through parched throats, while wildly waving their ten-cent flags."

The *Journal*, itself triumphant, sounded a defiant tocsin to the Old World. There was a new bully on the block: "The Heroes Have Come Home, but the Ships Have Their War Paint on Yet. Europe, Please Take Notice."

On Tuesday, September 13, Roosevelt was writing in his tent at Montauk when he heard a commotion. Several troopers appeared at the entrance and asked if he would come outside. He went out, and he saw that the entire regiment had formed in a hollow square. At its center were the officers, the color sergeant, and a table with something on it, concealed by a horse blanket. The regiment was about to muster out, and Roosevelt sensed what was coming; his eyes suddenly glistened in the bright sun.

Private William S. Murphy stepped from the ranks. He had been a judge in the Indian Territory, and was known in the West for his eloquence. Murphy began to speak in his commanding voice, enunciating carefully, but choking over some of his words: "I want to tell you, sir, that one and all of us, from the highest of us to the humblest of us, will always carry with us in our hearts a pleasant and loving memory of your every act, for there has not been one among them which has not been of the kindest ... as our colonel, you have taught us to love you deeply, as men love men."

He paused, and took hold of the blanket; there were sobs from some of the battle-scarred troopers. Then Murphy said, "It is our sincerest hope, now that we are about to separate, that this bronze 'Bronco Buster' will sometimes make you think of us, as we shall ever think of you." Gently, he pulled the blanket aside.

It was Remington's first sculpture. The painter had started it about three years earlier, encouraged by a friend who saw that he visualized action in three dimensions. The subject was enormously difficult. Remington had taken no lessons, had never worked in bronze, but he got it exactly right. There was his beloved horse, shining now on the sun-washed Montauk dune, rearing up on hind legs, forelegs tucked up by its head, and on its back the desperate rider in a sombrero, one hand flung out for balance, the other grimly hanging on to the bronco's mane.

Roosevelt had seen the bronze before; he adored it. And having it come to him, in this way, from his men, was almost more than he could bear. He began to speak, reaching for words in a shaky voice, and then found his way: "I am proud of this regiment beyond measure. I am proud of it because it is a typical American regiment, made up of typical American men. The foundation of this regiment was the bronco buster, and we have got him here in bronze. . . . Besides, the cow-punchers, this regiment contains men from every section of the country and from every state within the Union."

He went on to commend their fighting qualities, their heritage, and their devotion, and to thank them for their testimonial. "It comes to me from you who shared the hardships of the campaign with me. You gave me a piece of your hardtack when I had none, and you gave me your blankets when I had none to lie upon. . . . This is something I shall hand down to my children, and I shall value it more than I do the weapons I carried through the campaign.

"Now, boys, I wish to take each of you by the hand as a special privilege and to say goodbye to you individually."

The men formed a line and came by, one by one. Many wept; some felt the urge to hug him. Roosevelt knew each of the men, and spoke to them by name. Then it was over and a trooper gave a prophetic shout: "Three cheers for the next Governor of New York!" A great roar swept over the Montauk dunes.

On the morning of the fifteenth, the colors of the First Volunteer Cavalry came down for the last time. The glory-filled history of the regiment was ended, but the story of its commanding officer had barely begun.

On August 20, as Hearst staged the navy's victory parade in New York, George Dewey cabled Washington that he hoped he would not be ordered to Paris to advise the peace commissioners: "Should very much regret to leave here while matters are in their present critical condition."

Since his arrival at Manila on May 1, the admiral had faced

a number of imposing problems. Several of these "situations with which I had to deal promptly" were neatly resolved. Naval reinforcements, particularly two heavily gunned monitors, cemented his tenuous control of Manila Bay. Admiral Cámara's retreat from Suez ended the threat of a second naval engagement. The first three troop transports arrived on June 30, convoyed by the *Charleston*, fresh from her conquest of Guam. Within a month two more contingents of Major General Wesley Merritt's Eighth Corps arrived. They waded ashore along the sandy beaches stretching from Cavite to Manila and dug in.

Merritt, commander of the Department of the East, was, with reason, uncertain about McKinley's commitment to the Philippines. But his own goal was clear. He had long favored the conquest of the entire archipelago—some seven thousand islands of whch about a thousand were inhabited. He had little faith in Consul Oscar Williams's sanguine prediction that Emilio Aguinaldo's insurgents would fight the Spaniards under American command. Indeed, he forecast that "we will have the so-called insurgents to fight as well as the Spaniards."

McKinley had given Merritt the force considered necessary "for the two-fold purpose of completing the reduction of Spanish power in that quarter and giving order and security to the islands while in the possession of the United States." By July 25, when he arrived at Manila, over half of the twenty thousand troops designated for Merritt's Philippine operations were in place.

No one quite knew what to make of Emilio Aguinaldo y Famy, the "most complicated" problem Dewey faced. The twenty-nine-year-old mestizo of Chinese-Tagalog ancestry had little formal schooling, yet had studied law, the history of the American and French revolutions, and the Constitution of the United States, which, he realized, made no provision for colonies. Behind a cold and unsmiling facade some saw shrewdness and corruption, others childishness and integrity. Dewey characterized him as "a soft-spoken, unimpressive little man" with a "quaint" command of English, but sensed that he had become a charismatic figure to the Filipinos.

One thing was clear—Aguinaldo was a gifted guerrilla leader. In the 1896 uprising against the Spanish, insurgents under his command crushed a large force of troops led by Ramón Blanco, then governor-general of the islands. As Blanco was recalled, his successor launched a reign of terror patterned after Weyler's tactics in Cuba. "The hour has come to exterminate the savages," an officer told newly arrived troops. "Destroy! Kill!"

Aguinaldo appointed himself "generalissimo" and defiantly issued the first of his proclamations: "Filipino citizens! We are not a savage people; let us follow the example of European and American nations; now is the time for shedding our blood. . . . Spain . . . to our face calls us carabaos, drones, monkeys. . . . The time has come. . . ."

Aguinaldo took refuge in a mountain sanctuary north of Manila, but the Spanish pressed him hard. Finally, he agreed to a truce. In exchange for Spanish concessions and the payment of eight hundred thousand pesos in "reparations" (which he said would be used to buy arms for a future rebellion) Aguinaldo accepted exile in Hong Kong. Most of the Spanish reforms—they included freedom of the press and Filipino membership in the Spanish Cortes—failed to materialize, and the reparations were not paid in full. The insurgent struggle against Spain soon resumed.

After the outbreak of war between Spain and the United States, Aguinaldo was told the Americans had no designs on the Philippines. "As in Cuba, so in the Philippines," said U.S. Consul E. Spencer Pratt in Singapore. Acting on his own initiative, he suggested to the insurgent leader that Philippine independence could be secured if he returned to the islands to fight the Spaniards. In Hong Kong, Consul Rounseville Wildman considered Aguinaldo a "childish figure of petty moods," but he too encouraged him to support the American war effort and proposed to sell him guns.

Aguinaldo sought reassurance from Dewey. He arrived in Hong Kong after the commodore sailed for the Philippines, but in May, when the *McCulloch* made her second trip to Hong Kong, Dewey gave him a lift to Manila, thinking "he might have valuable information to impart at a time when no source of information was to be neglected."

On May 26, John Long cabled Dewey: "It is desirable . . .

not to have political alliances with the insurgents of any faction in the islands that would incur liability to maintain their cause in the future." Dewey responded on June 6 that he had entered no entangling alliances and later added, "I have refrained from assisting him in any way with the force under my command. . . ." He had, however, put Aguinaldo ashore at Cavite, where the insurgent planned to establish a civil government, and had given him Spanish arms and ammunition.

Once ashore, Aguinaldo swiftly united elements of his old command, pushed the Spanish out of Cavite Province, invested Manila, and commissioned a national anthem and a flag. On May 24, he proclaimed a "provisional dictatorship," with himself at its head, and announced grandly that "the great North American nation, the cradle of genuine liberty . . . has come to us manifesting a protection as decisive as it is undoubtedly disinterested toward our inhabitants, considering us as sufficiently civilized and capable of governing ourselves and our unfortunate country." And at a ceremony in Cavite on June 12, he read a long and flamboyant declaration of Philippine independence "under the protection of the mighty and humane" United States.

Dewey did not attend, saying he was too busy. Aguinaldo, who had sought his signature on the document, sent a copy to the admiral's flagship. Dewey would later testify that he attached little importance to the proclamation. "I never dreamed that they wanted independence." But by the end of July, when the third contingent of troops arrived with General Arthur MacArthur (who left behind him an eighteen-year-old son named Douglas), Dewey had grasped that the insurgents were to be taken seriously. He cabled Washington on July 30 that Aguinaldo had "become aggressive and even threatening toward our army."

The situation the American task force now faced was unusual. Correspondent Frank D. Millet of *Harper's Weekly*, who had arrived with MacArthur's troops, tried to explain its complexity: "Until the campaign before Manila I always believed it to be an elementary military axiom that if two armed bodies jointly occupy a territory they must be either enemies or allies. In the investment of Manila the insurgents were not recognized by us in either of these capacities."

Dewey hoped to add to his laurels by arranging a bloodless surrender of the city. The Spanish were not averse to surrendering as long as it was to the Americans and not the feared insurgents. Morale had plummeted when the news of Admiral Cámara's withdrawal to Spain reached Manila. "The disillusion has been horrible, it has killed all our hopes," one Spaniard noted.

The admiral began surrender negotiations with Don Basilio Augustín Dávila on July 24, but the Spanish governor-general was soon recalled for "defeatism" and replaced by General Firmín Jaudenes y Alvarez. Jaudenes, though urged by Madrid to defend the city, considered the preservation of honor a greater goal. He proposed to Dewey a sham, face-saving bombardment and a mock assault of the city; then the white flag of surrender could be raised. Jaudenes then procrastinated, asking for the usual time to consult Madrid, but the matter was finally arranged and scheduled for August 13.

While the chief contestants had reached an amicable agreement, the Aguinaldo problem was still unresolved. Jaudenes made it plain that he would surrender only "to white people, never to niggers." Dewey granted Jaudenes the point, if not the inapt way he put it. He, too, refused to consider "turning it [Manila] over to the undisciplined insurgents, who, I feared, might wreak their vengeance upon the Spaniards and indulge in a carnival of loot." That aside, he knew that Washington would not sanction an insurgent role in the surrender scenario. But Aguinaldo's troops were dug into trenches and other fortifications surrounding the city. The problem was how to wedge the American soldiers between the Spanish and the Filipinos.

General Francis Greene was given the assignment. He promised Aguinaldo modern artillery pieces and an official document, signed by General Merritt, formally requesting that American forces supplant insurgents in the trenches circling Manila's southern flank. Aguinaldo, eager for modern weapons, still hoping for some small sign of American recognition, agreed. Greene's troops took over the trenches; Aguinaldo never got the guns or the document.

At eight forty-five on the sweltering, cloudy morning of August 13, the curtain rose on the Dewey-Jaudenes charade as the admiral ranged his ships along the Manila shoreline.

Less than an hour later the *Olympia* and three other warships began to bombard Fort San Antonio Abad. When American troops were spotted moving along the beach toward the fort, the flagship signaled, "Cease firing." Soon the Stars and Stripes rose over the fort, which proved to be unoccupied. The troops continued their advance toward the old city as regimental bands blared "There'll Be a Hot Time in the Old Town Tonight"—so often played that many Filipinos thought it the American national anthem.

Not all the actors in the tropical drama had been given their lines, and there were understandable gaffes as the scenes unfolded. Spanish troops who thought themselves under legitimate attack fired at the advancing Americans; there were casualties on both sides. When the Spanish hoisted a white flag from a bastion of the walled city, no one on the *Olympia* saw it in the milky haze that shrouded Manila. Finally, Dewey himself spotted it flapping limply in a light breeze. A Spanish flag still flew over the city, to Dewey's surprise, but that came down late in the afternoon when Merritt had enough troops in the city to protect the Spanish from the insurgents. As a huge American ensign replaced it, the sun finally burst through the cloud cover and the guns of the fleet crashed out a salute.

For the most part, the insurgents had been kept offstage—though "with some difficulty," Dewey recalled. Aguinaldo, who had hoped to add legitimacy to his Philippine Republic by participating in the liberation of Manila, was bitterly disappointed in his role as understudy. He was not even asked to the surrender ceremonies. Told to keep his troops out of the city, he responded angrily, "My troops are forced by yours, by means of threats of violence, to retire from positions taken." On the night of the thirteenth his exasperated soldiers began to infiltrate the abandoned Spanish earthworks around the city and to dig siege trenches.

Three days later a cable from the Navy Department dated August 12 finally reached Dewey by way of his Hong Kong shuttle: "Peace protocol signed by President. Suspend all hostilities and blockade." The "battle" for Manila had been fought after the peace protocol was signed—in view of the time differential, on the day after.

On August 21, Dewey had the telegraph cable to Hong

Kong spliced and repaired. Now he could swiftly impart his major concern to Washington: Aguinaldo continued to recruit insurgent forces and to spread the gospel of Philippine independence throughout the archipelago.

With American troops occupying Manila, McKinley's options somehow seemed less open. Mr. Dooley put the Philippine conundrum to his friend Hennessy: "Oh, what shud I do with thim? I can't annex thim because I don't know where they ar-re. I can't let go iv thim because some wan else'll take thim if I do. They are eight thousan' iv them islands, with a population iv wan hundherd millyon savages; an' me bedroom's crowded now with me an' th' bed."

Ambassador John Hay wrote to anti-imperialist Andrew Carnegie: "The only question in my mind is how far it is now *possible* for us to withdraw from the Philippines. I am rather thankful it is not given to me to solve that momentous question." And he confided to a friend, "I hope the Lord will be good to us poor devils who have to take care of them."

Outwardly, McKinley appeared to drag his feet on the vexing Philippine question. He prayed, paced the White House corridors, and cautiously sought the opinion of Cabinet ministers, congressmen, and senior officers recalled from Manila. A jest of the day asked: "Why is McKinley's mind like a bed?" The answer: "Because it has to be made up for him every time he wants to use it."

The president's instructions to Merritt, however, were crisp and positive. Aguinaldo's ambitions must be curbed: "The insurgents and all others must recognize the military occupation and authority of the United States. . . ."

Moreover, three of the five commissioners the president selected to represent him in Paris favored annexation of the islands. As they left Washington for Paris in the middle of September, McKinley reminded them, "the presence and success of our arms at Manila imposes upon us obligations which we can not disregard. The march of events rules and overrules human action. . . ."

Early in the fall McKinley went off on a ten-day speaking tour of the Midwest, ostensibly to campaign for Republican candidates in the November elections. Washington pundits thought he meant also to test the pulse of the people on the Philippine question. He was, after all, more a follower than a leader. In fact, McKinley seemed more intent on guiding than gauging. He spoke of the obligations of humanity, "the courage of destiny" and the responsibilities "put upon us by the results of the war." Why, he asked, should Americans deny themselves "what the rest of the world so freely and so justly accords to us?" In Iowa he put it plainly: "Territory sometimes comes to us when we go to war in a holy cause, and whenever it does the banner of liberty will float over it and bring, I trust, blessings and benefits to all the people." McKinley's crowds were enthusiastic; there seemed to be a meeting of minds.

On his return to Washington the president made his position entirely clear to the peace commission. On Cuba, "the spirit and letter of the resolution of Congress" must be carried out; in the Philippines, "The cession must be of the whole archipelago or none. The latter is wholly inadmissible, and the former must therefore be required."

Later he claimed, "I didn't want the Philippine Islands . . . in the protocol to the treaty I left myself free not to take them; but, in the end, there was no alternative." The problem all along had been that the "options" he had insisted on were unacceptable not only to the American people, but to his own conscience. It would be fainthearted and dishonorable to restore the Philippines to the medieval dominion of Spain. Leaving them to Aguinaldo and his Tagalog party would, he felt, result in anarchy or despotism. Turning them over to other interested parties—Japan, France, Germany—"would be bad business and discreditable." There was only one reasonable alternative: take them all.

"We will do our duty," McKinley had told a crowd in Omaha on his western swing, and now he knew that "duty determines destiny."

On October 5, shortly before his fortieth birthday, as the peace commissioners quibbled in Paris with Sagasta's emissaries, Theodore Roosevelt gave a major address in his gubernatorial campaign in which he firmly articulated the obligations McKinley had solemnly grasped. "There comes a time in the life of a nation," he declared, "as in the life of an individual, when it must face great responsibilities. . . . We have now reached that time. . . . The guns of our warships in the tropic seas of the West and the remote East have awakened us to the knowledge of new duties. Our flag is a proud flag, and it stands for liberty and civilization. Where it has once floated, there must be no return to tyranny or savagery. . . ."

On November 7 underdog Roosevelt bested Boss Richard Croker's Tammany Hall candidate by a narrow but telling margin.

XII

DUTY
AND
DESTINY

Then conquer we must, for our cause it is just,
And this be our motto: "In God is our trust";
And the star-spangled banner, in triumph shall wave,
O'er the land of the free, and the home of the brave!

—FRANCIS SCOTT KEY

I oppose the un-American policy of imperialism . . . because
it would divorce the American flag from the American Constitution by sending one where the other cannot go; because
it is a policy of . . . inconceivable folly from a material point
of view, and a policy of unspeakable infamy from a moral
point of view.

—BOURKE COCKRAN

WHEN THE WAR WAS OVER, or seemed to be over, a
mood of exhilaration took hold in many of its major players. "I have played it in bull luck this summer," Roosevelt wrote Cecil Spring-Rice. "First, to get into the war;
then to get out of it; then to get elected."

Henry Cabot Lodge wrote John Hay a letter as bubbly as
the champagne benefactors had sent to the returning troops
at Montauk. "What a wonderful war it has been, what a navy
we have got. . . ." Hay exclaimed to Roosevelt in radiant en-

thusiasm, "It has been a splendid little war; begun with the highest motives, carried on with magnificent intelligence and spirit, favored by that fortune which loves the brave."

But when the flush of victory drained away, even the most fervent expansionist saw that the possessions over which the peace commissioners haggled in Paris would bring burdens as well as opportunities.

In Cuba, the last-minute Teller Amendment to the Senate resolution to intervene promised that when pacification was achieved the government of the island would be left to its people. Stephen Crane thought the Americans, though not "an immaculate race," would keep their word, but considered the Cubans unsuited to the rigors of self-government. They had not displayed enterprise or toughness at Santiago. "The Cuban says, 'We took San Juan Hill.' Any of us who were there know that there were no Cubans present within any other range than spent-shell range." And while the American soldier shed his blood for Cuba Libre, "the Cubans back of the firing line stole his blanket-roll and his coat, and maybe his hat."

Shafter, with his usual tact, announced that Cubans "are no more fit for self-government than gun-powder is for hell." General S.B.M. Young put the matter even plainer. He considered the insurgents "a lot of degenerates, absolutely devoid of honor or gratitude."

The image of the noble Cuban revolutionary so carefully limned by the Cuban Junta and nurtured by the *New York Journal* dissolved. It was replaced, curiously, by a romantic vision of the Spanish don. Once considered cruel, corrupt, and contemptible, he now seemed a model of chivalry and courage. The valiant defenders of El Caney were lionized by American troops. Cervera and his brave sailors had been rescued from Calixto García's bloodthirsty insurgents. The admiral himself, enjoying sumptuous quarters at Annapolis, wrote Marine Minister Auñón that he had been extended "a kindness and courtesy that have probably no equal in history in the treatment of prisoners." Wherever he went, "there were demonstrations of the greatest sympathy with our misfortune." In Florida a fund was started to buy Cervera a house should he decide to reside in the United States.

The American regard for the Spaniard was reciprocated.

A Spanish soldier, leaving for home, tipped his hat to the men of the Fifth Corps. While the Cuban insurgents "shot their noble victims from ambush and then immediately fled," Shafter's troops "fought us as men, face to face, and with great courage."

The insurgents considered the turnabout unfair play. Shafter had treated García contemptuously and used his troops as common laborers. He had not involved the Cuban general in the negotiations that led to Santiago's capitulation. García's son, General Carlos García Vélez, was disturbed but philosophical about the American attitude. He asked critics of the Cuban guerrillas to be reasonable. His insurgents had waged an exhausting campaign in the jungle for more than three years while "the free citizens of the north" were fresh to the fray.

As Leonard Wood, the new governor of Santiago, tried to clean up the city (he wrote his wife that he had at least gotten down to "*modern dirt*"), Crane endured the bedlam of Havana. On a Sunday morning, perhaps suffering the after-effects of the Inglaterra's postwar brandy, the inane clamor of resonating metal propelled him into consciousness: ". . . when at blear dawn you are sleeping a sleep of both the just and the unjust and a man climbs into an adjacent belfry and begins to hammer the everlasting, murdering Hades out of the bell with a club—your aroused mind seems to turn almost instinctively toward blasphemy. Religion commonly does not go off like an alarm clock, and, as symbolized by the bells, it does not usually sound like a brickbat riot in a tin store . . . I fancy they use no such term here as 'bell-ringer;' they probably use 'bell-fighter.'"

As the American occupation and administration took over Havana, certain wrongs were righted. Gambling—and bell-fighting—were proscribed.

In Paris, McKinley's five peace commissioners bravely tried to unscramble the tortuous negotiations on Cuba and the Philippines. The Spanish, as was their way, dragged their heels, still casting about for some diplomatic reprieve. United States sovereignty over Cuba was acknowledged, but the "Cuban" debt (the monies borrowed to finance the war) must accompany it. Washington made it instantly clear that the huge debt, some $400 million, was not a matter for discussion.

The question of Philippine annexation was muddied by legal questions. The American army held Manila, but this was only one city on one island of the archipelago and had in fact been taken after the peace protocol was signed.

At McKinley's request, debonair, articulate John Hay had reluctantly left his ambassadorial post in London and taken over the Department of State. The less assertive William Day was eased out with an appointment to the peace commission, where his legal background might prove valuable. The scrupulous judge soon made McKinley's adamant stand on annexation appear legally flimsy, cabling Washington: "Captures made after agreement of armistice must be disregarded and status quo restored as far as practicable." Hay could only counter that the destruction of Montojo's fleet on May 1 was tantamount to "the conquest of Manila, the capital of the Philippines."

As the peace commissioners labored through the golden days of October in comfortable chambers at the Quai d'Orsay, they considered compromise. McKinley had advised them to stick to well-established precedents; they were not to make unworthy conditions. But later in the month the president's talk turned tough. The Philippines had become a matter of all or nothing, and nothing was "inadmissable." The function of the commissioners was made clear: wring consent from the Spanish.

The Paris negotiations had come close to foundering on the Cuban debt issue. Now, grudgingly, the Spanish yielded the point, thinking they might crack the American hard line on the Philippines. To some small extent they did. As Prime Minister Sagasta, under fire from conservative political rivals, threatened to call off the negotiations and resume the war, senator and peace commissioner William P. Frye proposed that the United States "pay Spain from $10 million to $20 million" for the Philippines. McKinley reluctantly gave his consent.

On this crass basis—the figure of $20 million was selected—the matter was resolved. Spain, bankrupt, helpless to defend or supply her smithereens of empire, ceded most of what was left "for lofty reasons of patriotism and humanity,"

and to avoid resuming "the horrors of war." By the Treaty of
Paris, signed on December 10, 1898, she relinquished Cuba,
Puerto Rico, Guam in the Ladrones, and the entire archipelago of the Philippines. Her majestic empire—perhaps the
most extensive the world had known—was all but gone:
North Africa, Burgundy, Naples, Sicily, the Netherlands, Cey-
lon, Java, Portugal, Gibraltar, Santo Domingo, Louisiana,
Trinidad, Florida, Mexico, South and Central America—all
had been lost—and now virtually the last jewels were
plucked from her crown. As a naval officer remarked, "An
hour or two at Manila, an hour or two at Santiago, and the
maps of the world were changed."

Speaker Thomas Brackett Reed, moody and bitter, wea-
ried by fighting battles with the president he served, thought
the price of the Philippines too high. "We have bought ten
million Malays at $2.00 a head unpicked," he observed ac-
idly, "and nobody knows what it will cost to pick them."
Even George Dewey saw a flaw in the Paris treaty: "The delegates to the Peace Conference scarcely comprehended that a
rebellion was included with the purchase."

The treaty had yet to be ratified by the Senate, but Emilio
Aguinaldo's capture of Iloilo, a major Spanish base on the
island of Panay, forced McKinley's executive hand. On December 26 he cabled General Elwell S. Otis, who had taken
command of the Eighth Army Corps in Manila from Merritt,
that the military government practiced in Manila "is to be
extended with all possible despatch to the whole of the
ceded territory." The inhabitants were to be assured that
their rights and liberties would be preserved, and that "the
mission of the United States is one of benevolent assimilation."

Otis, confounded by what appeared to him an illegal and
unenforceable order, cabled in January 1899: "The least spark
may start a conflagration."

Early on, Lodge sensed there would be "trouble over the
treaty" in the Senate. A two-thirds majority was required for
ratification, and opposition to the annexation of the Philippines was bubbling to the surface. Lodge blamed the southern Democrats in the Congress, but antitreaty sentiment was

more pervasive than he suspected. Prominent jurists argued
that "colonies" were not compatible with the Constitution,
and there was a widespread reluctance to assume the duties
that came with destiny. Even the Republican *San Francisco
Argonaut* took exception to McKinley's vision, drawing a rac-
ist line between territory and Tagalogs: "We do not want the
Filipinos. We want the Philippines. The islands are enormously rich, but, unfortunately, they are infested by Filipinos. There are many millions of them there, and it is to be
feared their extinction will be slow."

The House was not directly concerned with the ratification of the treaty, but made bold to discuss it at length. Representative John Sharp Williams of Mississippi chipped away
at the arrogance of the expansionists. "Who," he asked,
"made us God's globe-trotting vice-regents to forestall misgovernment everywhere?" In the Senate, William E. Mason
of Illinois lashed out at the hypocrisy of annexation. "Will
you tell me, please," he begged, "how grand larceny and
criminal aggression [as McKinley had put it with regard to
Cuba] become high Christian civilization in the Philippines?
Is there some place in the Pacific Ocean where we change
the code of ethics ... as we change the calendar and the
ship's clock in crossing?"

The Anti-Imperialist League had organized in Boston's
Faneuil Hall in June with an eclectic and influential membership: steel magnate Andrew Carnegie; ex-President Grover
Cleveland; Harvard professor Charles Eliot Norton; labor
leader Samuel Gompers; *New York Evening Post* editor Edwin Godkin; author Mark Twain. The league, which soon had
branches in a dozen cities, petitioned the Senate, arguing, as
their platform stated, "that governments derive their just
powers from the consent of the governed," and that "the subjugation of any people is 'criminal aggression' and open dis-
loyalty to the distinctive principles of our Government."

In Atlanta, ostensibly to celebrate the unification of the
United States under one flag, McKinley veered off into the
Philippine issue: Who, he asked, will take that flag away
"from the people over whom it floats its protecting folds?
Who will haul it down?"

In Washington the venerable senior senator from Massachusetts, George Frisbie Hoar, answered him. Imperialism, he

declaimed, would make the United States "a cheap-jack country, raking after the cart for the leavings of European tyranny." The American empire would be "vulgar, commonplace . . . founded upon physical force, controlling subject races and vassal states, in which one class must forever rule, and other classes must forever obey." Noting that McKinley had once opposed forcible annexation, he issued his own challenge: "Who shall haul down the President."

Lodge, as chief whip, led the floor fight for McKinley. The Philippines posed difficult questions, but clearly possession established the right to govern. It was nip and tuck, Lodge wrote Roosevelt—"the closest, hardest fight I have ever known." Much of it went on behind closed doors. "We were down in the engine room and do not get flowers, but we did make the ship move." Even so, it moved reluctantly. For all the senator's political acumen, and pressure brought to bear from the White House, the fifty-six votes needed for ratification would not have been secured had it not been for the last-minute entry of three unlikely contestants in the fray: Rudyard Kipling, William Jennings Bryan, and Emilio Aguinaldo.

Kipling, who lived in America from 1892 to 1896, was baffled by the residual animosity Americans held for the mother country, yet loved the land "where the sun shines and oysters is cheap." On February 1, 1899, one of his poems—"The White Man's Burden"—was published by *McClure's Magazine*. It addressed the American dilemma in the Philippines as well as that of the British in Africa.

> Take up the White Man's Burden—
> Send forth the best ye breed—
> Go bind your sons to exile
> To serve your captives' need;
> To wait in heavy harness,
> On fluttered folk and wild—
> Your new-caught, sullen peoples,
> Half-devil and half-child.

The *New York Times* swiftly rebutted:

> Take up the White Man's burden;
> Send forth your sturdy sons,

402   A SHIP TO REMEMBER

>And load them down with whiskey
>And Testaments and guns.
>Throw in a few diseases
>To spread in tropic climes
>For there the healthy niggers
>Are quite behind the times.

But Kipling's stirring call to duty and destiny took root.

William Jennings Bryan made an eleventh-hour appearance in Washington with a proposal so devious and unprincipled that even some of his loyal supporters were shocked. The Democratic standard-bearer, realizing free silver was a dying issue, hoped to crucify the Republican Party in the 1900 elections on a cross of imperialism, most especially the costly involvement in the Philippines. For this and other political reasons he urged Democratic senators to vote *for* the treaty. Richard F. Pettigrew, a "silver" senator from South Dakota, bluntly told Bryan "he had no business in Washington on such an errand." Republican George Hoar was incensed by the sly expediency of the proposal. "Everything I tried to do," he said bitterly, "was brought to naught by the action of Mr. Bryan."

But in the end, Roosevelt thought, it was Aguinaldo who "pulled the treaty through for us."

The Senate vote was scheduled for Monday, February 6. On Sunday morning a cable arrived from Dewey in Manila: "Insurgents have inaugurated general engagement yesterday night which is continued today. . . ."

On the evening of February 4, just after Taps sounded over the American picket lines encircling Manila, Privates William W. Grayson and Orville Miller of the First Nebraska Volunteers patrolled the Santa Mesa suburb on the eastern edge of the city. Grayson thought it a bit bullheaded of Otis to put them there, since the insurgents claimed the sector, but he had his orders and he pushed on through the thick undergrowth near the San Juan River. Suddenly, a figure ap-

peared about twenty feet in front of him. "Halt!" he yelled.
The Filipino may have been drunk. "*¡Alto!*" he shouted
back.

"Well," Grayson reasoned, "I thought the best thing to do
was shoot him. He dropped."

Two more figures jumped through a gateway near the
body of the first Filipino and Grayson and Miller shot them,
then raced back to their lines as the sharp crack of Mauser
fire broke out behind them. "Line up fellows," Grayson
shouted, "the niggers are in here all through these yards!"

The firefight triggered by the two volunteers raged through
the night. On Sunday morning the guns of Dewey's ships
raked Aguinaldo's lines, setting fires around Manila as Otis's
restive troops burst out from the city. By noon, Otis estimated
in his report to the War Department, there had been 4,000
Filipino casualties, most of them civilians. His own command had suffered 250 dead and wounded.

In Washington it was not clear who had provoked the battle. General Otis claimed a representative of the insurgents in
Washington had ordered hostilities to begin on February 7.
Alger backed him up, blaming Aguinaldo for "an overt act"
that "succeeded in drawing the fire of our picket." The anti-
imperialists rumbled that the assault had been engineered by
the army to ensure the ratification of the peace treaty by the
Senate.

While the charge seemed far-fetched, the outbreak of hostilities skimmed a few more votes from the anti-imperialist
coalition. ("How foolish these people are," McKinley remarked. "This means ratification of the treaty.") Even so, it
was a close thing. When the roll was taken at 3 P.M., Monday,
fifty-seven senators cast their votes for ratification—one more
than required. The House then appropriated the $20 million
compensation to Spain by an overwhelming majority.
Speaker Thomas Reed, czar no more, watched in sullen despair and considered leaving politics for private practice. He
would do so, to the astonishment of his colleagues, in April.

In Manila, at least, there was optimism. On February 8,
Otis cabled: "Aguinaldo's influence throughout this section
is destroyed. He now applies for a cessation of hostilities and
a conference. I have declined to answer."

*   *   *

Frederic Remington left New York for Havana on February 11 as a special correspondent for *Collier's Weekly*. It was a four-day journey, and he must have arrived in the harbor as memorial ceremonies for the *Maine* and her dead took place. Tugs and water taxis nestled up to the twisted, rust-reddened debris. The *Maine* had settled into the mud and clay of the bottom—her poop deck was now awash—but someone had climbed up to the surviving fighting top and raised the flag to half-mast.

As members of the Daughters of the American Revolution placed flowers on her shattered superstructure, Major General Fitzhugh Lee, commanding the Seventh Army Corps, led a delegation of soldiers and sailors into Colón Cemetery to honor the dead. They put floral bouquets on the simple cross at the gravesite where dozens of little American flags sprouted from the ground. They remembered the *Maine*, and then formed up and marched out.

Remington wrote for *Collier's* that the Cubans were "gradually adjusting themselves to their freedom. Too much cannot be expected at once of a people who have always lived under Spanish misrule and abuse. Cuba is not a new-born country, peopled by wood-cutting, bear-fighting agricultural folks, who must be fresh and virtuous in order to exist. It is an old country, time-worn, decayed, and debauched by thieving officials and fire and sword. . . ."

Major General John Rutter Brooke, seated in Governor-General Valeriano Weyler's old chair at the palace, had taken over the military government of Cuba in January. His mission was to rule, with the aid of a Cuban "cabinet," until the Cubans could establish their own constitution and elect a congress and president. One of his staff officers, Colonel Hugh Lenox Scott, saw it as a long-term project. There were, he wrote, "situations where the strong hand of the benevolent despot is necessary. . . . The American people are prone to believe that a race can be civilized overnight; that it is sufficient to declare a republic on paper to have one in fact. . . . You may declare a republic on paper among the mules and monkeys, but you will never get one."

That January, Navy Secretary John Long had written fondly and frankly to his wife: "If I could have had my way, I wouldn't have had the war, and I wouldn't have been burdened with Porto Rico or Cuba or the Philippines. They are an elephant, just as everything else is an elephant that disturbs the even tenor of our national way. But here they are, and my shoulder goes to the wheel."

There was nothing else to do, he thought, but civilize and Americanize the elephant. It could always have independence, if it preferred. "America will not hold a people in subjugation, who do not desire it."

The first months of the war in the Philippines set the tone for the long struggle that followed. On the night of February 22, Aguinaldo's insurgents put the torch to Manila. Fires were started simultaneously in three sections of the city. American troops attempting to put out the blazes came under sniper attack. Eventually, the fires were contained, but a square mile of the city had been devastated.

General Otis struck back, hitting Aguinaldo's strongholds north and west of the city. A Civil War veteran and the founder of the army staff school at Fort Leavenworth, Kansas, he operated by the book. A head wound from a Confederate slug had rendered him insomniac; he worked at his desk from dawn until late at night, flyspecking operations, poring over sketchy campaign maps, second-guessing his generals, issuing meticulous orders that fettered his field commanders. They lamented his fussy, armchair approach to a conflict that called for initiative and freedom of action. General Arthur MacArthur pictured him as "a locomotive bottomside up on the track, with its wheels revolving at full speed."

Otis's first assaults on insurgent strongholds were successful. Body and village counts were encouraging. Aguinaldo was driven out of one city after another, and the deskbound American general sent rosy reports to Washington: The insurgent army was "defeated, discouraged and shattered." But as the conflict dragged on, even Otis saw there were serious flaws in his campaign. His forces were too few to hold the towns they captured; when American troops left, insurgents moved back in. Heat and humidity sapped the fitness of his blue-shirted veterans. The six-month rainy season—in parts of the archipelago two hundred inches fell annually—began in April. Troops slogged their way through the gluey muck of rice paddies in water up to their knees.

Otis cabled Washington for more troops, and then more. Eventually, over seventy thousand reached the islands, almost five times the number that fought at Santiago. Benevolent assimilation of the "new-caught, sullen peoples" was proving more difficult than expected.

The war got mean early on. The army reported that on February 6 an artillery sergeant was captured, killed, and his dead body mutilated. That same month Kansas volunteers accused their commanding officer of ordering them to kill prisoners. American troops burned churches, native villages, and crops. The "Gugus," as the Americans called the insurgents, buried prisoners alive, cut throats, exacted brutal vengeance on Filipino "amigos" sympathetic to the Americans. On Leyte an American soldier was buried to the neck and a stick forced through his lips to jam his mouth into an open position. When he was found by a patrol, an ant-thronged trail of sugar led from the remains of his head to the edge of the jungle.

Stories leaked out that Americans had used the "water cure" to extract intelligence or confession from a prisoner. Water was forced down his mouth or nose, swelling his belly, then violently expelled by stomping on his stomach. The procedure went on until, as a soldier put it, "he gave in and gave the information they sought."

"Why should I hate the man I'm paid to kill?" Kipling asked. Lodge thought it understandable: "When a soldier in a disturbed district going along the road found the body of his comrade . . . stabbed to death from behind with the private parts cut off and stuffed in the mouth of the corpse, he was very apt to do something pretty nasty to the next armed Filipino that he met."

The insurgents had modern rifles, but ancient weapons most unnerved the Americans. "Pitfalls" concealed by foliage were armed with upward-thrusting bamboo stakes that could spear through a man lengthwise. In the high-grassed swamps

· LIFE ·

THE HARVEST IN THE PHILIPPINES.

and jungles of the islands, the razor-sharp, bone-slicing bolo was a terrifying close-range weapon. Otis's troops fought back with Gatling guns and Krag-Jorgenson bolt-action rifles, and sang bitterly:

> "Damn, damn, damn the Filipinos!
> Cut-throat khakiac ladrones!
> Underneath the starry flag,
> Civilize them with a Krag . . ."

The most effective weapon, many of them thought, and the only one that could stop the dervish-like charge of a bolo-swinging Filipino, was the .45-caliber revolver armed with soft, snub-nosed bullets. Colonel Frederick Funston of the Twentieth Kansas Volunteers, who had filibustered with "Dynamite Johnny" O'Brien and served as an artillery adviser with Máximo Gómez, had remarked in Cuba that "the Spaniards do not fight revolutions with rose-water." In the Philippines, it seemed to him, maybe they were right.

*   *   *

In Boston, in February, McKinley gave a truculent speech
on the Philippines. The United States, under God, held the
islands in solemn trust, he declared, and it was hardly "a
good time for the liberator to submit important questions
concerning liberty and government to the liberated while
they are engaged in shooting down their rescuers." In Pittsburgh that summer, before a crowd packed with veterans of
the Luzon fighting, the president hammered at the anti-
imperialists, calling them seriously misguided and unpatriotic. He stoutly defended Otis's refusal to negotiate with Aguinaldo. There was no point to parley until American
authority was in place.

They were tough, uncompromising speeches that hardly
fit the image of McKinley as a dutiful follower of public opinion, a man, as Joe Cannon had it, "with his ear so close to
the ground it's always full of grasshoppers." Despite the
atrocities, the bodies piling up, the pesky, never-ending nagging of the anti-imperialists, McKinley seemed entirely at
peace with the firm course of expansion on which he had set
the nation.

William Allen White, the popular young editor of the *Em-
poria* (Kansas) *Gazette*, saw Roosevelt as a "great rumbling,
roaring, jocund tornado of a man" who brought "the inexorable coming of change of life, the passing of the old into the
new." He was eager to boom Roosevelt as a rival to McKinley
at the 1900 convention. In June, when Roosevelt traveled
through Kansas on his way to the first Rough Rider reunion
in Las Vegas, New Mexico, to carouse with his "great big,
goodhearted, homicidal children," White hopped aboard the
train as it looped through Kansas. Roosevelt tried to dampen
the editor's premature ardor: "I am not out for presidential
honors at present." Even so, he could not resist reporting to
Lodge that "at every station at which the train stopped . . .
I was received by dense throngs exactly as if I had been a
presidential candidate."

As Roosevelt whistle-stopped the county agricultural fairs
of New York in August, people cheered him as the next presi-

dent, but he only grinned and shouted back, "No, no, none of that. Dewey's not here."

But Dewey was almost there. In May the hero of Manila had finally left the Philippines. After passing through the Suez Canal he leisurely paraded the *Olympia* through the Mediterranean. At Trieste, Naples, Leghorn, Villefranche, and Gibraltar, cannon pounded out nineteen-gun salutes honoring his four-star flag—Congress had granted him the unique rank of Admiral of the Navy. It was all heady froth, but nothing compared to what was waiting in New York.

He arrived on Thursday, September 28, and the next day sailed the *Olympia* up the Hudson, escorted by the North Atlantic Squadron. On Saturday, a huge parade—the largest since the Civil War—formed on Fifth-ninth Street, headed west, and wheeled smartly down Fifth Avenue amid showers of confetti toward Madison Square. There a magnificent Dewey Arch, styled in the Roman manner, made of wood and plaster (until funds were raised for the permanent granite and marble memorial), spanned the avenue.

Dewey was given a gold loving cup and a 150-pound, silver-cased volume of newspaper clippings celebrating his victory. The admiral was understandably stirred: "Dewey arches," he wrote, "Dewey flags, and 'Welcome Dewey' in electric lights on the span of the Brooklyn Bridge! The great city of New York made holiday." His political stock was high. Yet no one knew what party he backed. When asked in Manila, he had replied, "Well, you see, I am a sailor. A sailor has no politics." He would point to his dog and say, "I know as much about politics as Bob here." As it turned out, he was right.

But Joseph Pulitzer began pushing Dewey as a bright alternative to William Jennings Bryan and his tarnished silver image. The admiral finally conceded to a *World* reporter that he would, in fact, be willing to serve. The job was not as difficult as he had once thought, the duties of the president "being mainly to execute the laws of Congress. Should I be chosen for this exalted position I would execute the laws of Congress as faithfully as I have always executed the orders of my superiors." He still had not chosen a party. Mrs. Dewey would speak on that matter.

Almost overnight Dewey became an absurdity. The *Atlanta Constitution* announced that the admiral had changed his mind and headlined, THE ADMIRAL SAYS HE WILL OBEY ORDERS AS USUAL. Cartoonists depicted the admiral floundering in a sea of politics as the *Olympia* steamed away. Even Charles Sigsbee, Dewey's friend and naval colleague, put his foot in it when he tried to explain the matter: The inappropriate nature of the statement was "characteristic of a man whose life has been spent at sea."

Dewey's ship of state sank the moment it was launched. The hero had become human. In the wake of the admiral's ill-advised plunge into politics, what glistened in the public mind most brightly was the image of the top-hatted figure proudly seated on a dark charger at the head of Dewey's parade down Fifth Avenue: the governor of New York.

A month after Dewey's return, Roosevelt explained to one of his admirers that he had no intention of running for the presidency in 1900, or in 1904. "By that time the kaleidoscope will have shifted completely and the odds are that an entirely new set of men and set of issues will be at the front." The pendulum swung, he said, from crest to hollow. "From Tom Reed down and up, how many men have I seen ruined by getting the presidential bee in their bonnets."

That December, Charles Sigsbee, now commanding the *Texas*, brought back the bodies of the *Maine* victims that had been buried in Havana. Navy Secretary John Long was at Arlington National Cemetery for the reinterment ceremonies. It was a chill day, and a scrim of snow sheeted the hard earth, but the 150 caskets, he wrote his daughter Helen "were arranged upon a pretty knoll, each covered with a flag and ornamented with a wreath of green." Beyond them he could see the Lee mansion and, through a mist over the Potomac, the majestic peak of the Washington Monument.

With him on the platform were the president and most of the Cabinet flanked by ranking army and navy officers. Dewey sat next to him wearing a cocked hat and a heavy navy overcoat. There was a detail of marines, and also a squad of cavalry, sunlight flashing from the yellow-stripes on their trousers. The marine band played, "a sweet dirge," and Father John Chidwick of the *Maine*, flanked by acolytes, read the service for the dead. Then the marines marched behind the caskets and raised their rifles toward the sky. Three sharp volleys ripped through the cold air.

There seemed to be a little tear in Long's heart that morning. He was deeply touched when a bugler stepped forward to sound Taps. "It was so absolutely quiet, the air so still, the notes of the cornet so sweet and prolonged, and the suggestion of putting out the light . . . was so significant of the close of life of these departed spirits that it made one of the most impressive occasions I have ever known. . . ."

Throughout 1899, Roosevelt had lobbied the president to have Brigadier General Leonard Wood appointed governor-general of Cuba. Wood had done an extraordinary job in Santiago and Oriente Province, cleaning up the city and its entrenched bureaucracy, building roads and schools, dredging the harbor, mapping the countryside, renovating hospitals, and perhaps most importantly, prescribing "liberal doses of the U.S. Constitution" as an alternative to the antiquated Spanish system of jurisprudence. Like so many others, Wood believed the Cubans incapable of self-government. After a brief and painful period of independence, he thought they would demand to be taken into the Union.

In December, Wood did replace General Brooke as military governor of Cuba. The president told him "to get the people ready for a Republican form of government. . . . Give them a good school system, try to straighten out their courts, and put them on their feet as best you can." McKinley's former physician set about the task with his usual efficiency. In less than six months municipal elections were held, and Wood began organizing a convention that would fashion a Cuban constitution.

The Republican National Convention met in June 1900 in the swelter of Philadelphia. Roosevelt, a delegate at large, appeared in town on Saturday the sixteenth, three days before the convention officially opened. Lodge urged the popular governor to seek the vice-presidential nomination—Garret Hobart had died in November—but Roosevelt protested that he was not a candidate for the job. He did not fancy being a figurehead. "I would be simply a presiding officer," he had written Senator Tom Platt, "and that I should find a bore."

Roosevelt was, in any case, bitterly opposed by Mark Hanna, the wily political infighter and Republican Party national chairman. Hanna, who had always thought Roosevelt—"that damned cowboy"—a bit crazy, pressed McKinley to approve some other candidate. The president was noncommittal—any of the distinguished names under discussion would be acceptable.

On Monday morning, returning from a weekend in the suburbs, Hanna railed at Wisconsin committeeman Henry C. Payne, a Roosevelt supporter, "Don't any of you realize that there's only one life between that madman and the Presidency?" But without McKinley's support his political clout was at a low ebb and he knew it. "I am not in control of the convention!" he shouted to Payne. That was fine with Payne. He considered Roosevelt not just New York's son, "but the nation's son." So did most of the delegates.

On June 21, Senator Joseph Foraker nominated William McKinley for the office of president of the United States, and the huge crowd at the West Philadelphia exposition building sang out "The Union Forever." Governor Theodore Roosevelt strode to the podium to second the nomination. Cabot Lodge, chairman of the convention, was there, and the two looked at each other for a moment as applause and cheering thundered through the hall. Then Roosevelt turned to the crowd, to the bright red, white, and blue banners and flags and streamers, and began to speak:

"We stand on the threshold of a new century big with the fate of mighty nations. . . . The young giant of the West stands on a continent and clasps the crest of an ocean in either hand. Our nation, glorious in youth and strength, looks into the future with eager eyes. . . ."

McKinley was elected by a unanimous vote of the delegates. Soon afterward, the governor of New York was nominated for the vice-presidency and given every vote but one—his own.

Hanna, bitterly disappointed, told McKinley, "Your duty to the Country is to live for four years from next March."

McKinley, after giving one speech, retired to his front porch in Canton, Ohio. Roosevelt filled the void, telling Hanna to use him to the limit—"I am as strong as a bull moose." He proved it that summer and fall, traveling over 21,000 miles and giving 673 speeches in 24 states. There were a number of issues, including silver (Bryan, nominated in Kansas City in July, with Adlai Ewing Stevenson as his running mate, had insisted on a silver plank), tariffs, trusts, "militarism," the Open Door policy in China.

Bryan, highlighting bad news from the Philippines, pushed hardest on the imperialism issue he had secured at such moral cost in urging the senators of his party to ratify the peace treaty with Spain. "We dare not educate the Filipinos," he cried out, "lest they learn to read the Declaration of Independence and the Constitution of the United States." The articulate voices of the anti-imperialists echoed his plaint in newspapers and journals across the country, and Bryan was encouraged. Andrew Carnegie, writing to a friend in the administration, summed up McKinley's predicament in the Far East: " . . . you seem to have about finished your work of civilizing the Filipinos; it is thought that about 8000 of them have been completely civilized and sent to Heaven; I hope you like it."

To Roosevelt imperialism was not an issue. "The simple truth is," he wrote, "there is nothing even remotely resembling 'imperialism' . . . in the present development of that policy of expansion which has been part of the history of America from the day she became a nation." As for expansion, that had already taken place. "The question now," he said on the stump, "is not whether we shall expand for we have already expanded—but whether we shall contract." Democratic support for Aguinaldo, Roosevelt suggested, was killing American soldiers. Bryanism meant anarchy; the great orator was cut from the same cloth as Marat and Robespierre.

On November 6, McKinley resoundingly defeated Bryan in both the popular and Electoral College votes. Roosevelt, who had done his duty by the party, wrote to a friend: "I do not expect to go any further in politics."

On Friday, September 6, 1901, William McKinley attended the Pan American Exposition in Buffalo. He had spoken there, the day before, to more than fifty thousand people, on how swiftly developments in transportation and communications had shrunk the world. "Isolation is no longer possible or desirable. . . . God and man have linked the nations together." This day he visited the Temple of Music, where, standing on a platform at the end of the spacious gallery filled with potted palms, he would shake hands with acquaintances and the public.

Shortly after 4 P.M., a short, boyish-looking man in a plain dark suit approached the president. He was, they later found out, Leon F. Czolgosz, a Polish anarchist with a history of depression and abnormal behavior. The man's right hand, McKinley saw, was wrapped in a bandagelike handkerchief, so the president reached out to grasp his left hand. The muffled crack of small-caliber revolver shots suddenly punctuated the murmur of the crowd. The handkerchief around the man's hand blazed into flame and smoke wisped out through two black holes.

As Czolgosz was wrestled to the ground by a Secret Service agent, McKinley was taken by ambulance to an emergency hospital at the exposition. There a bullet that had grazed his ribs fell to the floor, but there was a hole in his abdomen and the wound appeared serious. As surgeons prepared to operate, and an anesthetist began to administer ether, William McKinley was heard to murmur:

> "Our Father, who art in Heaven,
> Hallowed be thy name . . ."

A week later, McKinley was dead of gangrene poisoning. On the evening of September 14, Theodore Roosevelt solemnly took the oath of office in the Ansley Wilcox house in Buffalo and spoke a few reassuring words: "I wish to say that it shall be my aim to continue, absolutely unbroken, the policy of President McKinley for the peace, the prosperity, and the honor of our beloved country."

That did not mean, he wrote later, that his administration would be a "pale copy" of McKinley's. "If a man is fit to be President, he will speedily so impress himself in the office that the policies pursued will be his anyhow...."

Lodge had written Roosevelt from Paris: "It wrung my heart to think of your coming to the great place through an assassination, for I know how terribly that idea must be haunting you...."

Roosevelt agreed. "It is a dreadful thing to come into the presidency this way," he wrote Lodge, "but it would be a far worse thing to be morbid about it. Here is the task, and I have got to do it to the best of my ability...."

Roosevelt was, at the age of forty-two, the youngest president ever to take office, and his "fighting edge" was almost instantly challenged. Just two weeks after he was sworn in, a massacre took place in the Philippines that the press compared to that of Custer at the Little Bighorn.

At Balangiga on the island of Samar, in the Visayan chain southeast of Luzon, seventy-four troops of Company C, Ninth U.S. Infantry, were eating an early breakfast on the Saturday morning of September 28. The flag was at half-mast, in tribute to McKinley, and there were to be religious services afterward. At 6:30 A.M. they were surprised by hundreds of bolo-swinging guerrillas and native laborers who slashed and hacked their way through the unarmed Americans. A handful managed to escape in native canoes and sail to Leyte.

The next day, when a detachment of volunteers arrived at Balangiga, the horror was overwhelming. One man had been boiled alive; disembowled bodies were crammed with molasses; a dog, presumably the company mascot, had been blinded, its eyes replaced by stones; heads, arms, legs, blood, and brains littered the compound.

Roosevelt, informed of the massacre, ordered "the most stern measures to pacify Samar." On the island, his directive, after passing down the chain of command, was interpreted by General Jacob H. (Hell-Roaring Jake) Smith in Draconian terms. American soldiers and marines, told to take no prisoners, to "kill and burn," savaged their way across the island. They left it, as Smith had promised, "a howling wilderness."

Gradually, however, news from the Philippines improved. Aguinaldo had been captured in March in a daredevil raid commanded by Frederick Funston. The Tagalog leader performed an astonishing about-face by pledging his allegiance to "the great American nation." In so doing, he wrote, "I believe that I am serving thee, my beloved country." He called upon his followers to end resistance: "There has been enough blood, enough tears, enough desolation."

His capture and capitulation did not end the war—Balangiga alone proved that—but it did mark the beginning of the end. The *coup de grâce* came in December when army directives established plainly marked zones around towns under United States control. Filipinos were ordered to move into the camps with their food supplies and livestock by December 25. If they did not, "their property [found outside of said zone at said date] will become liable to confiscation or destruction." Army troops then moved through the countryside, scorching the earth, shooting insurgents and anyone suspected of being one.

In New York, Thomas Reed had struck up an acquaintance with Mark Twain, who wrote earlier in the year, "And as a flag for the Philippine Province, it is easily managed ... we can just have our usual flag, with the white stripes painted black and the stars replaced by the skull and crossbones." Now Reed, convinced the United States had taken on the "last colonial curse of Spain," joined in the sport, drafting fictive letters to the Congress from "Butcher" Weyler in which the architect of the Cuban concentration camps claimed credit for inventing the methods now employed by the United States army to separate the insurgents from their civilian base of support.

Whatever the ethical merits of the policy, it worked. On July 4, 1902, Roosevelt was able to declare the insurrection officially ended, though fighting and killing continued on a sporadic basis. The cost of the three-and-a-half-year war had been high. More than 4,000 American and 20,000 Filipino troops were dead; estimates of civilian deaths from starvation, disease, and killing by soldiers on both sides ranged up to 250,000.

The job now was literally to take up the White Man's Burden—to make the Filipinos, as Roosevelt put it, "fit for self-government after the fashion of the really free nations." Local elections had been held in parts of Luzon in 1901, and with the end of military government in July 1902, Congress passed an act enabling a popularly elected Philippine assembly. Transports at Manila disgorged the implements of peace— soap, toothpaste, sewing machines, educational materials, and baseball bats. There were reports that some tribal chiefs insisted on doing all the batting, leaving the more menial chores, such as base-running, to their underlings.

In Cuba, by this time, Wood had made formidable progress. The first municipal elections were held in 1900, and a constitutional convention began meeting in Havana late that year. By the following June it had produced, after considerable arm-twisting by Washington, a document acceptable to the president and the Congress. It incorporated a precautionary amendment proposed by Senator Orville H. Platt of Connecticut granting the United States "the right to intervene for the preservation of Cuban independence, the maintenance of a government adequate for the protection of life, property and individual liberty. . . ."

United States military authority was to end at noon on May 20, 1902, and the government turned over to Cuba's newly elected president, Tomás Estrada Palma, the old schoolteacher, junta chief, and "president" of the insurgent republic. On the night before his inauguration Estrada Palma was joined in his rooms by two ardent Cuban patriots, "Dynamite Johnny" O'Brien and Horatio Rubens, the Junta's former legal counsel. Estrada Palma was euphoric, O'Brien reported, almost hysterical with joy about the prospect of Cuban independence.

"The great moment is close at hand," he declared. "The hour for which we have been fighting for years is almost here. Cuba is coming into her own. And such enthusiasm!"

Rubens was cynical. "Yes," he replied, "until tomorrow." Then a reaction would set in; it was the law of human nature. With the war over, "the demagogue will return to his mob, the outlaw to his violence and crime and every man who does not get what he considers his share of the spoils of conquest will become your active enemy." Cubans were ignorant of self-government, he went on. They would not recognize the will of the people. He hoped he was wrong, "but I fear there are still dark days ahead for Cuba."

The next day, as unleashed church bells banged out the triumph of the revolution, Estrada Palma took over the reins of government from Wood in the Governor's Palace. American flags dipped and the lone-star banner of Cuba rose over Havana as the Seventh Cavalry presented arms and the guns of the *Brooklyn* roared in salute. Roosevelt was proud that his country and administration had fulfilled the terms of Senator Teller's 1898 amendment. England, he noted, had promised to get out of Egypt, and had not. Japan had promised to leave Korea, and probably had not even entertained the idea. "We made the promise to give Cuba independence; and we kept the promise."

As the years passed, Roosevelt stamped them with his imprint as vividly as he had branded the Maltese cross on his cattle in the Dakotas. In 1903 he established the Department of Commerce and Labor and appointed George B. Cortelyou, McKinley's accomplished aide and confidant, as its first secretary. Fearing "the portentous growth of corporations," he dusted off the moribund Sherman Antitrust Act of 1890 and asserted the government's right to regulate industrial monopoly. As the first batches of cuddly "Teddy Bears" tumbled off the assembly line, Roosevelt discreetly supported a "most just and proper" revolution in Panama, then governed by Colombia and its "irresponsible alien dictator," José Manuel Maroquín.

The Republic of Panama, immediately recognized by Washington, approved—as Colombia had not—a canal treaty, and work began in 1904. That same year, concerned by the general instability of the Caribbean and the kaiser's territorial ambitions, the president articulated the Roosevelt Corollary to the Monroe Doctrine in a letter to Elihu Root: "Brutal wrong-doing, or an impotence which results in a general loosening of the ties of civilized society, may finally require intervention by some civilized nation, and in the Western Hemisphere the United States cannot ignore this duty."

Roosevelt underscored his intent to the Congress in his

December annual message. "Interference would be a last resort," but, when required, the United States would police the area to keep the peace and enforce international obligations. The corollary was first imposed in 1905 when the debt-ridden Dominican Republic was forced to accept American control over its customs houses.

On March 4, 1905, Roosevelt was again inaugurated president of the United States. He had made it on his own this time, by thumping margins in the popular and electoral votes, and he rode triumphantly to the Capitol in a carriage surrounded by yipping Rough Riders. He rode in a submarine, too, John Holland's A-Class *Plunger,* an improved version of the submersible that had alarmed the *Vizcaya* in New York in 1898, and which Roosevelt had urged Secretary Long to purchase. In 1906 he won the Nobel Peace Prize for his skillful diplomacy in negotiating an end to the Russo-Japanese War.

That year, Horatio Rubens's gloomy appraisal of Cuba's capacity for self-government proved true. Estrada Palma's administration of moderates had become plagued by pension scandals, inflation, and elections that bordered on the farcical. In August the liberals declared a revolution, their standard a Cuban flag shrouded in black. Estrada Palma demanded United States intervention, then resigned, leaving Cuba without a government. Lodge, disgusted, thought the Cubans "ought to be taken by the scruff of the neck and shaken until they behave themselves."

Reluctantly, Roosevelt sent in marines and army units to restore order. A United States civilian provisional government maintained "peace and public confidence" for more than two years until fair elections could be held and a new president inaugurated.

The Philippines seemed a problem of a different sort. Roosevelt began to wonder whether the archipelago might prove to be "our heel of Achilles if we are attacked by a foreign power." The Japanese held Korea and parts of China. Lodge was wary, too. He thought the Japanese bumptious and sensitive, "disposed to attack anybody"—"the Prussia of the East." In 1907, as relations soured over United States' immigration policies and Japanese provocation in the Pacific, Lodge wrote that if the Japanese attacked, "there is nothing to prevent their seizing the Philippines [and] possibly Hawaii."

Roosevelt responded by proposing to send "the Great White Fleet" around the world to demonstrate that the Pacific Ocean was "home waters." European observers believed it would lead to war with Japan. In the United States, Mark Twain, who now considered the president "clearly insane," wrote disdainfully: "His excellency leaves for Washington today, to interest himself further in his scheme of provoking a war with Japan with his battleships. . . . I think he wants a war. He was in a skirmish once at San Juan Hill, and he got so much moonshine glory out of it that he has never been able to stop talking about it since. . . ."

Roosevelt had put naval appropriations at the top of his list. On December 16, 1907, at Hampton Roads, he watched with delight as a mighty armada, resplendent in peacetime white, buff, and gold hues, passed in review. Rear Admiral Robley Evans commanded the fleet, which included sixteen battleships with some fourteen thousand sailors aboard. Not a single one of the battlecraft was more than seven years in commission.

Roosevelt did not expect trouble. He believed the trip would be one "of absolute peace," but if trouble did come, the fleet was prepared for it. The ships put apprehensively into Yokohama in October 1908, and were given a grand welcome. Roosevelt wrote, "I had been very sure that the people of Japan would understand aright what the cruise meant, and would accept the visit of our fleet as the signal honor it was meant to be. . . . The event even surpassed my expectations."

The Great White Fleet timed its homecoming for Washington's Birthday, February 23, 1909. Roosevelt considered the unprecedented voyage one of his greatest accomplishments in office. The formidable ships and their crews had clearly shown the "fighting edge" and enhanced the nation's repute among the peoples of every continent. The president went down to Hampton Roads to greet "the first battle fleet ever to circumnavigate the globe."

As the first towering military mast appeared on the horizon—"on the minute," Roosevelt noted—he may have recalled, as he later did in his memoirs, a scene on the *Louisiana* bringing him back from an inspection tour of the Panama Canal construction. He had given a short speech to the crew at the end of the trip, and afterward an old sea dog of a petty officer shouted out, "Now then, men, three cheers for Theodore Roosevelt, the typical American citizen!" That was a very good way, Roosevelt thought, for seamen to think of their commander in chief.

Roosevelt had just ten more days in office. He did not believe a president should serve three consecutive terms and had turned over the Republican reins to William Howard Taft, who had been the first American governor-general in the Philippines. The triumphant voyage of the Great White Fleet seemed a fitting conclusion to his work in Washington.

But one almost forgotten project had been stillborn. In the spring of 1898, after the *Maine* blew up, Roosevelt had advised that funds be appropriated to raise the battleship from her muddy tomb in Havana Harbor so that she might be clearly and closely examined, and doubts put to rest. In the confusion of war, nothing came of it, but now, more than eleven years later, Congress finally authorized the first of a series of appropriations that would enable the ill-fated ship to rise from her muddy grave and once more put to sea.

XIII

TAPS

Let us hope that when we again find ourselves about to draw the sword to avenge an alleged insult or injury we may "remember the Maine" and pause before we unleash the dogs of war.

—ROBERT HENRY BEGGS

By this war our country became a world power. She gave the world to understand that she is a united country, a friend to the oppressed; and that she loves liberty, not merely for herself, but also for the people who have the capacity to enjoy it.

—MONSIGNOR JOHN P. CHIDWICK

OVER THE YEARS, the dark gray corpse of the *Maine* had slowly settled into the mud and clay of the harbor floor, but her main mast and the twisted steel bones of her superstructure still poked forlornly above the water. There were compelling reasons for raising and relocating the hulk. Havana was a busy port; the silted wreckage was a hazard to navigation. The remains of some seventy crewmen were still entombed on the ship; patriotic groups pushed hard for the recovery of the bodies so that they might be interred on American soil. And the mystery of the *Maine* lingered on. Charles Sigsbee and French Ensor Chadwick, among many others, felt that doubts about the findings of the 1898 court of inquiry would be resolved if a more thorough autopsy were performed.

In May 1910, by act of Congress, the Army Corps of Engineers was assigned the formidable task of floating the *Maine* and disposing of her remains. The engineers proposed to build a cofferdam of 20 interlocking cylinders, each 50 feet in diameter and constructed of 150 steel pilings. The 75-foot-long pilings, driven almost 40 feet into the harbor bottom, would extend a few feet above the surface of the water. The cylinders they formed would be filled with "stiff" clay and gravel to make them watertight. Then the water could be pumped out of the 400-foot-long cofferdam, the wreckage of the bow cut away, and the aft section of the battleship bulk-headed and refloated.

President William Howard Taft approved the plan on October 13. The elliptical cofferdam—the biggest ever built—was completed in six months. On June 3, 1911, the engineers began pumping out the water inside.

As the ship was unwatered, workmen shoveled and hosed away a thirteen-year accumulation of barnacles, oyster shells, seaweed, coralline formations, and harbor sediment. Barnacle cuts caused blood poisoning. The tropical sun cooked the crusted hulk and the salty stink of dying marine life became overpowering. In the dank tomb, bones and skeletons were discovered; corroded trinkets and personal effects sometimes made identification possible. Some objects had survived virtually intact: wool sweaters, light fixtures, rubber doormats for the officers' rooms, dumbbells, cigars, fifer Newton's cherished bugle, Sigsbee's bathtub, a gold watch with the name of John R. Bell, ship's steward, on the cover.

By the end of July, the water level had been taken down twenty-two feet. About half of the ship—the stern section—appeared to be intact. The bow section of the *Maine*, seen clearly for the first time since February 15, 1898, was skewed and shattered. It seemed to have capsized to starboard and pointed at an acute angle to the original fore-and-aft line of the ship. The three-hundred-ton starboard turret was finally found—twenty feet under the mud and thirty feet aft of its original position. Workers with acetylene torches began cutting their way through the wreckage.

Meanwhile, Taft had appointed a five-man Naval Board of Inspection and Survey to analyze the wreck and determine the cause of the explosion. Rear Admiral Charles E. Vreeland was its senior member. Navy experts in ordnance and ship construction, and an Army engineer who had worked on the wreck, completed the composition of the board. It convened in Havana on November 20 and met daily at the Plaza Hotel to study materials that had been readied—notes, plans, photographs, overlays, scale models of the *Maine*. An exhaustive on-site examination of the wreckage was conducted. Mud was pumped away from the key bottom and keel sections and the board members were able to actually see the effects of explosions on the ship's underbody.

Early in December, Vreeland and his experts returned to Washington to complete the inquiry and prepare their findings.

The verdict of the 1898 court of inquiry—that a mine had gone off under the *Maine* at about frame 18, lifting the ship, thrusting the keel up into its inverted V shape, and causing the partial explosion of the forward magazines—had been generally accepted as fair and accurate. Still, a number of naval architects, ordnance experts, and engineers on both sides of the Atlantic censured the court's findings. The British scientific journal *Engineering*, which thought the disaster accidental, provided a welcome harbor to several critical examinations of the evidence.

In May of 1898, a reader in Amsterdam, A.C.J. Vreedenberg, fired off one of the first salvos at the Sampson report. The Spanish, who sought to avoid war, would never have positioned the *Maine* over a mine. The explosion was most probably interior. The upward bursting of the protective deck, well connected to the ship's bottom, would have folded up the keel in the vicinity of frame 18.

Lieutenant Colonel John T. Bucknill of the Royal Engineers offered a long examination of the disaster in five May and June issues. He thought the mine theory highly unlikely—one powerful enough to bend the keel almost to the surface would have produced "dome-shaped" damage and blown the ammunition storage rooms out of the ship, and this had not happened. The sharp report heard by many on the *Maine* had instead come from the explosion of saluting powder in or near magazine A-14-M, probably heated to the ignition point by spontaneous combustion in coal bunker A-16.

The resulting blast fired into other forward shell rooms and magazines, and a great, roaring, catastrophic explosion followed. The bow sank like a shot, tipping to starboard as the aft end of the ship slid forward. These violent movements bent up the keel "like a knuckle joint."

Oddly, in view of his spontaneous-combustion bias, Bucknill cited mine experiments performed on HMS *Oberon* in which a five-hundred-pound mine filled with highly explosive gun cotton, detonated at a depth of fifty feet, had broken the back of the ship. And at the end of his argument, he added that a small contact mine might have initiated the disaster.

A well-reasoned case for accidental cause was advanced in November 1898 by Robert Henry Beggs in a lengthy article for the *Boston Transcript*. Beggs, whose meticulous critique reflected a knowledge of engineering and physics, argued that both the lifting of the *Maine* at the bow section and the dramatic bending of her keel into an inverted V shape, findings the Sampson court found conclusive evidence of a mine at about frame 18, could be explained by the explosion of the magazines located over the ship's double bottom.

As the powder exploded, everything in the vicinity would be shattered. "The outer [keel] plating, however, being water-tamped, would not be blown downward, but . . . seamed and fractured." As hot gases expanded, burst upward, cracked open the protective and berth decks, and blew out the ship's sides above the water line, the intact forward part of the vessel, some fifty feet long, would be lifted up and "tend to roll forward, lifting the keel at forward fracture and initiating a rotary motion." The two sections of the *Maine*, connected only by a strip of keel and bottom plating, drew together and forced the keel up into an acute angle. There was no mine, Beggs concluded. The *Maine* was destroyed by internal explosions alone.

Beggs's thesis was ingenious, if conjectural, and in the light of more modern investigations, plausible. He alluded to the proximity of bunker A-16 and magazine A-14-M, but did not cite a proximate cause. His study was also flawed by a political bias that cast a shadow of uncertainty over his conclusions. In a preface to an expanded version of his newspaper article, Beggs wrote candidly that he had an ax to grind. Since he abhorred war, he was "anxious that no evidence of a mine should be discovered . . . I was sadly disappointed when our special commission reported that the condition of the wreck proved that the chief damage to the ship was from without."

That judgment led him to seek "a weak place in the report" and, thinking that he had found one, his discovery spurned by "war hawk friends," he had secured the assistance of Professor Charles Eliot Norton of Harvard in having his polemic published in Boston. Norton, who detested imperialism and thought the war "a national crime," had been happy to oblige.

German naval commander Hermann Gercke did fix a prime cause of the magazine explosions—the ignition of gases generated from coal or fresh paints. The mine was a fiction, Gercke wrote, but added a caveat: If there had been one, then extensive changes in the bottom design of warships were required. *Scientific American* scoffed at his theory. Testimony given by officers and crewmen of the *Maine* had been full and explicit on the matter of paint and solvent storage, and the coal bunkers were inspected daily.

Critics of the 1898 report often lingered over the testimony that no geyser of water had been observed, and no dead fish found in the harbor. Sigsbee had, in fact, been naïve and vague on this question, and the matter was investigated by the Senate Committee on Foreign Relations in April 1898. Retired Admiral John Irwin, an expert on undersea explosions, testified on mine experiments he had supervised at Mobile Bay, Alabama, "fine fish-producing water." At a depth of six feet, he reported, a noticeable column of water was thrown up by an exploding mine. But at fifteen feet or more (the *Maine* was moored in thirty-six feet of water), hardly "a bubbling on the surface." In the month-long exercise, he had observed no dead fish.

There was also the convincing testimony of Captain Frederick Teasdale of the *Deva* to establish the existence of an underwater shock wave. Teasdale first thought his ship, over six hundred yards from the *Maine*, had been rammed. Afterward, there was "decided movement" to the *Deva* and his mate pointed out that the vessel was rolling. Captain C. C. Thomson of the English steamer *Vimeira* was not asked to testify but related, in a press interview, that his vessel "was lifted upon a tremendous wave and then bumped violently against the sides of the dock [at Havana]."

Finally, Captain French Chadwick posed a key question: If an internal explosion alone could crack the back of a warship and drive its bottom up to the surface, why hadn't the exploding magazines on Cervera's cruisers, similar in size and construction to the *Maine*, produced comparable effects?

As critics pecked away at discrepancies in the 1898 report, British naval historian Herbert Wrigley Wilson mustered a sound defense of the court's verdict. In his highly regarded *The Downfall of Spain*, published in London in 1900, Wilson carefully reviewed the testimony and concluded that the evidence "established the probability that the *Maine* was destroyed by a mine." Wilson had no ax to grind, though he was obviously piqued by "a French Admiral's statement that all American officers are liars, and that the *Maine* Court of Inquiry was a deliberate attempt to establish a falsehood."

Wilson admitted the mine theory posed difficulties. For example, the sharp report heard by some witnesses was not characteristic of an undersea explosion; "a dull heavy concussion . . . would be expected." In fact, as Beggs had pointed out, that was what many officers and crewmen on the *Maine* described. Some thought the ship had been torpedoed. Cadet David Boyd characterized the initial shock as like "the coupling up of a heavy freight train." Others sensed a jar, a shivering, trembling, vibration, or an underwater explosion more felt than heard.

Wilson was convinced that some exterior force had broken the ship's back and begun the movement which resulted in the inverted V shape of the ship's keel and bottom plating. There was, he observed, extensive damage well aft of frame 18, the point at which the Sampson court felt the mine had exploded. Between frames 23 and 30 the ship was almost completely destroyed. In the area of frames 29 and 30, the protective deck "stood straight up." And the keel itself, as Ensign Powelson had pointed out in his personal report to Captain Sigsbee, rose "at a gentle slope from frame 43 to about frame 22," where it was dramatically forced upward.

Wilson wondered whether Powelson might not have been right when he testified that a mine well aft of frame 18 could have exerted a "cushioned" but deadly force on the relatively weak bottom plating forward of the point where the *Maine's* midship armor belt ended. If so, following the magazine explosions, the two sinking ends of the ship might "buckle up" the twisted keel at frame 18. The event need not have been an act of treachery on the part of the Spanish. "Some unauthorized person" might have gained access to the mine station and fired the device.

Gradually, as other events took over the headlines and the war came to an end, the feverish analysis of the 1898 report ended. But in 1911, the corpse of the *Maine*, dry and bare in her man-made coffin, lay open to inspection and dissection.

The autopsy performed by the members of the Vreeland board was thorough, competent, and mercifully swift. Their eleven-page report to President Taft was transmitted to the Congress on December 14. It confirmed some findings of the 1898 inquiry, but on the basis of new evidence, came to a radically different conclusion.

The Vreeland board submitted twenty photographs and six plans of the wreck showing "breaks and bends" and divided the wreckage into four distinct sections. The first extended sixty feet from the bow to frame 18. It had tipped onto its starboard side but pointed sharply to port, with its ram nose down in the mud. The highest point of the inverted keel was 31 feet above its "intact" position.

The second section extended for 48 feet from frame 18 to frame 30. Here the upper part of the ship—all the side plating above the armor belt—was gone. A tongue of metal consisting of keel and starboard side bottom plating still connected sections one and three.

In section three, from frames 30 to 41, the protective deck was broken in several places and forced upward, mainly to starboard; decks above the armor deck were thrown up and aft with the pivot at about frame 41. The fifty-ton conning tower, attached to the main, superstructure, and bridge decks, had been exploded aft. It landed, upside down, some 85 feet behind its original position.

LONGITUDINAL SECTION

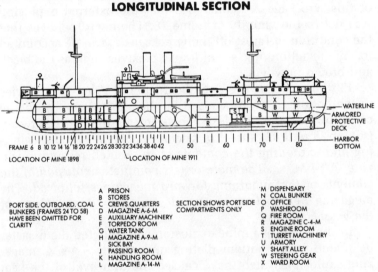

The 1898 and 1911 investigations both determined that a mine had exploded under the *Maine*, but located it at different frames.

Section four, the after half of the *Maine* from a point between her stacks to the stern, a distance of 172 feet, was relatively intact, though the main deck had been lifted perhaps 2 feet by the upward thrust of the armored deck.

Then the board announced key findings: The port garboard strake (the fore-and-aft strip of plating next to the keel) between frames 27½ and 31 was "dished" upward as much as two feet; rivets had popped along the inboard seam of the adjacent B strake; C strake in the same general area was "torn irregularly"; and most significantly, near the port side of the keel, between frames 28 and 33, about 100 square feet of bottom plating had been "displaced upward, inward and to starboard through approximately 180 degrees."

Some of this damage, the board reported, had been noticed in 1898. It called the attention of the Congress to the testimony of divers Olsen, Smith, and Rundquist. Eventually, the 1898 court placed an exterior explosion at frame 18, where the keel jackknifed to the surface. The Vreeland board, "because of its better opportunity for a detailed examination of this wreckage . . . concludes that the external explosion was not in the vicinity of frame 18. The board believes that the condition of [most of] the wreckage . . . can be accounted for by the action of gases of low explosives such as the black and brown powders. . . ."

Further aft, however, the board found "*that the injuries to the bottom . . . were caused by the explosion of a charge of a low form of explosive exterior to the ship between frames 28 and 31, strake B, port side. This resulted in igniting and exploding the contents of the 6-inch reserve magazine, A-14-M. . . . The more or less complete explosion of the contents of the remaining forward magazines followed. The magazine explosions resulted in the destruction of the vessel.*"

In short, while a mine explosion had initiated the disaster by pounding up bottom plating underneath A-14-M, magazine explosions might have caused the upheaval of the keel at frame 18. The board did not explain how this could have happened.

Robert Beggs pounced on the new findings. In the expanded version of his newspaper article, published in booklet form in 1912, he pointed out that the second report contradicted the first: "The damage [at frame 18] ascribed to a mine was not the work of a mine. The report on which we rushed to war was without foundation."

Bucknill's knuckle-joint scenario and Beggs's theory of rotary motion enlisted only token support. While doubts persisted, most qualified observers accepted the conclusion of the Vreeland board. The *Scientific American* headlined in

January of 1912: MAINE EXPLOSION NO LONGER A MYSTERY. An "incurved bottom plate" proved the first explosion was exterior. The magazine told its readers that a mine containing a low explosive charge (high explosive would have blown a hole in the bottom) had done the deed. It might even have been crude and amateurish—"an ordinary barrel, say the size of a sugar barrel, loaded with black powder . . . provided with a length of rope and an anchor." Placing it on a dark night was "a simple matter." The 6-inch reserve magazine, with its supplies of saluting powder, was just above the point of detonation. The heat of inrushing gases ignited it, and explosions in other forward magazines followed.

Once again, the matter was put to rest.

Then, sixty-two years later, as Admiral Hyman G. Rickover, the navy's nuclear submarine expert, browsed the *Washington Star-News*, he was intrigued by a headline: RETURNING TO THE RIDDLE OF THE EXPLOSION THAT SUNK THE MAINE. The article by John M. Taylor pointed out that the mystery of the ship had never been solved. It was still not known whether the *Maine* had been destroyed by a mine or an accidental magazine explosion.

Rickover accepted the challenge. As he researched the disaster, he asked Ib S. Hansen of the David W. Taylor Naval Ship Research and Development Center and Robert S. Price of the Naval Surface Weapons Center to examine the reports and supporting data of the Sampson and Vreeland boards. When Hansen and Price finished their study, they were persuaded the initial explosion on the night of February 15, 1898, was internal and accidental. In their scenario, after bunker A-16 was inspected at 10:00 A.M., spontaneous combustion in the soft, bituminous coal generated sufficient heat to ignite powder in magazine A-14-M. (Testimony given in 1898 revealed that while the bunker was accessible on three sides, and on the fourth through empty bunkers, it did abut the 6-inch reserve magazine in two places.) The explosion that resulted detonated part of the contents of adjacent magazines.

The explosions ruptured decks, peeling them forward and aft, and blew out the sides of the ship. The bow, now connected to the stern section only by a thin strip of keel and bottom plating, was seriously unbalanced by the weight of peeled-back decking. It capsized to starboard as it sank, twisting the attached keel up into a vertical position between frames 17 and 21. The bending of the keel was accentuated as the after section of the ship, sinking at its forward end, slid down to the bottom.

Examining the inward bends and bulges of hull sections under the reserve 6-inch magazine, the Vreeland board thought it had found the smoking gun. Hansen and Price were skeptical about the significance of the damage. While "dished" and torn, the strakes were not severely "mangled" as might be expected if a submarine explosion large enough to ignite the magazine had occurred. A simple explanation for the displaced plates was, they admitted, not to be found, and the V-shaped keel and bottom plating were "rather surprising phenomena."

But the dynamic effects of a magazine explosion could account for the bending in various ways. For example, explosive gases from the magazine could have expanded into the bottom structure and pushed aside water underneath the ship. "The subsequent return rush of the water . . . could have caused the unstiffened, unsupported outer bottom plating to be bent inward to its final position."

Rickover considered the Hansen-Price analysis convincing. The initial explosion had, he thought, occurred in the 6-inch reserve magazine. It had been caused, probably, by a fire in bunker A-16. Such slow-burning conflagrations had occurred on warships before. They were hard to detect. Rickover concluded: "There is no evidence that a mine destroyed the *Maine*." President McKinley, he wrote, "was unfortunate in the commanding officer of the *Maine* . . . there is no evidence he [Sigsbee] took more than routine measures in Havana to safeguard his ship from an accident. . . . Perhaps it is also significant that the *Kearsarge* and *Texas* while under his command were inspected and found dirty."

The admiral's verdict seems harsh. In fact, testimony given in 1898 shows that special precautions (such as the wearing of antistatic slippers, a Sigsbee innovation) had been put into effect, and all safety regulations and procedures fully met. And if there was a fire in bunker A-16, why was it not

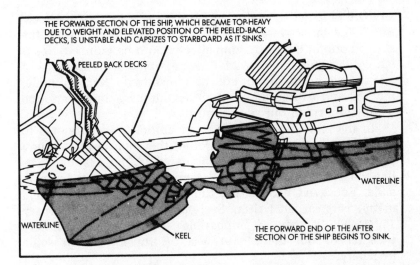

THE FORWARD SECTION OF THE SHIP, WHICH BECAME TOP-HEAVY
DUE TO WEIGHT AND ELEVATED POSITION OF THE PEELED-BACK
DECKS, IS UNSTABLE AND CAPSIZES TO STARBOARD AS IT SINKS.

PEELED BACK DECKS

WATERLINE

WATERLINE

KEEL

THE FORWARD END OF THE AFTER
SECTION OF THE SHIP BEGINS TO SINK.

Diagram from a study commissioned by Admiral Hyman Rickover shows
how keel and bottom plating could have been thrust upward as the bow
toppled to starboard and the aft end of the *Maine* sank and lurched
forward.

promptly discovered, as on the Schley's *Brooklyn* and other
vessels? As Herbert Wilson pointed out, "The bulkheads surrounding it on three sides could be felt by the hand, indeed
had to be felt by everyone who went by the wing passage
into the loading, hydraulic and dynamo rooms. . . ." Moreover, the bunker had been inspected that morning. And the
highly sensitive annunciators had not gone off. The *Army
and Navy Journal* considered these devices "no more reliable
than the electric front door bell," but they had the virtue of
simplicity. As heat rose in a bunker, a column of mercury
expanded, closed an electrical circuit, and set a bell to
ringing."

Hansen and Price found "no technical evidence in the
records examined that an external explosion initiated the destruction of the *Maine*," but in their discussion of mines
raised an element of doubt. A mine on the harbor floor, they
said, fourteen feet under the keel, could not have ignited the
suspect magazine since it would rupture the ship's bottom
and drive huge quantities of water into the hole, quenching

any fire or powder explosion caused by hot gases or shock. But if the burst were in contact with, or very close to, the ship's bottom, the quenching effect would be reduced. Spanish contact mines, they noted, were armed with a charge of one-to-two hundred pounds of guncotton. "Such a mine, moored and exploding close under the magazine, cannot be completely ruled out as the source. . . ."

In the end, like so many other authoritative attempts to unravel the mystery of the *Maine*, the Hansen-Price study proved conjectural and inconclusive. A bunker fire was likely, but could not be proved; a mine was unlikely, but possible. Roosevelt had sensed the dimensions of the enigma many years earlier, writing Secretary John Long on February 16, 1898: "It may be impossible to ever settle definitely whether or not the *Maine* was destroyed through some treachery. . . ."

Nevertheless, there was speculation as to who the culprit might have been. The 1898 court had taken testimony from a mystery witness (eventually identified as one Mr. Brondi) who claimed that the sinking of the *Maine* had been arranged by Spanish military officers. And Henry Drain, Lee's clerk, had read into the record the contents of a letter received at the consulate on February 18 from "An Admirer." It said that three men, including a diver named Pepe Barquin, also known as Pepe Taco, had taken a small boat from Regla on the evening of February 15 and rowed around the *Maine*. The family of one of the men was said to have received a payment of six thousand dollars after the *Maine* sank.

Both stories seemed far-fetched. The court paid them little heed, perhaps because there was not enough time to prove or disprove them. In any event, nothing came of the unsubstantiated testimony. And no one ever stepped forward to accept responsibility for the disaster.

For logical reasons William Randolph Hearst came under suspicion. He was close to the leaders of the Cuban Junta. His daring plan to liberate Evangelina Cisneros and the thwarted plot to sink a ship in the Suez Canal showed him capable of decisive—and illegal—action. Indeed, as Hearst bannered, WHILE OTHERS TALK, THE JOURNAL ACTS.

If he was not directly involved, wrote Ferdinand Lundberg, one of Hearst's biographers, he was at least an accessory: "If the Junta directed the explosion, then it was caused by a group with which the *Journal* had intimate connections." But the evidence is entirely circumstantial—guilt by association. Not a shred of proof links Hearst to the explosion.

In *Cuba: The Pursuit of Freedom*, British historian Hugh Thomas raises the possibility that the American millionaire and adventurer William Astor Chanler somehow contrived the explosion. Chanler, a veteran of "Dynamite Johnny" O'Brien's gun-running expeditions to Cuba, had allegedly discussed the matter with Máximo Gómez.

Chanler was fanatically devoted to Cuba Libre and a close friend of Junta attorney Horatio Rubens. On one of his 1897 filibustering ventures, a biographer reports, gunners blew a Spanish gunboat out of the water, thereby committing an act of piracy. Chanler confided to a friend that he was willing to give his life for the gallant Cuban struggle for liberty. Later on, Chanler served with distinction under Gereral Wheeler at Santiago. But not a tatter of evidence puts Chanler near Havana on February 15, 1898. He was almost certainly in Albany where he served as a New York State assemblyman. The story appears to be based, at best, on rumor.

For some of the same reasons, Captain John—"Dynamite Johnny"—O'Brien qualifies as a suspect. Consumed by the cause of Cuba Libre, he worked hand in glove with Estrada Palma and Rubens. He was an explosives expert and had carried to Cuba on his various filibustering vessels dynamite, fulminate-of-mercury detonators, "a corps of dynamite experts," and an "electrical engineer in command of a torpedo corps." At Banes Bay in March of 1897 he had shown how simple and unsophisticated an explosive device could be by mining the mouth of the channel "with two five-gallon demijohns of nitroglycerine, which were connected up with wires running to the shore."

Possibly O'Brien felt driving Spain and its "murderous misrule" out of the Caribbean of greater importance than one ship. Curiously, O'Brien was near Havana on the night of February 15, 1898. By his own account he was conning the *Dauntless* westward along the north Cuban coast, somewhere between Matanzas and Nuevitas, where she had landed guns and men.

But it is not credible that O'Brien, an American as well as Cuban patriot, placed a mine under a United States battleship. He did later offer one of the simpler solutions to the mystery. Powder decomposition had led to spontaneous combustion. The same thing had happened, he wrote in 1912, aboard the French battleship *Jena* in 1907 when she blew up in drydock.

The theory did not impress most experts. The *Jena* carried chemically unstable smokeless powder, a cellulose nitrate explosive rather like guncotton, which tended to deteriorate under certain conditions. The *Maine* stored the old-fashioned, stable, black and brown powders.

Dynamite Johnny did have disciples in explosives' technology, and if sabotage was indeed the cause, perhaps the most likely suspects were members of the Cuban Junta, who knew the explosion would almost certainly touch off war between the United States and Spain and bring about U.S. intervention. One of the ubiquitous harbor lighters, crewed by insurgents, might have dropped a primitive mine in the general area of the *Maine.* Charles Sigsbee had outlined to Sampson and Chadwick how it could be done, and they agreed it was possible.

If so, the ebb tide may have swung the battleship over the device. Then, as the Vreeland board concluded, a low form of explosive hammered up plates in the area of frame 30. At this first explosion the ship was violently heaved up; men were propelled from their bunks; Marine Sergeant Meehan was "lifted clean off the gangway and fired in the water."

Somehow—perhaps from the cushioned punch postulated by Powelson—the ship's back cracked in one of its more fragile sections near frame 18. As Marine Private William Anthony put it, the ship "apparently broke in the middle . . . and surged forward, and then canted over to port."

The terrifying, rumbling roar of exploding powder and ammunition followed immediately. Decks burst up and bent fore and aft. The bow section, weighed down by elevated decking, rolled over and dived, pivoting at the bow where it was still chain-moored to the bottom. As it rotated, the aft section, sliding forward as it sank, squeezed up bottom plating and keel near frame 18 into an inverted V. Water rushed into the open ends of the ship, quenching the magazine explosions, saving a few lives.

It may have been a mine; it may have been powder decomposition or spontaneous combustion in a coal bunker. It may have been treachery, an accident, or an act of God. But like the identity of Jack the Ripper in London, the killing of John F. Kennedy in Dallas, and the Tonkin Gulf "incident" of August, 1964, the mystery of the *Maine*—the "crime" of the nineteenth century—will forever remain unsolved.

What did become clear, over the years, was that the explosion of the *Maine* and the events that ensued should not be forgotten. Admiral Rickover wrote in 1976: "In the modern technological age, the battle cry 'Remember the *Maine*' should have a special meaning for us. With almost instantaneous communications that can command weapons of unprecedented power, we can no longer approach technical problems with the casualness and confidence held by Americans in 1898. The *Maine* should impress us that technical problems must be examined by competent and qualified people; and that the results of their investigation must be fully and fairly presented to their fellow citizens."

After the second autopsy was concluded by the Vreeland board in December 1911, the *Maine* was made ready for her last voyage. Army engineers bulkheaded the forward end of the intact stern section with wood and concrete. To overcome the suction of mud in which the hulk was embedded, holes were cut in her bottom and water jetted through under high pressure. The holes were then plugged with sea cocks; sluice gates were built into the bulkhead to further prepare the *Maine* for her final plunge.

On February 13, 1912, water was allowed to pour into the cofferdam until the *Maine* floated. After leakage tests, which proved negative, two of the cylinders were dismantled and the ship towed out and made fast to the outside of the cofferdam.

At sunrise on March 16, cannon boomed a salute from the Cabañas fortress. Like the tolling of a solemn bell, the cannonade was repeated every hour. At 9 A.M. the battleship *North Carolina* entered harbor. Coffins holding the remains of sixty-six victims of the explosion were ceremoniously placed aboard under the supervision of the *Maine's* old sky pilot, Monsignor John Chidwick.

On the *Maine*, a work crew passed a heavy chain through hawse pipes on the stern and shackled it together. A seven-inch manila towing line was reeved through a ring in the chain and made fast to the tug *Osceola*. To minimize water pressure on the makeshift bulkhead, the ship would be towed out backward. Lines were also passed to two other tugs from bitts at the fragile bulkheaded end of the *Maine* so that her uncertain progress up-channel might be steadied.

The *Maine* was warped away from her temporary berth abutting the cofferdam and squared away. The work party disembarked. One man, ceremonially dressed in black, was left aboard to pilot the hulk to her final resting place. At two-fifteen he hand-signaled the tugs to get underway. The guns of the Cabañas began minute-firing as the *Maine* was slowly towed toward the harbor entrance.

John Randolph Caldwell, the former *New York Herald* correspondent whose frantic code message requesting pistol ammunition ("Camera received but no plates . . .") may have hastened the *Maine's* departure for Havana fourteen years earlier, was on hand to record the scene for *Harper's Weekly*. It was appropriate, he thought, that little "Captain Dynamite" was conning the ship to her final resting place. O'Brien, "the skillful pilot, the renowned adventurer whose exploits in Caribbean waters may rank with those of Morgan and Drake," and for many years a valued member of the Corps of Port Pilots of Havana, deserved the honor.

There was no bridge on the *Maine* so O'Brien, in black hat, bow tie, and morning suit, stood at the foot of a tall jury mast stepped where the original main mast had risen. A huge American flag had been nailed to the pole—there was no way wind or water could tear it from its moorings. O'Brien thought it "the biggest and handsomest navy ensign . . . I ever saw." Looking across the deck, strewn with thousands of roses, he had a bright vision of it "bristling with cannon and crowded with strong sailormen. I never felt so much like crying in my life." Something caressed his cheek—the tip of Old

Glory. He took a fold of the flag, raised it to his lips, and kissed it.

The whole city of Havana had turned out for the funeral. Spectators swarmed along the waterfront and thronged rooftops. Soldiers lined the parapets of Cabañas and Morro. Chidwick noted how quiet it was; not a sound came from the crowds. As the *Maine* passed in review between two lines of American and Cuban warships, flags half-masted, marines presented arms and sailors snapped to attention. The sea was smooth and there was little wind in the harbor, but the *Maine* sheered nervously in the wake of the *Osceola*. O'Brien signaled the flanking tugs to tighten or ease the tension on their steering lines.

When the *Maine* reached the San Telmo buoy, where the channel turned to port for its last run to open water, the warships fell into line behind the tow. The marine band on the *North Carolina* played laments as the hulk bobbed seaward. Dark clouds shrouded the sun and waves began to break in the fresh tradewind as they passed the Morro, but the ship somehow behaved more peacefully in the open sea. She was a good tow, O'Brien reflected, pitching from side to side "as gently as a baby . . . the *Maine* as she used to be must have been a smart sea boat."

They went out beyond the three-mile limit, and another mile, and then three shrill whistle blasts and a gunshot from the *North Carolina* brought the cortège to a halt. The *Maine*'s last voyage was almost over. Beneath the surface of the sea, a submarine trench six hundred fathoms deep ran along the Cuban shore; this was to be her grave. The work party, again put aboard, opened the sea cocks and the sluice gates in the bulkhead, and left. The *Osceola* cast off. O'Brien climbed down the side of the ship and dropped into a pilot boat. The American vessels arranged themselves to the east of the sinking ship, the Cuban ships to the west. The marine band on the *North Carolina* began playing "The Star-Spangled Banner."

Almost imperceptibly, the *Maine* began to go down. Chidwick thought it a gallant sight. The ship seemed to struggle against her fate—"again and again, she seemed to defy all efforts to sink her." O'Brien thought so, too. It seemed to him hours passed by. Yet with every plunge she settled deeper by the bulkhead; waves began to wash over her decks. She staggered, her stern heaved up high, and the keel came into view.

Then, one final time, a bugler played Taps:

Go to sleep . . . go to sleep . . .

The ship let go. As a ray of sun shot through the clouds and flickered over the *Maine*, her stern heaved up almost vertically and she dove for the bottom. The mast struck the water flat, O'Brien saw, and "Old Glory vanished under the foam with a flash of red, white and blue as vivid as a flame." Air pressure inside the hull exploded decks and threw clouds of spray into the air. Pieces of timber shot to the surface.

Then, over her grave, a glistening slick of smooth water appeared, strewn with roses. The sirens of the surrounding ships wailed a funeral dirge. After firing a parting salute, the *North Carolina* set a course north, taking the bodies of the last victims of the *Maine* to Arlington.

As O'Brien watched, heavy rollers boiled over the smooth surface of the *Maine*'s grave. In a moment, there was nothing to mark the site. "In no way," he thought, "could she have met a sweeter or more peaceful end. The sea beckoned to her and she went swiftly and gladly to its bosom."

Rear Admiral Charles Sigsbee had not been present at the funeral, but watched the last rites on Pathé moving pictures. "The *Maine* lies in water clear and cold," he wrote. Her death marked "an epoch of new territorial possession, new policies, expanded military and naval power, increased commerce, wider international influence, and immensely greater responsibilities . . ." The nation's "slumbering energies" had been released.

It was the end of one chapter, but the beginning of another. No one saw that more clearly than Yeoman Fred Buenzle, Sampson's former clerk, who had sailored on for years after the great victory at Santiago. The Spanish defeat, he wrote, marked the end of the old navy, of sails and rigging, marlinspikes and capstan bars. "All hands now looked toward a navy of speedy cruisers of steel, floating fortresses bristling with mighty guns of hairbreadth precision."

The watch had changed; a new era had begun. But one could still dream: "My hammock slings enticingly on its hooks, and I can hear the soft tread of the officer of the deck overhead. . . . There is the music of restless wheel ropes, and the thrumming of cordage. The bugler rasps my hammock as he passes softly up the ladder. . . .

"Now I have heard the sweet refrain of taps; the old boatswain comes up from the berth deck, fingering his silver whistle. As the trilling notes reach the lower decks I coil up my last piece of gear, and hoist the signal of
'END HO!'"

EPILOGUE: THE PROTAGONISTS

THE NATIONS

Cuba

When the second American administration of Cuba came to an end in January 1909, General José Miguel Gómez became the Cuban republic's second president. His administration, like many of those that followed, was marked by corruption and violence. There was a bloody race conflict in 1912 and a revolt sparked by election fraud in 1917. President Woodrow Wilson declared, "I am going to teach the South American republics to elect good men."

The task was beyond him. As Winston Churchill had predicted, Cuban politics would be corrupt, capricious, and unstable. In 1928, General Gerardo Machado y Morales, an elected president, became Cuba's first full-fledged dictator.

The Platt Amendment, which seemed to guarantee American support or intervention to any insurgent cause—whether or not justified—was abrogated in 1934. In the years following, Cuban government was dominated by a junta led by Fulgencio Batista y Zaldívar, an army sergeant (later general) who had gained control over the Cuban military. Batista left Cuba in 1944 but returned in 1952. His second regime lasted until January 1, 1959, when Fidel Castro Ruz, the son of a Spaniard from Galicia, seized power. Castro was at first compared to José Martí, later with General Valeriano Weyler.

On January 3, 1961, the United States broke diplomatic relations with Castro's left-leaning government. The Bay of Pigs invasion and the Cuban missile crisis followed.

The Philippines

The history of the Philippines, as an old saying has it, is "three centuries in a Catholic convent and fifty years in Hollywood." American governors—William Howard Taft was the first—administered the affairs of the islands from 1900 to 1941. In 1934, however, the Philippines achieved commonwealth status; full independence was to be granted in 1946. In 1935 Manuel Luis Quezon y Molina became the first president of the commonwealth, defeating sixty-six-year-old Emilio Aguinaldo in the elections that year.

As Roosevelt and Lodge had foreseen, the archipelago became the Achilles heel of the United States. Two weeks after Pearl Harbor, Japanese troops invaded Luzon and in less than four months overwhelmed American and Filipino defense forces trained by General Douglas MacArthur, Arthur MacArthur's son. For three years the Japanese struggled to incorporate the Philippines into their Greater East Asia Co-Prosperity Sphere. The islands were liberated by American troops in 1945, and on July 4, 1946, the Republic of the Philippines was declared.

Ferdinand Edralin Marcos was elected president of the Philippines in 1965. His autocratic, corrupt, venal administration, cloaked in a protective veneer of anticommunism, sustained by economic and military support from Washington, lasted until 1986. In 1988, the new president of the Philippines, Corazon Cojuangco Aquino, admitted there was still work to be done. The task of achieving "a genuinely independent Filipino nation," she declared, one with "true nationalism," must be completed by 1998, the hundredth anniversary of Emilio Aguinaldo's declaration of independence from Spain.

Puerto Rico

Ceded to the United States by the Treaty of Paris, Puerto Rico was ruled by a military governor until May 1900, when a law establishing civil government under American control was enacted by Congress. To increase participation in Puerto Rican self-government, the law was broadened in 1909 and again in 1917 when the island became a territory of the United States. Key officials, however, including the governor, were still appointed by the president of the United States. Until 1946 they were Americans.

In that year President Harry S Truman appointed a Puerto Rican governor, and in 1947 Congress allowed the election of governors by popular vote. Under the administration of Luis Muñoz Marín a constitution was declared, and in 1952 Puerto Rico became a self-governing commonwealth. While that status is still favored, movements for statehood and independence persist.

Spain

In the nineteenth century Spain staggered under the burden of political division at home and the moral and financial costs of quelling independence movements in her far-flung colonies. Two naval battles, at Manila and Santiago, brought her hegemony to an end. As the gall of defeat eased, so did her colonial burdens. Historian Salvador de Madariaga wrote: "Spain felt then that the era of overseas adventures had gone, and that henceforth her future was at home. Her eyes, which for centuries had wandered to the ends of the world, were at last turned on her own home estate."

Pascual Cervera wrote to a friend before leaving Spain that he would do his duty, but also recited the words of Jesus Christ: "O, my Father, if it be possible, let this cup pass from me." The admiral's cup did not pass, but Spain's did—to the

United States. The political road ahead was potholed but, unfettered by colonial responsibilities, Spain made rapid progress in agriculture and industry, arts and letters. The distinguished group of philosophers, writers, and artists who broke new cultural ground for Spain was known as "the Generation of 1898."

The United States

Whether by "expansion" or "imperialism," the United States now governed possessions inhabited by Spanish-speaking peoples from San Juan to Subic Bay. She had become, as Europe was quick to notice, a world power. Her once-mocked navy had, by 1909, become the world's second most powerful. The expansionist gospel of Alfred Thayer Mahan and his disciples—at least for a time—held sway.

New opportunities for trade and power were vast, but over the years "the White Man's Burden" proved heavy. As anti-expansionist Moorfield Storey had warned, victory might be more costly than defeat, since it would lead to "the annexation of new regions which, unfit to govern themselves, would govern us." But it was not a time, as Roosevelt noted, for timidity, rather for decisiveness. The best course of action, he said, was embodied in a West African proverb: "Speak softly and carry a big stick, you will go far."

It was understandable, and perhaps even appropriate, that the nation's new mandate was carried out with a certain youthful brashness. We're a great people, Mr. Dooley remarked, "an' the best iv it is, we know we ar-re."

The Caribbean

In his autobiography Theodore Roosevelt underscored the fragile nature of government in the area when he offered a "partial list of the disturbances" in Panama for the period 1850–1902. In that time there were fifty-three revolutions, riots, outbreaks, counterrevolutions, and massacres. More or less under the umbrella of the Roosevelt Corollary to the Monroe Doctrine, in countries prey to "continuous revolutionary misrule," the United States has intervened in "banana wars" in Cuba, the Dominican Republic, Grenada, Haiti, Nicaragua, and Panama. The effort to export constitutional government to countries without democratic traditions, begun in Cuba in 1898, appears to be never-ending.

THE SHIPS

Infanta María Teresa

Pascual Cervera's flagship, similar in length, tonnage, armament, and age to the *Maine*, somehow survived the holocaust of fire and magazine explosions that tore through her on July 3, 1898. After bottom holes were patched, she was floated and taken to Guantánamo Bay for further repairs. Late in October, she was towed toward Norfolk, Virginia, for further refitting by the salvage vessels *Merritt* and *Vulcan*.

A tropical storm caught the three-thousand-foot-long tow in the Crooked Island Passage through the Bahamas. The *María Teresa* threatened to founder. Her crew was taken off by the *Merritt* and the great fifteen-inch manila cord connecting her with the *Vulcan* severed with an ax. Somehow the Spanish cruiser stayed afloat until she found a tongue of sea between two reefs and fetched up on Cat Island. Ten days later she was surveyed by Lieutenant George Blow and Naval Constructor Richmond Hobson. Clearly, her back was cracked and her bottom crushed by coral outcroppings. Like the *Maine*, she had endured conception, birth, death, and resurrection, and then found her final resting place.

The other ships of Cervera's squadron, because of the depth of water in which they sank or extensive damage to their hulls, were beyond salvaging.

Maine

The ill-fated battleship still exists as a ping on a submarine sonar recorder—and in thousands of collectibles: ashtrays, paperweights, models, bits of brass, scrapbooks. One of her large bow anchors, according to Navy records, is in place at a cemetery in Reading, Pennsylvania. Her mainmast carries the flag above the *Maine* Plot at the Arlington National Cemetery, and the foremast stands near the seawall that girds the Naval Academy at Annapolis, Maryland. For this reason, the *Maine* is sometimes called the longest ship in the navy.

She exists also in memory.

Oregon

The great gray "bulldog of the fleet," the mighty West Coast battleship that smashed her way around the Horn in record time and drove the *Cristóbal Colón* into the hard coast of Cuba, became a navy favorite. She served with Dewey in the Philippines and carried troops to China during the Boxer Rebellion of 1900. In 1918 she convoyed troop transports to Vladivostok.

Several times she was slated for destruction, but each time spared. Assistant Secretary of the Navy Franklin D. Roosevelt gave the *Oregon* a reprieve in 1920 when her sister ships *Indiana* and *Massachusetts* were used as target vessels and sunk. She found a safe harbor in Portland, Oregon, in 1925, and for sixteen years continued her charmed life as a floating monument.

No one loved her more, and perhaps not as much, as Ed "Guncotton" Murphy. In December 1941, when the Japanese struck Pearl Harbor, Murphy knew the *Oregon* "wanted to steam to battle once more, with Old Glory at the masthead. She tried to enlist, in this global war, when the State of Oregon offered her for active patrol duty. I tried to enlist, too, even if I am 65, but they found the both of us too old, my ship and me."

In fact, the gutted bulk of the *Oregon* served as an ammunition carrier in the Pacific. After the war, at Guam, she was torn from her moorings and flung out to sea by Hurricane Agnes. Her hull was found five hundred miles away, floating easily. Now fifty-five years old, she seemed immortal, but was not. The end finally came, ironically, in a shipyard in Kawasaki, Japan, where she was reduced to scrap iron in 1956.

THE MEN

Alfonso XIII

Alfonso XII's posthumous son finally ascended the throne of Spain in 1902, on his sixteenth birthday. The ubiquitous Richard Harding Davis covered the coronation in Madrid for *Collier's*. Davis described Alfonso as "an alert impulsive boy [who] looks like an invalid and has a funny little rabbit face," but gave him credit for grit: "He is young, strong, eager and intelligent, and every one wishes him well." Davis was surprised to find that Spain, now free of the "decayed parts" of her empire, was kempt and prosperous.

Alfonso XIII reigned until 1931 when, blamed for abrogating the Constitution and the collapse of parliamentary government, he left Spain (without formally abdicating) to an elected republican government.

Pascual Cervera y Topete

Understandably, the commander of the Spanish squadron was disturbed by the condition of his ships, Madrid politics, and, as Captain Víctor Concas put it, the "strategic absurdity" of his orders. Even so, his defeatist attitude and indecisive actions properly merit censure. He skirted the shoals of disobedience when he took the fleet to Martinique and Curaçao rather than San Juan; failed to take bold action in striking at the American coast or breaking through the weak blockade at Havana; missed several opportunities to escape Santiago when Schley convinced himself the Spanish were holed up at Cienfuegos; and made a poor choice of battle plan when he finally did sortie. His tactics, Commander Richard Wainwright noted, could be questioned, though his courage was never in doubt.

In September 1898, Cervera returned to Spain to face a military court of the realm which acquitted him, and his captains, of responsibility for the disaster at Santiago. Subsequently, he made vice admiral and was appointed chief of staff of the Spanish navy. He died in 1909, his honor—if not his military reputation—intact.

Stephen Crane

Crane finally left Havana in November 1898, still weakened by the malarial fever he had suffered at Santiago. He wrote a friend: "The truth is that *Cuba Libre* just about liberated me from this base blue world. The clockwork is juggling badly."

Probably his best postwar story was "The Price of the Harness," which concerned the cost in blood, hunger, and fever of putting on an army uniform. This became part of a memorable collection of stories and sketches based on his war experiences called *Wounds in the Rain*. Shortly before Crane died in June 1900, of tuberculosis, at the age of twenty-eight, Davis generously conceded that Crane outclassed the other correspondents in Cuba: "Of his power to make the public see what he sees it would be impertinent to speak."

Richard Harding Davis

After Greece, Cuba, and Puerto Rico, Davis covered the Boer and Russo-Japanese wars, and reported World War I from Belgium, France, and the Balkans. Between wars he wrote short stories, popular novels, and a number of slight but often successful Broadway plays. He died in 1916.

History treats Davis almost with disdain. The well-dressed raconteur and bon vivant seemed to many readers never to mature. *The New York Times* slighted him as "that supervisor and critic of the universe." But Davis's tough, colorful war reportage stands the test of time, and some of the best of it came toward the end of his life. He thought the Japanese "the most remarkable soldiers in the world . . . as cold-blooded in making war as Hill or Morgan are in a deal on Wall Street." In 1914 he watched in dismay as the kaiser's army quick-stepped through Brussels: "This was a machine, endless, tireless, with the delicate organization of a watch and the brute power of a steam roller. And for three days and three nights through Brussels it roared and rumbled, a cataract of molten lead. The infantry marched singing, with their iron-shod boots beating out the time . . . like the blows from giant pile-drivers. . . ."

George Dewey

Even Theodore Roosevelt considered Dewey's brief fling at politics "merely ridiculous." The Admiral of the Navy retreated to what he knew best—naval operations—becoming president of the newly established General Board. As a kind of chief staff officer, he backed naval aviation but failed to appreciate the potential of submarines. He died in January 1917.

William Randolph Hearst

Hearst never had to pay the fifty-thousand-dollar reward he put up for the detection of the "perpetrators" of the *Maine* disaster, which was just as well since the costs of war coverage—some fifty correspondents and a ten-boat press fleet— thrust the *Journal* deep into the red. After the war, as he boldly expanded his publishing empire, the shy but forceful entrepreneur took a fling at politics, won a seat in the House of Representatives, and almost became mayor of New York. He dreamed of the White House and at the Democratic National Convention of 1904 was nominated as "the friend of all who labor and are heavy laden." The 263 votes he received on one ballot were not enough to push him over the top, and his political aspirations withered when he lost the election for the New York governorship in 1906.

In 1913, Hearst tardily but grandly unveiled the colossal result of the *Maine* Monument Fund. President Taft, Charles Sigsbee, and a crowd of ten thousand helped him dedicate the monument on Columbus Circle at the southwest corner of New York's Central Park.

Possibly, Hearst exaggerated when he called the Spanish-American conflict "the *Journal*'s war." Certainly, Joseph Pulitzer and a number of other "yellow kids" could also stake a claim. But unquestionably he led the pack, heating public opinion to a flash point that demanded retribution for the victims of the *Maine* and "Butcher" Weyler's concentration camps. Hearst's critics wrote that the war was unnecessary, but Tomás Estrada Palma saw the matter in a different light. "I do not believe," he wrote, "we would have secured our independence without the aid which you have rendered." Evangelina Cisneros, who married a Cuban member of Karl Decker's rescue team on Fitzhugh Lee's Virginia farm, agreed: "My country and I owe everything to Mr. Hearst and the American people."

Alfred Thayer Mahan

The philosopher of sea power had as Naval Academy mates Dewey, Sampson, and Schley, but none of the renowned admirals influenced the course of world history as did Mahan. The seminal lessons of his lectures, articles, and books—that sea power determines whether empires stand or fall, and is rooted in capital ships grouped in cohesive fighting fleets—were not lost on England, Germany, and Japan. One Japanese translator wrote Mahan: "I trust that the great principles . . . set forth by your forcible pen may . . . awaken our nation and, as in Moses' time, be the pillar of fire leading our nation in the century to come."

After the war was over, Mahan observed that the Spanish fleet could have delayed American operations until the hurricane of September 1898 swept over the Caribbean. He warned: "We cannot expect ever again to have an enemy so entirely inapt as Spain showed herself to be. . . ."

Thomas Brackett Reed

Irascible, independent, and mutinous to the end, Reed continued to write ironical petitions from Valeriano Weyler to the American Congress: "I understand that some of your people think your conduct [regarding the Philippines] is justified by what your ancestors did to the Indians. If that be a justification, I can assure you that I am entitled to the same. . . ."

"Czar" Reed, the most powerful congressional leader of his time, died in December 1902. Henry Cabot Lodge wrote that he was "the finest, most effective debater that I have ever seen or heard." In the days of William Jennings Bryan, Bourke Cockran, and a host of other eloquent speakers, this was not faint praise.

Theodore Roosevelt

In his autobiography, published in 1913, Roosevelt wrote that there was a lesson to be learned from the Spanish-American War: "The true preachers of peace . . . are men who never hesitate to choose righteous war when it is the only alternative to unrighteous peace." In 1917, now blind in one eye, he entreated President Woodrow Wilson to allow him to raise and lead a division. Wilson rejected his request.

Roosevelt's sons, all four, did go to war. Archibald and Theodore were wounded on the Western Front. Quentin's aircraft was shot down behind German lines in July 1918. Colonel Roosevelt wrote of his youngest son's death: "Only those are fit to live who do not fear to die; and none are fit to die who have shrunk from the joy of life."

Theodore Roosevelt died of a coronary embolism early on the morning of January 6, 1919. Twenty-five years later, Brigadier General Theodore Roosevelt, Jr., gave a full measure of devotion to his father's ideals in Normandy, France. For his "unfaltering leadership" under savage fire on Utah Beach, a grateful nation posthumously awarded him the decoration his father had most coveted, and never received: the Medal of Honor.

William Thomas Sampson

In the popular eye Schley was the hero of Santiago, but most of the captains present, along with Navy Secretary John Long, credited Sampson, the architect of the close blockade that stifled Cervera's options, with the victory. After the battle the health of the exhausted fleet commander continued to deteriorate; he seemed depressed, bewildered, unable to function under stress. In February 1902 he was retired. Within three months, his contributions to navy and nation still disputed, he was dead. According to one obituary, the cause was paresis (motor paralysis); another cited "degeneration of the arterial system and softening of the brain." Today the diagnosis might be Alzheimer's disease.

"Those who knew Sampson best," wrote Yeoman Buenzle, "admired him most, and many loved him. . . . His name will shine among the resplendent names of American naval heroes forever."

Winfield Scott Schley

Acclaimed by the press, idolized by the public, Schley's star blazed high in the national firmament after the battle at Santiago. Privately, Long thought him guilty of "unpardonable vacillation and weakness in his approach to Santiago." And several of the captains told him the "loop" was an error—Schley had flinched. Even so, Long hoped "that the volcano, caused by the Sampson-Schley controversy, will cease to belch." It did not.

In 1901 the third volume of Edgar S. Maclay's *History of the United States Navy* was scheduled to be introduced in the Naval Academy curriculum. Maclay accused Schley of "turning tail" and "indulging in caitiff flight" at Santiago. Understandably, Schley demanded a court of inquiry. The book was withdrawn—but the court majority opinion cited Schley for vacillation and lack of enterprise. George Dewey, president of the court and an old friend of Schley's, issued a minority opinion stating that the commodore was "in absolute command" at the time of Cervera's sortie and was due the credit for the victory.

Schley appealed the majority finding to Roosevelt, who approved the court's decision and declared there was no excuse "for any further agitation on this unhappy controversy." Santiago had been, in fact, "a captain's fight." That was that. Shortly, Schley retired from the navy.

Charles Dwight Sigsbee

While there is some truth to Admiral Rickover's allegations against the *Maine*'s captain, the navy itself endorsed Sigsbee's stewardship by assigning him first the *Maine*, and then the *St. Paul* and the *Texas*. At San Juan in June 1898, Sigsbee won commendation when the *St. Paul* took on Cervera's refitted torpedo-boat destroyer *Terror* and drove it back into harbor badly hurt. In 1903 he was promoted to rear admiral.

Until his death in 1923, Sigsbee was convinced the *Maine* was blown up by a mine, and that the disaster "was the pivotal event of the conflict which . . . terminated Spanish possession in the Western World."

SOURCE NOTES

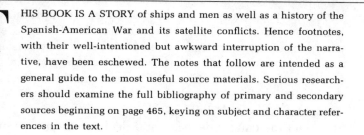

THIS BOOK IS A STORY of ships and men as well as a history of the Spanish-American War and its satellite conflicts. Hence footnotes, with their well-intentioned but awkward interruption of the narrative, have been eschewed. The notes that follow are intended as a general guide to the most useful source materials. Serious researchers should examine the full bibliography of primary and secondary sources beginning on page 465, keying on subject and character references in the text.

I. THE LAST SUPPER

The Cervera-Bermejo correspondence is given in Pascual Cervera's *The Spanish-American War*; interesting highlights and perspective on the Spanish situation are provided by Víctor Concas in *The Squadron of Admiral Cervera* and by Severo Gómez Núñez in *The Spanish American War: Blockades and Coast Defense*. The rationale for *trochas* and *reconcentrado* are outlined and elegantly illustrated in *Mi Mando en Cuba* by Valeriano Weyler. *The Letters of Theodore Roosevelt*, edited by Elting E. Morison, are published in eight volumes; the first two are most relevant to this book. Edmund Morris's splendid biography of Roosevelt, *The Rise of Theodore Roosevelt*, provides additional color and detail, as does *Henry Cabot Lodge* by John A. Garraty.

John D. Long's notes and comments on the navy and the

war with Spain are in *The Journal of John D. Long,* edited by his wife, Margaret Long, and in *America of Yesterday: The Journal of John D. Long,* edited by Lawrence Shaw Mayo. Roosevelt's relations with his alma mater are underscored in Henry F. Pringle's biography, *Theodore Roosevelt,* and by Howard K. Beale in *Theodore Roosevelt and the Rise of America to World Power.* Barbara Tuchman paints a marvelous portrait of Thomas Brackett Reed in *The Proud Tower;* see also Robert L. Beisner's *Twelve Against Empire.* Charles D. Sigsbee relates the story of the *Maine* in his book, *The Maine,* and in his *Cosmopolitan* magazine articles. Other accounts of note are in John Edward Weems's *The Fate of the Maine,* G.J.A. O'Toole's admirable *The Spanish War,* and Charles H. Brown's *The Correspondent's War,* a fascinating account of the role of the press in the 1895–1898 period. Fitzhugh Lee's wide-ranging history, *Cuba's Struggle Against Spain,* contains a vivid account of the *Maine's* appearance and destruction at Havana by Richard Wainwright and is of additional interest for its photographs.

The Life of Clara Barton by Percy H. Epler is perhaps the most useful biography of the American Red Cross founder. Of the many works on William Randolph Hearst, W. A. Swanberg's *Citizen Hearst* stands out. The background of the messages between Fitzhugh Lee and Washington is given in French Ensor Chadwick's comprehensive *The Relations of the United States and Spain: Diplomacy.* George Bronson Rea reports on the *Maine* disaster in *Harper's Weekly.* His *Facts and Fakes About Cuba* takes an interesting point of view on the "revolution" in Cuba. *Remember the Maine!* by Harry Cook relates the life of John P. Chidwick, chaplain of the *Maine.*

II. PEARL OF THE ANTILLES

Julia Ward Howe's *A Trip to Cuba* paints a lively, if antique, view of nineteenth-century Cuba. The story of the filibusters is told in numerous sources but most usefully in Philip S. Foner's *A History of Cuba and Its Relations to the United States,* and in Hugh Thomas's monumental *Cuba: The Pursuit of Freedom,* an invaluable source to the nation's history through 1971. Horace Smith relates the exploits of "Dynamite Johnny" O'Brien in *A Captain Unafraid*. Various books on Winston Churchill's early life portray his little-known service with the Spanish forces in Cuba, including his own *My Early Life* and Randolph S. Churchill's *Winston S. Churchill: Youth*. Bourke Cockran's biography is James McGurrin's *Bourke Cockran: A Free Lance in American Politics*.

On Hearst, see again Swanberg. Other accounts illuminate his approach to the "new journalism" of the day, notably John Tebbel's *The Life and Good Times of William Randolph Hearst* and James Creelman's *On the Great Highway*. An invaluable guide to Frederic Remington's artistic and journalistic efforts at this time is Douglas Allen's *Frederic Remington and the Spanish-American War*. Richard Harding Davis relates his adventures along the *trocha* in *Cuba in Wartime*. An engaging contemporary account of the Evangelina Cisneros caper is provided by George Clark Musgrave in *Under Three Flags in Cuba*. The plot to assassinate Cánovas is explored in Hugh Thomas. Theodore Roosevelt's letters are in Elting Morison, here and throughout.

Any number of naval histories tell the story of the navy's resurrection toward the end of the nineteenth century. Among the best are *A History of the United States Navy* by Dudley W. Knox; *The Rise of American Naval Power 1776–1918* by Harold and Margaret Sprout; *Our Navy in the War with Spain* by John R. Spears; and *A Leap to Arms* by Jack Cameron Dierks. More recent naval histories are *The United States Navy* by Edward L. Beach; *This People's Navy* by Kenneth J. Hagan; and *To Shining Sea* by Stephen Howarth. Invaluable insights to Alfred Thayer Mahan are found in William E. Livezey's *Mahan on Seapower*. For technical and historical information on the *Maine* itself, see *American Battleships 1886–1923* by John C. Reilly, Jr., and Robert L. Scheina, and *The American Steel Navy*, John Alden's stunning photographic history. Robley D. Evans tells his own story in *A Sailor's Log* and Edwin Falk explores his role in the building of the *Maine* in *Fighting Bob Evans*.

III. "A BURST OF THUNDER"

A passel of books deal with William McKinley's political options and initiatives at this time. French Ensor Chadwick's *Diplomacy*, H. Wayne Morgan's *William McKinley and His America*, and Lewis L. Gould's *The Presidency of William McKinley* are commendable, but for depth and readability, Margaret Leech's *In the Days of McKinley* is in a class of its own. The story of the mysterious Dupuy de Lôme affair is assembled mainly from accounts in Hugh Thomas, O'Toole, Brown, Swanberg, and also from Walter Millis's *The Martial Spirit* and David F. Trask's *The War with Spain in 1898*, probably the most thorough account of army and navy operations in the Spanish war.

Sigsbee's book and magazine articles provide the underpinning for the account of the *Maine* explosion. The principal source for this section, however, is the testimony taken by the court of inquiry in Havana and Key West, document 207, Government Printing Office. Crewmen and correspondents on the scene embellish the official account. Those by Walter Meriwether and Cadet Wat T. Cluverius in the U.S. Naval Institute *Proceedings* were particularly useful. John Weems's book includes interviews with survivors of the *Maine*. Interesting observations on the physical and chemical aspects of the explosion are in Admiral Hyman Rickover's *How the Battleship Maine Was Destroyed* and in *Scientific American* reportage. John Long's journals and Lieutenant W. Nephew King's *The Story of the War of 1898* flesh out more general accounts of how the news reached Washington.

IV. THE YELLOW KID AND THE CHINA-SHOP BULL

Over seventy sources, many of them already mentioned, were used to relate the events of the critical three-week period following the explosion of the *Maine*. For the situation in Havana and the diving activity over the battleship, Sigsbee, Rickover, and the report of the court of inquiry are especially useful. Accounts of the funeral of the victims are given by

Sigsbee, Cluverius, and Chidwick among others. The formation of the court is documented by Rickover and fleshed out
by Fred J. Buenzle, the court's first stenographer, in *Bluejacket*. Roosevelt's concern about his ailing wife and son are
best understood through Roosevelt's letters and Morris's biography. The very real concern over the *Vizcaya's* safety on
her visit to New York is illustrated by the precautions outlined in Appendix B of Sigsbee's book. Cervera's anguish at
this time is reflected in his correspondence.

McKinley's reaction to the disaster, and the Washington
scene in general, are again highlighted by Leech, Morgan,
Millis, and by Ernest R. May in *Imperial Democracy*. Lodge's
role in the sending of orders to Dewey in Long's absence is
confirmed by Roosevelt's later letters; a facsimile of the cable
is reproduced in Frank Freidel's profusely illustrated *The
Splendid Little War*. Hearst's journalistic responses to the explosion are in Brown and various biographies including *William Randolph Hearst* by John K. Winkler. The photographs
in King's history, probably the most complete visual record
of the war published, help to confirm innumerable details.

V. COURT OF INQUIRY

The report of the court of inquiry forms the basis for this
chapter though testimony given by witnesses is sometimes
embellished by later accounts. The *Maine's* East River incident is related in her log at the National Archives. Meriwether tells the story of the *Maine's* keel in Naval Institute
Proceedings. The biography of the remarkable Chanler family
is Lately Thomas's *A Pride of Lions*. Various sources including Chadwick, Millis, and May relate the tense Madrid-Wash-
ington negotiations of the period. Tuchman and Beisner,
again, provide color for the portrait of Thomas Brackett Reed.
Redfield Proctor's critical speech on Cuba is given in full in
The American-Spanish War, which also contains accounts by
a number of "war leaders." Sigsbee's book relates his fears of
the *Montgomery* being moored over a mine and also contains,
as Appendix E, Ensign Wilfred Powelson's personal report to
the captain. The delivery of the report is narrated dramatically by Leech and in *Spanish-American War Clippings*. The

findings of the Spanish Court of Instruction are in Sigsbee as Appendix F. Sigsbee's book, and the report of the Senate Committee on Foreign Relations, include his concept of how a mine might have been set near the *Maine*.

VI. THE DOGS OF WAR

Stewart Woodford's diplomatic efforts are in *The American-Spanish War* and in Chadwick's *Diplomacy*, Leech, Morgan, May, Millis, Trask, Hugh Thomas, and other sources. For Spanish naval movements, and strategy, see Cervera and Concas. Ralph D. Paine writes an entertaining account of filibustering and the war in *Roads of Adventure*. French Ensor Chadwick's appraisal of the naval strengths of the protagonists is in *The Relations of the United States and Spain: The Spanish-American War*, vols. 1 and 2. The *Scientific American Special Navy Supplement* also offers data on the ships of the fleets. War plans and games are discussed in Chadwick, the *Scientific American*, O'Toole, and other naval sources already listed. The substance of McKinley's message to the Congress is given in Chadwick's *Diplomacy*, and congressional reaction is highlighted by the Senate Foreign Relations Committee Report. Horatio Rubens's lobbying efforts are related by Hugh Thomas.

Don Russell, in *The Lives and Legends of Buffalo Bill*, along with Lately Thomas, Swanberg, Brown, and others recount the rush to arms. The scene at Key West is pictured by Paine, Meriwether, Evans, and Richard Harding Davis in *The Cuban and Porto Rican Campaigns* (hereafter cited as Davis). Sources for George Dewey's Hong Kong operations are listed in the notes to Chapter VII. Various sources portray the panic along the Atlantic coast, including Theodore Roosevelt in his letters and autobiography. The war songs at the end of the chapter are from *Bamie* by Lilian Rixey, and from Hugh Thomas.

VII. WOLFHOUND AT MANILA BAY

Dewey's victory at Manila Bay spawned a vast body of literature. Virtually every naval history at the least takes a sidelong glance at the operation and some consider it as important to American history as Trafalgar was to English history. Of these accounts and appraisals, I found Beach, Howarth, and King most valuable. Dewey's autobiography, with its perceptive introduction and useful appendices, is a cornerstone for the chapter, and Ronald Spector's *Admiral of the New Empire* fills in some of the gaps left by Dewey.

Eyewitness accounts, other than Dewey's, are scarce, but I have spliced three of them into the narrative: *Drawn from Memory* by John T. McCutcheon, *Admiral Dewey at Manila* by Joseph L. Stickney, and navigator Carlos G. Calkins's report which is in *The American-Spanish War*. Additional information was found in a number of general histories including O'Toole, Freidel, Leech, Morgan, Brown, Trask, Chadwick, and Mark Sullivan's *Our Times*.

Finley Peter Dunne's Mr. Dooley, featured in *Mr. Dooley at His Best* and *Mr. Dooley in Peace and War*, adds his wry view of the operation. The story of how James Keeley woke the president is told by McCutcheon and Sullivan. The famous fanfaronade is given in its entirety by King. Dierks supplies the recipe for a Dewey cocktail.

VIII. HIDE AND GO SEEK

The story of the blockade of Havana and the bombardment of San Juan is told by various correspondents and naval officers including Remington (in Allen), Davis, Evans, Paine, Buenzle, and Chadwick. W.A.M. Goode's *With Sampson Through the War* is also a vital source. Stephen Crane's contributions and background are in *The War Dispatches of Stephen Crane*, creatively annotated by R. W. Stallman and E. R. Hageman, and in Stallman's biography, *Stephen Crane*. Cervera's wanderings in the Caribbean and his fatal inaction at Santiago are detailed in his correspondence and in Concas. Beach, Buenzle, and Winfield Scott Schley, in *Forty-Five Years Under the Flag*, underscore the serious nature of Sampson's illness. The complex geography and timing of the navy's orders to Schley, and his dilatory response, are best understood through Goode, Chadwick, Schley, Long, Trask, Brown, and O'Toole, and also George Edward Graham's

Schley and Santiago and James Parker's *Rear Admirals Schley, Sampson and Cervera.*

The account of Crane's failed venture is in Stallman, Brown, and Cecil Carnes's *Jimmy Hare.* Long, Leech, and Trask describe the consternation in Washington on receipt of Schley's message of withdrawal from Santiago. And Paine and Charles E. Clark, in *My Fifty Years in the Navy*, portray the arrival of the *Oregon* and her reception by the fleet.

IX. "CHILDREN OF THE DRAGON'S BLOOD"

Three key sources support the events told in this chapter: Theodore Roosevelt's *The Rough Riders*; Virgil Carrington Jones's *Roosevelt's Rough Riders*; and Roosevelt's letters in Morison. Morris's biography and Roosevelt's autobiography are also invaluable, and Charles Johnson Post's lively *The Little War of Private Post* deserves a special nod of appreciation. Behind these prime sources lie numerous histories of the army expedition to Cuba, most important those of Trask, Freidel, O'Toole, Millis, Leech, and Brown. A.C.M. Azoy gives a spirited account of the fighting at Santiago in *Charge!* Swanberg and Creelman offer insights on William Randolph Hearst in Cuba. The most complete account of the *Merrimac* adventure is Richmond Pearson Hobson's *The Sinking of the Merrimac.*

The army's arrival at Tampa, its voyage to Cuba, the landings at Guantánamo, Daiquirí, and Siboney and the battles of Guásimas and San Juan Heights are largely told by eyewitnesses, among them: Remington (in Allen), Davis (backstopped by Gerald Langford's biography, *The Richard Harding Davis Years*), Roosevelt, Post, Creelman, Crane (in the Stallman volumes), and Paine. Rear Admiral Daniel P. Mannix III offers colorful observations on the chaos at Tampa, and subsequent naval operations, in *The Old Navy.* Admiral Cámara's threat to the Philippines is thoroughly covered in Trask and in an appendix to Cervera. *Cannon and Camera* by photographer John C. Hemment adds to the portrait of Hearst in Cuba and is also informative on the prewar situation in Havana.

X. LAMBS TO SLAUGHTER

In the short takes on army operations at the beginning and end of this chapter, sources are generally evident. For the naval battle off Santiago, eyewitnesses include Evans, Chadwick, Clark, Buenzle, Schley, Mannix, Cross (in Clark), Philip (in Edgar Stanton Maclay's *The Life and Adventures of Jack Philip*), Ed Murphy (in Naval Institute *Proceedings*), Cyrus S. Radford and R. K. Crank (in *The American-Spanish War*), Goode, and Graham; also, for the Spanish, Cervera, Concas, Núñez, the reports of the Spanish commanders (in Cervera), and José Müller y Tejeiro (in Lee). Useful overviews are in Azoy *(Signal 250!)*, Long *(The New American Navy)*, King, Falk, Parker, Beach, Freidel, Dierks, Knox, Trask, O'Toole, Brown, Millis, and the *Scientific American*. The log of the *Gloucester* was a helpful document.

XI. THE COST OF CONQUEST

A broad spectrum of histories, biographies, and eyewitness accounts were used to wind up the war in Cuba, cover the little-known invasion of Puerto Rico, document the peace negotiations in Washington and Paris, and bring the decimated Fifth Army Corps back to its mustering-out base on Long Island. Most of them have been cited; the text often reflects their identity. Many are also vital to the Philippine dilemma, and I am indebted to these additional sources: *In Our Image*, Stanley Karnow's lively ramble through Philippine history; *Cuba, the Philippines and Manifest Destiny* by Richard Hofstadter; *Expansionists of 1898* by Julius W. Pratt; and *Little Brown Brother* by Leon Wolff.

XII. DUTY AND DESTINY

The Cuban image problem is remarked in Crane (Stallman), Thomas, Millis, and Karnow, among others. Of the many sources on the Paris peace negotiations, I found Leech, Millis, Trask, and Tuchman the most useful. The battle for ratification of the peace treaty, and anti-imperialist opposition, is detailed in Millis, Morgan, Leech, O'Toole, Beisner, and Pratt. Sullivan reprints *The New York Times's* spoof of "The White Man's Burden." Trask, Leech, Tuchman, and Millis record aspects of Bryan's political flip-flop. The start of the Philippine uprising is well told in Karnow, King, Leech, and O'Toole; see also Frederick Funston's *Memories of Two Wars*. The various sections on postwar government in Cuba are from Morgan, Millis, Thomas, Leech, and Gould, among others.

Roosevelt's path to the vice-presidency is traced in his autobiography, in the collected letters in Morison, by biographers Morris, Pringle, Beale, William H. Harbaugh (in *The Life and Times of Theodore Roosevelt*), and by Morgan, Garraty, and Harold Howland (in *Theodore Roosevelt and His Times*). Dewey's return from Manila and his political pratfall are highlighted in his autobiography and in Morris, Leech, and Sullivan. John Long tells the story of the reburial of *Maine* victims at Arlington in his journals. Of the many accounts of McKinley's assassination, those by Leech, Sullivan, Morgan, and Gould stand out. The massacre at Balangiga is vividly related in Karnow, O'Toole, and in *Naval History*. The Roosevelt years are limned, largely, by his autobiography and the biographies of him.

XIII. TAPS

The unwatering and floating of the hulk of the *Maine* is given in the report of the Vreeland board, Rickover, magazine articles in *Naval History*, *Engineering*, *Naval Institute Proceedings*, and in the Lackawanna Steel Company report on raising the wreck. The series of photographs in *The Story of the Maine* proved a useful visual check to these narratives. Various theories on the explosion are taken from *Engineering*, *Scientific American*, and the *Army and Navy Journal*; *The Mystery of the Maine* by Robert H. Beggs; and *The Downfall of Spain* by Herbert W. Wilson. The Thomas account of the shock wave in Havana Harbor, never noted by investigators of the explosion, was found in *Spanish-American War Clippings*, vol. 2. The formation and composition of the Vreeland board is reported and commented on by Rickover and Naval Institute *Proceedings*. Rickover gives the Hansen-Price study.

The Pepe Taco plot is explored in *American History Illustrated*. The Hearst accusation is in Ferdinand Lundberg's *Imperial Hearst*. Lately Thomas relates William Astor Chanler's filibustering activities, and Hugh Thomas the hearsay of his responsibility for the explosion. John O'Brien's exploits are in his own account (Smith). Sources for the *Maine's* last voyage include Rickover, O'Toole, Weems, Chadwick (Cook), and magazine articles in *Cosmopolitan, Harper's Weekly,* and *Scientific American*.

EPILOGUE: THE PROTAGONISTS

A congeries of reference works, biographies, and other sources, in many cases evident in the text, were used for this section. Of special interest, however, are Hugh Thomas on Cuba; Karnow on the Philippines; and Ivan Musicant's *The Banana Wars* on the Caribbean. Family papers, and documents in the Naval Historical Center, were used in the stories of both the *Maine* and the *María Teresa*. The introduction to Clark by Jack Sweetman records the charmed life of one of the navy's most revered ships. Langford notes some of Richard Harding Davis's postwar reportage in Spain and Europe; Dierks reports the honors granted the Spanish admiral, Pascual Cervera, who disclaimed all responsibility for his failed campaign; Stallman writes the obituary of Stephen Crane. Hearst's political career, and the dedication of the *Maine* Memorial, are in Swanberg and Winkler. Livezey underscores the importance of Mahan's lessons to the Japanese. In *The Day Before Yesterday* Mrs. Theodore Roosevelt, Jr., reminisces about Theodore Roosevelt and his children. For Reed, see especially Samuel W. McCall's biography, *The Life of Thomas Brackett Reed.*

BIBLIOGRAPHY

BOOKS

Abbott, Willis John. *Watching the World Go By*. Little, Brown, 1933.

Alden, John D. *The American Steel Navy*. Naval Institute Press/American Heritage Press, 1989.

Allen, Douglas. *Frederic Remington and the Spanish-American War*. Crown Publishers, 1971.

American-Spanish War: A History by the War Leaders, The. Charles C. Haskell & Son, 1899.

Atkins, Edwin F. *Sixty Years in Cuba*. Harvard University Press, 1926.

Azoy, A.C.M. *Charge! The Story of the Battle of San Juan Hill*. Longmans, Green, 1961.

————. *Signal 250! The Sea Fight Off Santiago.* Van Rees Press, 1964.

Bartholomew, C. A. *Mud, Muscle, and Miracles: Marine Salvage in the United States Navy.* Naval Historical Center and Naval Sea Systems Command, 1990.

Barton, William E. *The Life of Clara Barton.* Houghton Mifflin, 1922.

Beach, Edward L. *The United States Navy: A 200-Year History.* Houghton Mifflin, 1987.

Beale, Howard K. *Theodore Roosevelt and the Rise of America to World Power.* Johns Hopkins University Press, 1956.

Beer, Thomas. *The Mauve Decade: American Life at the End of the 19th Century.* Random House/Vintage, 1960.

Beggs, Robert H. *The Mystery of the Maine: An Examination of Public Documents Relating to the Destruction of the U.S.S. Maine.* The Carnahan Press, 1912.

Beisner, Robert L. *Twelve Against Empire: The Anti-Imperialists 1898–1900.* McGraw-Hill, 1968.

Birkenhead, Lord Frederick. *Rudyard Kipling.* Random House, 1978.

Bishop, Joseph Bucklin, ed. *Theodore Roosevelt's Letters to His Children.* Charles Scribner's Sons, 1919.

Brown, Charles H. *The Correspondents' War: Journalists in the Spanish-American War.* Charles Scribner's Sons, 1967.

Buenzle, Fred J. *Bluejacket: An Autobiography.* Naval Institute Press, 1986.

Carnes, Cecil. *Jimmy Hare, News Photographer.* Macmillan, 1940.

Chadwick, French Ensor. *The Relations of the United States and Spain: Diplomacy.* Charles Scribner's Sons, 1909.

————. *The Relations of the United States and Spain: The Spanish American War.* Vols. 1 and 2. Charles Scribner's Sons, 1911.

Churchill, Randolph S., *Winston S. Churchill: Youth, 1874–1900.* Houghton Mifflin, 1966.

Churchill, Winston S., *My Early Life: A Roving Commission.* Oldham Press Ltd., 1930.

————. *Amid These Storms: Thoughts and Adventures.* Charles Scribner's Sons, 1932.

Clark, Charles E. *My Fifty Years in the Navy.* Naval Institute Press, 1984.

Clifford, Deborah Pickman. *Mine Eyes Have Seen the Glory.* Atlantic–Little, Brown, 1979.

Coblentz, Edmond D. *William Randolph Hearst: A Portrait in His Own Words.* Simon & Schuster, 1952.

Cook, Harry. *Remember the Maine! An Historic Narrative of the Battleship as Told by Its Chaplain.* Winchester Printers, 1935.

Creelman, James. *On the Great Highway.* Lothrup Publishing, 1901.

Cuba and the Wrecked Maine: Photographs with an Introduction. Belford, Middlebrook, 1898.

Cushing, Harvey. *The Life of Sir William Osler.* Oxford University Press, 1940.

Davis, George T. *A Navy Second to None.* Yale University Press, 1940.

Davis, Richard Harding. *The Cuban and Porto Rican Campaigns.* Charles Scribner's Sons, 1898.

———. *Cuba In Wartime.* R. H. Russell, 1899.

DeVoto, Bernard, ed. *Mark Twain in Eruption.* Harper & Bros., 1940.

Dewey, George. *Autobiography of George Dewey.* Naval Institute Press, 1987.

Dierks, Jack Cameron. *A Leap to Arms: The Cuban Campaign of 1898.* J. B. Lippincott, 1970.

Downey, Fairfax. *Richard Harding Davis and His Day.* Charles Scribner's Sons, 1933.

Dunne, Finley Peter. *Mr. Dooley in Peace and in War.* Charles Scribner's Sons, 1898.

———. *Mr. Dooley at His Best.* Charles Scribner's Sons, 1938.

Epler, Percy H. *The Life of Clara Barton.* MacMillan, 1941.

Evans, Robley D. *A Sailor's Log.* D. Appleton, 1901.

Falk, Edwin. *Fighting Bob Evans.* Jonathan Cape, 1931.

Fish, Carl Russell. *The Path of Empire: A Chronicle of the United States as a World Power.* Yale University Press, 1921.

Foner, Philip S. *A History of Cuba and Its Relations to the United States.* Vols. 1 and 2. International Publishers, 1962.

Freidel, Frank, *The Splendid Little War.* Little, Brown, 1958.

Funston, Frederick. *Memories of Two Wars*. Charles Scribner's Sons, 1914.

Garraty, John A. *Henry Cabot Lodge: A Biography*. Alfred A. Knopf, 1953.

Gilkes, Lilian. *Cora Crane: A Biography*. Indiana University Press, 1960.

Goode, W.A.M. *With Sampson Through the War*. Doubleday & McClure, 1899.

Gould, Lewis L. *The Presidency of William McKinley*. The Regents Press of Kansas, 1980.

Graham, George Edward. *Schley and Santiago*. W. B. Conkey. 1902.

Hagan, Kenneth J. *This People's Navy: The Making of American Sea Power*. The Free Press, 1991.

Hagedorn, Hermann. *The Roosevelt Family of Sagamore Hill*. Macmillan, 1954.

Halliburton, Richard. *Seven League Boots*. Bobbs-Merrill, 1935.

Harbaugh, William H. *The Life and Times of Theodore Roosevelt*. Oxford University Press, 1975.

Harper's Pictorial History of the War with Spain. Vols. 1 and 2. 1899.

Hartmann, Gregory K. *Weapons That Wait: Mine Warfare in the United States Navy*. Naval Institute Press, 1979.

Hemment, John C. *Cannon and Camera*. D. Appleton, 1898.

Hobart, Mrs. Garrett (Jennie). *Memories*. Carroll Hall (privately printed), 1930.

Hobson, Richmond P. *The Sinking of the Merrimac*. Naval Institute Press, 1987.

Hofstadter, Richard. *Cuba, the Philippines and Manifest Destiny: The Paranoid Style in American Politics and Other Essays*. Alfred A. Knopf, 1965.

Howarth, Stephen. *To Shining Sea: A History of the United States Navy 1775–1991*. Random House, 1991.

Howe, Julia Ward. *A Trip to Cuba*. Negro Universities Press, 1969.

Howland, Harold. *Theodore Roosevelt and His Times*. Yale University Press, 1921.

Jane, Fred T., ed. *Jane's Fighting Ships—1898*. Arco Publishers, 1898.

Jones, Virgil Carrington, *Roosevelt's Rough Riders*. Doubleday, 1971.

Karnow, Stanley. *In Our Image: America's Empire in the Philippines*. Random House, 1989.

Kennan, George. *Campaigning in Cuba*. Kennikat Press, 1971.

King, Rear Admiral Randolph W., ed. *Naval Engineering and American Sea Power*. The Nautical and Aviation Publishing Company of America, 1989.

King, W. Nephew. *The Story of the War of 1898*. P. F. Collier & Son, 1900.

Knox, Dudley W. *A History of the United States Navy*. G. P. Putnam's Sons, 1948.

Langford, Gerald. *The Richard Harding Davis Years: A Biography of a Mother and Son*. Holt, Rinehart, & Winston, 1961.

Langley, Lester D. *The United States and the Caribbean in the Twentieth Century*. University of Georgia Press, 1985.

Lee, Fitzhugh. *Cuba's Struggle Against Spain*. New York Historical Press, 1899.

Leech, Margaret. *In the Days of McKinley*. Harper & Brothers, 1959.

Livezey, William E. *Mahan on Sea Power*. University of Oklahoma Press, 1981.

Long, John Davis. *The New American Navy*. Outlook, 1903.
———. *America of Yesterday: The Journal of John D. Long*. Edited by Lawrence Shaw Mayo. Atlantic Monthly Press, 1923.

Long, Margaret, ed. *The Journal of John D. Long*. Richard R. Smith, 1956.

Lovette, Leland P. *Naval Traditions and Usage*. Naval Institute Press, 1959.

Lundberg, Ferdinand. *Imperial Hearst: A Social Biography*. Equinox Cooperative Press, 1936.

McCall, Samuel W. *The Life of Thomas Brackett Reed*. The Riverside Press, 1914.

McCullough, David. *Brave Companions: Portraits in History*. Prentice Hall Press, 1992.
———. *Mornings on Horseback*. Simon & Schuster, 1981.

McCutcheon, John T. *Drawn from Memory*. Bobbs-Merrill, 1950.

McGurrin, James. *Bourke Cockran: A Free Lance in American Politics.* Charles Scribner's Sons, 1948.

Maclay, Edgar Stanton. *The Life and Adventures of Jack Philip, Rear Admiral, United States Navy.* The Illustrated Navy, 1904.

Mahan, Alfred Thayer. *The Influence of Sea Power Upon History.* Little, Brown, 1890.

Manchester, William. *The Last Lion: Winston Spencer Churchill, Visions of Glory.* Little, Brown, 1983.

Mannix, Daniel P. III. *The Old Navy.* Macmillan, 1983.

Mason, Gregory. *Remember the Maine.* Henry Holt, 1939.

May, Ernest R. *Imperial Democracy: The Emergence of America as a Great Power.* Harcourt Brace & World, 1961.

Mazarr, Michael J. *Semper Fidel: America and Cuba 1776–1988.* The Nautical and Aviation Publishing Company of America, 1988.

Millett, Allen R. *Semper Fidelis: The History of the United States Marine Corps.* Macmillan, 1980.

Millis, Walter. *The Martial Spirit.* The Riverside Press, 1931.

Morgan, H. Wayne. *William McKinley and His America.* Syracuse University Press, 1963.

Morison, Elting E., ed. *The Letters of Theodore Roosevelt: The Years of Preparation, 1868–1900.* Vols. 1 and 2. Harvard University Press, 1951.

Morris, Edmund. *The Rise of Theodore Roosevelt.* Ballantine Books, 1980.

Musgrave, George Clark. *Under Three Flags in Cuba: A Personal Account of the Cuban Insurrection and Spanish-American War.* Little, Brown, 1899.

Musicant, Ivan. *The Banana Wars: A History of the United States Military Intervention in Latin America from the Spanish-American War to the Invasion of Panama.* Macmillan, 1990.

Neely's Photographs: Panoramic Views of Cuba, Porto Rico, Manila and the Philippines. F. Tennyson Neely, 1899.

Neeser, Robert W. *A Landsman's Log.* Yale University Press, 1913.

Neider, Charles, ed. *The Autobiography of Mark Twain.* Harper & Bros., 1959.

O'Connell, Robert L. *Of Arms and Men: A History of War,*

Weapons, and Aggression. Oxford University Press, 1989.

O'Toole, G.J.A. *The Spanish War: An American Epic, 1898.* Norton, 1984.

Paine, Ralph D. *Roads of Adventure.* Houghton Mifflin, 1922.

Parker, James. *Rear Admirals Schley, Sampson and Cervera.* Neale Publishing, 1910.

Post, Charles Johnson. *The Little War of Private Post.* Little, Brown, 1960.

Pratt, Fletcher. *The Compact History of the United States Navy.* Hawthorn Books, 1957.

Pratt, Julius W. *Expansionists of 1898.* Johns Hopkins University Press, 1959.

Pringle, Henry F. *Theodore Roosevelt: A Biography.* Harcourt Brace Jovanovich, 1984.

Rea, George Bronson. *Facts and Fakes About Cuba.* G. Munro's Sons, 1897.

Reilly, John C., Jr., and Robert L. Scheina. *American Battleships 1886–1923: Predreadnought Design and Construction.* Naval Institute Press, 1988.

Rickover, Hyman G. *How the Battleship Maine Was Destroyed.* U.S. Government Printing Office, 1976.

Rixie, Lilian. *Bamie: Theodore Roosevelt's Remarkable Sister.* David McKay Co., 1963.

Roosevelt, Mrs. Theodore, Jr. *Day Before Yesterday: The Reminiscences of Mrs. Theodore Roosevelt, Jr.* Doubleday, 1959.

Roosevelt, Theodore. *An Autobiography.* Macmillan, 1914.

——. *The Naval War of 1812.* Naval Institute Press, 1987.

——. *The Rough Riders.* Charles Scribner's Sons, 1925.

Ross, Ishbel. *Angel of the Battlefield.* Harper & Bros., 1956.

Russell, Don. *The Lives and Legends of Buffalo Bill.* University of Oklahoma Press, 1960.

Russell, Francis. *The Confident Years.* American Heritage, 1969.

Schley, Winfield Scott. *Forty-Five Years Under the Flag.* D. Appleton, 1904.

Scott, Hugh L. *Some Memories of a Soldier.* Century, 1928.

Sigsbee, Charles D. *The "Maine": An Account of Her Destruction in Havana Harbor.* Century, 1899.

Smith, Horace. *A Captain Unafraid: The Strange Adventures*

of Dynamite Johnny O'Brien. Harper & Bros., 1912.

Smith, Page. *America Enters the World.* Vol. 7. McGraw-Hill, 1985.

Spears, John R. *Our Navy in the War with Spain.* Charles Scribner's Sons, 1898.

Spector, Ronald. *Admiral of the New Empire.* Louisiana State University Press, 1974.

Sprout, Harold, and Margaret Sprout. *The Rise of American Naval Power, 1776–1918.* Princeton University Press, 1939.

————. *Toward a New Order of Sea Power: American Naval Policy and the World Scene.* Princeton University Press, 1940.

Stallman, R. W. *Stephen Crane: A Biography.* George Braziller, 1968.

Stallman, R. W. and Hagemann, E. R., eds. *The War Dispatches of Stephen Crane.* New York University Press, 1964.

Stickney, Joseph L. *Admiral Dewey at Manila: Life and Glorious Deeds of Admiral George Dewey.* 1899.

Story of the Maine, The. American Photo Co. (Havana), 1911.

Sullivan, Mark. *Our Times: The Turn of the Century.* Charles Scribner's Sons, 1926.

Swanberg, W. A. *Citizen Hearst: A Biography of William Randolph Hearst.* Charles Scribner's Sons, 1961.

————. *Pulitzer.* Charles Scribners' Sons, 1967.

Teague, Michael. *Mrs. L.* Doubleday, 1981.

Tebbel, John. *The Life and Good Times of William Randolph Hearst.* E. P. Dutton, 1952.

Thomas, Hugh. *Cuba: The Pursuit of Freedom.* Harper & Row, 1971.

Thomas, Lately. *A Pride of Lions: The Astor Orphans.* William Morrow, 1971.

Time-Life Editors. *The Fabulous Century.* Time/Life Books, 1970.

Trask, David F. *The War with Spain in 1898.* Macmillan, 1981.

Tuchman, Barbara. *The Proud Tower: A Portrait of the World Before the War: 1890–1914.* Macmillan, 1966.

————. *The First Salute: A View of the American Revolution.* Alfred A. Knopf, 1988.

Weems, John Edward. *The Fate of the Maine*. Henry Holt, 1958.

Werstein, Irving. *The Spanish-American War*. Cooper Square, 1966.

Westcott, Allan, ed. *Mahan and Naval Warfare*. Little, Brown, 1941.

Weyler, Don Valeriano y Nicolau. *Mi Mando en Cuba*. Madrid, 1910.

White, Leonard D. *The Republican Era: 1869–1901*. Macmillan, 1958.

Williams, Eric. *From Columbus to Castro: The History of the Caribbean 1492–1969*. Harper & Row, 1970.

Wilson, Herbert W. *The Downfall of Spain: Naval History of the Spanish-American War*. Sampson, Low, Marston and Co., London, 1900.

Winkler, John K. *William Randolph Hearst: A New Appraisal*. Hastings House, 1965.

Wolff, Leon. *Little Brown Brother*. Longmans, Green, 1961.

REFERENCE BOOKS

Bibliography of American Naval History, A. Compiled by Paolo E. Coletta. Naval Institute Press, 1981.

Book of Navy Songs, The. Collected and edited by the Trident Society. Naval Institute Press, 1987.

Dictionary of American Biography, The. Edited by Allen Johnson. Charles Scribner's Sons, 1964.

Dictionary of Military and Naval Quotations. Edited by Robert Debs Heinl, Jr. Naval Institute Press, 1966.

Encyclopaedia Britannica. Encyclopaedia Britannica, Inc., 1969.

List of Officers of the United States and of the Marine Corps from 1775–1900. Edited by Edward W. Callahan. L. R. Hamersly, 1901.

Map Catalogue, The. Edited by Joel Makower. Vintage Books, 1990.

Maritime Museums of North America. Edited by Robert H. Smith. Naval Institute Press, 1990.

Naval Historical Foundation Manuscript Collection. A Catalogue. U.S. Government Printing Office, 1974.

Oxford Companion to English Literature, The. Edited by Margaret Drabble. Oxford University Press, 1985.

Rand McNally Indexed Atlas of the World, The. Vol. 1. Rand McNally, 1899.

Times Concise Atlas of World History, The. Edited by Geoffrey Barraclough. Hammond, 1986.

Timetables of History: A Horizontal Linkage of People and Events, The. Edited by Bernard Grun. Simon & Schuster, 1979.

Webster's American Biographies. Edited by Charles Van Doren. G. & C. Merriam Co., 1974.

West Point Atlas of American Wars, The. Vol. 1. Frederick A. Praeger, 1959.

DOCUMENTS AND RECORDS

Cervera y Topete, Pascual. *The Spanish-American War: A Collection of Documents Relative to the Squadron Operations in the West Indies.* Government Printing Office, 1899.

Concas y Palau, Víctor M. *The Squadron of Admiral Cervera.* Government Printing Office, 1900.

Hydrographic Office Chart of the Harbor of Havana. No. 307, corrected to March 1898; also 1882 chart corrected to November 1890, at the National Archives.

Hydrographic Office Chart of the West Indies; Cuba. No. 2145, 1904, at the National Archives.

Log of the U.S. gunboat *Gloucester.* Richard Wainwright, 1899, The U.S. Naval Institute.

Log of the U.S.S. *Maine.* Captains Crowninshield and Sigsbee, April 1, 1897–September 30, 1897, at the Library of Congress.

Nuñez, Severo Gómez. *The Spanish-American War: Blockades and Coast Defense.* Government Printing Office, 1899.

Report of the Secretary of the Navy. 1898.

Scrapbook and naval records of Lieutenant George Preston Blow, in author's collection and at the Naval Historical Center.

Spanish-American War Clippings. Vol. 2, 1898. Presented to

the New York Public Library by Frank Wilstach.

U.S. Congress. Senate. *Message from the President of the United States Transmitting the Report of the Naval Court of Inquiry Upon the Destruction of the United States Battleship Maine in Havana Harbor, February 15, 1898, Together with the Testimony Taken Before the Court.* 55th Cong., 2nd sess., 1898, Doc. 207.

U.S. Congress. Senate. Committee on Foreign Relations. *Report of the Committee on Foreign Relations Relative to Affairs in Cuba.* 55th Cong., 2nd sess., 1898. No. 885.

U.S. Congress. House. *Letter from the Acting Secretary of War, Transmitting Copy of Report by the Board of Engineers Appointed to Raise the Wreck of the Battleship Maine in Havana Harbor, and Calling Atttention to the Necessity for Additional Funds to Complete the Work.* 62nd. Cong., 1st sess., Doc. 96.

U.S. Congress. House. *Report of Board Convened at Havana, Cuba, by Order of the Secretary of Navy, to Inspect and Report on the Wreck of the Maine.* 62nd Cong., 2nd sess., Doc. 310.

U.S. Congress. House. *Final Report on Removing Wreck of Battleship Maine from the Harbor of Havana, Cuba.* 63rd Cong., 2nd sess., Doc. 480.

MAGAZINE ARTICLES AND BOOKLETS

Basoco, Richard M. "What Really Happened to the *Maine.*" *American History Illustrated,* June 1966.

Bucknill, John T. "The Destruction of the United States Battleship *Maine.*" *Engineering, An Illlustrated Journal* (London), May 27, June 3, 10, 17, 21, 1898.

———. "The Raising of the Wreck of the Battleship *Maine.*" Ibid., March 15, 1912.

Caldwell, J. R. "Most Mournful of Sea Pageants." *Harper's Weekly,* May 11, 1912.

Cluverius, W. T. "A Midshipman on the *Maine.*" *The U.S. Naval Institute Proceedings,* February 1918.

Dawley, Thomas R., Jr. "Along the Trocha." *Harper's Weekly,* May 30, 1896.

Duncan, John E. "Remember the *Maine*, One More Time." *Naval History*, Spring 1990.

Feuer, A. B. "The Maine Remembered." *Sea Classics*, December 1988.

Homan, Wayne E. "Is the *Maine* Anchor Authentic?" *Historical Review of Berks County*, Fall 1960.

Lackawanna Steel Company. "Raising the Wreck of the Battleship *Maine*." Havana Harbor. *Lackawanna Steel Company Bulletin*, 1912.

Linn, Brian M. "The 'Howling Wilderness.'" *Naval History*, Fall 1990.

Meriwether, Walter Scott. "Remembering the *Maine*." The U.S. Naval Institute *Proceedings*, May 1948.

Murphy, Ed "Guncotton." "We Remember the *Maine*." The U.S. Naval Institute *Proceedings*, January 1944.

Naisawald, L. VanLoan. "The Destruction of the *Maine*: Accident or Sabotage?" The U.S. Naval Institute *Proceedings*, February 1972.

New York Naval Shipyard. *Souvenir Journal of the New York Naval Shipyard (1801–1951)*, 1951.

Post, Charles Johnson. "G.I. View of the War in Cuba." *American Heritage*, February 1957.

Professional Notes. "Wreck of the *Maine*." The U.S. Naval Institute *Proceedings*, March 1912.

Rea, George Bronson. "The Night of the Explosion in Havana." *Harper's Weekly*, March 5, 1898.

Santovenia y Echaide, Emeterio S. The Memorial Book of the Inauguration of the Maine Plaza at Havana, 1928.

Scientific American. Analysis of the Vreeland report, January 27, 1912; analysis of war games, March 26, 1898; Commander Hermann Gercke's analysis of the explosion; July 28, 1898; editorial and an account of the *Maine*'s destruction, February 26, 1898; the *Maine* laid to rest, March 30, 1912; observations on submarine mines, March 5, 1898; story of the *Maine*'s launching, November 29, 1890; summary and comment on the "Report of the Naval Court of Inquiry on the Destruction of the United States Battleship *Maine*," April 9, 1898; views and comments on Spanish destroyers and torpedo boats, March 19, 1898; and wrecking operations company, March 12, 1898.

The Scientific American Special Navy Supplement
(1893–1898), 1898.

Sigsbee, Charles D. "My Story of the Maine." Cosmopolitan,
July and August, 1912.

The United States Army and Navy Journal. "The Maine Disaster Explained," May 21, 1898.

————. Material regarding testimony before the Senate Committee on Foreign Relations on the effects of subsurface
explosions, April 23, 1898.

Wainwright, Richard. "Sinking of the Maine." Sunday Magazine, August 12, 1906.

Warren, Arthur. "The Fighting Engineers at Santiago." Factory and Industrial Management (Engineering Magazine), January 1899.

Index

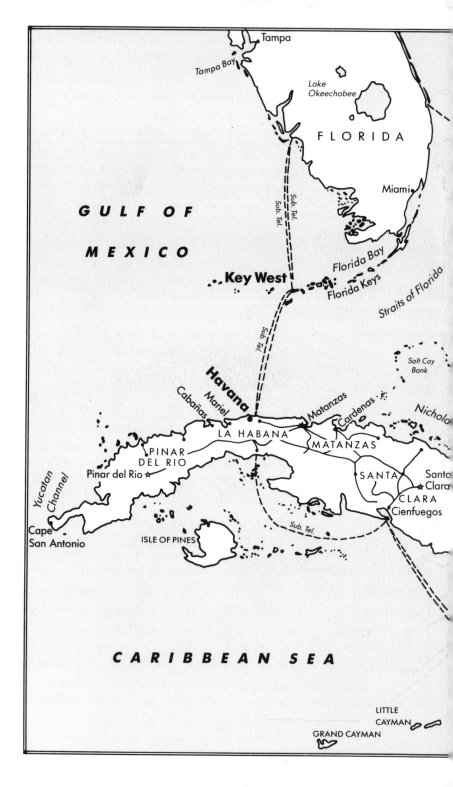